Giggles in the Middle

Caught'ya!
Grammar with a Giggle
for Middle School

Jane Bell Kiester

Maupin House *by*
capstone·
professional

Giggles in the Middle:
Caught'ya! Grammar with a Giggle for Middle School

Cover Design: David Dishman
Layout Design: Billie J. Hermansen

Library of Congress Cataloging-in-Publication Data

Kiester, Jane Bell, 1945-
  Giggles in the middle : caught 'ya! grammar with a giggle for middle
school / Jane Bell Kiester.
      p. cm.
  Includes bibliographical references.
  ISBN-13: 978-0-929895-88-8 (pbk.)
  ISBN-10: 0-929895-88-6 (pbk.)
  1. English language—Grammar—Study and teaching (Middle school) 2.
Humor
in education. I. Title.
  LB1631.K465 2006
  428.2—dc22
                                2005025653

Also by Jane Bell Kiester
> *Caught'ya! Grammar with a Giggle*
> *Caught'ya Again! More Grammar with a Giggle*
> *The Chortling Bard: Caught'ya! Grammar with a Giggle for High School*
> *Elementary, My Dear: Caught'ya! Grammar with a Giggle for Grades 1-3*
> *Blowing Away the State Writing Assessment Test*

Maupin House Publishing, Inc. by Capstone Professional
1710 Roe Crest Drive
North Mankato, MN 56003

www.maupinhouse.com
800-524-0634
352-373-5546 (fax)
info@maupinhouse.com

Printed in the United States of America in Eau Claire, Wisconsin.
012915 008760

Dedication

I dedicate this book with much love
To my best friend and most ardent fan,
My mother, Perra Somers Bell.

For six decades (so far)
You have filled my life
With an abundance of love,
Laughter, approval, and moral support.

You impart to me your wisdom
Of kindness and positive attitudes,
Your sense of history,
Your fondness of literature
(Dickens and Shakespeare in particular),
Your delight in superlative writing,
And your love of words.

How fortunate I am to be your daughter.

A Special Acknowledgement

To my former students,

I would like to give special thanks (with a hug) to all the middle-school students whom I have had the pleasure to teach for the more than thirty-one years of my career. It is you who have inspired this book.

You gave me years filled with an abundance of mirth, affection, energy, challenge, and mutual learning. Because of you, my teaching career spanned over 6,000 days that were never dull. I hope that *your* chosen career paths will be as fulfilling and rewarding as you made mine.

You wrote all those stories, plays, and essays for me to read. Grading them kept me occupied, inspired, laughing, out of trouble, and occasionally groaning.

You also willingly served as my fervent "guinea pigs" who tried out most of the earlier twelve Caught'ya stories as I wrote them (and, in unguarded moments, even said you enjoyed them).

Many of you even learned to love (and use) hundred-dollar words as you honed and improved your writing. I am proud of you.

Without all of you, my professional life would have lacked its luster and zest. You added the glitter and the pizzazz, the "woo-woo factor," as we used to say in class, and I thank you.

Acknowledgements

First, I wish to express my love and gratitude to my husband, Chuck Kiester, and my mother, Perra Bell. You cheerfully edited, slashed, cleaned up, clarified, and improved the manuscript of this book without complaint. I would not dare to send it to the publisher without your input (and outtake). Thank you. I couldn't have done it without you.

Joyce Kohfeldt, good friend and fellow octogenarian-mother-appreciator, gave me the idea of inserting writing ideas within the Caught'yas and linking them to the subject matter at hand. Thank you, Joyce. Thank you also for loving my books and spreading the word. What a dear friend to have in my corner!

I want to thank Lee Lyons, my big brother (forget the in-law stuff), for being the older brother I never had. During the writing of this book, you unstintingly gave me wise council, rides galore, a trustworthy "Plan B," and a friend who can tell me "woof" when I need it. And, Nancy, thank you for reading the story, being honest, and loving me just as I am. I love you both.

Again, I wish to thank Renée Trufant. You provided encouragement, humorous insight, and invaluable, currently-in-the-trenches input to the story of the robot teachers. Thank you for editing at the end of the school year when you were going nuts. You take the meaning of "true friend" to new heights!

I also would like to thank Bridget Mann at Marco Island Charter Middle School who polled her seventh-graders for the current middle-school vernacular so that my characters wouldn't sound out-of-date. Thank you also for showing me how Caught'yas worked for you. You are an inspired teacher.

A delightful young lady, seventh-grader Georgia Cudmore, let me use her Caught'yas for the sample. Thank you, Georgia, for your help with this book. It was truly a pleasure to work with you.

And, finally, I give a grateful thanks to Emily Gorovsky of Maupin House Publishing for your insightful ideas and superb, creative editing.

Table of Contents

On the CD

Complete Story for Grades Six, Seven, and Eight: "The Bizarre Mystery of Horribly Hard Middle School"

Caught'yas for Sixth, Seventh, and Eighth Grade

***Grammar, Usage, and Mechanics Guide** – Everything You Never Wanted to Know about Grammar, Usage, and Mechanics, but I'm Going to Tell You Anyway*

Introduction

A Love Affair with Middle School

A joke that periodically circulates in teachers' lounges of middle schools goes as follows: Sixth-graders run in a scattered manner everywhere, and when they get to where they were originally headed, they hit someone and say something silly in a loud voice. Seventh-graders either run or saunter everywhere, and when they get to where they are going, either hit someone or touch someone inappropriately while saying something silly in a loud voice or muttering something rude under their breath loud enough for nearby peers to hear. Eighth-graders saunter everywhere, and when they finally get to where they were originally headed, they touch someone inappropriately and mutter a rude remark loud enough for half the class to hear.

This description is not much of an exaggeration. One day, you face little angelic cherubs who feel love for you and the world, and twenty-four hours later those same angels turn into vitriolic spitfires who hate each other and refuse to work on the assignment for the day. Teaching middle school certainly never is boring. It is a circus, a challenging one that requires good planning, quick thinking, and a healthy dose of humor.

I fell in love with teaching middle school in 1972 and continued that love affair for more than thirty years. It is only fitting, therefore, that I finally write a book designed exclusively for middle schools. Because of the ever-changing nature and hormonally volatile age of our clientele, we middle-school teachers face problems and situations that teachers of other grades only can imagine.

If you line up seventh-graders, for example, you find that they vary in size, hairiness, and maturity—from the ones who resemble eight-year-olds to little girls who look (and dress, changing clothes in the bathroom before school) like eighteen-year-olds and from little boys who still think kissing is icky to big, hairy, six-foot young men who have only one thing on their minds (and it isn't English).

Students who are perceived as "different" suffer most from the slings and arrows of their peers. The "difference" does not matter. They can be too intelligent or not intelligent enough, overweight or underweight, too hairy or not hairy enough, over- or underdeveloped, too tall or too short, too immature or too mature, too effeminate (males) or too masculine (girls), like to read or have difficulty reading, have a physical deformity of any kind, be shy, suffer from low self-esteem, come from a dysfunctional home, live with poverty or alcoholism or abuse or neglect or lack of love or too much responsibility or...The list is as numerous as middle-school students.

The world is fraught with lures, pitfalls, and dangers that appeal to middle-schoolers' desire to be "cool" and a part of some group or follow some weird fad like "sagging" that irritates any adult. Dealing with this peer and media pressure to be "in" makes it doubly difficult for the students to concentrate on learning, doubly difficult for teachers to deal with the resulting behavior, and doubly difficult for us to come up with ways to teach our material so that we reach our students.

Perhaps this is why Mark Twain suggested that one should put a twelve-year-old in the middle of a field, place a barrel over his head, and feed him through a small hole in the barrel until he or she reaches the age of "reason."

I disagree with Mr. Twain and the rest of the adult world who, when I tell them how much I adored teaching middle school, look at me in horror and amazement and think I have a screw loose. *We* who teach this age group know differently. Or maybe we just enjoy that loose screw!

Middle-school students are to be enjoyed for their humor, their antics, their bluntness, their unpredictability, and their many contradictions. If they trust you, they will confide in you and write without the restraint or the stiltedness of adults. If they are feeling positive and good about themselves, they will give you heartfelt hugs as if you were their own mother or father.

This book attempts to address the particular needs, moods, and tastes of middle-school students. The story was written just for them, keeping in mind the kinds of stories they like to read (often under the desk) and their particular brand of humor.

I Can't Help but Brag about My Special Students!

I invented Caught'yas in 1978 out of desperation (nothing else worked). It is one of those teaching tools that proved so effective that I used it and improved it for the rest of my teaching career. This method of teaching English improved my students' writing whether I taught basic skills, "regular," advanced, or gifted classes.

One class in particular remains my greatest Caught'ya success story. I'll never forget them. The class was a special, seventh-grade basic-skills language arts group who had never had success in reading or writing or language skills. I taught them the period after lunch, and you veteran teachers *know* what that means... Among the students in this class were those who already had accumulated more than several felony charges, had previously failed language arts, had been tossed out of various programs because of behavior problems, whose only meals of the day were at school, who had the weight of the world on their shoulders, who currently lived in the detention center, who sold drugs, who drank alcohol, who had already had a baby, or who lived mostly on the streets, etc. They were, as one North Carolina teacher lovingly put it, "beloved thugs."

After an initial difficult month or so, my students and I developed a positive learning atmosphere in the classroom with mutual respect and genuine affection (although they just knew that I was a "crazy lady"). I attribute my success at reaching most of these previously unreachable students primarily to the use of the Caught'ya method.

It took my kids six weeks before they consistently began a sentence with a capital letter and put some kind of punctuation at the end, but they felt so good about themselves once they had mastered this basic skill. It took another month to punctuate a quote correctly and paragraph when a new person spoke. Vocabulary words started appearing in their speech. One young man fell in love with the word "dulcet." Why, I don't know. He just used it whenever he could. Other students adored equally sophisticated words and used them as often as possible. These words gave them power. Soon they were learning and writing simple but good paragraphs with real detail and great vocabulary.

Besides doing Caught'yas, we read and read and wrote and wrote. I took one or two great sentences (using active verbs) from among each student's paragraphs and essays, typed them up in a huge font, laminated the collection, and hung it on a "Great Writers" wall. This marked another turning point. My students were thrilled. No one had ever publicly recognized them for their writing. They worked even harder to write better. What a great group of kids!

The criterion for a student to get into this special class was a stanine in language arts of 1.2 or below on the previous year's state language arts test. After almost a year of completing Caught'yas and experiencing great success, the majority of my students again took the standardized test for language arts. All but one or two of them earned stanines of 3 or better. At least a quarter of them earned a 4 or 5, an average score.

We all were thrilled and held a huge party. If Caught'yas could work to improve the writing of my "beloved thugs," they will work for ANY student.

What You Will Find in the Chapters of This Book

Chapter 1 briefly summarizes the Caught'ya method. It also includes an explanation of why there are only 125 Caught'yas for each of the three years. This is included because when I do a workshop, someone always asks the question, "Will 125 Caught'yas get me through a year?"

Chapter 2 will regale you with ten easy steps that explain all the details and tricks necessary for implementing the Caught'ya method in your classroom. Even those of you who have used Caught'yas for years and could do a Caught'ya in your sleep will want to read this chapter. In it I have included ideas specifically for middle school as well as new ideas that I discovered or thought of after the last Caught'ya book was written. Teaching, after all, is a continuous learning process.

Chapter 3 answers questions you may have as you begin to use the Caught'yas. You will want to read this chapter before beginning the actual Caught'yas in **Chapters 6, 7, and 8**. Also included in **Chapter 3** is a brief history of each of the three types of poetry the characters in the story use—limericks for sixth grade, cinquains for seventh grade, and haiku for eighth grade. I did this to save you the trouble of looking them up. I know how little extra time you have...

Chapter 4 lists all the vocabulary words used in the Caught'yas, including the characters' bizarre names, listed by the number of the Caught'ya in which they appear in each grade-level story.

Chapter 5 contains the entire, uninterrupted, corrected Caught'ya story. This allows you to see the story in its entirety.

Chapters 6, 7, and 8 are the Caught'yas that will span three school years, one section for each year of middle school. Within each chapter, the story has been broken up into two- to four-sentence segments to teach the skills. Each segment has an error-laden "B" (for board) sentence with its corresponding, corrected "C" sentence. In addition to the Caught'yas, the following is included in each of the three chapters:

→ Twenty-five writing ideas for each grade level, one after every five Caught'yas. Although the topics of the seventy-five writing ideas are related to the plot of the Caught'ya story, these writing assignments are not part of the daily Caught'ya routine. Whether you use all of them, some of them, or none of them is up to you. As your sympathetic colleague (who just retired from active teaching and whose memories are still very vivid), I am attempting to make your life a bit easier by supplying a writing topic a week so that you don't have to think up one yourself. I have tried to include all the genres of writing that can be found on state writing assessment tests around the country. These writing ideas include the different types of writing that most of us are required to teach at the middle-school level plus some that are just for fun, like writing a crazy poem or two.

→ Suggestions about how to teach the skills most effectively, listed by the Caught'yas in which those skills appear.

→ Passages to be read aloud to your students or turned into extra Caught'yas if needed. These are continuing parts of the story.

→ A formal, three-part "Almost Midterm Caught'ya Test" near the halfway point of the 125 Caught'yas and a final exam at the end.

On the **CD**, you'll find files that save you time and allow you to customize the Caught'yas to your needs. Chapters marked with this icon (🔘) are on the CD.

→ The *Grammar, Usage, and Mechanics Guide (Everything You Never Wanted to Know about Grammar, Usage, and Mechanics, but I'm Going to Tell You Anyway)*. I referred to this useful addendum almost daily when I taught Caught'yas (and I wrote it). Who among us doesn't sometimes confuse a participle with a gerund (a verb acting as an adjective vs. a verb acting as a noun) or forget the difference between a restrictive (essential) and non-restrictive (non-essential) modifier? The *GUM Guide* and the Caught'yas cover every skill listed in *Warriner's English Grammar and Composition: Complete Course*—the big white book that bored so many of us when we were in school. This also means that all the skills you are required by your state to teach (and then some) are covered.

Besides providing a quick reference for those picky points of grammar that elude our memory, the *Grammar, Usage, and Mechanics Guide* contains simple examples you can use in your instruction and mnemonic devices to help your students learn some of the more difficult concepts.

→ **The entire, uninterrupted, corrected Caught'ya story**. You easily can print and run off a copy of the story up to the point where you begin Caught'yas in order to read it aloud to your students. Students who join your class after the beginning of the year also can read this to catch up on the story so far.

➔ **The sixth-, seventh-, and eighth-grade Caught'yas.** These are provided so that you do not have to copy or type the student Caught'yas (or tests) as you do in the earlier Caught'ya books. Middle-school English teachers have enough work to deal with, so you need as many shortcuts as possible.

Now I invite you, my fellow middle-school teachers, to stuff that pile of papers you need to grade into your bag for later (along with the guilt for not grading them right away), get comfortable in your favorite chair, take off your shoes and any restrictive clothing you are wearing, put up your feet, pour a glass of your favorite beverage, take a deep, cleansing breath, and read the rest of this book.

CHAPTER I

Caught'yas in a Nutshell

What is the Caught'ya Method?

The Caught'ya method is an integrated approach to teaching language skills in context. It allows you to teach grammar, usage, mechanics, vocabulary, paragraphing, varied sentence structure, spelling of homophones and commonly misspelled words, use of literary devices, and how to avoid fragments, all within the context of a story.

In this book, each two- to four-sentence Caught'ya is part of the ongoing story, "The Bizarre Mystery of Horribly Hard Middle School." Each is fraught with errors for your students to correct. The type and number of errors left in the Caught'ya depend on *you*. You can adjust the difficulty of each day's Caught'ya to match your students' needs. To the left of each Caught'ya, I have listed most of the skills included in that Caught'ya to make it easier for you to pick and choose. **Flexibility** is the key to using the Caught'ya method and one of the most important traits necessary for successfully teaching middle school.

In almost every Caught'ya, students are required to capitalize the first word of each sentence, capitalize proper nouns, and supply end punctuation. These, therefore, are not included in the skills list beside each Caught'ya. Although I have taught more than a few sixth-, seventh-, and eighth-graders (like my beloved "thugs") who, when I inherited them at the beginning of the year, could (or would) not put a capital letter at the beginning of a sentence nor a period at the end, the majority of middle-school students already have mastered those skills. After a month of completing Caught'yas, even my "basic skills" students had learned to do so consistently in Caught'yas and in their writing. Now, mastering the comma rules was another matter...

Each Caught'ya contains at least one challenging word (usually more) that should be new to most of your students. Many Caught'yas also include literary devices and writing conventions. You introduce and elicit the meaning of the vocabulary word(s), wait while students write it (them) into their vocabulary notebooks (more on these in **Chapter 2**), read the Caught'ya dramatically, and, until your students get the hang of it, initiate a discussion as to whether the Caught'ya begins a new paragraph in the story.

Students enter your room, and, as soon as the bell rings (or even before), they open the Caught'ya section of their binders and write the Caught'ya that you have put on the board or overhead as correctly as they can. Then you walk around the room and give immediate, tinged-with-humor feedback (like saying "Caught'ya" and sticking out your tongue) to individual students. As you move quickly around the room, you can provide mini-lessons to some students and encourage, challenge, or tease others to find the errors on their own.

Please note that a teacher can get around to each student in a class of thirty-five in fewer than five minutes by glancing at each paper and looking for one particular error (usually the hardest skill—like antecedent/pronoun agreement). If, and only if, you find that particular error already has been discovered and corrected by a student, you read the rest of the Caught'ya and search for errors.

When students finish the Caught'ya, they complete a short task you may have assigned and then write a page in their journals. Topic? Anything they wish or, for those who can't think of anything to write, a topic suggested by you. For ease, I suggest that you wing it daily and suggest a topic that is related to something in the Caught'ya. For example, if "hair" is mentioned, you could suggest that students write about the weirdest hairdo they ever have seen.

Then, when you have glanced at each student's effort, and nearly all your students have completed the Caught'ya as well as written the required amount in their journals, you go to the board or overhead, review the meaning of the vocabulary word(s), and go over any literary devices or new skills. Then, with you or one of your students writing in the corrections on the overhead or board, you elicit the correct answers from your students and go over the reasons and rules for each correction. Students use simple proofreading symbols (or just corrections in another color ink) to mark errors that were missed. They also take notes on their papers—how detailed is up to you—on the reasons for the corrections.

When the entire Caught'ya has been corrected communally, corrections discussed thoroughly, and, most importantly, the reasons for each error noted on their papers, students count the errors they missed the *first* time—i.e., when they attempted to correct the Caught'ya on their own. They then indicate the number of their initial errors in the margin of their papers. Several skills have been introduced, reinforced, or practiced; a new word has been learned; and maybe the class has enjoyed a giggle from the story, the vocabulary word, or your antics as you cavorted around the room.

As you know, success breeds success, a fact that Caught'yas exploit in the assessment. Assessment is based on whether your students catch the errors and note them on their papers when the class reviews the Caught'ya, *not* on the number of errors made when they attempted to correct the Caught'ya on their own. All you are grading is whether your students *paid attention* when you went over the Caught'ya and caught the mistakes they missed. In this manner, your students, no matter how weak their English skills are, can experience success.

You may be surprised that your weakest students often get the highest grades on their Caught'yas. Why? They pay attention because they know that this is something in which they can experience success if they just listen and correct carefully. In fact, I invented Caught'yas in an attempt to reach my students with learning disabilities and emotional handicaps. The method eliminates feelings of failure and frustration previously associated with language arts. The more advanced students often think that they "know it all" and get careless. For most advanced and gifted students, however, Caught'yas can offer a welcome challenge.

Caught'yas are short so that those with limited attention spans don't get lost. The method allows for immediate success and feedback as you always can praise a student for *something* he or she did correctly. Students can have public success in front of their peers when you call on them for something you know (because you have just seen it) they got right. Caught'yas are good self-esteem boosters.

Do not worry if you are an introvert, are not naturally a ham, or know that your students prefer you to be serious and scholarly. Caught'yas will work in your classroom if you are at all enthusiastic (in your own way) about them and about the subsequent improvement in your students' writing.

How Many Caught'yas and Why?

If your entire school chooses to use this book, you will use only the corresponding sixth-, seventh-, or eighth-grade part of the story for your class. The 125 two- to four-sentence Caught'yas in each part are enough to last you for the entire year if you do four or five a week and add a few more of your own when needed. And, if you complete the year's worth of Caught'yas with time to spare and need more to finish up the year, there are several passages that you easily can turn into Caught'yas.

However, if you teach eighth grade, for example, and the sixth- and seventh-grade teachers in your school do not use this book, you can use the Caught'yas from one or both of the other two chapters and do more than one Caught'ya per day. Of course, you will need to read aloud any parts of the story you do not use as Caught'ya sentences in order to keep with the storyline. You also can choose not to do additional Caught'yas from the other two chapters and simply read those parts of the story out loud to your class before beginning the eighth-grade Caught'yas. Any way you choose to use the Caught'yas, they allow for much-needed flexibility during the hectic school year.

Constant interruptions to lesson plans and constant cuts into time with students are the bane of middle-school teachers. Assemblies, state assessment testing, special P.E. events, band concerts, chorus concerts, an entire grade being held over at lunch to be chastised by the dean, lock-downs, field trips, reward trips, the occasional really unruly student who is having a worse day than usual and who makes teaching that day an impossibility, and other such events cut into language arts periods all too often. We English teachers need leeway and "wiggle room" in our curriculum.

Having only 125 Caught'yas for the year (with options for more if desired) when there are 180 days in the school year gives us fifty-five days for all the above distractions while still allowing us the organized flexibility to add a few Caught'yas of our own if students need more practice in a particular skill.

The midterm and final exam found in each of the three Caught'ya chapters can be adapted as well. Each exam has three parts, but you do not need to use all three. You even can shorten the main part of the tests, reading the rest to your students so that they don't lose the storyline as the tests are continuing parts of the story. I have tried to compose the tests from one of the more exciting parts to keep student interest alive.

Depending on the needs of your class, you also can change the existing Caught'yas and/or the exams to make them simpler or more difficult or to repeat skills that still need work. Unlike more traditional methods of teaching English skills, you can repeat skills *ad nauseam* until every student in the class masters them or begs for mercy. Student: "Please, Mrs. Kiester, (loud groan) don't go over compound sentences again. We know what they are. Want me to write one on the board?"

To this end, you will want to peruse the ***Grammar, Usage, and Mechanics Guide*** on the CD for an annotated list of the skills that are included in the Caught'yas to see if your students need more practice in any of them. I liked to analyze my students' writing frequently to see how their grammar, mechanics, usage, and use of vocabulary were improving and which skills needed to be practiced further in subsequent Caught'yas.

Those of you who teach "English-challenged" students in basic skills or self-contained "VE" classes can simplify the Caught'yas or put in most of the correct punctuation to model and leave only one or two errors for your students to spot and correct. Or, since there are two to four sentences in each Caught'ya, you might prefer to require students to write only one of the sentences and go over the others orally as a class. I did this with my "regular" classes at least once every two weeks when I felt that they needed a break. They loved the change of pace, thought that they were getting away with murder, and learned the skills anyway. They had to write the vocabulary word(s) and their meanings in their vocabulary notebooks no matter how we completed the Caught'ya.

Conversely, if you teach advanced or gifted language arts classes, you can make the Caught'ya sentences more complicated, adding more of the sophisticated skills such as antecedent/pronoun agreement and the use of participles.

As the year progresses, you will find that you can model less and less and ask students to correct more and more. Each class is unique. Each teacher alone knows how much his or her students can handle and what they are capable of doing.

Benefits You Can See

Caught'yas save time.

The beauty of Caught'yas for middle-school students is that they take only ten to fifteen minutes to complete each day (twenty for block classes if you do two a day), thus matching middle-schoolers' attention spans for studying English conventions. This leaves the rest of the period or block to be spent writing, playing vocabulary games, and reading literature.

Caught'yas eliminate "waste time."

Another hallmark of the Caught'ya method that especially helps middle-school teachers is the elimination of "waste time" at the beginning of each period. Students soon get used to entering your classroom and immediately settling down to write the Caught'ya or looking up the vocabulary word (so that they can be the one to supply the meaning when you ask). Because most students crave attention, the immediate feedback the method provides while they work on the Caught'ya usually spurs them to get started quickly. Why? So that they have something completed by the time you reach their desks and can give them the positive attention they want.

In my last six years of teaching, my classroom was a run-down portable (with its own bathroom—significant to this story). Insulation was non-existent, and when a student used the bathroom, he or she (or I) turned on the water to hide any other sounds. That portable had character, and I loved it! I drink lots of water, so, in between classes, I always hit the potty (turning on the faucet, of course). Often I was still in there when the bell rang and students began to arrive. Sometimes, I couldn't help but listen in on them when they did not know that I was there. I stood near the door, ears tuned.

First, they came in and sat down. I heard rustlings and the click of binders and notebooks opening. If it wasn't already turned on, someone turned on the overhead. I heard discussions of the meanings of vocabulary words, placement of commas, etc., music to any teacher's ears. I listened to brief arguments about who was going to look up the vocabulary words or about who had whose vocabulary notebook. Basically, without my being there, class began as usual.

They often didn't even notice that I was missing! I was thrilled! When I came out of the bathroom, usually as the final bell rang, we quickly recited the poem of the month, went over the Caught'ya that students already had started, discussed the vocabulary word(s) for which some student (who had looked it up in the dictionary before class began) was proud to regale us with its meaning, and continued the routine of completing the Caught'ya, the short English activity, and the journal entries. As they continued writing, I walked around the room, checking for one error and giving a quick mini-lesson if it was needed.

Caught'yas eliminate boring, rote work.

For many years, my colleagues and I used only Caught'yas to teach the conventions. Our students always scored very high on the language arts part of the state achievement test (FCAT in Florida). On the new component on the SAT that our students will take in high school, knowledge of what is correct and what is not in a sentence is essential to success.

Caught'yas eliminate the need not only for those dull grammar books but also for those repetitive worksheets. By the way, you can use those grammar books with their chalk-dry exercises for diabolical punishments for miscreants who are particularly annoying! (Middle-school students loathe doing textbook exercises!) All I had to do to quiet some querulous or talkative student was to grab a book and wave it in the air. The offender usually ceased the offensive activity immediately. Thus, the traditional grammar books are very useful, just not for the purpose for which they were intended. Other teachers have confided to me that they did the same.

Caught'yas raise students' test scores.

Since the publication of the first Caught'ya book in 1990, teachers all over the country have contacted me with the exciting news that their students, too, vastly improved their writing skills and earned higher test scores on their state achievement tests. One first-year teacher in Texas even reported that her students scored so far above everyone else's that she won a trip to Las Vegas!

Student scores on the new, multiple-choice and "pick-the-correct-sentence" components of most states' writing assessment tests rise as well. Since the Caught'yas are similar to how the new components are presented, by doing one daily, your students are set up for success. The state-mandated test will be just like doing a few more Caught'yas, only they will not be part of a story. Like my drop-out-prevention students, even the most dyslexic, dysgraphic child will know to put capital letters at the beginning of a sentence, to use end punctuation, to indent, and to avoid fragments.

Caught'yas build teacher/student trust.

Other teachers and I found an added, non-English-related benefit of doing Caught'yas. Because of the daily, brief, positive contact with each student in the class, teachers who use Caught'yas forge a strong bond with their students. Once that bond is forged, the students feel as though they can trust us with their confidences, their hopes, and their fears. Because of this trust, they even occasionally listen to our "sage" words of experience and gift us with heartfelt hugs worthy of a first-grader.

One of my students was the terror of the seventh grade. I will call him "Keith" to protect the guilty. Keith did not, however, misbehave in my class. I knew that he adored the daily hug and attention I gave him as we completed the daily Caught'ya for, although he pretended nonchalance, his eyes followed me eagerly during my daily trek up and down the aisles until I reached his desk.

One day, after a meeting in which I had listened to my colleagues discuss Keith's latest antics in their classes, I asked this miscreant why he did not misbehave in my class.

He replied, "It wouldn't be fair."

Keith was not the most verbally acute person in the world, and this was the extent of his explanation. I pressed him further anyway.

He kept saying "*You* know" with emphasis on the first word. Finally, when he saw I wouldn't give up until I understood, he added, "You talk just to me every day."

I knew that I had forged a bond with Keith while completing the daily Caught'yas, a bond that he would not violate with aberrant behavior that would disrupt my class. He wanted that daily hug, that daily talk "just to him" to continue. By the way, Keith's state achievement test scores in language arts rose dramatically that year!

Caught'yas build students' self-esteem.

The success that the Caught'ya method engenders typically raises the self-esteem of our students which, in turn, translates into better grades and a more positive attitude about school. The Caught'ya method has proven to be successful with low-achieving students, "regular" students (if there is such a thing), gifted students, advanced students, and all those in between.

A Caveat

I have a warning, though. I have had parents complain that their child was not "learning grammar" in my class because we weren't using a book with exercises and accompanying xeroxed sheets for homework. After initially being taken aback by this accusation, I learned to ask the student various questions, like "Can you give us an example of a complex sentence?" or "When should you paragraph?" or "Can you recite the subordinating conjunctions and tell us when you use them?" When they heard their children give prompt, correct answers to these questions, the parents always withdrew their complaint.

CHAPTER 2

Implementing and Assessing

Ten Easy Steps to a Successful Caught'ya

1. Choose the story you wish to use from this book. If you teach seventh or eighth grade, read the earlier parts of the story to your class from Chapter 5 so that they know what already happened.

2. Decide whether you want to change the level of difficulty of the Caught'yas, and then A) pull up the student Caught'yas from the CD; B) make the changes; C) print out the student Caught'yas; and D) make overheads.

3. Put the day's Caught'ya on the overhead (or write it on the board) with the day and date at the top. Write the suggested journal topic. Assign an extra task.

4. Read the Caught'ya dramatically; review the vocabulary word(s); discuss the need for a new paragraph; and warn of a difficult skill.

5. Students then enter the vocabulary words into their vocabulary notebooks, write the Caught'ya as correctly as they can with a heading at the top of their papers, write an entry in their journals, and complete whatever extra task you assigned for the day.

6. Walk around the room, commenting on each student's efforts, praising, teasing, or giving a hint or a quick mini-lesson.

7. Go to the board or overhead and check the Caught'ya out loud with the class, eliciting answers and reasons for corrections from students.

8. Students mark mistakes and take notes.

9. Students count and indicate the number of errors in the margin of their papers.

10. Collect one paper per student after five Caught'yas have been completed, and grade only one Caught'ya per paper, noting the errors still missed so that the skills can be repeated in subsequent Caught'yas.

Even if you have used the Caught'ya method before, you still should read this chapter before going on to the next. While I do repeat the basic information necessary to implement Caught'yas successfully in your classroom, I have added a few embellishments and insights from thirty-one years of teaching middle-school students. I also proffer teaching suggestions that other middle-school teachers around the country and I discovered after publication of the earlier Caught'ya books.

As you know, middle-school students require a different approach to learning than other children. We have to work harder to grab their interest and attention. We middle-school teachers, because of our clientele, tend to be a little bizarre and different ourselves. This, in my opinion, is a good thing. Once exposed to a classroom full of hormone-raging middle-school students, you either fall in love with the age group or run to avoid it at all costs. We have to have a well-honed sense of humor to deal effectively with our students. We have to be a bit (or more than a bit) weird to reach them. The execution of the Caught'ya method plays to those strengths.

Step 1: Choose the story you wish to use from this book. If you teach seventh or eighth grade, read the earlier parts of the story to your class from Chapter 5 so that they know what already happened.

In **Chapter 5**, you will find the story in its entirety (for all three grades), not broken up into Caught'yas. If you teach sixth grade, you will not need to read **Chapter 5** to your students and can begin with **Chapter 6**. You might, however, want to read all of **Chapter 5** for yourself so that you know how far the story is going to go in the sixth grade and how the mystery will end in the eighth grade.

If you teach seventh or eighth grade, you will want to read the part of the story for the previous grade(s) to your students to establish the characters, the setting, and the mystery as well as apprise them of the plot up to the point where you want to begin the Caught'yas for your grade level. In addition, no matter what grade you teach, you will want to run off a hard copy of **Chapter 5** (from the CD) up to the point where your class is in the Caught'yas. Keep it in your classroom, updating it as you progress further into the story for your grade level. In this way, any students who join your class after you begin doing the Caught'yas can spend a period or two reading the story and catching up with the plot.

Before you begin doing the Caught'yas, you also will want to teach your students the meanings of the last names of the characters. You will find the names and their meanings in **Chapter 4**. By learning these new words before beginning the Caught'yas, students become so familiar with the superlative vocabulary in those names that it will become a part of their daily parlance and will be included in their writing. Using these words should be as natural as using their simpler synonyms. (For example: **puerile** = childish, infantile, or immature.)

Step 2: Decide whether you want to change the level of difficulty of the Caught'yas, and then A) pull up the student Caught'yas from the CD; B) make the changes; C) print out the student Caught'yas; and D) make overheads.

Each class is different. Each year students are spectacularly deficient in certain skills. One year, for example, you may have classes of students who may barely be able to remember to put any end punctuation and to whom indenting for a paragraph is an anathema. Another year you may have a group of students who play "verb ping-pong" when they write. They characteristically switch tenses back and forth from present to past to present to past, etc.

This lack of consistency usually improves as students mature (one hopes), as their attention spans increase, with how the teachers in the previous grades taught English skills, and with the number of sun spots. I'm just kidding with the last one, but I'm sure you seasoned teachers have all taught "the class from Hell" that began its reputation in kindergarten and, despite the efforts of all the teachers in between kindergarten and middle school, retained its label. Teachers in my school, for lack of any other explanation, blamed sun spots the few times we experienced one of those groups because the problem extended to every middle school in the county.

Caught'yas address the diverse nature of the classes we teach because they can be adapted to fit the needs of every student. After you read the Caught'yas in **Chapters 6, 7, or 8**, decide if the skill level is, like the porridge in *Goldilocks and the Three Bears*, too difficult, too easy, or just right. Only you know what your students can handle before they become frustrated.

Before you print the student Caught'yas to put on overheads, make the changes you wish. Then print them out, **only ten at a time**. This gives you the flexibility to change subsequent Caught'yas to cover skills that need more work. You also can print out a few copies for your more challenged students whose copying skills are not up to par.

With an advanced, gifted, or a pre-IB class, you can add more sentences to the existing 125 Caught'yas, inserting more sophisticated skills like dangling modifiers, antecedent/pronoun agreement, etc.

There are plenty of places within the story where an extra Caught'ya or two can be inserted without interrupting the continuity.

TEACHING NOTE:

Remember, however, that if you add a complete Caught'ya of your own, you will need to insert a vocabulary word or two. The difficulty of the word doesn't matter. Just write the sentences, and find a good place in that sentence to substitute a more sophisticated word. One of those little electronic thesauruses is perfect for finding delicious synonyms. I find that the one on my computer often offers limited alternatives.

With a learning-disabled or basic-skills class, you can concentrate on a few skills, such as end punctuation, paragraphing, the comma rules, and the use of similes, and model all the rest. You also can simplify the sentences, turning complex ones into two simple ones.

If you have a class of low-achieving students, you also might want to run off the first five or so student Caught'yas so that you can begin the year with your students pasting the day's Caught'ya into their notebooks and making the corrections on the typed copy instead of copying the sentences themselves. It is, however, a good idea to wean students off this after a week or two and make them copy the Caught'ya themselves.

Why? The skill of copying from the board or overhead is a necessary one that needs early mastery and practice. Of course, if your students did Caught'yas in previous grades, this transition will not be necessary, and they will be ready to copy the sentences themselves at the beginning of the year.

If you have classes that vary widely in ability as I did when I taught a class of drop-out prevention, several classes of "regular" students, and a class or two of advanced students, you can use this same story, utilizing the overhead for one class and writing the Caught'ya on the board for the others. I even made changes to the Caught'ya on the board between periods to meet the difficulty level of the next class.

When I had totally heterogeneous classes with kids who read on a second-grade to college level, it was easy. As I walked around the room (**Step 6**) looking at student Caught'ya papers, I adjusted my reaction to student ability level. For some students, "comma" was a foreign word. Others, after instruction, had little difficulty inserting them where needed.

Step 3: Put the day's Caught'ya on the overhead (or write it on the board) with the day and date at the top. Write the suggested journal topic. Assign an extra task.

Write the day (spelled incorrectly) and date (without commas or capital letters) at the top. Even my most English-challenged students liked catching the misspelling of a day of the week or month or the comma in a date. My gifted eighth-graders, for the life of them, just couldn't spell "Wednesday" or "February." Constant repetition and reminders quickly cure these common problems.

Next, put up the day's suggestion for a journal topic for those students who can't think of their own topic. To make it simple, I always read the Caught'ya and just winged it, writing a topic reflected in a word or sentence of the Caught'ya. For example, the corrected Caught'ya #53 in the seventh-grade part of the story reads as follows:

Sam gently put his hand on her shoulder and said, "He is a 'bogus' cad. No one listens to him. My friends and I pay him no heed."

Several journal topics may come to mind, but try to choose one that allows students to connect the story to their own lives (like the example below). The added questions help stimulate stagnant minds:

Write about a time when someone insulted you. How did that person insult you? How did you feel? What did your friends say? Were they supportive? How did you react to the insult?

Sometimes I even asked my students for an appropriate journal topic to write about the following day.

Finally, in addition to the suggested journal topic, you also may want to post a small task for your students to complete every day. This task should be something that uses the Caught'ya in some way and takes only two to three minutes to complete. Some suggested tasks could be

→ identifying a part of speech or literary device
→ writing an example of a type of sentence
→ circling all the nouns
→ writing above each prepositional phrase whether it is used as an adjective or adverb
→ changing one of the sentences to add a certain literary device (like a simile)
→ finding a synonym for one or more of the words
→ diagramming only the subject and verb of the first sentence or diagramming one complete sentence (see **Chapter 3, #7**)

Step 4: Read the Caught'ya dramatically; review the vocabulary word(s); discuss the need for a new paragraph; and warn of a difficult skill.

This is the step in which it is especially important to challenge your students to correct the sentences. Middle-school students love challenges, dares, and bets. As you read the Caught'ya dramatically, *dare* them to put in all the commas. Tease them and tell them that they'll never find all the errors. Do whatever it takes to intrigue your students enough to work hard to correct the sentences and learn the vocabulary word(s) well enough to recall skills and words when writing their own compositions.

After reading the sentences dramatically, review what happened previously in the story (for those who have been absent). Elicit the meaning of the vocabulary word(s) in a way that makes your students remember it for more than five minutes, or ask a child to look up the word(s) and inform the class of the meaning.

One good way to learn a new word is to associate it with an image. For example, when I taught the word "elevation," I gave my students the image of me wobbling on a table. When I taught the word "puerile," I gave them the meaning with my thumb in my mouth. When I taught the word "waggish," I ran around the room taking pencils, ruffling hair, and generally acting in a mischievous manner. And, aimed at my students with learning disabilities but helpful to all, I always made everyone take a finger (not the finger) and write the word out on his or her arm. This kinesthetic technique really helps (more on these in **Chapter 3**).

Next, if it is appropriate, warn students of any difficult skill in that day's Caught'ya and, at least the first few months of school, have a daily discussion of "to paragraph or not to paragraph." I liked to have a show of hands: "Should there be a new paragraph here? How many say 'yes'? How many say 'no'?" If a new paragraph was debatable, the arguments began, and my students and I enjoyed many a lively discussion! Except for an obvious paragraph change (like a new person speaking or a change of time), paragraphing can be personal. If a student could justify his or her point of view, I accepted that opinion as correct.

Step 5: Students then enter the vocabulary words into their vocabulary notebooks, write the Caught'ya as correctly as they can with a heading at the top of their papers, write an entry in their journals, and complete whatever extra task you assigned for the day.

I highly recommend that you require your students to keep a vocabulary notebook in which they progressively list all the Caught'ya vocabulary along with the part of speech and the meaning of each word. The vocabulary notebook is best kept in a composition book as those pages cannot be ripped out. Former students tell me that they found the vocabulary notebooks they made in my class to be useful in high school when they had to take the state writing assessment test and, later, the SAT. You, too, can make a big deal about students saving their vocabulary notebooks for just that purpose.

It is important to say at this point that if your students have never done Caught'yas before, you will need to ease them into the routine. Walk them slowly through the first five Caught'yas or so, doing one with the class, writing the Caught'ya on the board, debating out loud whether to put in commas, etc., just as your students will do when they complete a Caught'ya on their own. Students copy the Caught'ya on their own papers and put in the corrections as you model the thought process necessary to making those corrections. After a week or so, students can begin working independently by following these steps.

First, students should write the day of the week, the month, and the date. Students MUST write the number of each Caught'ya beside it or above it to stay organized and make grading easier for you. In addition, students should have a heading at the top of their paper that includes the items you require, such as their full name, their period, and a title. I required the latter in order to accustom my students to writing a title with correct capitalization and without using quotations or underlining. A two- to four-word title works best for this purpose. We used the title "Caught'ya Sentences # _____ to _____." This put in a preposition that wasn't supposed to be capitalized and made students practice the spelling of the word "sentences."

Second, students write the Caught'ya as correctly as they can individually, in pairs, in groups, or as a game—whatever way you decided to do it that week. (Variation is good—read about alternative Caught'ya execution methods in **Chapter 3**.) They do not use any proofreading symbols at this point. They simply write the sentences as correctly as they know how, but each student must have his or her own paper.

Third, students complete whatever extra task you assigned for the day. (See **Step 3** for suggested tasks.)

Finally, students write in their journals using a topic of their own choosing or the one you put on the board (see **Step 3**). You determine the length of each entry.

TEACHING NOTE:

I had three rules for the journal entries. First, entries had to be the specified length, and if the writing was huge, I took that into account. (This really made some students mad!) Second, swearing (except in Shakespearean) was not allowed at all. Even though I didn't read the journals unless a student indicated "Read Me" on top of a page, I told my students that swear words just leapt out at me like neon signs, and I just had to read that page. Third, writing the same sentence or phrase over and over again also was not acceptable and received no credit. My students trusted me not to read their journals if they desired privacy and abided by my three rules.

Step 6: Walk around the room, commenting on each student's efforts, praising, teasing, or giving a hint or a quick mini-lesson.

This is where the fun begins! As students work on the Caught'yas, the daily mini-assignment, or their journal entry, you and/or the pupil(s) or group assigned to that day's Caught'ya, walk around the room, making sure to reach each student.

You can issue a challenge, goad a lazy student good-naturedly, offer individual encouragement to a student low on self-esteem, praise a struggling pupil for putting a capital letter or a period (or doing *anything* right), help a dyslexic student keep a straight margin, or provide a thirty-second mini-lesson to anyone who needs it. Encourage your students to read and reread the sentences on their own as they do (we hope) when they edit and proofread their own papers.

Time yourself very carefully. You do not want to spend more than five to eight minutes doing this. After practice, you will find that it takes about five to six minutes to circulate around a class of thirty students. Impossible, you say? Follow these tricks:

Give your students a few minutes to get started. (You cannot wait until all your students have completed the Caught'yas to begin circulating around the desks, or you will have pandemonium and student boredom on your hands.) Then simply glance at the Caught'yas of the first few students, and praise those who have not yet made errors.

Look for *one* **error** as you continue to perambulate the room and students' work is more complete. Choose the most difficult correction in the Caught'ya so that many of your students probably will miss it at first glance. If that error still exists in a student's paper, tease, make a brief comment (I said, "Caught'ya"), and move on. If, on the other hand, a student has found and corrected the targeted error, take a few more seconds to check the rest of the Caught'ya. In this way, you can move very quickly around the room. I sometimes hummed a tune (one at least twenty years old) as I circulated, stopping only occasionally to praise, tease, or encourage a student. My pupils especially hated my hummed rendition of "She'll Be Coming 'Round the Mountain."

Use the kinesthetic techniques described in **Chapter 3** as you go around the room. As you, say, stomp a foot for one student to remember to put end punctuation on a sentence, you will find that students within hearing distance also will peruse their papers for missing end punctuation.

Enlist student peer-checkers. Ask students on whose papers you find no errors to join you in checking their peers' work by assigning each student a row or table. In this way, the number of checkers increases as you move around the room. If any student is rude to someone as he or she walks around the room, he or she loses the privilege of helping you for at least a month.

Challenge students who have not even begun the Caught'ya when you arrive at their desks to begin work a bit faster. I always liked to dare them to complete at least one sentence by the time I got to their desks. I also greeted those students at the door when they entered my room and encouraged (and reminded) them to begin immediately since it took them longer than the other students to finish. If you have a student who is truly slow and *can't* finish a Caught'ya in time, make allowances—like only asking for one completed sentence each day instead of the entire Caught'ya.

Vary where you begin checking the papers. (I started at the right side of the room for even-numbered Caught'yas and on the left for the odd-numbered ones. Of course, I often forgot which side I started with the previous day, but my students always kept me straight as to where I was to begin checking.) Doing this keeps the feedback fair because the first few Caught'yas you check never will have all the sentences completed.

Every few years you will get a class (usually right after lunch) which just can't keep quiet and on task while you amble around the room to every student's desk. To gain control of that class, I found that it was *very* effective simply to stop dead, walk to the front of the room, cross my arms, and wait. I did not resume walking around the classroom giving feedback. I said nothing. They usually got the point quickly. If not, in the case of a really "challenging" group, I only went to half the class each day, not even attempting to get to the other half. Things like this get around amazingly quickly in middle schools. At lunch and in the halls, students gossiped about the class that wouldn't allow me to get around the entire room. Peer pressure works well. Sadly to say, "I like the way John is working," doesn't work as well in middle school as it does in elementary school. It doesn't hurt to try, though.

Step 7: Go to the board or overhead and check the Caught'ya out loud with the class, eliciting answers and reasons for corrections from students.

Now you return to the board or overhead, go over the corrections in the Caught'ya, eliciting the answers from your students. Review the *why* of each correction, and if necessary, give a mini-lesson. Be sure to use the kinesthetic symbols for each indent, punctuation mark, and capital letter. You want your students to associate the sound, symbol, or gesture with a correction. It helps them correct their papers when they write. (See **Chapter 3**.)

To the left of each Caught'ya in **Chapters 6, 7, and 8** of this book, you will find the *why* listed for each correction. The corrections have been broken down into categories like "Paragraphs," "Commas," "Verbs," "Homophones," "Types of Sentences," etc. If several of your students missed a certain correction (for example, mixing up "lay" and "laid"), you can launch into more explanation.

Keep your explanations bizarre, funny, and *short*. When teaching middle school, the more humor and strangeness you can inject into your explanations, the better your students will remember what you are teaching. Try to make your explanations fewer than three to four minutes. Absorbing correct English grammar, usage, and mechanics (GUM) must be done in short but intense bursts if retention and carry-over into writing are to take place.

I'm sure that you already use all kinds of techniques to wrest your students' attention from their bodies and friends to teach them English. One teacher at a conference where I was presenting told me that he had his students write a brief opera using the irregular verbs. I would have loved to have heard it!

A few classroom-tested suggestions on how to approach some of the hard-to-teach points with humor, simple-to-understand explanations, mnemonic devices, etc. that you can use to supplement your own ideas are listed with the actual Caught'yas, as well as in the ***Grammar, Usage, and Mechanics Guide*** on the CD. You will find more suggestions in Chapter 4, "Mini-Lessons," of ***Caught'ya Again! More Grammar with a Giggle***.

Repetition is the true key! Keep on plugging, a little bit each day, and keep on repeating *ad nauseam* until your students get the point and, most importantly, begin to use a skill correctly in their writing. A professor once told me that everyone, in order to truly learn something, needs to have it repeated from fifteen to sixty times, depending on that person's learning curve. And, the older you are, the more times you need things repeated! This is bad news for those of us getting up in years, but good news for our students.

Step 8: Students mark mistakes and take notes.

As you (or your students) go over the Caught'ya with the class, students must make sure their corrections can be seen easily.

They can, for example, use simple proofreading symbols to correct any error they did not catch on their own. Of course, don't require the use of proofreading symbols if you think it will only confuse your students.

Another option is for students to mark the corrections with a different ink color from the one with which they wrote the Caught'ya. After trying unsuccessfully to get my students to do this by demanding it, I offered them five extra points for doing so and got better results. When students use a different color for corrections, they stand out better, making it easier for them to study the errors that they did not catch when

indent	⌗	take out indent	
add words here	∧	take out, delete	
capitalize		make a small letter	
move word	⟶	reverse order	
add punctuation (whatever is inside circle)			○

they did the Caught'ya on their own. In this way, they tend not to miss the same errors in the future.

Listed on the previous page are a few of the most commonly used proofreading symbols that I used in my classroom.

By the second half of the year, your students should be capable of identifying the reason behind each correction and taking notes on them. You can require that they write the notes above the corrected error or in the margin. This helps cement the skills. If students know *why* they need to put a comma in a compound sentence, for example, and write the rule that applies, there is a better chance that they will remember that rule as they write their own compositions.

Step 9: Students count and indicate the number of errors in the margin of their papers.

This process has two advantages: It makes students leave good, healthy, margins, and it provides students with immediate feedback when they study.

Encourage, cajole, forbid, threaten, or do anything you can think of to keep your students honest when they correct the Caught'ya on their own and mark the missed corrections. Since the grade they receive has nothing to do with the number of errors made when they attempted to write the Caught'yas on their own, it would be pointless to try to hide errors and correct them surreptitiously when the answers are divulged. Moreover, explain to students that cheating only prevents learning from their mistakes when studying for a test.

I told all the above to my students, but the perfectionists still had trouble and didn't want to show any errors. What finally worked to make the majority of my students honest was to warn in a very ominous tone that anyone who *never* (or rarely) missed anything in the Caught'yas would be expected to earn an "A" on every Caught'ya test I planned to give that year. Since no student ever made a perfect score on the pretest I gave at the beginning of the year, my students heeded the warning.

Step 10: Collect one paper per student after five Caught'yas have been completed, and grade only one Caught'ya per paper, noting the errors still missed so that the skills can be repeated in subsequent Caught'yas.

I found it most efficient for all concerned to require that five Caught'yas be put on one piece of paper (even if they had to go over to the back). This helped students organize themselves and hang on to only one sheet of paper, and it helped me when I graded because I only had one sheet to grade per student. This paper can be kept in a separate Caught'ya section of their binders.

TEACHING NOTE:

Of course, there are always the students who, for the life of them, can't hang on to a paper for more than a class period. For those students, I made a Caught'ya folder to hold the Caught'yas. Then the student and I found a place in the room to put this folder. When the student arrived in class, he or she surreptitiously got the folder and began work. The other students never realized that the student in question couldn't hold on to a paper and thus wasn't a target for teasing. A child's dignity was preserved, and the Caught'ya papers were saved and turned in with the rest when I collected them.

Now we proceed to assessing students' progress. Grading the Caught'yas is as important as doing them because it also supports learning by keeping your students careful and paying attention.

Assessing Your Students' Progress

The most important thing to remember about grading Caught'yas is that the sentences are *not* graded on how well a student initially corrects the Caught'ya sentences on his or her own. Rather, they are scored on how carefully that student corrected the sentences when you and the class reviewed the Caught'ya. In other words, you are grading them for three reasons: To get a grade for your gradebook, to keep your students honest, and to reinforce skill mastery.

A student can make one or twenty errors in any Caught'ya and still earn an "A" if he or she has been careful with the format, caught all of the errors and corrected them, and taken notes—how detailed is up to you—as to the reasons or rules for the corrections. You can assess students' progress through frequent, short Caught'ya tests and by observation (more details later in this chapter).

The title of this book promises you "grammar with a giggle." Well, get ready to have a giggle yourself! A week's worth of Caught'yas takes only ten minutes to grade for a class of thirty-five students! You probably are thinking that I've lost my mind, but there are some tricks you can use to shorten the time spent grading. Depending on your district, you may have up to 180 Caught'ya papers a week to grade.

The following section will reduce the grading time for those 180 students to fewer than fifty minutes each week! I promise.

The following steps assume that you have a paper in front of you. If you do not, look at the sample paper at the end of this section, and use it for clarification as you read the steps.

Decide on a format.

I suggest the following format. You, of course, will decide on what heading you require. Be adamant about it.

→ Student's full name
→ Full date written out underneath the name
→ A two- to four-word title (for capitalization practice)
→ A fairly even margin on the left and a margin that leaves space on the right, either of which can be used to indicate the number of errors missed
→ Use of a different color for corrections, clearly marked so that you (and the student when he/she studies it—Ha!) can tell at a glance what has been missed and then corrected by that student
→ Number of Caught'ya errors indicated and circled in the margin
→ Notes alongside many of the corrections that clearly indicate the reasons or rules for some of the more difficult corrections
→ All five Caught'yas on the same sheet of paper

Check the format.

Now get out your green, pink, and purple pens. You are ready to grade some Caught'yas. The grading is based on a one hundred-point scale. I suggest the following for scoring the format of the paper:

→ Deduct a full ten points total if there is *any* error in the format.
→ Take off five points each for uneven margins (the bane of dyslexic students, so please do not subtract points for those students).
→ Take off ten points (in addition to the ten points you subtracted for the format) if a student misspells a day of the week or month, though. This may seem harsh, but it encourages students to be careful.
→ Withhold the extra credit points (however many you decided to bestow) if a student failed to use a different color for corrections.

Check the content of *one* Caught'ya.

After checking the format, choose *one* Caught'ya from among the five to grade, and deduct ten points per error that the student *did not catch* when you went over that Caught'ya at the board. This is what really saves you time. I assure you that if you read all five Caught'yas and take off fewer points per error, the results will be the same, and you will have wasted precious time that could have been spent reading a good book or grading your students' writing.

For six years, I graded every Caught'ya of every student every week. Then, I noticed that if I increased the number of points per error to ten and graded only *one* Caught'ya per student per week, the grade almost always came out the same. The careless students were careless, and the careful students continued to be careful. In fact, some of the careless students (perhaps because I was taking off more points per error) became more careful. Carol Harrell, a colleague who used Caught'yas, independently came to the same conclusion. One day, in the hall in between classes, we talked it over, pooled our collective guilt at not reading every Caught'ya, and chucked it out our classroom doors with glee about the extra time per week we were giving ourselves.

I advise you *not* to tell students which Caught'ya you plan to grade, however. If you succumb to your students' pleas to tell them, they will be careful only with that particular Caught'ya. I also recommend that you do not always choose the most difficult Caught'ya of the week to grade. This will keep your students hopping and guessing.

Even the grading of Caught'yas is flexible because you easily can individualize the evaluation of them. Grade an easier one for your weaker students or classes in which the majority of the students are below grade level. Choose a harder one to grade for your more advanced students. In twenty-four years of doing Caught'yas, I was amazed to find that not one of my students *ever* figured out that I was grading different Caught'yas for different students!

The whole point of individualizing the grading of Caught'yas is to encourage your students to like editing and to think of it as a fun game rather than an onerous, teacher-imposed chore only to be done when coerced. Those of you who have taught language arts for years know how difficult it is to convince students to even glance at a paper when they have finished writing the first draft. You *want* your students to receive high grades on the Caught'yas.

Choose which Caught'ya you want to grade for the week. Out of a score of one hundred, I suggest going no lower than a grade of fifty (giving fifty points for breathing). This way, their GPA isn't damaged.

And, after all, they were there when the lesson was taught and must have absorbed *something*. When grading, ask yourself the following questions and deduct ten points for each "No" answer:

→ Did the student clearly mark the errors with proofreading symbols or correct them clearly in a different color?

→ Did the student make notes as to the reasons for some of the corrections?

→ Did the student catch every error?

→ Is the number of errors indicated in the margin?

→ Are all the words (including the vocabulary word(s), months, and days) spelled correctly?

→ Has the student correctly copied the Caught'ya from the board or overhead without leaving out any words?

→ Are all capital letters and punctuation marks placed properly (no extra commas)?

You will be pleasantly surprised at the results. Even your weakest student can earn an "A+." This can be very exciting for these students because they know that their papers are graded on the same scale as all the other students. In fact, I often found that my "regular" and below-level students were more careful about checking each sentence. They tended to be less cocksure than the more advanced and gifted students who often "knew it all."

After you have added the number of points to be deducted for errors in the format to the number of points lost for errors not caught, subtract the total from one hundred. Put that grade at the top of the student's paper with an encouraging or positive comment. Since you grade only one Caught'ya per week, you have the luxury of making a brief, private comment on each paper. Encouragement and success breed success.

TEACHING NOTE:

On the day you collect the Caught'ya papers, ask your students to put their journals out on their desks. With your gradebook in hand as you walk around the room checking the Caught'ya, take a few extra minutes to check that each student has the required number of pages in his/her journal. If a student wants you to read the entry, put a marker on the page and collect it for later perusal and comments. If you see a forbidden curse word or repetition of a phrase when you glance at the journal, the child gets half or no credit. I gave a check for complete or a zero for incomplete. When I tallied points for a letter grade, ten checks equaled an "A" and so on.

Take notes. Give rewards.

As you grade the Caught'yas, take notes somewhere to keep track of the errors your students are still having difficulty catching. I liked to use the big calendar blotter on my desk because it was always handy; I never had to search for it; and I never lost it as I did a piece of paper. No names were recorded, only the error that a significant number of students did not catch. You then can concentrate on those errors and not harp on already-mastered skills.

Each year different errors seem to be popular with the students. I have no clue as to the cause since most of the teachers at our feeder schools don't change their teaching methods or texts from one year to the next. One year I struggled for six months with improper verb tense use—you know, the "ping-pong syndrome." Present, past, present, past, etc. until you want to scream! Another year, students only infrequently made verb tense errors and did not play "verb ping-pong" after November, but they had a terrible time with correct pronoun use. Each year I wondered what the current error fad would be.

In regard to a reward system, some teachers maintain that public displays of success are more important at lower grade levels, but I think that middle-school students crave peer recognition more than any other age group. This added reinforcement engenders more enthusiasm for learning English, a big factor in the Caught'ya method's success. Play up the reward system to the hilt!

After trying other less successful and more labor-intensive-on-my-part methods of heralding student success, I experimented with a Caught'ya lottery in my classroom. This did the trick. It was almost no work for me, and my students loved it. The lottery system is simple. When you pass back the Caught'ya papers, give one-quarter of a three-by-five index card to each student who earned an "A+" on his/her paper. Announce the "A+" students out loud with a challenge, a grin, or some comment designed to bring notice to the students being rewarded. I always liked to say, "I'll get you next time." This, of course, evoked comments of, "No, you won't," accompanied by renewed care in correcting subsequent Caught'yas.

Students who receive a card write their name, the date, and the class period on the card. Rather than just collecting the cards, make each "A+" student walk to the front of the classroom in full view of the rest of the class. Relishing the moment of public recognition, the students deposit the cards in a box. Once a month, open the box and draw out one card from each class. Those students receive a prize—a candy bar, a lunch period in your room with three friends, a coupon for something, a "teacher dollar" or two to be saved, added to others, and redeemed later for a larger prize, etc.

Be flexible with testing.

With Caught'yas, teachers have several quickie, fairly painless (for both students *and* teacher), even amusing ways to test how much correct English is being absorbed and to make sure students are being honest when they write the number of errors they made in each day's Caught'ya.

In addition to the midterm and final exam in **Chapters 6, 7,** and **8** of this book, you may want to give mini-tests about once every three weeks. Here are three variations.

→ Use the next uncorrected Caught'ya (or two) as a test. Please note that this should be done only on days when the Caught'ya in question does not contain any new skills. The day of the "test," we conducted the Caught'ya as usual except that when I found errors on a student's paper, I only said that there *was* at least one error. But, I did not give any mini-lessons. Sometimes I let the students do it without even that help.

→ Write a new, uncorrected Caught'ya that follows the storyline. Cram into it as many of the skills as you can from those you have taught in the previous few weeks. Then conduct the test as suggested above.

→ Announce to your students that *one* of the last five (or ten) Caught'yas will be a test the following day. If students study these previous Caught'yas, they have a good chance of doing well on the mini-test. This test gets your students' attention and makes the point that it is important to listen when you go over the Caught'yas with the class.

TEACHING NOTE:

I added a twist to this third method of testing. A colleague and I had a t-shirt made with one of the Caught'ya characters on it, and we wore it the day we gave the Caught'ya test. Word spread the minute homeroom students hit the halls, and kids scrambled to review the previous five (or ten) Caught'yas. To be fair, I sometimes let the first-period class take the test the following morning, but the Caught'ya used was not the same in every class. I varied between two Caught'yas of equal difficulty so that students in subsequent periods never knew from their peers which Caught'ya would be the actual test.

When I picked the Caught'yas to be used for the test, I chose ones that contained the most examples of the skills we already had covered. Except in the case of a low-achieving class, I selected two Caught'yas of equal difficulty level.

To determine the grading scale of these tests, I counted the possible errors in the chosen Caught'ya, divided that number into one hundred, and came up with the number of points to subtract for each error.

In order to swell the number of possible mistakes and thus reduce the number of points taken off for each error, I subtract the following points:

→ Two points for not capitalizing their own names
→ One point for incorrect format
→ Several points for all the possible errors in writing the date
→ One point for each capital letter missed in the heading
→ Several points for incorrect margins, etc.

Sometimes, I simply applied an arbitrary number to subtract for each error (like three or four) to obtain an indication of which students were listening, and no one had his or her grade destroyed.

An example of a corrected student paper follows on the next page. The teacher's marks and comments are indicated in dark black lines. The Caught'yas are from the seventh-grade part of the story.

A sample student Caught'ya paper. The thick, dark marks are the teacher's. Please note:

→ Format is correct. Days of the week are spelled correctly. (See checks.)
→ Thursday's Caught'ya, #84, was graded. There were two errors that Georgia didn't catch—the spelling of "finally" and splitting a verb = -10 each.
→ Although Georgia did not correct the use of "further" to "farther" in Caught'ya #81 and misspelled "offense" in Caught'ya #85, neither count against her as those Caught'yas were not the ones graded.

NOTE:
   Georgia was given an extra 5 points to encourage continued careful note-taking.

85

March 7, 2005
Period 5

Caught 'ya Sentences #81-85

81 Monday, March 7, 2005   sub clause

complex sen.   If they had run five steps (further,) the (miscreants) might have escaped Dean

new subject

Dread's eye. Dean Dread, however, moved
                                    interrupt.
-2   quickly.

82 Tuesday, March 8, 2005   long intro

Quicker than the blink of an eye, he had
the (malefactors) by the back of their

new speaker   shirts. "You two (rapscallions), come with
me to my office. We need to investigate
-2   this incident," he said in a low, menacing
voice.   2 adj.

83 Wednesday, March 9, 2005   Great job
     ABSENT   jubilently jeered   of note
                                    taking!
                                    +5

(84) Thursday, March 10, 2005   AP -10
The class tormenters (finaly) had been
-10 (apprehended) for something. (Rather they
                                  can't count
-2   might (even) be (castigated) and then
suspended for their (transgression.)

85 Friday, March 11, 2005   interrupt.
Setting off a stink bomb, after all,
was a major (offence.)
complex
sen.   When the (putrescent) smoke had
-1   been cleared, everyone (congregated)
                sub clause
around Felicia Fey.

CHAPTER 3

Questions You May Have about the Caught'yas

1) Can I vary the Caught'ya method?

2) What should I do when students miss a Caught'ya?

3) Should I reveal the number of errors in a Caught'ya?

4) How can I teach proper English without boring my students?

5) How do I use kinesthetic learning techniques?

6) Is it worth my time to teach the parts of speech?

7) Are diagramming sentences a waste of time?

8) Can Caught'yas teach students to vary sentence structure?

9) Can Caught'yas help students to stop inserting extraneous capital letters?

10) What's with the lousy poetry used in the Caught'yas?

11) How did you choose the vocabulary for the Caught'yas?

12) How can I encourage students to use in everyday life what they've learned in the Caught'yas?

13) Do Caught'yas work with block scheduling?

14) How do I contact you with corrections to this book?

1) Can I vary the Caught'ya method?

At the elementary level, it is the teacher who always directs all ten steps. At the middle- and high-school levels, however, some teachers find it extremely effective to assign each student (or a pair or group of students) a Caught'ya or two and make it his, her, or their responsibility to teach **Steps 4 through 10** (see **Chapter 2**). Students must prepare lesson plans and notes beforehand and then teach the assigned Caught'ya(s) on the appointed day(s). You simply make copies of the assigned Caught'yas, the overhead, and the outline of the **Ten Easy Steps** to aid students in this task.

Of course, you cannot begin doing this until students are totally familiar with the Caught'ya method and have observed many times the techniques you used as you taught the Caught'yas. When they are involved in their own learning process, students learn more and buy into it. When kids teach the Caught'yas, you will want to help them by taking half of the room for **Step 6**. If you assign a group of students to teach a Caught'ya, I suggest giving each student in the group a section of the class.

You always can step in and re-teach a skill yourself on the days you direct the proceedings because you don't want your students to have to unlearn something. Challenge students to come up with a weird and different way to teach the skills in their Caught'ya. They can be very inventive. Some teachers turn doing Caught'yas into a game with tables or groups working together to correct the Caught'yas (each student with his or her own paper, though). The group with the most correct Caught'ya gets a point for the day.

Bridget Mann, who teaches seventh-grade English in Marco Island, Florida, turned doing Caught'yas into "Grammar Football." She had a huge felt football "field" on her wall. Each period was a football team and competed with another (i.e., first-period Gators vs. second-period Eagles). She held this competition every other day, doing Caught'yas in the regular fashion the rest of the time.

Going in alphabetical order, Bridget called on a different student for each competition. That student chose four friends to help correct the day's Caught'ya and write it on the board. Bridget set a timer (after her students got the hang of the game) for three to four minutes.

When Bridget started the timer, the designee and friends ran to the board to begin. One group member ran to the dictionary to look up the vocabulary word(s) and shared the meaning with the class. As the group at the board wrote the Caught'ya, the students in the "stands" pointed out corrections that the team had missed and counted down the last few seconds, creating a lot of excitement.

If the group had caught all the errors in the Caught'ya, Bridget gave the class a certain number of yards. The class with the most points at the end of nine weeks got a party. The rivalries created were legendary. Remember, all's fair in love, war, and the teaching of middle-school English!

Another variation is to do a Caught'ya orally as the mood strikes you or when you feel your students need a break (of course, they still are responsible for the vocabulary words). When I did this, my students felt as if they were getting away with murder, but they were learning English just the same. The next day they resumed writing the Caught'yas with renewed enthusiasm.

2) What should I do when students miss a Caught'ya?

Please, do not require that students who missed a Caught'ya due to absence or being called out of the room make up the missed Caught'yas. That makes life too difficult for you and for them, and the skills will be repeated all year anyway.

I suggest that you *do*, however, require two things of your students who miss doing a Caught'ya or two: The absent student should write the number of the missed Caught'ya(s) and the word "absent" in the space where the Caught'ya(s) should have gone, and the student should get the vocabulary word(s) from a friend and make the entry in his or her vocabulary notebook. In this way, students don't feel pressured; you know that the skills will be taught anyway in future Caught'yas; and everyone is happy. You also will want to check in your grade book to make sure a student who wrote "absent" on his or her Caught'ya paper indeed was absent that day.

If you do a Caught'ya orally with the entire class (to give them a break every week or two), students still will need to write the number of the Caught'ya, the date, and the vocabulary words. Then, instead of writing the Caught'ya on their papers, they write the words "done orally," just as they write "absent" if they miss a Caught'ya.

3) Should I reveal the number of errors in a Caught'ya?

I offer a word of caution here. I have found that students like to know how many errors there are in the Caught'ya sentences. They argue that it helps them find the errors. I used to fall for this and, against my better judgment, indulged them for a few weeks. There are a few major problems that arise. First, we never seem to count correctly, and some commas are debatable. Second, it frustrates the perfectionists to the point of getting really upset. Third, our more challenged students, too, get frustrated if they can't find all the errors and just give up. Thus, I have found such a practice counterproductive and to be avoided no matter how earnestly your students plead.

4) How can I teach proper English without boring my students?

As you complete the Caught'yas with your students, I again implore you to keep in mind that, although we are preparing them for high school, middle-schoolers' eyes glaze over at the mere mention of the more technical terms of English. In other words, in order for middle-school students to have a chance to understand the reasons behind the corrections, we must keep the explanations in simple terms to which kids can relate. Within the actual Caught'yas, you will find suggestions, such as mnemonic devices, for how to avoid using the technical terms.

Thus a "non-restrictive relative pronoun clause" can become "an unnecessary who clause," and "intransitive and transitive verbs" become "verbs that are not followed by an object and those that are," etc. Subordinating conjunctions can be called "A WHITE BUS words" (mnemonic device). Similarly, coordinating conjunctions can be renamed "FANBOYS" (mnemonic device).

At this level, the goal of teaching correct English is to help young people learn how to write correctly, not learn the correct terms..

If our students can write a clear paragraph or two with few egregious English errors and, in the process, use complete and varied sentences with a few great vocabulary words and a literary device or two thrown in, we have accomplished much!

5) How do I use kinesthetic learning techniques?

As you probably know, students learn more quickly if they involve their bodies in the process. To this end, I suggest that you employ what I call the "Victor Borge Technique" as you teach the Caught'yas. Musical humorist Victor Borge had a monologue in which he used pantomimes of stamped feet or sounds accompanied by appropriate air painting with fingers for each punctuation mark. I cannot imitate Mr. Borge's sounds or gestures in words, nor can I remember the exact ones he used. My students and I used the following ones:

→ Paragraph – say "move it over" accompanied by a step to the side
→ Period – a stamp of a foot
→ Comma – draw one in the air accompanied by a weird sound, but be careful not to spit
→ Capital letter – one clap of hands
→ Question mark – draw one in the air accompanied by an appropriate sound that ends going up in tone like a question
→ Exclamation point – draw one in the air accompanied by an appropriate sound with a smack of the lips at the end
→ Quotation marks – make finger gestures in the air (at least twice), and make a clicking sound two times to accompany the fingers

While you go over the Caught'ya each day, you might want to use the "Victor Borge Technique" at several points in the process. Students can mimic you. As you wander through the classroom, commenting and helping students, you can stand by a child who, for example, has forgotten to put in a period, and stomp your foot. That child (and often students sitting nearby), when he or she learns the appropriate kinesthetic action and sound that symbolizes it, will put in the missing period on his or her own. Then, as you go over the corrections, you can use the stomps, claps, etc. one more time.

6) Is it worth my time to teach the parts of speech?

That is a resounding "yes." As both a French and an English teacher, I had the unenviable task of teaching the grammar of two languages to middle-school minds. Since I didn't use the official terms when I taught grammar, usage, and mechanics (except to mention in passing in the vain hope that *one* student might remember), I had to use something to give my students a general frame of reference. The eight parts of speech worked perfectly. In my eighth-grade French classes, those who had *not* had a teacher who used Caught'yas to teach English in the seventh grade needed to be taught the eight parts of speech so that we could have a frame of reference. After all, a pronoun in French may sound different, but it is still a pronoun.

So, how do we go about teaching the parts of speech? I put large letters in my window for the first month of school and offered a prize if anyone could figure out what the letters represented. Each year, because kids from the previous year "blabbed," I changed the order of the letters. One of the following appeared in huge letters on a window the first day of school:

NIPPAVAC   PAVPANIC   CAPPAVIN   VANPAPIC

These are mnemonics for the eight parts of speech—noun, interjection, preposition, pronoun, adverb, verb, adjective, conjunction.

After someone guessed the "riddle" and won the prize (and someone always did—siblings can be such snitches), my students and I chanted the parts of speech several times daily for another two weeks until all the students knew them backwards and forwards. Then, they were ready to begin to work with them in the Caught'yas.

Some teachers like to teach the functions of each part of speech. Then, they ask students to identify the part of speech of each word in subsequent Caught'yas. I found this to be a bit much for my middle-school students. Instead, I found it worked best to focus on one part of speech at a time. For example, after briefly reviewing the functions of an adjective, students circled all adjectives (including adjective phrases) in the next ten Caught'yas or so. We proceeded in the same manner through all eight parts of speech. In addition, I required students to put the part of speech by each entry in their vocabulary notebooks.

When we had done this with *all* eight parts of speech, I still did not ask my students to identify the part of speech of all the words in a Caught'ya. Instead, each day, students circled examples of only one of them. They never knew which part of speech would be targeted. This became a sort of game. Students vied to find all the adverbs, for example. We even broke into groups to see if they could find all of them. One teacher I met, who has her desks set up in groups of four, has an ongoing contest to see which group can log the most days of correctly identifying the examples of the targeted part of speech.

Whatever *modus operandi* you choose, the Caught'yas can become the vehicle to teach your students the eight parts of speech. Once students are able to recognize each part of speech in a sentence, they easily can learn its function and hence can use it correctly and effectively in their writing.

7) Are diagramming sentences a waste of time?

Some may scoff at diagramming sentences, but I have found that it helps students to visualize the form of the sentence and the relevance of each part. Diagramming makes the parts of a sentence (especially the modifiers) clearer, and the punctuation and parts of speech then make more sense, especially to your left-brained students. Please note that I do not recommend diagramming every Caught'ya sentence. This would get tedious for your students. Diagramming one sentence once or twice every week or two for a couple of months should suffice.

The second half of the year, I always taught my seventh- and eighth-graders simple diagramming. Once or twice a week, I asked them to diagram a part of a Caught'ya. In the beginning, students diagrammed only the subject and verb of one sentence. Then I added modifiers, prepositional phrases, and compound and complex sentences. My students actually understood why a subordinate clause was not a complete sentence and that it was, indeed, just a long adverb.

8) Can Caught'yas teach my students to vary sentence structure?

Because most states require varying sentence structure on the writing assessment tests, it is important to point out the types of sentences that comprise each day's Caught'ya. According to the powers that be, all students at the middle-school level should have mastered the use of all four types of sentences—simple, compound, complex, and compound/

complex. The reality is somewhat different, so we need to push the concept. Caught'yas can help.

You will notice that the types of sentences used in each Caught'ya are identified to the left of that Caught'ya. Sometimes, to practice varying sentence structure, you might ask students to change a simple sentence in a Caught'ya to a compound or complex one; I found this effective. In addition, frequent discussions about fragments help students to recognize and ultimately avoid them. You can program a few fragments into the Caught'yas if you find that your students still are using them.

Since identifying a type of sentence and actually producing one are totally different animals, I suggest that, as the extra skill in the Caught'ya, you often ask your students to write an example of *one* of the four types of sentences. Diagramming sentences, believe it or not, also helps as students then get a picture of how each type of sentence is constructed.

9) Can Caught'yas help students to stop inserting extraneous capital letters?

For some inexplicable reason, many middle-school students wildly and inappropriately insert extraneous capital letters into their writing. This is especially true of sixth-graders. Perhaps somehow in an earlier grade, they became confused about common and proper nouns. Perhaps they like the appearance of the capital letters. Perhaps they just don't think. Who knows? The problem is how to cure students of this practice.

To this end, if many of your students suffer from what I call "capitalization craziness," you may wish to put extraneous capital letters or capitalize all the letters in the "B" sentence of many Caught'yas until you cure your students of this disease. With a daily discussion of what needed to be capitalized and what did not, it usually took my students a month or so to get the point.

10) What's with the lousy poetry used in the Caught'yas?

I do apologize for the corny poems (especially the limericks in the sixth-grade story), but they were fun to write. Sometimes the syllable stress is misplaced, but I took such liberties in order to get the desired content and syllable count.

As you use the Caught'yas with your students and get into the story, you will notice sometimes outlandish but droll limericks, cinquains, and haiku that distress most of the teachers in a strange way. These short poems are the clues that eventually lead the students to solve the mystery of the bizarre teachers. The secret will be revealed at the end of the eighth-grade story, but I'm sure your students will figure it out much earlier. To this end, I beseech you not to tell them the end of the story. **Let them speculate!** However, should students guess correctly, hopefully they will keep their mouths shut, and the unfolding of the plot as well as the goofy poems will keep them interested.

The poems may contain vocabulary words but **do not** contain any spelling errors. However, capitalization and punctuation may be omitted in obvious places in the seventh- and eighth-grade Caught'yas. I felt that any more errors would be too much since poems often are punctuated according to the poet's whimsy (like E. E. Cummings). You simply can write the poems under the day's Caught'ya in which they appear and teach the vocabulary where appropriate.

All the names of places mentioned in the limericks in the sixth-grade story, are real places, believe it or not, found in the *National Geographic Atlas*. Since the state appears in parentheses, you and your sixth-grade students might enjoy looking up the town on a map.

Middle-school students really "get into" the short poetic forms of limericks, cinquains, and haiku. You may find that your students begin to compose them on their own to try to annoy you and your colleagues. This is good! You can tell them that these three forms of poetry have been around for a long time.

Limericks – Sixth Grade

Maybe you have heard this already, but limericks were invented in twelfth-century China as a marching ditty for the army. Later, the poetic form of five lines with successively eight syllables, eight syllables, five syllables, five syllables, and a last line of eight syllables that often repeats the first line, combined with a rhyme scheme of AABBA (with the accent on the last syllable of each line), became popular during the eighteenth century in Europe. That was when this type of poem finally was called by the name we know today—limericks. Traditionally, limericks went beyond the silly and often smutty ones we usually associate with the genre these days.

Cinquains – Seventh Grade

The form of poetry called "cinquain" was invented by Adelaide Crapsy in 1907. She had translated some Japanese forms of poetry, tanka and haiku, from the French and was inspired to develop her own poetic system. She called her invention "cinquain."

A cinquain is a short, unrhymed poem that consists of twenty-two syllables. The syllables are distributed in five lines as follows:

Line One – 2 syllables
Line Two – 4 syllables
Line Three – 6 syllables
Line Four – 8 syllables
Line Five – 2 syllables

The most famous cinquain is probably the following:

> These be
> Three silent things:
> The falling snow...the hour
> Before the dawn...the mouth of one
> Just dead.

Guidelines to writing cinquains:

→ Write in iambs (two-syllable groupings in which the first syllable is unstressed and the second syllable is stressed).
→ Write about a noun or something concrete.
→ Don't try to make each line complete or express a single thought. Each line should flow into the next.
→ Cinquains work best if you avoid adverbs and adjectives as much as possible.
→ The poem should build toward a climax with the last line as a conclusion or link to the topic.

Haiku – Eighth Grade

Haiku is an ancient Oriental form of poetry that first appeared in the fifteenth century and became popular for over 600 years, especially in Japan. A contemplative, deceptively simple poetic form that emphasizes nature, seasons, colors, contrasts, and surprises, Haiku attempts to use a vivid image to get beyond the usual limitations of language and linear thinking and reach the spiritual realm.

A haiku poem might be a splash of sunlight on a leaf, a little girl's laugh, or the sight of a falling flower petal. Any experience that can arouse a sense of beauty, humor, wisdom, sadness, or joy for even a moment is a subject for a haiku. Each haiku is supposed to register a moment in time, a brief memory, a sensation, or a momentary impression of an aspect of our earth. Haiku tend to be beautiful because they are almost like a photograph or painting of some specific moment.

The form has changed only slightly over the years. There are variations, of course, but today's haiku remain three lines with seventeen syllables total—five in the first line, seven in the second line, and five in the last line. There is no rhyme scheme.

Here is a famous haiku by Basho Matsuo, the first well-known haiku poet, who lived from 1644 to 1694.

> Old pond...
> a frog leaps in
> water's sound.

You will notice that there are only nine syllables in the poem above. For the purpose of this Caught'ya story, all the haiku will be of the modern, seventeen-syllable type like the example below by Ryuho.

> I scooped up the moon
> In my water bucket...and
> Spilled it on the grass.

11) How did you choose the vocabulary for the Caught'yas?

There is no set list of vocabulary words for upper-elementary or middle-school students as there is for the primary grades or for tenth-graders (SAT list), so the vocabulary words we teach are up to each individual teacher. This leaves us free to teach our students the hundred-dollar words that we adore and would use naturally anyway in our normal parlance. It also leaves us free to use any list of words (as from a literature book) and to employ diverse approaches to teaching those vocabulary words. In my classroom, I always chose words I found in the literature my students were reading, words I already loved, and, of course, the vocabulary words in the Caught'yas.

When Mr. Walt Frazier, the basketball star, wanted to increase his vocabulary, he ended up writing a book, *Word Jam* (Frazier, 2001), that can be used with middle-school students. Where did Mr. Frazier get his list of words for his vocabulary book? To increase his vocabulary in order to become a better sportscaster, Mr. Frazier searched wordbooks and pocket dictionaries for "words that jump out and grab you with their rhythm and reason" (Frazier, 2001).

While much of the vocabulary used in this book *is* on the SAT list, that august list is not the criterion for a word's use. The important element to remember is that the carry-over of superlative vocabulary into student writing is the objective of teaching those hundred-dollar words. Every language arts teacher wants to have his or her students "fall in love" with words so thoroughly that they *want* to use those words in their speech and ultimately in their writing. The source of the vocabulary does not matter—Caught'yas, Walt Frazier, SAT list—as long as the students learn the words, use them in their writing and speech, and recognize them when they encounter them in books.

How do we middle-school teachers find words that will appeal to our students? I suggest listening to *them*. Perhaps because of constant association with them, I am sparked by the same motives as those of the students with whom I have spent so many years of my life on a daily basis. Words that I encounter, fall in love with, and soon wear like a comfortable old sweatshirt seize me with their power, feel good in my head, look delicious on paper, or roll around on my tongue in a pleasant fashion when uttered. I kept these sensations and my students' interests (bathroom talk, violence, love, friendship, the opposite sex, not being different, external beauty, etc.) in mind when coming up with the vocabulary words to insert in the story.

The key to teaching vocabulary to young, otherwise occupied minds is to teach only words that have a simple synonym or that would appeal to them either by the sound of the word or its meaning.

For example, "masticate" was a personal favorite of my eighth-graders for obvious reasons. Their minds may have been thinking of a word with a similar sound, but their mouths were saying and using a synonym for "chew." "Flatulent" was a popular word with my seventh-graders. This time the word was enjoyed for its meaning, not a lofty one but acceptable to adults and much preferable to its cruder synonym.

All of my students, of whatever middle-school grade I taught, always adored the words "a plethora of" as they could never remember whether "a lot" was one word or two, but they had no difficulty with the former, and they loved the sound of it. Other words that have caught my students' fancy over the years are "dulcet," "a dearth of," "pulchritudinous" (which sounds like something a cat hacks up), "comely," "obese," "loathe," "abhor," "blithe," "egregious," "puerile," "pugilist," and more. Many students, in fact, became true "wordaholics," always trying to find a new, "cool" word to use or searching for one the meaning of which I did not know.

12) How can I encourage students to use in everyday life what they've learned in the Caught'yas?

There is almost nothing middle-school students love more than besting someone, especially an adult. Keeping in mind that all's fair in love, war, and the teaching of middle-school English, I challenged my students to find English errors in books, newspapers, television programs, and adults. I gave them two extra credit points if they caught me in an error (like using "like" instead of "as" or ending a sentence with a preposition) and one point for an error found anywhere else.

Students had to produce the example. With something said on television, they had to write down the place or program, the time, and what the error was, and get the signature of an adult. Confusion of possessives vs. plurals, fewer vs. less, and who vs. whom were the most prevalent errors my students found.

If students heard an error voiced by an adult, I instructed them to quietly write down the error and get the adult to sign the paper when the student could be alone with that person. In other words, they were not supposed to embarrass the adult. It is a good idea to get the permission of a few of your colleagues in advance and then tell your students that those particular teachers are "fair game," but you will not give credit for or allow them to note English errors of any teacher other than the ones who have previously agreed to join the fun.

This worked well! In addition, extra credit is always popular with students who find (and bring in) the Caught'ya vocabulary words in books, newspapers, and other printed material. One day, I received a pile of copies of a newspaper headline that included the words "a plethora of."

I must make a couple of caveats to this activity, though. You can incur the indignation and wrath of other adults! When I challenged my students to find as many errors as they could in the yearbook, they found quite a few (of course) and somehow, it got to the teacher in charge of the yearbook. I almost lost a friend. I just assumed that she, being an English teacher as well, wouldn't mind. She did mind. But, when she saw the enthusiasm of the students, she relented and encouraged her own students to find even more errors in the yearbook.

It is also a good idea to cover your rear by sending a letter home to parents explaining what you are doing and why and asking that any parent who objects please let you know. Only one parent ever objected, and she hadn't been given the note.

When students find English errors in store signs, it can have thrilling, far-reaching effects, and students can see the result of their knowledge of English! The local supermarket, a Florida chain, was bombarded with students (mine and those of other English teachers using Caught'yas) who went up to the manager and told him in no uncertain terms (as indignant middle-schoolers are wont to do) that the store was setting a bad example for the children of the town by displaying signs with incorrect English on them. First our local store changed its sign. Within a few years, the entire chain of stores, all over Florida, changed the "10 Items or Less" signs to "10 Items or Fewer." My students were delighted and felt very powerful. It encouraged them to learn more rules of English! Our students *can* make a difference in this world.

13) Do Caught'yas work with block scheduling?

Yes. Caught'yas work well no matter how your school schedules the day. If you are lucky enough (as I was) to have block scheduling in which you keep the same students all year long, count your blessings and proceed to do a Caught'ya every day. Caught'yas can be a perfect starter for the period or can be used as a break between two different activities when you want to change the pace.

If, on the other hand, you have one set of students the first semester and another the second semester, you have my sympathy. Students only can absorb so much in one day and forget most of it in six months. In order to finish the Caught'ya story for your grade and include all the skills your students need to learn for the year, I suggest that you do two Caught'yas a day, one in the regular, written fashion and the other orally with the class as a whole. Teachers who have used Caught'yas with that kind of block scheduling found that this solution worked best. But, you will want to make students responsible for the vocabulary words in both Caught'yas.

If you suffer the "A" and "B" days type of block scheduling, doing two Caught'yas a day—one written, one oral—works well as long as you keep reminding your students of what is going on in the plot of the story.

14) How do I contact you with corrections to this book?

Keep in mind that English rules are not always hard and fast! In fact, many are debatable. I, for example, always put a comma before the "and" in a series of three or more. Others do not. In other words, feel free to disagree with me. I was not even the "absolute word" in my own classroom. My students and I had hot debates over optional comma use and paragraphing. By the way, just so you know how far I do go in order to be comfortable with the rules—the apostrophe in Caught'ya is a contraction of the made-up word, "caughtchya."

Don't be shy. Contact me if you find an error so that it can be corrected for the next printing of this book. You can reach me directly at my e-mail address, janekiester@comcast.net, or via Maupin House Publishing.

CHAPTER 4

List of Vocabulary and Character Names

This chapter includes four lists of vocabulary words: a list of the characters' names and one list each for the sixth-, seventh-, and eighth-grade parts of the Caught'ya story. The words are listed by the number of the Caught'ya in which they appear.

All the vocabulary used in the book is in this chapter as a reference and a teaching tool. I always liked to see, in advance, the words my students might encounter in any book we read as a class. Usually, I had to go through the book and write them down myself, making my own list. I liked to use those words as I spoke, thus making them even more familiar to my students.

Use the lists as you wish. You may just want to refer to the list for your grade level to play vocabulary games with your students. You may want to print copies to give to students who come into your classroom later in the year to catch up on their vocabulary notebooks. You may want to have students paste the list in the back of their vocabulary notebooks for easy review.

You will note that, except for the characters' names, I do not provide the meanings of the words. If you use one of the lists with your students, you will want *them* to look up the meanings of the words they do not know. Keeping in mind the keys to choosing vocabulary words for middle-school students (see **Chapter 3**), most words can be substituted for a simple synonym and have kid-appeal.

If you do not know the meaning of a word and forget (or just don't have the time) to look it up before class, there is no shame in saying, "Hey, here's a word even *I* don't know! Let's look it up." My students *loved* when I did this. It made me human and fallible, like them. They delighted in their teacher learning something along with them. The words I admitted to not knowing were invariably the ones that the students learned well! Anything that works to motivate our students to learn is fair game!

You also will note that some of the vocabulary words are repeated in subsequent Caught'yas. Children of any age revel in being able to recognize those really big words and delight in being able to spout their meaning when they encounter them. My students just loved it when they recognized vocabulary words they already knew from previous Caught'yas. Besides, the more we repeat a word, the better the chances are that our students will place it in their long-term memory and use it in their writing.

Student Names and Meanings in Alphabetical Order

Alessandra **Amorous**
  loving, ardent, passionate, affectionate, romantic
Beth **Bibliophilic**
  book-loving
Carolyn **Clamorous**
  noisy, loud, rowdy, boisterous, vociferous, raucous
Danny **Dapper**
  handsome, neat, well-dressed, debonair, well-groomed
Dalbert **Devious**
  deceitful, sneaky, tricky, cunning, scheming, underhanded, sly, shifty, mean
Felicia **Fey**
  use only the meaning that has to do with being like a wizard, magical
Isabelle **Ingenuous**
  free from reserve or dissimulation, frank, candid, open, sincere, innocent
John **Jabbering**
  prattling, talkative
Jesse **Jocose**
  jovial, joking, jesting, humorous, playful
Mark **Meticulous**
  careful, scrupulous, thorough, particular, painstaking
Orson **Odious**
  hateful, horrible, abhorrent, loathsome, obnoxious, repellant, detestable
Olivia **Otiose**
  lazy, idle, indolent
Pauline **Puerile**
  childish, immature, silly, infantile
Petra **Pulchritudinous**
  beautiful, comely
Quincy **Querulous**
  argumentative, difficult, cantankerous, irritable, petulant, confrontational
Sam **Sagacious**
  wise, sage, clever, learned, perceptive, erudite, astute

Skateboarding Steven **Slovenly**
  sloppy, careless, disheveled, untidy, messy
Vivian **Virtuous**
  good, honest, righteous, upright, moral, worthy, honorable
William **Waggish**
  roguish (only in merriment and good humor), mischievous, jocular, fun-loving

Names and Meanings of Custodian, Teachers, and Administrators

Mr. **Adept** Fixit
  adroit, competent
Ms. **Amicable** Artist
  friendly, good-natured, agreeable, harmonious, kind
Mr. Dean **Dread**
  fear, anxiety, terror
Ms. Grammar **Grouch**
  moaner, complainer, nasty-tempered
Ms. **Grumpy** Geography
  irritable, grouchy, cantankerous
Mr. **Horrendous** History
  hideous, revolting, dreadful
Ms. **Humdrum** History
  boring, ordinary, dull
Mr. Math **Martinet**
  disciplinarian, stickler, despot, tyrant, hardliner
Mr. **Melodious** Music
  harmonious, tuneful, musical, mellow
Mr. **Punctilious** Principal
  painstaking, assiduous, meticulous, socially correct, thorough, conscientious
Ms. **Stern** Science
  severe, strict, harsh, firm, demanding, unyielding, uncompromising, hardhearted
Ms. **Stringent** Social Studies
  severe, strict, righteous, stern, harsh, tough, inflexible, rigid
Mr. **Scintillating** Social Studies
  entertaining, amusing, stimulating, sparkling, dazzling, brilliant, shining, bright, amusing
Ms. **Witty** Writing Wizard
  amusing, humorous, droll, clever, sharp

Sixth-Grade Caught'ya Vocabulary

Introduction to story

eerie	dormant	puerile	fey
sported	trekked	waggish	evoked
ablaze	adept	titters	sagacious
punctilious	portals	clamor	reluctant
blousy	myriad	myriad	rebounded
ambled	askew	trudged	harass
gaggle	foyer	loomed	emulate
otiose	ingenuous	cadence	

Caught'yas

1. tedious — nestled — verdant
2. shrilled — ingenuous — auburn
3. insipid — waggish
4. sagacious — otiose
5. retorted — fey — meager — awry
6. mane — portal
7. sextet — monotone
8. puerile — commenced — snivel
9. somber
10. *sotto voce*
11. mausoleum — surreptitiously — surveyed
12. uttered — loquacious
13. ushered — tittered
14. mortified — jocose — quell — proximity
15. distraught — garbed
16. formidable — somber
17. perceptive — blousy — tresses
18. quailed
19. sentries — glowering
20. punctilious — mete
21. subvocalize — utterance
22. uttered — wisps
23. muffle — glowered — swiveled
24. phenomenon — colleague
25. incident — paid heed
26. striplings
27. intrepid — stern — martinet
28. shenanigans — confiscated — querulous — articulated — puerile
29. inimitable — malevolent — wrathful — wrath — stifled
30. peer — demise — uncompromising
31. resumed — emitting
32. pandemonium
33. intrepid — amicable — melodious
34. pealed
35. daunted
36. titanic
37. petite
38. jocose — wrath — jocularity
39. appropriate — encountered

40.	proboscis			
41.	eerie			
42.	queried			
43.	differentiate	consternation		
44.	amiable	terse		
45.	blurted	coiffure	tittered	
46.	juncture	emitted		
47.	penned	furtive	micturated	
48.	loathed	latter		
49.	perceive			
50.	countered	unison	infamous	livid
51.	nostrils	anomalies		

Almost Midterm Caught'ya Test

bizarre	clad	maliciously	expounded
nemesis	odious	verbal	reigned

Caught'yas continued

52.	stern	monotone	a plethora of	a dearth of
53.	slumped	woe		
54.	ominous	pontificate		
55.	elude	wretched	commenced	
56.	unsightly			
57.	portal	proboscis		
58.	boisterous	pandemonium	rumor-monger	purportedly
59.	peers	forebodingly		
60.	compatriot			
61.	malevolent	visage	marred	pursed
62.	amicable			
63.	opted			
64.	commenced	Impressionist	touts	
65.	periodically	ambled	perused	
66.	hued	coiffure	spiel	rapt
67.	mused			
68.	neophyte	melodious		
69.	arduous			
70.	compel			
71.	plodded			
72.	invariable			
73.	comely	pulchritudinous	amorous	dapper
74.	afoot	atrocious	hilarious	
75.	evoked	infamous	monotone	
76.	*apropos*			
77.	indolent			
78.	innovative			
79.	apathetic	superlative	noxious	
80.	insufferable	taunts	pugnacious	
81.	countered	visage	fray	rapscallions
82.	goaded			
83.	jeered	quiescent	exacerbate	
84.	loathes	pacifistic		
85.	orchestrated	obstreperous		
86.	ushered	miscreants		

87.	miscreants		
88.	docile	bibliophilic	secreted
89.	meticulous	elated	
90.	warrant	scoffed	
91.	retorted	daunt	mutual	nurturing
92.	widespread	species	
93.	habitat		
94.	larvae	chrysalis	metamorphosis
95.	stupendous	exhilaration	oozed
96.	shrilled		
97.	concur		
98.	adamant	retched	animated
99.	problematical	horrendous	
100.	spectacles	puckishly	stripling	barbs
101.	doggerel		
102.	protruded		
103.	manifesting	gargoyles	
104.	omnipresent	interlude	proboscis
105.	latter	untoward	
106.	regale	bellowed	
107.	articulated	awe	replica	tresses
108.	oblivious	barbs	jabs
109.	crammed	massive	
110.	approximately		
111.	reproached		
112.	discourse		
113.	metamorphose	chrysalises	
114.	marveled		
115.	*caveat*	refrain	
116.	reigned	mesmerized	clamor
117.	puled	petulant	querulous	peevishly
118.	mollified		
119.	querulous	peers	adept

Passage to be read out loud to students

insensitive	warily	obnoxious	pastoral
adhered	abodes	lilting	assiduously
consternation	unruly	abode	
whooped	hence	frangible	

Caught'yas continued

120.	balmy				
121.	aggressive	banished			
122.	vicarious				
123.	flabbergasted	diligent			
124.	noxious	deem	abodes		
125.	simultaneously	unison	hues	dispersed	diverse

Another passage to be read out loud to students

dispersed	prodigious	insignificant	ameliorated
majority	alacrity	strolled	apprehensive
bane	annual	scurried	
outlandish	inappropriate	adept	

Caught'ya Final Exam

bustled	vantage	in accord
concur	assent	exasperation

Seventh-Grade Caught'ya Vocabulary

Introduction to story

eerie	dormant	askew	vehicle
punctilious	adept	careened	decrepit
sported	harried	animatedly	genially
myriad	trekked	stout	brimful
ambled	ablaze	leverage	disgorged
adept	punctilious	ambled	diverse
portals	strolled	foyer	ingenuous
dapper	ambled	otiose	languid

Caught'yas

1. ingenuous — animated — excess — puerile — tardiness — otiose
2. garbed — fey — awry
3. otiose — ingenuous — uttering
4. putrid
5. waggish — lame — vapid
6. sagacious — clamor — erudite
7. waggish — regaled — aspiration — eloquent — articulate
8. sagacious — fey — deter
9. affront — glowered
10. insipid
11. deftly — ensued — amicable — odious
12. concurred — fervor — queried
13. otiose — chartreuse — abode
14. sniped — ineptitude
15. intrepid — trekked — abode — paucity
16. mutely
17. jocose
18. dejection — puerile
19. incessant — predicted — eerie
20. virtuous — odious
21. coiffed — ebony
22. odious — crony — dapper
23. malevolent
24. coerced — shenanigans
25. appropriate
26. whimpered — nemesis — torment
27. odious — maliciously — lobbed — wrath — martinet

28.	fidgeting	sagacious	ambled	portal
29.	comely	demurely	pulchritudinous	
30.	comely			
31.	pulchritudinous	ebony	tresses	
32.	novel (original)			
33.	unison			
34.	dapper	abhorrent	vindictive	grimace
35.	skirmish	nemesis		obstreperous
36.	queried			
37.	vernacular	concurred	jocose	slang
38.	reiterated			
39.	taunted	somber		
40.	glowered	perilous		
41.	comeuppance			
42.	enamored	avail	oblivious	aloof
43.	blithe			
44.	a plethora of			
45.	bibliophilic	cad		
46.	pulchritudinous	abounded	atrocious	
47.	sycophant	incorrigible		
48.	amicable	melodious	witty	appalling
49.	deplorable	cinquain		witty
50.	penned	martinet	audacity	utter
51.	drones (to drone on)			

Almost Midterm Caught'ya Test

uttered	exuded	latter	spurning
bizarre	amorous	spitefully	primped
sycophant	disenchanted	uncomplimentary	affront

Caught'yas continued

52.	proboscis	refrained	cringed		
53.	cad	heed			
54.	sycophant	noisome			
55.	awe-inspiring	*sotto voce*			
56.	protrusion	utterance			
57.	monotonous	droned	latter	laboriously	drivel
58.	regale				
59.	fervent				
60.	amicable	hue			
61.	audibly				
62.	emitted				
63.	unremittingly				
64.	majority	to critique			
65.	perplexed	blatant	pondered		
66.	odoriferous	milled			
67.	noxious	reeked	a plethora of	noisome	billowed
68.	perdition	dearth of			
69.	stentorian	bellowed	garbed	foreboding	
70.	ubiquitous	loomed			
71.	putrescent	stench			
72.	incantation	dispel			

73.	mauve	reeked		
74.	culprits	obstreperous		
75.	cadence			
76.	stellar			
77.	lapse			
78.	striplings			
79.	receding			
80.	brisk	pace	exacerbated	
81.	miscreants			
82.	malefactors		reprobates	
83.	jubilantly	jeered		scalawags
84.	apprehended		castigated	transgression
85.	putrescent		congregated	
86.	diffidently		extolled	
87.	lauded	cuffed		contritely
88.	magnanimously	loathed	attire	
89.	dénouement		incident	nefarious	duo
90.	reprehensible	preyed	posterior	intrepid
91.	abruptly			
92.	awry			
93.	rationalized	putrid		
94.	relegated	cropped up	clamorous	obstreperous
95.	jabbering	incessant	inane	audible	querulous	quarrels
96.	vociferously			
97.	droll	slovenly	monotony	
98.	slovenly	inadvertently		
99.	retribution			
100.	quest	unravel	otiose	
101.	loathe	buffoon		
102.	pique	fervent	pithy	
103.	oeuvre	devotee	sentiment	
104.	engross			
105.	anomalous			
106.	mulled over	peers		
107.	*sotto voce*			
108.	subordinating	conjunctions		
109.	critiqued	stringent	customary	
110.	mock	dreary	stringent	unethical
111.	spontaneous	lank		
112.	overtaxed			
113.	barrage	egregious		
114.	articulate	epitome		
115.	reek			
116.	upbraided	pejorative		
117.	flourish	blathering		
118.	exuberantly	extemporaneous	aversion	guise

Passage to be read out loud to students

otiose	abhorred	amassing	intractable
stringent	cadence	spontaneous	strident
emanated	abruptly	inflexible	surreptitiously
punctilious	overt	launched	sodden
adept	latter	rife	visages
grimace	epithet	cacophony	futilely

Caught'yas continued

119.	visage	wrath		
120.	din	amplification	raucous	
121.	stentorian	fearsome		
122.	appalling	boded	dire	intoned
123.	jabbering	mute	querulous	bristled
124.	querulous	ominously	miscreants	
125.	postponed	gobbet	persisted	comport

Caught'ya Final Exam
Part 1:

maw	jabbering	aghast	livid
mute	mutely	lashed	posterior
salvo	retorted	withering	loathed
sycophant	jeered	dubbed	

Part 3:

diverse	hone	epithets	vague
mages			

Eighth-Grade Caught'ya Vocabulary

Introduction to story

eerie	dormant	disgorged	ambled
punctilious	adept	hordes	precariously
sported	harried	foreboding	dreaded
myriad	tandem	dread	garbed
trekked	ambled	menacing	miscreant
ablaze	adept	slovenly	banned
punctilious	portals	twine	outsized
strolled	dapper	culpable	latter
ambled	askew	jeered	trudged
vehicle	careened	dejectedly	ingenuous
decrepit	animatedly	animated	otiose
genially	stout	puerile	amorous
brimful	leverage	assemblage	
nabbed	perpetrators	awry	

Caught'yas

1.	puerile	ingenuous	uttering	
2.	obliterate			
3.	retorted	indignant		
4.	garbed	puckish	waggish	
5.	fey	retorted	waggish	egregious
6.	lame	vapid	barbs	
7.	sagacious	mutely	clamor	
8.	regaled	pupils	eloquent	
9.	emanated			
10.	protruded	sagacious		
11.	discombobulate			

12.	exasperating					
13.	deter	tittered				
14.	insipid					
15.	jibe	loped	malevolent	odious	dapper	pulchritudinous
16.	derided	odious	nemesis	reek	wafted	
17.	putrescent	misdeed	culpability			
18.	sycophants	dapper	pulchritudinous			
19.	cohorts	epithets	ominously			
20.	bravado	infuriate	'pulchritudinous	ingenuous		
21.	putrid	jocose	alacrity			
22.	regale	sultry	simmering			
23.	ambled	ebony				
24.	virtuous	bailiwick				
25.	rejoined	portals	lingered			
26.	insufferable	dejection				
27.	intolerable					
28.	reiterated	discombobulate				
29.	diffidently	earnestly				
30.	noisome	alleged				
31.	sniggered					
32.	emitted	garbled	incoherently			
33.	perceive					
34.	amicable	melodious	martinet			
35.	scintillating	pondered	omnipresent			
36.	despicable	automaton	witty			
37.	griped	arduous				
38.	incessant	predicted	eerie			
39.	promptly	a plethora of	assess	omnipresent		
40.	astute	manifesting	protrusion			
41.	mirth	speculated	superlative	devoid	vision	
42.	exasperated	mused				
43.	scintillating	disregarded	uttered			
44.	arduous					
45.	malicious	bibliophilic				
46.	dapper	comeliness	bibliophilic	derision		
47.	malevolent	devious	insecure			

Almost Midterm Caught'ya Test

drastic	edifice	varlets	tolerate
miscreants	monotone	egregious	transgressions
voluminous	scorched	subdued	conniving
inadvertently	devious	haughty	

Caught'yas continued

48.	stickler	manifested	lisped			
49.	adroit	prose	surreptitiously	bibliophilic	dumbfounded	antics
50.	pondered	discombobulated				
51.	entreated	rejoined				
52.	regaled	apparent	bizarre			
53.	beseeched	implore	affable			
54.	shoddy	stern	topple			
55.	wily	automaton	incessant			
56.	deviousness	cogitating	peers			
57.	slovenly	unanticipated				

58.	subdued	sycophant	scurrilous	superlative
59.	fervently	heeded	foreboding	garbed
60.	foreboding	garbed		
61.	marveled	palpable	metaphor	
62.	mammoth	wind-milled		
63.	lisped	authority	buckled	
64.	blatant			
65.	loped	gawked	ajar	uncharacteristic
66.	reiterated			
67.	pulchritudinous	*modus vivendi*	episode	
68.	subdued	adorned		
69.	cascaded	garlands	strident	strummers
70.	strident	reverberated		
71.	azure	garments	inappropriateness	
72.	comely	pulchritudinous		
73.	ebony			
74.	surreptitiously	perilously	posterior	garb
75.	shrilled	compounded	gyrate	
76.	bailiwick			
77.	laden			
78.	amid	visage	wailed	wrath
79.	snivled			
80.	ominous			
81.	wily	egregious		
82.	décolletage	comely		
83.	escorted	mortified		
84.	lavatory	optimistically	intolerant	
85.	blithe	episode		
86.	scintillating	predecessor	humdrum	
87.	bizarre	unadulterated	lackluster	vernacular
88.	extensive			
89.	garbed			
90.	probed	era	innovative	clad
91.	dangled	a plethora of		
92.	conveyance	regalia	careened	crescent-shaped
93.	ominous			
94.	constable	replica	facsimile	
95.	horde			
96.	implored	unison	incarcerate	cacophony
97.	beseeched			
98.	din	assessment		
99.	dénouement	chortled		
100.	sauntered	impart		
101.	commemorate	yore		
102.	peers	unison		
103.	ebony	proboscises	plummeted	
104.	inaudible	scurried		
105.	remonstrated			
106.	reiterated	conjectured		
107.	scurry	weathered	visage	
108.	atypical			
109.	rampant	eccentric	persevered	endeavor
110.	diversion			
111.	maliciousness	superlative		
112.	elated	colossal		

113. correlated   academic
114. a plethora of
115. animatedly   clambered
116. intrepid   flummox
117. compiling   stealth   fabricated
118. jabbering   loquacious
119. forte   meticulous   glee

Passage to be read out loud to students

> **NOTE:**
> Meanings have been given because, with all the hoopla at the end of the year, you need a break, and this is a long passage with lots of words.

objective (goal)
clandestine (hidden)
peers (contemporaries)
meandered (wandered)
punctual (on time)
soupçon (French word meaning "a suspicion or hint")
baffling (confusing)
sweltering (super hot and sweaty)
mitigate (make less)
alacrity (quickness)
tresses (hair)
egregious (really bad)
meticulous (super careful, thorough)
asserted (said forcefully)
inert (not moving)
gracelessly (clumsily)
commenced (began)
illustrious (famous)
wreak havoc (cause great devastation)
orifices (holes)
rigid (stiff)
inflexible (stiff)
vaulted (leapt)
rejoined (said back quickly)
credibility (believability)
glitches (problems occurring)
copious (lots of)
timorous (shy)
ecstatic (delighted)
pretext (excuse)
ajar (open)
redundant (extra)
quiver (shake)
lingered (stayed)
warily (cautiously)
immobile (unmoving)
oblivious (totally unaware)

tedious (boring)
devoured (ate ravenously)
laden (piled high)
conveyances (vehicles)
wrathful (angry)
sotto voce (softly)
sultry (hot)
indolent (lazy)
wafted (floated lightly)
chartreuse (yellow-green mix)
gawked (stared)
zephyr (light breeze)
lethargically (without energy)
monotone (boring, no variation)
secreted (hidden)
eminent (well-known)
affably (nicely)
emanate (come out)
incomparable (the very best)
placated (tried to make feel better)
transversely (sideways)
understatement (means less)
stealth (sneakiness)
comestibles (eats)
solidifying (making sure of)
jabbering (talking non-stop)
opted (chose)
bogus (fake)
witty (clever)
cohorts (buddies)
trepidation (fear)
omnipresent (always there)
mutely (silently)
utter incredulity (absolute amazement)
sentinel (watching soldier)
static (unmoving)

visage (face)

cravat (tie)

unison (together)

crevices (little cracks)

innovative (creative, imaginative)

assess (check out)

sullied (dirty)

bolstered (propped up)

cacophonous (noisy and jangling)

secreting (hiding)

lingered (stayed)

intrepid (loyal)

surmise (guess)

affirmed (agreed)

diverse (different)

interjected (added in)

queried (asked)

deduce (figure out)

grubby (grimy)

fitfully (restlessly)

ablutions (washings)

resonated (echoed)

myriad (lot of different kinds)

mingled (mixed)

conspirators (people who get together to plan something secretively)

covert (secret)

appalling (horrible)

implausible (not explainable)

stagnant (non-moving)

enhanced (intensified)

exemplary (perfect)

Caught'yas continued

120. *coup de grace*
121. capacity   latter
122. tome   rapt
123. clandestine
124. *coup de grace*   egregious   abound
125. orifice   uttering

Caught'ya Final Exam

| perdition | vociferously | ruckus | din |
| automatons | pandemonium | vigilant | superlative |

CHAPTER 5

The Bizarre Mystery of Horribly Hard Middle School

Unlike the other Caught'ya books, each of which contains three totally different stories turned into Caught'ya sentences, this book includes only one story that is broken up into three parts. The story, "The Bizarre Mystery of Horribly Hard Middle School," is long enough to produce more than three years' worth of Caught'ya sentences. A group of kids (whose personalities you will recognize in your own students) progress through three years at Horribly Hard Middle School doing the usual middle-school things and suffering from typical middle-school-kid dilemmas and problems. They write awful poetry, deal with obnoxious miscreants, live in a world where magic is possible, and try to figure out what is wrong with many of their teachers who don't seem quite normal.

I felt it would be better to have a story that would span the three years of middle school because middle-school students need continuity. They like books in a series with the same characters. They enjoy reading about themselves (thinly disguised) and their lives at school, and they love reading about adults with foibles—hence the popularity of *Harry Potter* and other *series* of books about pre-teens and teens.

As you read, you will notice that each year's worth of Caught'yas has a basic introduction repeated almost verbatim at the beginning. Obviously this would not be done in a regular children's novel, but I wanted to re-introduce the story and the main characters to the students each year. After all, summers are long, and adolescent memories are short. While they never forget lyrics to a popular tune, middle-school kids tend to forget anything having to do with school in a break of more than a few days. In addition, students will not have a personal copy of the story to read and reread as they so often do with beloved books before the next in the series appears.

Some sentences in the story may sound stilted and others may seem repetitious or redundant. This is because the primary purpose of this story is to teach English grammar, mechanics, usage, vocabulary, literary devices, spelling, etc. Obviously, while retaining the story's appeal to middle-school students, the main purpose had to take precedence.

You will recognize most of your students and some of their antics as the story unweaves. I based the characters on the beloved (and sometimes challenging) "characters" who have passed through my classroom over the years. Almost all the non-magical and non-robotic incidents that take place in the story have occurred at the middle school where I taught (like the accidental mooning of the dean or butterfly releasing or food fights, etc.). I wanted to keep the story "real" and amusing for students in a typical middle school.

I hope you enjoy a chuckle or two as you and your students read about the antics of Isabelle Ingenuous, William Waggish, and their friends and enemies.

NOTE:
The numbers in the margin of this chapter correspond with the Caught'yas in **Chapters 6, 7,** and **8.**

Sixth-Grade Part of Story

As the August morning sun chased the shadows from the roofs of houses and painted the sky gold, there was an **eerie** silence at Horribly Hard Middle School. In the dawning light, you could not see into the classrooms because of the dark curtains at every window. No early teacher rushed out of a car in the parking lot to set up a lab or to get an early start on preparation for the first day of school. Horribly Hard Middle School was like a spooky mansion: closed, dark, and abandoned.

Introduction

In contrast, across town, as the sun rose a bit higher in the sky, Marvelously Magic Magnet Middle School (known popularly as MMMMS) burst with energy and noise. Coffee perked in the teachers' lounge. Cars roared into the parking lot, parked, and spilled out teachers of different sizes, shapes, and complexions. Boxes, books, bags, and piles of "stuff" filled their arms as they walked into the school early to be ready for the first day of classes for the year.

Finally, two cars drove up to the **dormant** and silent Horribly Hard Middle School; one a new mauve Lexus and the other an old blue Ford pick-up truck. A man stepped out of each. The man who exited the Lexus wore a suit and tie and carried a battered briefcase. His face mirrored anxiety. The owner of the pick-up climbed out of his truck and lifted a large black tool case out of the bed of his truck. He **sported** a denim shirt and overalls, a red handkerchief in his upper pocket, a wrench hanging out of his lower pocket, and an air of excitement and purpose.

The two men nodded solemnly to each other as they **trekked** in different directions, the suited one toward the school office and the man in overalls toward the sixth-grade wing and the custodian's office. No other human soul could be seen in the dim light of early morning.

Slowly, one after the other, classroom lights came on in HHMS. Soon the school was **ablaze** with light, and all classrooms were lit, but apart from Mr. **Adept** Fixit, the custodian, rushing from room to room to open the doors and turn on the lights, no sounds of people could be heard on the campus. If you listened carefully in the main office near the door to the principal's room, you could hear the faint click of computer keys as Mr. **Punctilious** Principal, a man who was always concerned with correct procedure, checked and rechecked the procedures which would be followed that first day as well as the list of students who would enter the **portals** of the HHMS in about an hour.

Half an hour later several more cars pulled up in front of the still silent Horribly Hard Middle School.

Introduction

A lady, dressed in a long pink skirt and a **blousy** white shirt spattered with paint, hurried towards one of the still-dark classrooms with rolls of paper under her arm and a **myriad** of paint brushes in her mouth and hands. A man **ambled** toward a nearby dark classroom. He was burdened with various-sized instrument cases. His purple tie, decorated with yellow musical notes, was **askew**, and his glasses perched unevenly on his large nose.

Meanwhile, in a house not far from Horribly Hard Middle School, a **gaggle** of sixth-graders had gathered to gossip about the upcoming first day of school. They stood in the **foyer** of Isabelle's house, waiting for Olivia **Otiose** whose lazy nature always made her late to everything. Isabelle **Ingenuous**, always **animated**, twirled in nervousness and an excess of energy. Pauline **Puerile** whined in a babyish manner about Olivia's tardiness. Felicia **Fey**, always acting in a bizarre manner, muttered words of a spell, parts of which she could not remember, under her breath to encourage her friend Olivia **Otiose** to hurry. William **Waggish** made a tasteless but funny joke that **evoked titters** from the gathered friends. The last member of the troop, Sam **Sagacious**, simply stood wisely and silently with his backpack in his hand, waiting for the **clamor** to die down.

Isabelle **Ingenuous** danced out the open door, swiftly followed by her friends, with Pauline **Puerile** taking up the rear as she picked up her teddy bear that had fallen from her backpack and tucked it into the front pouch. Another girl joined them as they walked down the steps of Isabelle's house onto the sidewalk. Olivia **Otiose** had arrived, hair half combed and wrinkled blouse hanging out of her jeans. The group was ready but **reluctant** to face their first day of their new middle school: Horribly Hard Middle School.

A **myriad** of thoughts echoed and **rebounded** in each student's mind as the six sixth-graders **trudged** to their new school, a mile away, as if walking the plank of a pirate ship to their doom.

What would the new school be like? Would the new teachers be mean and hard? Were they going to have too much homework? Were the big eighth-graders going to **harass** them? Would they be able to remember the combinations of those shiny new locks in their backpacks? Were they dressed appropriately? Were the teachers nice? Would middle school be much different from elementary school? How would they find all their classes? Would their friends be in their classes? Would they get lost? Was the dean mean?

These questions and many more circled around in the six friends' heads as they silently **ambled**

towards the place where they would find out all the answers. All too soon, the brick walls of Horribly Hard Middle School **loomed** in front of them.

Brown-faced with dark, expressive eyes, William **Waggish** recited a silly limerick to break the tension. (He always was composing poetry to try to **emulate** his hero, Langston Hughes.) The friends' steps matched the **cadence** of the hopeful poem.

> There is a bizarre middle school
> Where teachers are easy to fool.
> They fall for our jokes
> And don't call our folks
> Even when we break every rule.

Horribly Hard Middle School did not look much different from their elementary school which was nearby in their town of **Tedious**, Florida. A big, one-story brick building sat **nestled** among large trees and a **verdant** lawn, and a small city of white portables dotted the field behind the school like white lily pads in a green pond.

"Look!" **shrilled** Isabelle **Ingenuous** in her high voice as she nervously twirled the purple, plastic butterfly that was perched in her wild, curly, **auburn** hair. Always upbeat, Isabelle was dressed in her new outfit of matching purple shorts and bright-green top. "All the lights are on, and there is a teacher gazing out the window of each classroom!" Isabelle Ingenuous continued.

"I wish we were going to Marvelously Magic Magnet Middle School instead of this old, ordinary, **insipid** one," groaned William **Waggish**, who was not his usual teasing, cheerful self.

"Yeah," sighed Sam **Sagacious**, who was usually reserved behind his horn-rimmed glasses, "I hear the teachers there are great!"

"Yes, I hear they don't give much homework, either," added Olivia **Otiose**, who hated homework with a passion.

"Well, we don't have enough magic in us, so we can't go to MMMMS," **retorted** Felicia **Fey** whose **meager** magic always went **awry**. "If I were better at magic, I would be going there with all the neat teachers and cool classes, but I failed the entry test when I accidentally gave Ms. Vice Principal a big, juicy zit right between her eyes."

"At least you *have* some magic, even if it always screws up," Isabelle Ingenuous reminded her friend as she twirled the purple butterfly that perched in her **mane** of auburn hair. "The rest of us can't even open a classroom **portal**," she concluded.

Suddenly, right in front of this **sextet**, stood a tall man who was dressed all in black with a shiny, new, black hat perched on his slick black hair. He peered down at the group and boomed in a loud, **monotone** voice, "Welcome to Horribly Hard Middle School."

The frightening man then announced that he was the dean of the school and that his name was Dean **Dread**.

Pauline **Puerile commenced** to **snivel** (she was such a baby), and Felicia Fey muttered a "cheer-up spell" but only succeeded in frizzing her friend's hair.

Dean Dread, a disturbing figure in his **somber** suit and tie, directed the group to go to the "cafetorium," a combination of cafeteria and auditorium. There, the friends found other sixth-graders whom they already knew from elementary school.

"What a bizarre dean," whispered Sam Sagacious *sotto voce* to William Waggish. "You and I wouldn't want to cross him nor meet him in a dark alley."

"From what **mausoleum** did he crawl out, Sam?" murmured William Waggish **surreptitiously** so no one else could hear.

"Hey, William, look at the other weird teachers standing against the wall," whispered always observant Sam Sagacious as he **surveyed** the room.

As Sam **uttered** this last statement, Dean Dread suddenly appeared and loomed menacingly over the two boys.

"**Loquacious** ones, eh? You two, come here," the dean ordered. His voice had the flatness of a cockroach crunching under a shoe.

Dean Dread put one huge, ham-sized hand on the back of each boy and **ushered** them to the front of the "cafetorium." All the other new sixth-graders, of course, **tittered** at the sight of William and Sam being caught talking.

"Quiet, students," said Dean Dread in a deadly tone of voice as he placed William Waggish and the **mortified** Sam Sagacious in the second row next to Jesse **Jocose**, another talker.

When Dean Dread said this, he nodded his head, and teachers lined up in the aisles to **quell** the noise with **proximity** control. The new sixth-graders squirmed in fear and became **distraught** as they got a closer look at their new teachers. Only a few of them had genuine, welcoming smiles on their faces, and most were **garbed** in grey or black, too.

Among the teachers, only a few didn't look too mean or **formidable**. They just didn't look like the friendly teachers the kids had had in elementary school, and most of them dressed in **somber** clothes that looked as if they were stiff and uncomfortable.

Olivia Otiose, who was more **perceptive** than most sixth-graders but lazy when it came to work, saw that one teacher's smile was genuine. This teacher wore a **blousy** white shirt and a long pink skirt, and she had stuck a pink flower in her thick blonde **tresses**.

"Felicia, that must be the art teacher," Isabelle Ingenuous dared to whisper to her friend Felicia Fey.

Dean Dread and two teachers glared at the two girls who **quailed** under their gaze.

All the teachers still stood in the aisles like **sentries**, most of them **glowering** at the kids as if daring them to speak. The principal stood up on the stage, and Dean Dread joined him there.

"Children, I am the school's principal, the captain of your ship," said the principal. My name is Mr. **Punctilious** Principal, and this is Dean Dread who will **mete** out any discipline for misbehaving students," he continued as he put a hand on the dean's broad, right shoulder.

William Waggish, always playfully humorous, chose that moment to **subvocalize** a limerick under his breath, his favorite way to deal with tension. He entitled it "The Mean Dean." Several people heard its **utterance**, and Jesse Jocose, who sat nearby, snorted in laughter.

> There was an old dean from Salt Lick   (Kentucky)
> Who made all the kids very sick.
> One look at his face
> And students would race,
> Well-aided by steps that were quick.

As William Waggish **uttered** the last word of his limerick, the teacher nearest him twitched and nodded his head. His eyelids fluttered; his tongue protruded between his closed lips; and **wisps** of smoke curled from his ears.

Jesse Jocose pointed to that teacher with his one hand and held the other over his mouth to **muffle** his giggles. The other teachers turned and **glowered** at him as students **swiveled** their heads in the direction Jesse pointed.

Only the teacher with the pink flower in her hair and the paint on her shirt smiled at the strange **phenomenon** of her eye-fluttering, ear-smoking, tongue-sticking-out **colleague**. She, somehow, was different, like a cool, glacier breeze in a hot classroom.

After that **incident**, everyone quieted down, turned his or her face towards the stage, and **paid heed** to Mr. Punctilious Principal as he instructed students on where to go and what to do next.

"I hope my friends and I are in the same homeroom, too," whispered Isabelle Ingenuous to her two friends, Olivia Otiose and Pauline Puerile.

Finally, the assembly was over. Teachers filed out, directed the **striplings** to the homeroom lists on the walls of the sixth-grade hall, and then pointed out the various classrooms.

26

The **intrepid** group who had begun the first day of school together found themselves in the same homeroom. Their teacher was a very **stern**-looking man, Mr. Math **Martinet,** who promptly announced that he was also their math teacher.

He told the students, too, that he would tolerate no **shenanigans**, and then he **confiscated** a headset from Quincy **Querulous**, a student in the back of the room who made faces as his headset was taken, opened his mouth as if to argue, and then thought better of it.

"Hey, Pauline, that's the teacher who stuck out his tongue," **articulated** Felicia Fey to her **puerile** friend who was crying silently.

William Waggish, worried about Pauline, whispered another of his **inimitable** limericks, this one about a **malevolent** math teacher entitled "**Wrathful** Math." Faint curls of smoke wisped from Mr. Math Martinet's ears, and his eyelids fluttered, too.

> The nasty man, teacher of math,
> Was utterly filled with such **wrath**.
> He yelled at the boys
> And **stifled** their joys.
> He took a malevolent path.

At this, you could have heard a pin drop as the students' mouths gaped open at their **peer**'s boldness and their teacher's antics. The class waited for William's painful **demise** at the hands of the stern, **uncompromising** teacher.

Nothing happened! Absolutely nothing! After fewer than three seconds, Mr. Math Martinet **resumed** his announcements as if he neither had been interrupted nor had wisps of smoke **emitting** from his ears. After he went over the school rules, Mr. Math Martinet handed out a schedule and a map of the school to everyone.

As soon as the students' schedules were in their hands, **pandemonium** broke out as everyone tried to see who was in his or her classes. The **intrepid** six compared notes and found that they shared some of the same classes: math, English, and science. Pauline, Isabelle, Jesse, William, and Felicia had art with Ms. **Amicable** Artist, and the other two had music with Mr. **Melodious** Music.

The bell **pealed**, signaling the end of homeroom. Although the group was going to the same place, Pauline Puerile got lost. Things were not going well for her. First, she became separated from her friends. Then, she turned her map upside down. Next, the size of

35

the eighth-graders **daunted** her, and finally, she got lost. As Pauline
Puerile stood in the crowded hallway blubbering while others
laughed and pointed fingers at her, a kind, **titanic** eighth-grader
took pity on her and pointed her in the right direction.

Meanwhile, Isabelle Ingenuous and Felicia Fey found the girls'
bathroom, but there were too many eighth-graders for comfort in there,
so they left hurriedly. Felicia and Isabelle found their first class (which,
thankfully, was only ten steps farther). Before entering the classroom,
Felicia Fey, who should have known better, tried to fix her flyaway hair
with a **petite** spell. As usual, it backfired; this time it turned her hair
purple.

At the same time, William Waggish found a new friend, Jesse
Jocose, the boy who had experienced the **wrath** of Dean Dread, too.
The two of them discovered their love for **jocularity** and limericks.
Since, like William's other friends, they were headed for English class,
they composed an **appropriate** poem and entitled it "Awful Teacher,"
even though they had not yet **encountered** the teacher.

> An English teacher from Slade   (Kentucky)
> Confused the verbs "lay" and "laid."
> She didn't know squat
> And was put on the spot,
> So she quit and didn't get paid.

Standing at her door, their new English teacher, Ms. Grammar
Grouch, heard the limerick. Her eyes fluttered, and she stuck out her
tongue while curls of smoke wisped from her **proboscis** and rose to
the ceiling.

"Hey, Jesse, look at that," giggled William Waggish, pleased with
their poetic efforts and their effect on the teachers. "These teachers are
eerie! Maybe my friends and I are wrong, and this year will be fun
after all."

Sam Sagacious just made a further notation in his pocket notebook.

Jesse Jocose **queried** with a grin as they stepped into the room of
the slightly smoking teacher, "I wonder what makes them do that?"

Just then they spied Felicia Fey in her newly purpled hair.

"Uh oh, William, I bet the teachers are not going to find *that*
amusing," said Jesse Jocose.

Ms. Grammar Grouch *could* **differentiate** between the verbs "lay"
and "laid," and, much to the **consternation** of Olivia Otiose, she loaded
the class with a list of vocabulary words to learn. In addition, Ms.
Grammar Grouch did not permit any student to end a sentence with
a preposition nor to split a verb. She was a true Grammar Grouch.

35

44

She also was not very **amiable** and was going to send Felicia
Fey to the dean with a **terse** note to call Felicia's parents about her
coming to school with purple hair.

44

"Wait, Ms. Grouch, I can fix it. It's fixable," **blurted** Felicia as she
muttered another spell which turned her hair back to its normal color but
put a purple streak in Ms. Grouch's **coiffure**.

Jesse Jocose composed a limerick on the spot that he entitled
"My New Friend, Felicia" and sent it in a note to William Waggish who
whispered it to Felicia who **tittered**.

> There was a young lady from Day   (Florida)
> Whose nature was quirkily fey.
> She purpled her hair,
> But she didn't care
> And merrily did things her way.

At this **juncture**, Ms. Grammar Grouch stuck out her tongue,
fluttered her eyes, and **emitted** smoke from her ears. She stopped
teaching, froze for fewer than three seconds, mumbled, "That is
unanswerable," and then resumed her grammar lecture as if nothing
had occurred.

"Weirder and weirder," **penned** William to Jesse in another **furtive**
note.

"I don't think I like that teacher very much," said Isabelle to her
friends as they exited the room at the peal of the bell, and Felicia and she
dashed into the ladies' room, **micturated** quickly, washed their hands in
the filthy sink, and ran out to join their friends.

"I wonder if the science teacher will be any better. We already
know what the math teacher is like," said Sam Sagacious who liked the
vocabulary lesson of Ms. Grammar Grouch but **loathed** the way the
latter had wanted to send his friend to Dean Dread.

"Well, she couldn't be worse," said Felicia Fey whose narrow escape
had scared them all further. "I hope she doesn't **perceive** that purple
streak in her hair until she gets home."

"She's the one who deserved it," **countered** Felicia's friends William
Waggish and Pauline Puerile in **unison**. They shared a "high five" as
William proceeded to recite another one of his **infamous** limericks, this
one entitled "Frigid English."

> Our grammar teacher is rigid.
> On English rules, she is frigid.
> She never splits verbs
> And teaches hard words,
> And errors make her quite **livid**.

50

Nearby, two teachers in unison fluttered their eyelids, stuck out their tongues between closed lips, froze in place for fewer than three seconds, and emitted wisps of smoke from their **nostrils**. Sam Sagacious noted the **anomalies** in their reactions.

"**Bizarre**," Sam Sagacious muttered to himself as he took notes.

The rest of the day went pretty much the same. The teachers, for the most part, were **clad** in somber colors, and they had no sense of humor. Unfortunately, in science class, the friends found their old **nemesis**, Orson **Odious**. As they entered the room, Orson was "holding court" in the back among many of the popular kids.

"Ah, guys, look at the weird ones who just entered science class," Orson said **maliciously**. "There's the witch who can't do a spell right, the four-eyed wise guy who knows it all, the free spirit who even wears stupid, plastic butterflies in her hair, the crybaby, the lazy one who never has her homework, and the two who think they're funny. What losers," he stated, and he chuckled to his audience and encouraged them to laugh.

"I'm sorry my parents made my buds and me late this morning, and my buds and I missed two of the "geeks" getting caught by the Dean," **expounded** Orson Odious as he concluded his **verbal** attack.

The intrepid six and Jesse Jocose, heads down, slunk into seats in the front of the room just as the science teacher entered and closed the door behind him. When the class saw the teacher, silence **reigned**, even from the back of the room where Orson's gang sat.

"I am Ms. **Stern** Science," the teacher said in a **monotone** voice. "I believe in a lot of hard tests, **a plethora of** homework, and **a dearth of** student talking in my class, but I also expect students to do well."

At this, Olivia Otiose **slumped** in her desk in **woe**. "Oh, no," she whined as she sank farther into her seat. "This year is starting out badly."

Ms. Stern Science stared at Olivia Otiose with her bird-like, beady eyes, and she said in a low, **ominous** tone, "There always will be silence in this classroom when I **pontificate**."

Olivia Otiose thought she heard a snicker from Orson Odious in the back, but the teacher did not catch it.

As the seven friends left the room, they tried to **elude** Orson Odious who knew all the tricks of making other students' lives **wretched** without getting caught by the teachers himself. William Waggish and his new friend Jesse Jocose **commenced** composing another limerick, this one about the stern science teacher, and they entitled it "Crude, Rude Science."

55

> Our old science teacher is rude.
> She also is horribly crude.
> She picks at her nose;
> She sports ugly toes;
> And always is in a bad mood.

Isabelle Ingenuous and her friends laughed, imagining their teacher's **unsightly** toes. They forgot about the toad Orson Odious and all that he liked to do to make their lives miserable.

By her desk near the **portal** of the room, Ms. Stern Science stuck out her tongue, smoked slightly from her **proboscis**, fluttered her eyes like a blinking lizard, and froze mid-step for fewer than three seconds.

"Stranger and weirder," murmured Sam Sagacious who noticed these things.

Lunch was the usual **boisterous pandemonium** typical of a middle-school lunchroom. A fight broke out between two girls over something a **rumor-monger** had reported that the other had **purportedly** said, and both were suspended on the spot. Dean Dread called their parents from the lunchroom, right in front of the girls' **peers**.

After that incident, Dean Dread stood on the stage with his ham-sized hands on his hips, glaring **forebodingly** at the students as if he dared them to try anything else except talking and eating.

"It's amazing he lets us talk at all, Sam" said William Waggish to his **compatriot** at the table. He also composed another limerick for the occasion, entitled it "Mean Green Dean," and caused everyone at his table to hoot with laughter like a bunch of hyenas. After a brief flutter of his eyelids and one wisp of smoke curling from his left ear, Dean Dread turned to stare at their table with a **malevolent** expression on his **visage**, **marred** only by his tongue that still stuck out between his **pursed** lips.

> The dean of students is mean.
> His face in anger turns bright green.
> He maintains his right
> To stop any fight
> And suspend those who are obscene.

Art and music were the only relief for the rest of the week. In art, the teacher, Ms. **Amicable** Artist, smiled a lot and promised the class that they would release butterflies on Earth Day and celebrate the event further with an art project of their own choosing as well. Pauline, Isabelle, Jesse, William, and Felicia, who had **opted** to take Art, were delighted.

"This teacher seems almost human, girlfriend," whispered Isabelle to Felicia who nodded in agreement.

Chapter 5: The Bizarre Mystery of Horribly Hard Middle School   73

With only a small frown at Isabelle, Ms. Amicable Artist quietly moved by the two girls and **commenced** a lecture about the **Impressionist** artists.

William Waggish took out a pencil and a piece of paper, and he composed another limerick entitled "Art."

> We have a bizarre art teacher
> Who **touts** painters like a preacher.
> Cassat and Van Go
> And Monet, now we know,
> Are the ones who really reach her.

Ms. Amicable Artist, still lecturing and **periodically** showing pictures from a stack in her hand, **ambled** over to William, confiscated the paper, swiftly **perused** its contents, smiled, and said, "You spelled Van Gogh's name incorrectly, William. It is spelled 'G-o-g-h,' not 'G-o.'"

Nothing else happened except that the pink-**hued** flower in her **coiffure** fell onto William's desk as she nodded her head at him, handed back William's paper, and continued her **spiel** on the Impressionists.

William Waggish corrected the spelling of the Dutch painter's name and paid **rapt** attention for the rest of the period.

"Hey," **mused** William Waggish to himself, "maybe the limerick has to be said out loud for it to affect the teachers. I must tell Sam as he would want to make a note."

Meanwhile in music, Mr. **Melodious** Music told his class all about band, and he let the untried, **neophyte** sixth-graders choose their instruments. Sam Sagacious played the guitar at home but wanted to take up a new challenge. He chose the oboe, an **arduous** instrument to learn to play. Olivia Otiose, who had not signed up for any exploratory class and who had been randomly assigned to band by the school's computer, wanted the instrument that was the easiest to play. She wanted to play the triangle but was given a clarinet.

"'Bummer,'" she said. "If I have to learn to play this instrument, I will be forced to carry this home every day, and my mother will **compel** me to practice."

That day, the six friends (Jesse Jocose took a bus to school) **plodded** home, piled with science and math homework. Olivia Otiose was not pleased, so she did none of it and lied to her mother when her mother asked if she ever had been assigned any. Olivia's lying about homework was nothing new.

Months passed in a similar, **invariable** manner. The six walked to school, met up with their friends who bussed to school, suffered through classes with their bizarre teachers, and tried to avoid Orson Odious and his popular pals, the **comely** Petra **Pulchritudinous**, lovely Alessandra **Amorous**, and handsome Danny **Dapper**. Except in art and music, the nasty, annoying teachers gave tons of homework.

While middle school is always a weird place, they knew that something strange was **afoot** at Horribly Hard Middle School. Sam kept notes on the effects that William's and Jesse's **atrocious** but **hilarious** limericks had on their teachers. One of their best, a wicked limerick about the social studies teacher, Ms. Grumpy Geography, **evoked** more than smoke from her ears and fluttering eyes.

> There is a teacher from Noodle　　　　　　　(Texas)
> Whose hair looks like a French poodle.
> She paints her nails green;
> She taps on the screen;
> Her face looks like pale apple strudel.

In addition to the usual teachers' reactions to hearing one of their **infamous** verses, Ms. Grumpy Geography repeated over and over in a **monotone** voice for more than two seconds but fewer than three, "You must read the book <u>Great Geography</u>. You must read the book <u>Great Geography</u>."

As usual, Sam Sagacious took notes *apropos* of the incident, but neither he nor anyone else could draw any conclusions. There was just something different about their school, but no one could put a finger on what its difference was.

Art continued to be "awesome." Band was challenging, and even lazy, **indolent** Olivia Otiose was getting into playing her clarinet well.

Then, there was this **innovative** teacher who visited their English class from time to time to teach creative writing. Her humor and enthusiasm inspired students to write well. Usually **apathetic** Olivia Otiose wrote a personal narrative that won a prize. In addition, William Waggish even abandoned his favorite form of writing—the limerick—and composed a **superlative** argumentative essay defending his position that school uniforms were a **noxious** idea.

One day in science, Orson Odious was particularly **insufferable**. His **taunts** provoked the usually cheerful Jesse Jocose to become **pugnacious** and to swing at him in fury. Orson **countered** with a blow to Jesse's **visage**. William jumped into the **fray** to support his friend, and then Ms. Stern Science stepped into the act.

"You three **rapscallions**," she said in a loud voice, "go to the dean's office immediately. Isabelle, take this note, go see that they arrive in the appropriate place, and get a return note from the dean," she concluded, punching the call button to inform the office that Dean Dread had some "customers."

As the group walked to the dean's office, Orson **goaded** and teased Jesse, William, and Isabelle.

"You're nothing but unpopular little geeks," he **jeered**.

The three remained **quiescent** at this insult, for they dared not **exacerbate** the situation.

"Everyone **loathes** your stupid poems," he continued. "They are written badly."

"Now you've gone too far," growled the usually **pacifistic** William Waggish as he rushed in on his tormentor.

As if they had **orchestrated** it beforehand, the three friends jumped on Orson, all at the same time. Orson fell to the ground, and Jesse, William, and Isabelle sat on him and called him an **obstreperous** jerk. Orson Odious was shocked into silence.

At that moment, Dean Dread appeared suddenly, like a huge, swooping bat, and **ushered** all four **miscreants** into his office. Orson Odious tried to blame the three for the entire incident, but luckily Ms. Stern Science had seen him take a swing at Jesse Jocose. Dean Dread called everyone's parents to come get their **miscreants**, and then he suspended all four of them for two days. William Waggish didn't even have time to compose a limerick appropriate for the occasion.

When the suspension had ended, and all were back in school, things got better for a while. Orson Odious remained unusually **docile**. He did, however, start targeting a girl named Beth **Bibliophilic** who had read Harry Potter more than four times and who always **secreted** a book on her knees under her desk.

Orson also picked on a boy named Mark **Meticulous**, a perfectionist who always rewrote his papers many times. These two, of course, were not **elated** with this turn of events. Beth Bibliophilic and Mark Meticulous, to be sure, preferred it when Orson Odious had ignored them as if they weren't there.

"Weirdos who sit on people don't **warrant** my attention," Orson **scoffed**.

"Bullies who taunt my friends deserve to be expelled," **retorted** Isabelle Ingenuous, the free spirit whom even Dean Dread did not **daunt**.

Then, in art and in music, Ms. Amicable Artist and Mr. Melodious Music joined their classes to present a **mutual** art/music project— **nurturing** and releasing butterflies.

"We have ordered your kits, and you will raise Painted Lady butterflies," said Ms. Amicable Artist. "Painted Lady butterflies are probably the most **widespread** butterfly **species** and are found all over the world," she said. "They particularly like living in mountains and flowery meadows, and they love the following flowers: aster, cosmos, thistle, and buttonbush. After we release the butterflies on Earth Day, art students will paint an appropriate **habitat** with their butterfly in it," she lectured, "and music students will compose a short tune.

"Each student will raise his or her own butterfly from a caterpillar (which is the **larvae**) to the **chrysalis** (in which the caterpillar **metamorphosis** will occur) and, finally, into a Painted Lady butterfly," Mr. Melodious Music concluded.

"This will be **stupendous**," Felicia Fey informed her pals. Then, in her **exhilaration**, she accidentally waved her hands the wrong way, enacting a spell, and a white maggot **oozed** out of Sam's left ear.

"EEWWW, that's gross, Felicia," **shrilled** Isabelle and Pauline in unison.

Sam Sagacious and the other boys collected the disgusting maggot Felicia's spell had produced and admired its properties. They plotted to leave it on some unsuspecting teacher's desk. Which teacher deserved their "present"? They couldn't **concur**.

"It came out of my ear, so I get to decide," insisted an **adamant** Sam.

The three girls almost **retched** in disgust, but they quickly turned their thoughts to butterflies. "Oh, you guys, I can't wait until the caterpillars arrive," said Isabelle, her face **animated** by the thought of raising a butterfly.

Then, on a day that had been particularly **problematical**, the group arrived in art and music and breathed a sigh of relief.

"Boy, Pauline, this has been a **horrendous** day," said Isabelle Ingenuous.

Pauline Puerile just nodded in agreement as she didn't trust herself not to cry.

"Yeah, Orson Odious forgot his truce, and he insulted Sam about his **spectacles**," groaned Jesse Jocose. "We must make up a limerick about him, William," he grinned **puckishly**.

A nasty young **stripling** from Toast   (North Carolina)
Was meaner and crueler than most.
His **barbs** were so cruel
That we hated school
Where he made his nastiest boasts.

Ms. Grammar Grouch and Mr. Math Martinet, who were passing by the group just as Jesse Jocose recited his **doggerel**, stopped dead in their tracks, one foot raised as if to take another step.

Their eyelids fluttered wildly. Their lips clamped shut but their tongues still **protruded** like pink taffy. Wisps of smoke curled from their ears as they stood there, unmoving. There they froze, **manifesting** their bizarre behavior for fewer than three seconds. It wasn't a pretty sight; they looked like ugly, stone **gargoyles**!

101

"Stranger and stranger," murmured Sam as he made a note in his **omnipresent** notebook.

During the peculiar **interlude,** William gently dared to touch Mr. Math Martinet on the tip of his large, Pinocchio-like **proboscis.** The **latter** did not even notice. William Waggish quickly withdrew before both teachers resumed walking as if nothing **untoward** had occurred.

As William and Jesse continued to **regale** the rest with their account of their horrendous day, the crew saw a big box being delivered to the art room!

"Caterpillars!" **bellowed** Felicia Fey in her loudest voice.

"Future butterflies!" **articulated** Isabelle Ingenuous with **awe** in her tone. As usual, she wore a plastic **replica** of one in her auburn **tresses,** and it bobbed as she spoke.

The rest of the day passed, and the group remained **oblivious** to Orson's verbal **barbs** and **jabs,** the teachers' love affair with homework, and the usual battle to walk in the crowded halls with the bigger students.

Finally, it was time for art and music! Ms. Amicable Artist and Mr. Melodious Music stood in the front of the art room as their students **crammed** themselves into a room made for many fewer bodies. A **massive,** opened box sat on the front table.

"These are the caterpillars," said Ms. Amicable Artist in a quiet voice. "The caterpillar-to-butterfly life cycle is **approximately** twenty-one days, so three weeks from now, on Earth Day, we will release butterflies." She added, "First, you will choose a partner."

Murmurs erupted from the students as they searched for partners. "Silence, students, you may choose partners after you receive all the instructions," Ms. Amicable Artist gently **reproached** the kids. "Next, each pair of you will receive one of these cups," she continued as Mr. Melodious Music held up several small, covered cups in his hand.

Mr. Melodious Music continued Ms. Amicable Artist's **discourse.** "Each one of these," he said, indicating the covered cups, "contains four to five caterpillars. Because not all of the caterpillars will live, each pair of students will have between three to five butterflies to release. The caterpillar cup has all the food the caterpillars need to **metamorphose.** Finally, keep the lid on the cup until the caterpillars form their **chrysalises,**" he warned the students. "Completing the chrysalis will take only about ten days," he concluded.

"Awesome," **marveled** Isabelle Ingenuous who adored butterflies.

Ms. Amicable Artist resumed the lecture with a *caveat*. "Handle your cups as little and as gently as possible so that you do not disturb the caterpillars. Occasionally, you may open the lid to peer inside, but **refrain** from touching the caterpillars; it will stop them from changing."

Even though there were sixty sixth-graders in the overcrowded room, silence **reigned**. Suddenly, one student coughed, and the **mesmerized** crowd resumed its usual **clamor**.

"I can't wait three weeks!" **puled** Pauline Puerile in a **petulant** tone.

A boy named Quincy **Querulous** echoed Pauline's whine. "Why can't we speed up the things?" he asked **peevishly**.

"Nature takes her own time," **mollified** Sam Sagacious.

Nature did take its own time. In three weeks, each pair of students opened a box, revealing several **chrysalises** on the sides and little green balls on the bottom.

"EEWWW! What are those little green balls?" asked Pauline Puerile who was totally grossed out.

"They are caterpillar poop, you dummy," piped up Quincy **Querulous** who actually had done his homework. (He liked to insult his **peers** almost as much as Orson Odious but wasn't as **adept** at it.)

After the teachers sent Quincy Querulous out of the room for his **insensitive** remark, the rest of the class **warily** removed the small pieces of paper to which the chrysalis had **adhered**. They then taped them to the inside wall of one of the butterfly **abodes** that the art class had constructed. They also placed twigs inside the abodes. Pauline Puerile, of course, dropped a chrysalis and cried with **consternation**.

In science, Orson Odious, who took P.E. instead of art or music, yanked the plastic butterfly from Isabelle's hair, put it in his **unruly**, uncombed mop, flapped his arms, and pretended to fly around the room like a butterfly to make fun of the students who were excited about the project. In reality, the **obnoxious** pest was jealous.

In art, each student drew a picture of his or her chrysalis, and in music, they played a **pastoral** piece with a **lilting** melody that gave the airy feeling of a butterfly in flight. Even Olivia Otiose practiced her part **assiduously** and played it beautifully. Everyone was anxious for the final metamorphosis to happen.

A little more than a week later, William Waggish arrived in art. To his amazement, he spied lovely Painted Lady butterflies in the butterfly **abode**. They clung to the side. Their wings looked as if they had been painted with black, brown, and orange paint with spots of

Read-aloud passage

white, red, and blue thrown in. They were lovely! They perched on the twigs and pumped their **frangible** wings to unfurl them.

Read-aloud passage

"Oh, look, guys," William Waggish gleefully **whooped** to his classmates, "the butterflies are emerging!"

As the class supplied the newly formed insects with food (sugar water), they impatiently waited for Earth Day which was two days **hence**, at the end of April.

Finally Earth Day arrived. The entire sixth-grade class, Orson Odious included, gathered around the butterfly houses that were on tables in the middle of the P.E. field. The weather was **balmy**, and there was a slight breeze. Orson Odious pushed and pinched his way to the front of the crowd, and Ms. Amicable Artist, who did not feel amicable towards **aggressive** bullies, **banished** him farther back because Dean Dread was there.

Ms. Amicable Artist then asked Isabelle and William to come forward. Pauline whined in disappointment, and Felicia Fey danced in a circle of **vicarious** joy for her friends. Two brown moths flew out of Ms. Grammar Grouch's hair.

Mr. Melodious Music called upon Sam Sagacious and, much to her surprise, a **flabbergasted** Olivia Otiose. "You, Sam, are a talented and **diligent** student," he said.

Orson Odious made **noxious** faces from the last row of students.

You, Olivia Otiose, have improved so much, that I **deem** that you, too, deserve this honor," Mr. Melodious Music stated as he beckoned with his finger for the two students to come up close to the butterfly **abodes**.

Then, at a nod from the two teachers, Isabelle, William, Sam, and Olivia **simultaneously** lifted the lid to a butterfly abode. As the crowd gasped, "Ahhh," in **unison**, a fluttering cloud of brown, black, and orange **hues** rose from the boxes and **dispersed** in **diverse** directions.

Orson Odious tried to catch one to crush it; thankfully, he failed. As the cloud of butterflies rose into the air and **dispersed** with the breeze, the sixth-graders craned their necks to watch their departure. This had been a truly **prodigious** experience for the **majority** of the sixth-graders. Even Orson Odious was impressed although he did not admit it.

The last six weeks of school sped by with **alacrity**. The band concert went well, and although she earned her usual "Ds" and "Fs" in the majority of her classes, Olivia Otiose and her clarinet wowed the audience. Sam Sagacious aced all the exams with ease, and Isabelle Ingenuous earned all "As" and "Bs" except for a "C" in math,

Read-aloud passage

the **bane** of her existence (besides Orson Odious). Her drawing of her butterfly astounded all at the **annual** art show. William Waggish and his new friend, Jesse Jocose, continued to compose **outlandish** limericks. Felicia Fey only let fly a few **inappropriate** spells that had minor, **insignificant** results, usually involving Ms. Grammar Grouch. Pauline Puerile still cried when frustrated, but even she **ameliorated** her grades. Thus, their sixth-grade year drew to a close.

Read-aloud passage

One gorgeous morning at the end of May, the sextet **strolled** to school. They were unusually early. (Olivia Otiose, who had spent the night at Isabelle's house, actually was on time!) They reached the parking lot at the school just as the custodian, Mr. **Adept** Fixit, got out of his blue pick-up truck. Mr. Adept Fixit waved at the group of friends, grabbed a strange-looking tool from his truck, and **scurried** into the building. He had an **apprehensive** look on his face.

The friends watched in amazement as Mr. Adept Fixit **bustled** from room to room with only one tool. As he exited each room, the lights went on quickly, and the blinds rose. From their **vantage** point on the sidewalk, the friends could see well the outlines of their teachers in the rooms.

"Where did they come from?" **astutely** asked Sam. I see fewer than three cars in the parking lot, and the teachers aren't moving, too.

"This is a mystery to be solved next year when we are in the seventh grade," said William in a rare serious tone.

"Yes, William, I **concur**," said Sam Sagacious. "There are neither enough time nor enough clues, and I only want to think about my summer and the book The Mystery of the Terrible Teachers," he agreed.

"Yeah," said Isabelle as she nodded her head in **assent**, and her plastic butterfly bobbed **in accord**.

"I don't like this," whined Pauline.

Everyone else heaved his or her shoulders in **exasperation**. Was Pauline going to grow up, and was she ever going to stop her sniveling?

"I think I will wear all black next year in the seventh grade," announced Felicia who had not produced a single successful spell the entire sixth-grade year.

The friends, except Sam, of course, promptly forgot about their strange teachers and concentrated on the end-of-year activities and their summer plans.

On the last day of school (after all the students had left), all was silent except for muffled sounds from the art and music rooms and the "clack" of computer keys in the main office.

Final Exam

Seventh-Grade Part of the Story

As the August morning sun chased the shadows from the roofs of houses and painted the sky gold, once again there was an **eerie** silence at Horribly **Introduction** Hard Middle School. In the dawning light, you could not see into the classrooms because of the light-blocking curtains at every window. No early teacher rushed out of a car in the parking lot to set up a lab or to get an early start on preparation for the first day of school. Horribly Hard Middle School was like a spooky mansion: closed, dark, and abandoned.

In contrast, across town, as the sun rose a bit higher in the sky, Marvelously Magic Magnet Middle School (known popularly as MMMMS) burst with energy and noise. Coffee perked in the teachers' lounge. Cars roared into the parking lot, parked, and spilled out teachers of different sizes, shapes, and complexions. Boxes, books, bags, and piles of "stuff" filled their arms as they walked into the school early to be ready for the first day of classes for the year. Finally, three cars drove up to the **dormant** and silent Horribly Hard Middle School—a new mauve Lexus sedan, an old blue Ford pick-up truck, and an old, battered, tan Subaru station wagon that had seen better days. A middle-aged man, Mr. **Punctilious** Principal, stepped out of the Lexus. Another middle-aged man, the custodian, Mr. **Adept** Fixit, exited the blue pick-up.

The man who exited the Lexus wore a suit and tie, and carried a battered briefcase. The owner of the Ford climbed out of his pick-up, walked to the back, and lifted a tool chest from the bed of his truck. He **sported** a denim shirt and overalls, a red handkerchief in his upper pocket, a wrench that hung out of his lower pocket, and a purposeful air.

The door of the Subaru creaked open and out fell construction paper and magazines, followed by a **harried**-looking woman. She was dressed in a long, loose pink dress with a pink flower in her thick blonde hair and a **myriad** of new paint brushes in her mouth. The two men nodded solemnly to each other and smiled at the woman as she gathered the stuff that had fallen from her car.

The men **trekked** in different directions, the suited one toward the school office and the man in overalls toward the custodian's office. The woman gathered her materials from the pavement and **ambled** slowly to a building set slightly off from the main part of the school. No other human soul could be seen in the dim light of early morning.

Slowly, one after the other, classroom lights came on in HHMS. Soon the school was **ablaze**, and all classrooms were lit, but apart from Mr. **Adept** Fixit, the **Introduction** custodian, rushing from room to room to open the

82 **Giggles in the Middle**

doors and turn on the lights, no sounds of people could be heard on the campus. This was the first day of school?

Introduction

If you listened carefully in the main office near the door to the principal's room, you could hear the faint click of computer keys as Mr. **Punctilious** Principal, a man who was always concerned with correct procedure, checked and rechecked the procedures which would be followed that first day of school as well as the list of students who would enter the **portals** of the HHMS in about an hour. If you **strolled** over to the art room, and listened very carefully, you could hear faint singing of an old Beatles tune and the rustling of paper.

Ten minutes later another car pulled up in front of the still silent Horribly Hard Middle School. A man in a **dapper** suit who was humming a Mozart sonata **ambled** toward a nearby dark classroom. He was burdened with various-sized instrument cases. He wore his favorite purple tie that was decorated with yellow musical notes. His tie was **askew**, and his glasses perched unevenly on his nose, ruining the effect of his handsome suit.

Before the man with the instrument cases could close the trunk of his car, a final **vehicle**, an ancient white Volvo sedan, **careened** into the lot and parked next to the **decrepit** tan Subaru. A pleasingly-plump middle-aged woman with curly grey hair jumped **animatedly** out of the Volvo and dashed up to the man who hummed the Mozart sonata.

She spoke briefly to him, gesturing with both hands. The man pointed to a building, nodded **genially** in farewell (since his arms were filled), turned around, shifted his burden of instrument cases, and walked in the opposite direction from where he had pointed.

The **stout** woman returned to her car, opened the trunk, and removed an obviously heavy box that was **brimful** with books. She heaved the box for better **leverage** and trudged slowly with her heavy burden in the direction the Mozart-humming man had indicated. The staff parking lot of Horribly Hard Middle School once again fell silent. Only five cars awaited their drivers.

On another side of the school, school busses arrived, one by one. Each **disgorged** a bunch of chattering students. Other students who had walked to school **ambled** slowly onto the school grounds to join the mobs being let off by the busses. Horribly Hard Middle School came alive with voices. A new school year was about to begin.

Meanwhile, in a house not far from Horribly Hard Middle School, a group of five **diverse** seventh-graders had gathered to gossip about the upcoming first day of school.

Introduction

They stood in the **foyer** of Isabelle **Ingenuous's** house, waiting for Olivia **Otiose** whose **languid** (yet delightful) nature usually made her late to everything, even the first day of seventh grade.

Isabelle **Ingenuous**, always **animated**, twirled in nervousness and an **excess** of energy. Pauline **Puerile** whined in a babyish manner about the **tardiness** of Olivia **Otiose**, about having to return to Horribly Hard Middle School for another year, and about the homework the teachers loved to pile on her.

Another girl was **garbed** all in black. Even her hair was dyed black. It was Felicia **Fey**, who acted in a bizarre manner and who was known for her spells that always went **awry**. Felicia began to mutter words of a spell to encourage her friend Olivia **Otiose** to hurry. Isabelle **Ingenuous** put her hand over Felicia's mouth to stop her from **uttering** her spell, and she warned her friend.

"You know it will backfire on you, Felicia," warned Isabelle Ingenuous. "You don't want to ruin your new black hairdo or start the seventh grade with **putrid** purple streaks in your hair as you did in the sixth grade last year, do you?"

William **Waggish** made a tasteless but funny joke about girls and their weird habits, but no one listened. They were used to his **lame** limericks, **vapid** jokes, and strange sense of humor. The last member of the troop, Sam **Sagacious**, simply stood wisely and silently, waiting for the **clamor** to die down. An **erudite** young man, Sam held a book in his hand, The Count of Monte Cristo by Alexandre Dumas, and he read as he waited.

Since his joke had fallen flat, and no one had laughed, William **Waggish regaled** his friends with a new limerick about girls who wear black. Brown-faced with expressive dark pupils, William composed mischievous poems to hide his real **aspiration**: to be as **eloquent** and **articulate** a poet as his secret hero, Langston Hughes.

> There once was a strange girl from Mack   (Colorado)
> Whose hair and clothes were all black.
> She looked like a crow,
> And she should have said "No"
> To trying a magical act.

Sam **Sagacious** put his book in his backpack and laughed. Felicia **Fey** threatened to zap William with a spell, but that didn't **deter** him. Isabelle Ingenuous smiled at William's poem and the image of Felicia as a crow, but she dared not laugh because she didn't want to **affront** her friend Felicia.

9

Felicia **glowered**, stuck out her tongue at William, and then muttered something rude under her breath.

"William, can't you write anything except those **insipid** limericks?" she snapped. "How about giving us a break and trying another form of poetry for a change?"

Isabelle Ingenuous **deftly** changed the subject before an argument **ensued**. "I dread going back to Horribly Hard Middle School for another year," she groaned. "I dislike all the teachers except Ms. **Amicable** Artist, and I don't want to be laughed at by Orson **Odious** and his stuck-up friends," she concluded.

"Yes, I'm with you, Isabelle," **concurred** Sam Sagacious with **fervor**, "but we also need to curb William and his limericks. Doesn't he know any other form of poetry? Would other types of poetry have the same effect on the teachers?" he **queried** further, always curious.

Finally Olivia **Otiose** arrived, late as usual, shrugging on her new **chartreuse** backpack as she hurried up to the door of Isabelle's **abode**. "Hola, amigos," she said in Spanish she had learned over the summer, "Am I late?" she queried as she approached her friends.

"Aren't you always, Olivia?" **sniped** Felicia, who still smarted from William's limerick about her magical **ineptitude**. "Are we ready to go face school for another year?" she finished as she waltzed out the door and onto the sidewalk.

As they slung their backpacks over their shoulders, the **intrepid** friends followed Felicia out of Isabelle's **abode**. There was a **paucity** of talk as the group **trekked** the short walk to Horribly Hard Middle School.

At the edge of the campus, each wondered **mutely** what the new school year in the seventh grade would be like. All too soon, they had reached their school. At the school by the bus port, they were joined by another friend, Jesse **Jocose**, who rode the school bus. Each of them found his or her name on lists posted on the doors to the seventh-grade wing of the school.

"Oh, no, guys, it's bad. It looks as if many of our sixth-grade teachers followed us to the seventh grade, too," moaned Pauline **Puerile** in **dejection**.

"I see a lot of homework in our future, and I see William getting into trouble with his **incessant**, stupid limericks," **predicted** Felicia Fey in an **eerie**, spooky voice.

"Hey, wait up, people," chirped a soft, cheery tone.

"It's Vivian **Virtuous**," whispered Isabelle to her friends. "I remember her from last year as she was in a few of my classes.

She always did her work, and she got straight 'As.' She was the one on whom Orson **Odious** picked whenever he could," she finished.

"Remember me?" murmured the girl with a quiet voice and carefully **coiffed**, intricately braided, **ebony** hair. She clutched a huge hard-back book in her hand entitled <u>War and Peace</u> by Leo Tolstoy. "I was in your science class last year, and I sat in the last row as far away from Orson **Odious** and his **crony** Danny **Dapper** as I could get. They used to lie in wait for me between classes.

"Orson always whispered **malevolent** things under his breath in my direction, too," she sighed, "and he called me a 'suck-up.' Unfortunately, the teacher never caught him doing it.

Danny, on the other hand, threatened and **coerced** me into doing his homework so that he could go to parties. No adult ever caught on to his **shenanigans** either."

Vivian Virtuous joined the group of seven seventh-graders as each member searched for the correct homeroom. When everyone had found his or her **appropriate** classroom, the friends found that they had different homerooms.

When she arrived in her homeroom, Pauline Puerile whined at the unfairness of it all.

"It's not fair," Pauline **whimpered** to herself. "It's just not fair. Not only do I have to go back to school, but my worst **nemesis** is in homeroom to **torment** me first thing every morning."

Orson **Odious**, who, indeed, was in Pauline's homeroom, grinned **maliciously** at her and **lobbed** a slimy spit wad in her direction. Pauline ducked, and she incurred the **wrath** of the homeroom teacher, Mr. Math **Martinet**.

"Stop **fidgeting**, young lady, and sit still," he ordered Pauline in a menacing tone of voice.

Sam **Sagacious ambled** to his new homeroom a few doors down from Pauline's. As he entered the room's **portal**, he froze mid-stride.

"Oh, my," Sam Sagacious muttered in awe as he spied a **comely** girl who sat **demurely** in the third row of desks. Sam hastily grabbed a seat in the fourth row, right behind the **pulchritudinous** girl.

The young, **comely** lady wore a tight, ribbed, aqua top that barely met the top of her equally-tight jeans. Her medium-length black hair curled gently around her ears and flipped up in the back like birds' tail-feathers, only softer. Sam Sagacious, for once in his life, was struck "dumb." (**pun—meaning for "dumb" = "silent, speechless"**)

Sam, by the way, knew that he had seen this **pulchritudinous** girl before among other students, but he couldn't place her. He sat there in the fourth row, right behind the "vision," and breathed in the fresh, shampoo scent from her cute **ebony tresses**.

"This is a **novel (meaning "new")** twist. She's extremely 'hott' with two 'Ts,'" Sam thought to himself as, busily writing, he copied the daily schedule.

As the day progressed, the eight friends met periodically in the hall to compare gossip and the latest news flashes.

"My friend and I think that Orson Odious is worse than ever this year," proclaimed Isabelle and Vivian almost in **unison**.

"Danny **Dapper** is worse than ever as well. Most of the girls think he is so handsome and good, but I think he is **abhorrent** and **vindictive**," added Isabelle with a **grimace**.

"Too right," said William, who already had experienced a **skirmish** with his arch **nemesis**, the **obstreperous** Orson, and his pal Danny.

"They're *both* in my homeroom," **carped** Pauline Puerile. "It's unfair."

"Have you seen the new English teacher yet?" **queried** Sam. "She's one for whom even Olivia Otiose will work! She does well."

"She's 'boss,'" William concluded in the current **vernacular**.

"Oh, yeah, William, she's 'tubular,'" **concurred** Jesse **Jocose**, who was not to be outdone in his knowledge of **slang**.

"Yeah, she's not like Ms. Grammar Grouch at all," **reiterated** Felicia Fey. "She's, like, almost human, and I think she has a touch of magic in her. She has such a way with words; she almost paints pictures with them."

At that moment, Orson Odious passed by. "There's the girl who can't do anything right," he **taunted**. "You're weird, Felicia. Your **somber** outfit is ugly, and your hair looks like a muddy broom. You don't have any class."

Felicia Fey **glowered** at Orson and prepared to zap him with a spell, but her friend's warnings stopped her before she could mouth the first word.

"Careful, Felicia," counseled Isabelle, "your spells don't always work the way you want. It's too **perilous** to try one."

Felicia held back and just stared in the direction of the rapidly retreating Orson. "You're going to get your **comeuppance** some day," she muttered to his back.

After that, the first few months of school passed in the usual fashion except that Sam was **enamored** of the girl in his homeroom and kept trying to get her to notice him—to no **avail**. She seemed **oblivious** of his presence and very **aloof**. Something was troubling her.

She didn't seem to be too **blithe**, and she always looked as if something was wrong.

Teachers assigned **a plethora of** homework but less than at the end of the previous year. Vivian Virtuous raised her hand no fewer than three times each period, even in science class. Orson continued to call her a "suck-up" at every opportunity. As usual, Beth **Bibliophilic** won the "Million Minutes of Reading" Contest. Orson, the **cad**, picked on her as much as he could, and he reduced her to tears on more than one but fewer than ten occasions.

Petra **Pulchritudinous**, as beautiful as ever, spent as much time as possible in the girls' bathroom. Gossip **abounded** in the halls and students' bathrooms (which still smelled **atrocious**). Orson Odious and his main **sycophant**, Danny Dapper, attempted to make everyone's life as miserable as possible; they were **incorrigible**. They made nasty comments to everyone.

The teachers, with the exception of Ms. **Amicable** Artist, Mr. **Melodious** Music, and the new, amazing English teacher, Ms. **Witty** Writing Wizard, were their usual, stern selves. They also still did their usual routine when William or Sam recited one of their **appalling** limericks: stick out their tongues, smoke slightly from their ears and noses, and flicker their eyes.

Happily for the crew of friends who were getting tired of William Waggish's **deplorable** limericks, the new English teacher, Ms. **Witty** Writing Wizard, taught them a new form of poetry—**cinquain**. William, thankfully, abandoned limericks and began to write cinquains. (**NOTE TO TEACHER: See Chapter 5 for definition of "cinquain" and how to write one.**)

William Waggish, as soon as he was comfortable with the new poetic form, **penned** several cinquains. William's first effort was about Mr. Math **Martinet**, his least favorite teacher, and he had the **audacity** to **utter** it as he entered class that same day. He titled his poem "Mindless Math."

> Math class,
> It's deadly dull.
> The old teacher **drones** on...
> Numbers, equations, formulas.
> Boring.

Out of the corner of his eye, William spied Mr. Math Martinet who was standing at the front of the classroom. As William **uttered** the last few words of the poem, Mr. Martinet's eyes fluttered fewer than eight times, his tongue protruded, and his ears **exuded** curls of smoke.

Midterm

"Aha," muttered William to no one in particular, "cinquains work as well as limericks on these **bizarre** teachers."

Sam Sagacious pursued his new interest, the girl in homeroom whose name was Alessandra **Amorous**. She was a former **sycophant** of Orson Odious. Alessandra had become **disenchanted** with the **latter** when Orson (who secretly loved Alessandra) had popped her bra in the back, right in front of everyone in the lunchroom. She hadn't spoken to Orson since then.

Orson Odious, of course, was not pleased with this turn of events, and he went out of his way to embarrass Alessandra every chance he got. Alessandra also avoided Danny Dapper and Petra Pulchritudinous who still hung with their leader, Orson.

"Still stuck-up, aren't you, Alessandra?" Orson said to Alessandra one day in front of Sam and at least nine other students as he passed by.

"Yes, are you **spurning** me, too?" queried Petra **spitefully**. Petra secretly missed the company of her former friend, Alessandra, when she **primped** in the girls' bathroom between every class, but she would never let Orson, Danny, or Alessandra know.

Alessandra muttered something **uncomplimentary** in Spanish under her breath, but no one else heard the **affront**. Orson certainly wouldn't have understood it anyway.

There, in the middle of the lunchroom, Sam wanted to punch Orson in his big, ugly **proboscis**, but he **refrained** from doing so. Alessandra **cringed**.

Sam gently put his hand on her shoulder and said, "He is a 'bogus' **cad**. No one listens to him. My friends and I pay him no **heed**."

Alessandra smiled at Sam, and as he grinned back, Sam's heart sang with hope.

Meanwhile, Orson Odious and his **sycophant**, Danny Dapper (whom the girls thought handsome despite his mean nature), had big plans for a particularly **noisome** event.

Ms. Stern Science displayed a particularly **awe-inspiring** demonstration of teacher weirdness after William recited *sotto voce* one of his new cinquains to see how it would affect the teacher. Sam concluded that cinquains had an even greater effect on the bizarre teachers than limericks. Ms. Stern Science not only had done the usual eye fluttering, smoke curling, and tongue **protrusion**, but she also had raised and lowered both arms no fewer than five times during the recitation of the poem, once with the **utterance** of each line.

This poem was entitled, "Ms. **Monotonous** Science" because Ms. Stern Science **droned** on and on about the day's science topic

57

(which sounded like all the other days' topics) while covering the board with her notes. She required each student to copy the **latter laboriously** into his or her notebook.

> Science,
> Dreary subject...
> **Monotonous drivel**...
> Every day the same thing from one
> Dull prof.

"Wowzer, man!" whispered Jesse to his friend Sam, who also had witnessed the effect of William's poem on the teacher. "This 'rocks.' I can't wait to **regale** the rest of our friends with this latest effect of William's poems."

Yes, this was another piece to add to the puzzle of the bizarre teachers. Inspired by William's success and by Ms. Witty Writing Wizard's **fervent** teaching, Jesse wrote a cinquain of his own. He dedicated his to his favorite teacher, Ms. **Amicable** Artist, on whom he had a small crush. He entitled his composition "Art in Pink" because Ms. **Amicable** Artist loved to wear that **hue**.

> Frothy
> Teacher in pink.
> Daily we create and mold.
> She guides our hands...Creative things
> Spring forth.

When Jesse repeated his poem **audibly** in art class, within hearing of his favorite teacher, he watched her actions. Nothing happened! He said the poem again.

"That's a nice cinquain, Jesse," said Ms. Amicable Artist, but her eyes never fluttered; her tongue never protruded; and her ears and nose never **emitted** smoke.

"Yes, this gets weirder and weirder," Jesse muttered.

The group **unremittingly** continued to test its teachers with the new poetry form. Everybody wrote his or her own cinquain and then tried it out. It was "sweet" to watch the **majority** of the teachers' reactions to the poems. Ms. Amicable Artist, Mr. Melodious Music, and Ms. Witty Writing Wizard, however, still did not react in any way except to **critique** the poems. The crew was getting even more **perplexed**. The cinquain had the most **blatant** effect on Ms. Stern Science and Dean Dread. Sam **pondered** this new development in the mystery.

A few weeks later, though, there was an **odoriferous** incident that distracted the group from their experiments with the bizarre teachers. One day, as the students **milled** about in the halls between classes, a loud "boom" erupted from the boys' bathroom in the seventh-grade hallway. The "boom" immediately was followed by a bad, **noxious** odor that **reeked** badly of rotten eggs.

The door to the boys' bathroom suddenly burst open, and **a plethora of noisome** grey smoke **billowed** out. Two boys emerged from the smoke, coughing, hacking, giggling, and holding their noses. Isabelle and Felicia, who were standing nearby, thought they recognized Orson and Danny as they ran out of the bathroom. Then, all **perdition** broke loose as students scattered in all directions to flee the noxious smoke and the **dearth of** fresh air.

A booming, **stentorian** voice echoed from down the hall. "Who set off a stink bomb in the boys' bathroom?" **bellowed** a tall, black-**garbed, foreboding**-looking man. It was the feared, seemingly **ubiquitous** Dean Dread who was ever present in the halls and lunchroom. He **loomed** over and rushed among the scurrying seventh-graders as he proceeded towards the still-smoking bathroom.

Felicia, for whom spells never worked, panicked. The **putrescent stench** of the stink bomb filled her nostrils, and it gagged her. Without thinking, she muttered an **incantation** to **dispel** the smoke and odor. Of course, it backfired badly. Felicia's fingernails turned **mauve**. The smoke changed from grey to mauve, but it still **reeked** badly of rotten eggs. Oddly enough, there were mauve streaks in the hair of the two fleeing **culprits**, Orson Odious and Danny Dapper.

William Waggish, also on the scene, muttered his newest cinquain entitled "Orson, the **Obstreperous**."

> There is
> One bad person.
> A mean boy…A troublemaker...
> He loves to torment the helpless.
> Bad kid.

Immediately, Dean Dread waved his arms up and down in **cadence** with the poem as smoke curled from his ears and nostrils. His tongue protruded from his mouth, and his eyes fluttered uncontrollably. In addition, his legs seemed to buckle completely, and he wobbled like the scarecrow from the movie <u>The Wizard of Oz</u>. It was a **stellar** performance of teacher weirdness. When Dean Dread recovered from his momentary **lapse**, he took charge of the situation.

"Get the custodian, Mr. Fixit," he bellowed to a nearby teacher.

Then as he frowned, the dean's eyes bulged when he spied the mauve smoke that had been grey fewer than four seconds before. He also saw two **striplings** with matching mauve streaks in their hair sprint out the door of the seventh-grade wing. He made a connection between the two in less than a second.

"You, boys, STOP!" Dean Dread roared to the **receding** backs of Orson and Danny.

All boys in the hallway stopped except the two in question who were headed for the sixth-grade wing at a **brisk pace**. This **exacerbated** the possibility of their guilt.

If they had run five steps farther, the **miscreants** might have escaped Dean Dread's eye. Dean Dread, however, moved quickly. Quicker than the blink of an eye, he had the **malefactors** by the back of their shirts.

"You two **reprobates**, come with me to my office. We need to investigate this incident," he said in a low, menacing tone.

Orson and Danny cringed. The crowd of seventh-graders who witnessed this clapped their hands in delight and **jubilantly jeered** at the two **scalawags**! The class tormenters finally had been **apprehended** for something. Further, they even might be **castigated** and then suspended for their **transgression**. Setting off a stink bomb, after all, was a major offense.

When the **putrescent** smoke had been cleared, everyone **congregated** around Felicia Fey.

"You did well, girlfriend," praised Isabelle Ingenuous.

"You really nailed them, Felicia," **extolled** Sam Sagacious.

"Astounding, Felicia," said Vivian Virtuous **diffidently**.

"Way to go, girl," **lauded** Jesse Jocose as he **cuffed** Felicia gently on her back.

"I take back all those poems about your magic, Felicia," William Waggish apologized **contritely**.

"That's all right, William," returned Felicia **magnanimously**, for she really **loathed** William's teasing poems. "What am I going to do with these mauve nails? They clash with my black **attire**."

The **dénouement** of the entire stink-bomb **incident** was that Orson and Danny (over whom all the girls still drooled and for whom some still did an extra copy of their homework) were suspended for ten days. The **nefarious duo** was sentenced to cafeteria clean-up for a month after their return, too.

After that incident, Dean Dread and the rest of the teachers kept a watchful eye on the **reprehensible** pair for the remainder of the school year. Orson still gave evil looks; Danny still **preyed** on the girls; but the two ceased to be a major pain in the **posterior** of the **intrepid** friends.

Now, Felicia **abruptly** became "Miss Popular." One of the teachers even recommended her for the special school for magically gifted kids, Marvelously Magic Magnet Middle School.

On the day she was tested for admission to that school, however, Felicia's entry spell, as usual, went **awry**. Instead of raising a pencil more than one foot but fewer than two feet off the desk as required, Felicia turned the pencil and her hair green.

"I didn't want to go there anyway," she **rationalized** later to Isabelle, her best friend, "and I didn't want to leave all of you stuck here without me. At whom would William direct his **putrid** poems?" she concluded.

Now that Orson and Danny were **relegated** to nasty stares only, new problem students **cropped up**. Carolyn **Clamorous** became even more **obstreperous** with her persistent, but pointed, questions in math. John **Jabbering** and his **incessant**, **inane** chatter grew to be more **audible** and more annoying. Quincy **Querulous**, who always argued with everyone, tried to pick more **quarrels**. Quincy went so far as to complain **vociferously** to Ms. Stern Science about copying the notes from the board. She punished him by requiring him to make an extra copy of the notes for someone who was absent. Even Jesse's usually **droll** jokes fell flatter than usual.

Skateboarding Steven **Slovenly** provided a welcome break in the **monotony** of school when he accidentally dropped his sagging jeans to his ankles as he jumped to touch the top of a doorway. It seemed that Dean Dread was right behind him. Steven **Slovenly** thus **inadvertently** "mooned" Dean Dread with his bright, orange and blue, striped boxer shorts. Steven maintained afterwards that the **retribution** of three days of in-school detention was worth mooning the dean. Everyone talked about the incident for weeks, and Steven became the new hero for that time.

William, Jesse, and Sam intensified their **quest** to **unravel** the mystery of the bizarre teachers and their strange behavior.

Sam, Jesse, and Olivia **Otiose** had taken music for the second year. Sam, as he had the previous year, played the oboe. Olivia, **loathe** to learn a new instrument, stuck to her clarinet, and Jesse, always the **buffoon**, played the trombone which allowed him some "tubular slides." For the most part, the trio liked the subject and the teacher, but classical music did not **pique** their interest.

Jesse, whose attitude towards classical music was less than **fervent**, directed a **pithy** cinquain at the music teacher, Mr. Melodious Music. Jesse entitled his **oeuvre** "Music Misery."

> We play
> Poorly, off-key.
> Bach, Beethoven, Mozart,
> Three ancient composers, long dead,
> Haunt us.

In spite of the mention of his favorite composers, Mr. Melodious Music, a **devotee** of classical music, did not appreciate the **sentiment**. He sentenced Jesse to playing Bach on the trombone to **engross** the crowd at lunch for a day, but Mr. Melodious Music did not react in any other way to the poem.

"Strange," murmured Sam.

"'Bogus,' you're toast, my friend," whispered Olivia for whom writing a poem for the fun of it would be **anomalous** even though she was good at it.

"'Bummer, dudes,'" said Jesse Jocose to his friends as he **mulled over** the misery of having to play Bach on his trombone before his **peers**. "If only he had let me play jazz..."

In English, Ms. Witty Writing Wizard also did not react to the poems in any way except to analyze them for form. William Waggish recited *sotto voce* one of his best efforts. He had entitled it "Writing Wacko" because the new English teacher was, indeed, a little crazy. Ms. Writing Wizard required her students to sing "dead" verbs and the **subordinating conjunctions** and to chant prepositions and the coordinating conjunctions.

> Writing.
> Weird stuff.
> Poems, essays, stories.
> Singing "dead" verbs; chanting the preps.
> Strange class.

"William," **critiqued** Ms. Writing Wizard, "your last line needs work."

In social studies, however, the new teacher, Ms. **Stringent** Social Studies, reacted in the **customary** fashion to the poems. Isabelle Ingenuous, who usually didn't like to **mock** anyone, wrote a cinquain for her least favorite class.

> History (Say it in two syllables.)
> We study dates, facts,
> And people who are dead...
> A good class to catch a good nap.
> **Dreary**.

Towards the end of the period, Isabelle recited her poem under her breath when Ms. **Stringent** Social Studies was walking the aisle to make sure no one was being **unethical** on the test.

There was an immediate and **spontaneous** reaction by Ms. Stringent Social Studies. Not only did her eyelids flutter, her tongue protrude, and smoke curl from her ears, but her **lank** grey hair stood on end for more than two but fewer than three seconds.

"Oh, wow, that 'rocks,'" said Jesse who witnessed the event.

"What is all this?" whined Pauline for whom anything out of the ordinary **overtaxed** her ability to cope. "I had gotten used to the smoke, the flutter, and the tongue, but hair standing on end? What's next?" she moaned. "Sparks?"

Jesse, William, and Sam then wrote and recited a **barrage** of **egregious** cinquains. Alessandra also wrote one which she gave to Sam to **articulate**. Sam, for whom Alessandra was the **epitome** of female beauty, was thrilled right down to his toes. Of course, he tried her cinquain on every teacher with whom he came into contact. Alessandra's cinquain was entitled "Horribly Hard Middle School 'Bites;'" it went like this:

> School "bites."
> Teachers assign
> Piles of homework and projects.
> Bathrooms **reek**; lunchroom is noisy.
> Why us?

Ms. Witty Writing Wizard **upbraided** Sam for his use of the **pejorative** word "bites."

"As you know, young man, your use use of the verb 'to bite' is improper," she scolded. "You have to bite something; it is a transitive verb. You're using it as an intransitive verb," she finished with a **flourish** as she lay down the chalk.

"What is she **blathering** about?" whispered Olivia to Isabelle since Olivia rarely listened in class when a teacher spoke.

Ms. Witty Writing Wizard overheard Olivia's question, and she **exuberantly** launched into an extensive, **extemporaneous** lesson on verbs that take an object and verbs that do not.

"Oh, brother," murmured Olivia as she rolled her eyes upwards in **aversion**, "she is a grammar book in the **guise** of a person."

Isabelle and Sam just grinned; Olivia Otiose was being her usual **otiose** self. She was very intelligent, but somehow **abhorred** to do anything that might make her do homework or study.

Other teachers reacted differently to Alessandra's poem. Mr. Math Martinet, Ms. Stern Science, and Ms. **Stringent** Social Studies did the usual: fluttering eyes, smoking ears, protruding tongue. In addition, their hair either stood on end for fewer than three seconds, or they raised their arms in the air in **cadence** with each syllable of the poem. When Sam recited Alessandra's poem in the vicinity

Read-aloud passage

of Dean Dread in the cafeteria, he rewarded the seventh-graders with a startling show of silver sparks that **emanated** from the tips of his fingers. The show stopped as **abruptly** as it had begun.

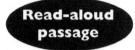

"Wow, Pauline," said Jesse Jocose in admiration, "you called it! Sparks!"

Principal **Punctilious**, who had lunchroom duty that day and who did not show any **overt** reaction to the poem, promptly used his radio and called Mr. **Adept** Fixit. The **latter** arrived in fewer than five seconds and then exited with Dean Dread following behind him. Jesse Jocose recited the poem again as the two passed by his table, but while Dean Dread reacted in the usual manner, Mr. Adept Fixit did not even **grimace**.

The art and music teachers, like the new creative writing teacher, showed no overt reaction except utter disgust at the use of the **epithet** "bites."

One day at lunch, Sam, William, Jesse, Isabelle, Pauline, Vivian, Alessandra (who now hung around with her hero, Sam), Felicia, and Pauline analyzed the new information that they were **amassing** on their bizarre teachers.

"This is getting stranger and stranger," said Sam. "Why did our **intractable** English teacher last year react to the poems while the creative writing teacher this year does not?"

"Hey, guys, why are they all reacting more obviously this year?" asked Vivian Virtuous.

Jesse Jocose, who always looked for an excuse to be funny, suddenly stood up on the bench and recited a **spontaneous** cinqain in a **strident** voice.

> There are
> Five things I hate
> About lunch: awful food,
> Piercing noise, hard seats, no freedom,
> Stale rolls.

When he had finished his poem, Jesse sat down on the **inflexible** seat mentioned in Jesse's poem. Felicia (who secretly liked Jesse) **surreptitiously** threw a stale roll in Jesse's direction. Jesse, laughing, pitched an apple core into Felicia's lap.

William, not to be outdone and remembering that Dean Dread had left the room, flicked his tray and **launched** his uneaten, **sodden** vegetables into the air and yelled, "Food fight!"

Immediately, the air became **rife** with flying bits of food and trash. Bits of spaghetti dangled from the ceiling fans. Greasy sauce plastered everyone's hair and smeared most **visages**. Bits of "mystery meat" lay in brown blobs on the now-filthy floor. The **cacophony** of shouting and laughing student voices drowned out Mr. Punctilious Principal who stood on stage and shrieked **futilely** into his microphone.

All at once, the doors to the cafeteria flung open. A tall, menacing figure stood there, his **visage** a picture of righteous **wrath**.

"Students, stop this immediately," he boomed over the **din**. Even without **amplification**, his **raucous** voice could be heard by all.

Amazingly, the cafeteria was suddenly silent except for the drip of the spaghetti as it fell from the fans. Students froze in place. They stood, leaned, or sat, mid-hurl, at the sound of Dean Dread's **stentorian** and **fearsome** voice, and they stared in his direction.

"I absolutely will not tolerate such **appalling** behavior," Dean Dread continued in a deadly, low tone that **boded** disaster and punishment. "Sit down, children," he ordered. "There will be **dire** consequences for this," he **intoned**.

Everyone sat, stunned into silence. Even John **Jabbering** was **mute**.

Then Quincy **Querulous**, who always had to argue with everybody, broke the silence and said, "But..."

"I said 'silence,'" repeated Dean Dread as he **bristled** like an angry warthog.

Quincy **Querulous** was **querulous**, but he was not stupid. He did not attempt to speak again. Dean Dread stalked **ominously** to the front of the cafeteria where he stood, hands on hips, and glared at the **miscreants**.

"First," he said, "classes will be **postponed**, and you will stay here until every strand of spaghetti, every drop of milk, every piece of paper, and every **gobbet** of sauce is cleaned, and this cafeteria shines. Second," he **persisted**, "all end-of-the-year field trips are cancelled for all seventh-grade students; instead, you're required to write a series of essays on how to **comport** yourselves in public. Third," he pronounced, "there will now be assigned seats in the cafeteria for the rest of the year."

After Dean Dread made this pronouncement, he crossed his arms in front of his enormous chest and just stared. The seventh-graders cleaned the cafeteria under his watchful eye, and no one opened his or her **maw**. No one, not even Orson, misbehaved in any way. Even John **Jabbering** was **mute**, and Beth Bibliophilic didn't turn pages in her book, <u>Little Women</u>, by Louisa May Alcott until Dean Dread stopped talking.

After they cleaned up the mess, the seventh-graders filed **mutely** out of the cafeteria. No one spoke until the cafeteria was no longer in sight.

Final Exam

"It's not fair to cancel our field trips!" exclaimed William.

"Why do we have to write essays, too?" complained Olivia who hated to write.

"Why is he so mean?" whined Pauline to her friends.

"Hey, you guys," said Isabelle who always calmed her friends when they were agitated, "we *were* guilty, you know. We *did* throw food, and, in fact, we began the food fight because we threw the first **salvo**."

"I know," **retorted** Sam, "but did he have to take away all our end-of-year field trips? It's too much," he concluded.

Orson and his **sycophant** Danny, a too handsome young man, chose that moment to pass by angrily. "Nice going, losers," **jeered** Orson to whom everyone who was not in his crowd was a "loser."

Danny, **aghast** at the thought of having to write a bunch of essays in front of the teachers which meant he would actually have to write them by himself, really was **livid** at the thought. He **lashed** out.

"You're nothing but unsightly, stupid trash," he hissed. "You're a pimple on Dean Dread's **posterior**, too."

Everyone in the group of friends glared at Orson with his or her best **withering** gaze. They still **loathed** Orson and Danny because the two were so mean.

Luckily, the end of the school year quickly arrived. Despite the lack of the much-desired field trip to the amusement park and the extra essays they had to write, the school year ended on an upbeat note. Ms. Amicable Artist, Mr. Melodious Music, and Ms. Witty Writing Wizard got together and staged an afternoon in a nearby park. The HHMS Jazz Band's members provided music, and they played well. Students made impressions of leaves and flowers onto special paper. Vivian recited some of her favorite poetry, including "I Dream a World" by Langston Hughes. All three subjects were covered so that it could be **dubbed** "educational."

Soon the last day of school arrived. Exams had ended. The friends, except Sam Sagacious, of course, promptly forgot about their strange teachers and concentrated on their summer plans.

The girls had **diverse** ideas about how to spend their summer. Isabelle Ingenuous had imaginative projects to do. Olivia Otiose had to go to summer school for math because she had been lazy and had not done her homework; nor had she studied for tests. She hoped to spend time with her new friend, Alessandra, though, because she also thought that learning more

Final Exam

Spanish might be fun. Felicia Fey planned to **hone** her magical skills (but she really didn't want to leave her friends to go to the school for **mages**). Pauline Puerile didn't know what she was going to do that summer since no one yet had suggested anything that appealed to her. Alessandra Amorous and her family planned a trip to Puerto Rico to visit relatives. Vivian Virtuous had signed up for a writing course. Beth Bibliophilic would, of course, read as much as she could, but she hoped to travel with her family as well.

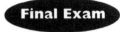

Final Exam

The boys had plans as well. William Waggish hoped to laze around in the morning, write poetry, and play sports at the local Boys Club in the afternoons. Sam Sagacious decided to go to the library daily for research but also was on a baseball team with William and Jesse. Jesse Jocose was going to summer school by choice to learn about computers. He hoped to spend his afternoons playing basketball and baseball.

It looked as if it would be a good summer for all the friends. They didn't have to deal with Orson Odious or Danny Dapper (whose parents were going to send them to their grandmothers for two months), and homework (except for Olivia Otiose) already was a **vague** memory.

On the last day of school (after all the students had left), all was silent at Horribly Hard Middle School except for muffled sounds from the art, music, and seventh-grade language arts rooms, the "clack" of computer keys in the main office, and the muttered **epithets** of Mr. Adept Fixit in the dean's office.

Final Exam

Eighth-Grade Part of the Story

As the August morning sun chased the shadows from the roofs of houses and painted the sky gold, once again there was an **eerie** silence at Horribly **Introduction**
Hard Middle School. In the dawning light, you could not see into the classrooms because of the light-blocking curtains at every window. No early teacher rushed out of a car in the parking lot to set up a lab or to get an early start on preparation for the first day of school. Horribly Hard Middle School was like a spooky mansion: closed, dark, and abandoned.

In contrast, across town, as the sun rose a bit higher in the sky, Marvelously Magic Magnet Middle School (popularly known as MMMMS) burst with energy and noise. Coffee perked in the teachers' lounge. Cars roared into the parking lot, parked, and spilled out teachers of different sizes, shapes, and complexions. Boxes, books, bags, and piles of "stuff" filled their arms as they walked into the school early to be ready for the first day of classes for the year.

Finally, four cars drove up to the **dormant** and silent Horribly Hard Middle School: a new mauve Lexus sedan, an old blue Ford pick-up truck, a new red Chevy sedan, and an old, battered, tan Subaru station wagon that had seen better days. A middle-aged man, Mr. **Punctilious** Principal, stepped out of the Lexus. Another middle-aged man, the custodian, Mr. **Adept** Fixit, exited the blue pick-up.

The man who exited the Lexus wore a suit and tie, and carried a battered briefcase. The owner of the Ford climbed out of his pick-up, walked to the back, and lifted a tool chest from the bed of his truck. He **sported** a denim shirt and overalls, a red handkerchief in his upper pocket, a wrench that hung out of his lower pocket, a purposeful air, and a worried look on his face.

The door of the Subaru creaked open and out fell construction paper and magazines, followed by a **harried**-looking woman. She was dressed in a long, loose purple dress with a purple flower in her thick blonde hair and a **myriad** of colored pencils in her mouth. The two men nodded solemnly to each other and smiled at the woman as she gathered the stuff that had fallen from her car.

The red Chevy parked next to the Subaru. The door swung open in **tandem** with the trunk. A man, dressed in a tri-corner hat and military uniform of 300 years ago, awkwardly stepped out of the car. He nodded to the lady in the purple dress, smiled, and walked to the open trunk. After lifting out the biggest of the boxes in the trunk and placing it on the ground, he closed the trunk, **Introduction**
picked up the box, and headed towards the eighth-grade wing of the school.

The men **trekked** in different directions: the suited one toward the school office, the man in overalls toward the custodian's office, and the one with the box towards the farthest wing of the school. The woman gathered her materials from the pavement and **ambled** slowly to a building set slightly off from the main part of the school. No other human soul could be seen in the dim light of early morning.

Slowly, one after the other, classroom lights came on in HHMS. Soon the school was **ablaze**, and all classrooms were lit, but apart from Mr. **Adept** Fixit, who rushed from room to room to open doors and turn on lights, no sounds of people could be heard on the campus. This was the first day of school?

If you listened carefully in the main office near the door to the principal's room, you could hear the faint click of computer keys as Mr. **Punctilious** Principal, a man who was always concerned with correct procedure, checked and rechecked the procedures which would be followed that first day of school as well as the list of students who would enter the **portals** of the HHMS in less than an hour.

If you **strolled** over to the art room, you could hear faint singing of an old Beatles tune and the rustling of paper.

Five minutes later another car pulled up in front of the still silent Horribly Hard Middle School. A man in a **dapper** blue suit who was humming a Mozart sonata **ambled** toward a nearby dark classroom. He was burdened with various-sized instrument cases. He wore his favorite purple tie that was decorated with yellow musical notes. His tie was **askew**, and his glasses perched unevenly on his nose, ruining the effect of his handsome blue suit.

Before the man with the instrument cases could close the trunk of his car, a final **vehicle**, an ancient white Volvo sedan, **careened** into the lot and parked next to the **decrepit** tan Subaru. A pleasingly-plump middle-aged woman with curly grey hair jumped **animatedly** out of the Volvo, nodded **genially** to the man who hummed the Mozart sonata, and turned back to her car.

The **stout** woman then opened the hatch and removed an obviously heavy box that was **brimful** with books. She heaved the box for better **leverage** and trudged slowly with her heavy burden in the direction of the seventh-grade wing of the school.

The staff parking lot of Horribly Hard Middle School once again fell silent. Only six cars awaited their drivers.

On another side of the school, forty-five minutes later, a long, curved line of school busses arrived, one by one. Each **disgorged** a bunch of chattering students, each with his or her backpack. Other students who had walked to school **ambled** slowly onto the school grounds to join the **hordes** being let off by the busses. Horribly Hard Middle School came alive with voices, and a new school year began.

A young man, whose vast, faded, too-big trousers sat **precariously** low on his hips, rode a much-decorated skateboard on one of the sidewalks. Mysteriously, a **foreboding** figure appeared. It was the **dreaded** Dean **Dread**. As usual, he was **garbed** in black. His long, narrow face showed neither humor nor compassion.

Dean **Dread** raised his **menacing** voice so that the **miscreant** could hear, and he said in a deadly tone, "Steven **Slovenly**, give me that skateboard. Skateboards are **banned** on campus. Sagging pants without belts also are not allowed. Come to my office right now to get a piece of **twine** to use as a belt for those **outsized** pants you insist on wearing. Didn't you learn anything last year when your pants dropped to your ankles right in front of me?"

Steven Slovenly knew he was **culpable**. He hung his head, mumbled something about "forgetting," got off his board, put it under his right arm, gripped the waistband of his trousers, and followed Dean Dread to the **latter**'s office. Every few steps, Steven hitched up his pants with his left hand. A few students pointed at Steven and **jeered**.

Steven Slovenly kept repeating, "I forgot. I forgot," as he **trudged dejectedly** after Dean Dread.

Meanwhile on the other side of the school, seven students, who had just walked to school together, stood on a corner of the sidewalk waiting for the bus of one of their friends to arrive.

Isabelle **Ingenuous**, an **animated**, perky young lady, twirled with an excess of energy. One of Isabelle's friends, Olivia **Otiose**, slouched next to her. Another friend, Pauline **Puerile**, whined in a babyish manner about the summer being over, but she perked up when Alessandra **Amorous**, another member of the group, diverted her attention by recounting a story of her summer in Puerto Rico with her relatives. The fourth girl in the **assemblage** was dressed and **coiffed** in an odd manner. Her long hair was light sea green. Her shorts and t-shirt also were green, but their color was more like that of a lime. This was Felicia **Fey**, who was known for casting spells that always went **awry** (except once in the seventh grade when one of her spells **nabbed** the **perpetrators** of a stink bomb in the boys' bathroom).

Felicia began to mutter words of a spell to encourage her friend Pauline **Puerile** to cheer up. Isabelle **Ingenuous** put her hand over Felicia's mouth to stop her from **uttering** her spell.

"You know it will backfire on you, Felicia," cautioned Isabelle Ingenuous. "You don't want to **obliterate** your new hairdo, do you?"

"My other magic friends and I practiced all summer," **retorted** a slightly **indignant** Felicia. "I'm getting a little better at it. I'm doing well."

"Hey, Felicia, how come you're not **garbed** in black as you were all last year?" asked a boy whose **puckish** expression mirrored his **waggish** personality.

Felicia **Fey** rolled her eyes and **retorted**, "Hey, William **Waggish**, I may dress weirdly, and my spells backfire, but you write the most **egregious** poetry."

To hide his admiration of Felicia, William Waggish made a tasteless but funny joke about girls. No one listened, and everyone turned his or her head in Alessandra's direction to hear her story. They, too, were used to William's **lame** poems, **vapid** jokes, and friendly **barbs**.

The last member of the troop, Sam **Sagacious**, simply stood wisely and **mutely** as he waited for the **clamor** to die down. He held a huge, heavy book (Norton's Anthology of Poetry) in his hand and pretended to read it, but he really was watching Alessandra Amorous whom he liked.

Since his joke had fallen flat, and no one had laughed, William Waggish **regaled** his friends with a new limerick about girls who wear green. Brown-faced with expressive dark **pupils**, William composed mischievous poems to hide his real aspiration: to be as **eloquent** a poet as his secret hero, Langston Hughes. He entitled it "The Heroine."

> There was a young lady in green
> Whose spells often cause a big scene.
> She's "fey" as they come
> But smarter than some,
> Like Orson who really is mean.

A faint wisp of smoke **emanated** from both ears of a teacher who was standing just barely within earshot. First, her tongue **protruded** slightly, and next, she froze in place for fewer than three seconds. This was nothing new.

Sam **Sagacious** glanced at the teacher, put his book in his backpack, and laughed. "It's working. You haven't lost your touch, William. Yes, you still can affect and **discombobulate** some of the teachers, and last year, in fact, you recited cinquains which had an even greater effect on the teachers than the limericks. Are you going to go back to limericks this year?"

"Nah," said his friend William Waggish, "I still like composing limericks just to be **exasperating**, like a constant drip. I do well at annoying you all, and, besides, it's fun."

Six pairs of eyeballs rolled at this comment. Felicia Fey threatened to zap William, but that didn't **deter** him. She then furrowed her brow, stuck out her tongue at him, and good-naturedly muttered something rude under her breath as the rest of the girls **tittered**.

"For the benefit of your friends, William, can't you and your friend Jesse write anything except those **insipid** limericks and cinquains?" Felicia teased. "Hey, how about giving us a break and trying another form of poetry this year?"

Isabelle Ingenuous, of course, smiled at William's poem and Felicia's friendly **jibe**, but her smile immediately turned to a frown at the sight of a recognizable, hulking figure that **loped** towards them with a **malevolent** grin on its face. It was Orson **Odious** followed by his two pals, Danny **Dapper** and Petra **Pulchritudinous**.

"Well, if it isn't the super-strange cast of 'Weirdo, Incorporated' and its famous witch," **derided** Orson **Odious**, the **nemesis** of the group.

"Seen Dean Dread today, Orson?" asked Sam Sagacious, wrinkling his nose against the **reek** of stale cigarette smoke that **wafted** from Orson's clothes and breath.

"Set off any **putrescent** stink bombs lately?" inquired William with a trace of sarcasm in his voice as he referred to the incident in the seventh grade when Orson had been caught for his **misdeed** by Dean Dread. His **culpability** was revealed when a misfired spell of Felicia's put mauve streaks in his hair that matched the smoke.

Suddenly, Orson's **sycophants**, Danny **Dapper** and Petra **Pulchritudinous**, came up behind him, ready to back up their friend, just as Orson spied a teacher approaching. When Orson and his **cohorts** strutted by Isabelle and friends, they muttered a few nasty, choice **epithets** and threats under their breath as they passed by.

As he raised a fisted hand into the air, Orson threatened **ominously**, "My friends and I will make 'toast' of you later."

"My friends and I are trembling," William said with false **bravado**.

Isabelle hushed him before he could **infuriate** Orson any further.

"I see that Petra **Pulchritudinous** already has changed her clothes in the girls' bathroom," commented Isabelle **Ingenuous**. "I know her family, and her mother never would let her wear a skirt that short to school," she finished.

Another **putrid** yellow school bus pulled up to the curb. Jesse **Jocose** leapt off the bus with **alacrity**; he walked quickly up to his friends.

"Hey, Dudes and Lades, how's it going? I can't wait to **regale** you with all I learned at the 'tubular' computer camp I attended this **sultry, simmering** summer. Now I can really 'hack.' Hey, William," he said as he thumped his buddy on the back, "got any new poems?"

22

Everyone else rolled his or her eyes and groaned. Another girl exited her bus and **ambled** over to the group, too. She had intricately braided **ebony** hair and a hardback book, as usual, in her hand. This one was entitled Pride and Prejudice. As she was greeted, the usually shy Vivian **Virtuous** turned to the boys with excitement.

"William, Jesse, I learned a new form of poetry in my summer writing course," she bubbled. "You'll love it. It's in your **bailiwick**. Haiku!"

"At least it's different from limericks and cinquains," **rejoined** Isabelle who really liked William's poems but pretended otherwise.

On that note, the nine friends gathered their stuff, walked to the double **portals** where eighth-grade homerooms were posted, checked out the lists, found their names, and then **lingered** together until the warning bell rang.

"Oh, no, guys, it looks as if some of the most **insufferable** teachers followed us to the eighth grade," moaned Pauline Puerile in **dejection** as she frowned.

"Hey, Vivian, tell me about haiku poetry. Maybe we really can flip out the **intolerable** ones this year as we did last year, and then we can discover why they react to our poems," said William.

"Yeah," **reiterated** Jesse who always was ready to try any prank that would **discombobulate** their teachers. "I've heard of haiku; it's 'sweet.' It's only three lines, too. That's two fewer lines than in a cinquain."

"I made up one this summer," said Vivian Virtuous **diffidently**.

"Let's hear your poem," said Isabelle Ingenuous **earnestly**.

Vivian recited her haiku. It was about her new friend, Felicia, and it was entitled "My Friend."

> My friend casts her spells
> Upon the wind, and she hopes
> That one will go right.

Isabelle pointed out, "Your spell on that **noisome** stink bomb sure worked well last year, Felicia! Maybe fewer of your spells will go wrong this year!"

"There are a few I've been practicing," **alleged** Felicia hopefully.

Pauline, Olivia, and Alessandra smiled. William and Jesse, who stood among the girls, **sniggered**, but they really were impressed with Vivian's poem. Sam, who always was observant, noticed that

32

two teachers standing in nearby classroom doorways twitched, **emitted** curls of smoke from their ears and noses, **garbled** almost **incoherently** some phrase over and over, and stuck out their tongues with each word like lizards. Sam couldn't **perceive** exactly what they muttered, but he was determined to find out.

Indeed, the group of friends did have some of the same teachers from previous years. Mr. Math Martinet had followed them to the eighth grade, much to Olivia's dismay. Ms. **Amicable** Artist and Mr. **Melodious** Music, however, taught eighth-graders, too. And, there was a new teacher for social studies, Mr. **Scintillating** Social Studies.

"I wonder what he's like," **pondered** Isabelle as she played with one of the **omnipresent**, plastic butterflies in her hair.

"It's probably just another horrible, **despicable**, boring **automaton**," moaned Pauline who always saw only the negative.

"Oh, no, that nice English teacher we had last year, Ms. **Witty** Writing Wizard, stayed in seventh grade," complained Olivia. "We have Ms. Grammar Grouch again, and there's Ms. Stern Science on the eighth-grade list, too," Olivia **griped** further. "It's going to be an **arduous** year."

"Well, between Ms. Grammar Grouch and Mr. Math Martinet, I see lots of homework. I also see William and Jesse getting into trouble with their **incessant**, stupid poems," **predicted** Felicia Fey in an **eerie**, spooky voice.

William and Jesse wasted no time, and after they received a few lessons from Vivian Virtuous, they **promptly** composed **a plethora of** haiku with which to **assess** their teachers' reactions. Sam kept notes on the various instructors' reactions in his **omnipresent** notebook.

One day, when one particularly **astute** poem of Jesse's made Mr. Math Martinet freeze in his tracks and raise his arms in the air for no fewer than two entire minutes (besides **manifesting** the usual ear-smoke, eye-flutter, and tongue **protrusion**), Sam knew that they were on the right track. Jesse Jocose entitled the poem "No **Mirth**." Sam Sagacious **speculated** that it was the **superlative** vocabulary that produced the added effect.

Numbers and homework
Fill his mind that seems **devoid**
Of **mirth** and **vision**.

Sam also noted further that Ms. Amicable Artist had no reaction except a sweet, **exasperated** smile for William's poem that was entitled "Brush Magic."

Her brush strokes paper,
And colorful images
Appear like magic.

42

"Mr. Melodious Music didn't react to the haiku either except to comment on their content. I wonder," **mused** Sam.

Surprisingly, the new history teacher, Mr. **Scintillating** Social Studies, didn't react to the poems either. Usually, he simply **disregarded** them as he went on with his lesson as if no poem had been **uttered**.

"This is becoming more and more curious," noted Sam to William.

Since the students had even more homework, eighth grade proved more **arduous** than seventh grade. Orson Odious was again up to his usual, **malicious** tricks, and this year he picked mainly on three victims: Isabelle Ingenuous, shy Beth **Bibliophilic**, and, of course, Felicia Fey who had "ratted" on him the previous year.

Once again, otiose Danny **Dapper** took advantage of his **comeliness** and preyed on super-shy girls like Beth **Bibliophilic** to do his homework for him. Petra Pulchritudinous showed **derision** toward any girl who didn't dress as she did. To make matters worse, the **malevolent** trio was joined by a new student, Dalbert **Devious**. Dalbert, too, liked to pick on anyone whom he perceived as weaker, more **insecure**, or smaller than he.

One morning, however, just before school, Orson, Danny, and Dalbert were caught smoking behind the eighth-grade wing. This effected some **drastic** changes for the better, and it got rid of a problem. It seems that just as Orson was taking a last drag behind the eighth-grade **edifice**, Dean Dread came around the corner, and he spied the **miscreants**.

"What do you think you're doing?" he said in his deadly, **monotone** voice.

"My friends and I didn't do anything," coughed Orson as he swallowed the cigarette's smoke.

"Oh, it's nothing, sir," mumbled Dalbert and Danny in unison as Danny stuck his hand with the still-lit cigarette, which he held between two fingers, into his **voluminous** trousers. "Ouch!" he yelped as the lit cigarette **scorched** his leg, and he **inadvertently** revealed his guilt.

Dalbert **Devious**, living up to his sneaky personality, quickly had crushed the evidence of his guilt under his shoe, and Dean Dread saw nothing. Orson and Danny, on the other hand, could not plead innocence.

"Follow me, you **varlets**," (**commonly known Shakespearean insult meaning a knavish person, a rascal**) snarled Dean Dread as he marched them toward his office.

Midterm

"Your parents will be notified immediately, and you're suspended for no fewer than ten days. We do not **tolerate** illegal use of substances of any kind on this campus, and you're guilty."

Midterm

The result of this incident was that Orson, who had a long list of **egregious transgressions** in his records, was sent to the alternative school. Danny came back after ten days of suspension a **subdued** young man who no longer made fun of others. Dalbert escaped with a few days of in-school detention because there was a **lack** of evidence in his case, but he remained as **conniving** as ever.

Now the group of friends only had to contend with one tormentor and, of course, the ever-**haughty** Petra Pulchritudinous, too. William and Jesse continued to recite their haiku poems in an attempt to discover the mystery of their teachers' reactions.

One day, Ms. Grammar Grouch, ever the **stickler** for correct punctuation and grammar, **manifested** her usual symptoms, froze for ten seconds, and **lisped** over and over for more than thirty seconds but for fewer than sixty seconds the following phrase: "There are four uses of semicolons; there are four uses of semicolons."

William had recited an **adroit**, clever poem he entitled "No Fire."

> She likes correct **prose**.
> Where's her imagination,
> Her creative fire?

Dalbert Devious, who sat in his usual place in the back row of Ms. Grouch's class, stopped **surreptitiously** poking Beth **Bibliophilic** (who sat in front of him) with his feet, and he stared, **dumbfounded**, at the **antics** of the teacher.

"Whoa," he **pondered**, "this is really 'bogus.' Maybe these 'weirdo nerds' aren't so weird after all."

After they left the class, Dalbert asked William what he had said that had **discombobulated** their instructor and made her freeze.

"Please tell me what you did to make the teachers do all that," he **entreated** William. "It's too 'sweet' for words."

"Words, that's all it is. It's just poetry," **rejoined** William Waggish.

When William **regaled** him about the limerick's effects on the teachers in the sixth grade, the cinquain's effects on the teachers in the seventh grade, and the even more **apparent** effects of the haiku this year, Dalbert resolved to join whole-heartedly in the effort to unravel the mystery of HHMS's **bizarre** teachers. He even politely **beseeched** Vivian Virtuous to teach him quickly how to write a haiku poem.

53

"Please, Vivian, as I live and breathe, I **implore** you to teach me how to write a haiku," pleaded Dalbert who suddenly was **affable**.

Dalbert's first effort was not **shoddy**. Its effect on Ms. **Stern** Science was amazing. Not only did she do the usual smoking, tongue-wagging, and freezing, but she wobbled as well as if she were going to **topple** over. This pleased Dalbert to no end as he loved to be **wily**. Dalbert entitled his poetic effort "The **Automaton**."

> Science is her life.
> Facts, figures, **incessant** notes.
> She is not human.

The effect of Dalbert's poem on Dalbert himself was to focus his **deviousness** on composing haiku instead of **cogitating** how to torment his **peers**. Writing haiku became the "in" thing among the eighth-graders that year. Even Skateboarding Steven **Slovenly** wrote on his skateboard in huge, block letters the phrase "Haiku Rules."

The year progressed, and William, Jesse, and the other friends were joined in their efforts at haiku writing from an **unanticipated** source— Danny Dapper.

A **subdued** Danny, former **sycophant** of the **scurrilous** Orson Odious, even composed a haiku himself. "It's easy," he marveled. "They're short!"

"Use **superlative** vocabulary in it so that it has an even greater effect on the teachers," instructed Sam Sagacious.

"I will," said Danny **fervently**.

Danny **heeded** Sam's advice, and he asked Beth Bibliophilic (in a nice tone for a change) for some suggestions. He used the following words: "**foreboding**" and "**garbed**." He entitled his poem "My Favorite Dean." It was the first piece of work Danny had completed by himself all year.

> A **foreboding** man
> **Garbed** in a black expression
> Looms over students.

"That's not bad!" **marveled** William, whose dislike of Danny was **palpable**. "My friends and I are impressed with your **metaphor**, and you're actually a good poet," he **marveled**.

In reaction to Danny's poetic effort, Dean Dread did the usual eye-fluttering, ear-smoking, and tongue-protruding, but he also raised his **mammoth**, trunk-like arms into the air and **wind-milled** them as if he were a plane revving up to take off. In addition, he also **lisped**

the clause, "I am the **authority**; I am the authority." He repeated
this for more than four but fewer than five seconds. Dean Dread
buckled at the knees, too, almost falling over.

63

"There is something weird going on here," said Sam. "Their
reactions are becoming more and more **blatant**. I never thought I'd say
this, but 'way to go,' Danny."

"It was nothing," murmured Danny as he blushed at the
unaccustomed praise and **loped** off.

Alessandra Amorous, who had hung around with Danny in the
sixth grade, **gawked** at Danny, her mouth **ajar** in shock at his
uncharacteristic behavior.

"Es increíble! It's unbelievable!" she said in Spanish and then
reiterated in English to anyone who listened. "Danny truly wrote
something himself!"

Danny may have written something on his own, but Petra
Pulchritudinous hadn't changed her *modus vivendi*. That same evening
at the second school dance of the year, there was an **episode** with Petra
Pulchritudinous that, temporarily at least, pushed thoughts of the bizarre
teachers out of the friends' minds.

The cafeteria was beautiful with **subdued** light. All the tables lined
the walls with red and blue paper draped over them. Mounds of artfully
arranged chips, cookies, cakes, veggies, and fruit **adorned** tablecloths in
the school's colors. A fountain of pink punch **cascaded** into a huge
bowl, and **garlands** of paper flowers hung from the ceiling. A live band,
The **Strident Strummers**, warmed up on a low platform. Their **strident**
music boomed from large speakers, and the walls **reverberated** with the
bass.

"Ah," breathed Petra as she entered the room, glanced around, and
heard the music. "My friends and I are going to have a blast tonight,"
she said as she ducked into the girls' bathroom to change to her too-short,
too-tight black skirt and spaghetti-string **azure** blouse, **garments** that her
mother would not let her wear because of their "**inappropriateness** for
her age."

Since Petra had plastered so much make-up on her now not-so-
comely face, she looked as if she had been painted. Petra, who thought
she looked **pulchritudinous**, exited the girls' bathroom and found her
friends. Orson no longer attended HHMS, but Dalbert Devious, dressed
in an **ebony** tank top and tight, black, leather pants, found Petra without
delay.

He swept Petra up in his arms to dance. As the dance moved to
a slow tune, Dalbert **surreptitiously** moved his hands further down

74

Petra's back until they rested **perilously** close to her **posterior**. Their improper behavior and **garb** were spotted immediately.

"Stop that at once!" **shrilled** Ms. Grammar Grouch to the two students who further **compounded** their guilt by ignoring her and continuing to **gyrate** slowly to the music. "Dean Dread, you must come see this! This is your **bailiwick**. These two students must leave this dance at once; we must call their parents."

As Dean Dread approached, Petra, who already was in trouble with her mother, panicked and ran. In her haste to further the distance between herself and Dean Dread, she tripped over a tablecloth and toppled over a food-**laden** table. She fell face down **amid** the food with her painted **visage** in a chocolate cake. As Petra lay there among the cakes, fruit, and cookies, she **wailed** her distress and **wrath**.

"Why me? I'm so beautiful. My friends and I are so popular. Things like this don't happen to *me*," she **sniveled** as Dean Dread and Ms. Grammar Grouch plucked her off the cake and then walked her to the office to phone her parents.

Dean Dread firmly gripped Dalbert's arm with his other hand.

"I wish I had written a poem to use right about now," Dalbert muttered.

"You're in big trouble, young man, and you must not speak unless spoken to," said Dean Dread in an **ominous** tone.

Dalbert Devious, for once in his **wily** life, couldn't think of a way to squirm out of trouble. He didn't even think he had done anything that **egregious**.

The next week all anyone could talk about was Petra Pulchritudinous.

"It's amazing," said Vivian Virtuous, "Petra actually is wearing long pants and tops without any **décolletage**. She looks like the rest of us; she's really **comely** without all that makeup. She should have done this sooner."

"Wow, I can't believe it," said Alessandra Amorous. "Petra's mother actually came to school every morning for a week, sat in homeroom with her, and **escorted** her to first period. I bet Petra was **mortified**; I certainly would be 'mucho' humiliated."

"Maybe she'll be nice when we bump into her in the girls' **lavatory**," said Felicia **optimistically**.

"Don't get your hopes up," said Pauline Puerile. "She scoffed at my blouse today, so I think this only is going to make her more **intolerant**."

"She's not a **blithe** camper this week," added Isabelle who always looked for the best in everyone.

Soon, as it usually happens with gossip, talk about the **episode** at the dance and its aftermath died down. The new topic of conversation centered around Mr. **Scintillating** Social Studies and his "Living History Day" incident.

85

Mr. Scintillating Social Studies turned out to be an exciting, creative teacher, and he certainly was different from his **predecessor**, Ms. **Humdrum** History. His teaching methods were somewhat **bizarre** since he liked to spark lively discussions and to hold panels instead of **unadulterated**, **lackluster** study out of the text.

"He's 'tubular,'" murmured Jesse who always used **vernacular**.

His "Living History Days" had become legendary, even though he only held one or two every unit, or fewer than four every six weeks. On "Living History Days," Mr. Scintillating Social Studies dressed up in a soldier's costume from his **extensive** wardrobe. If they were studying the Revolutionary War, then he **garbed** himself in the uniform of a foot soldier one day, and then he came as a sergeant or a high-ranking officer the next day. The third day he arrived as a cavalry officer. He even brought the mess kit and an authentic (unloaded, of course) rifle from the period. The class then held lively discussions, or students **probed** the history of the **era** in an **innovative** manner.

One morning, Mr. Scintillating Social Studies stepped out of his red Chevy, **clad**, like a true soldier, in the full uniform of a sergeant in the Civil War. A duffel bag and mess kit hung from one shoulder, and an authentic rifle **dangled** from the other.

As he sauntered to the eighth-grade wing of the school, he passed by the bus port where **a plethora of** school busses were disgorging students.

"Oh, boy, it's 'Living History Day!'" enthused Jesse as he descended from his public **conveyance** and spied his history teacher in full soldier **regalia**. "Hi, Mr. S."

Suddenly, a police car, sirens blaring, **careened** around the **crescent-shaped** driveway. Two officers got out, and they quickly surrounded Mr. Scintillating Social Studies, guns drawn.

"You're under arrest," one of them said in an **ominous** tone. "Firearms are not permitted on school grounds."

"You're violating the law," said the other **constable**.

"But, it's a **replica** of an antique gun, "spluttered Mr. S. "It's only a **facsimile**, and it has no bullets."

"Well, it looks like a rifle to my partner and me," said one of the officers angrily.

As the two officers prepared to drag Mr. S. to their car, a **horde** of students, Jesse in front, surrounded the trio.

95

"You can't arrest Mr. S, Officers; it's 'Living History Day!'" **implored** a bunch of students in **unison**. "Those are fun days, and we learn a lot!"

96

"No, no, you can't **incarcerate** Mr. S.," shouted Jesse over the **cacophony** of protesting students and police sirens. "He's one of the few good teachers whom we have, and we learn a lot from him," he added. "Please don't take our teacher," he **beseeched**.

At that moment, Mr. Punctilious Principal, roused from his office by the **din**, appeared on the scene. He surveyed the situation, made a quick **assessment** of the crisis, made a decision, and then he quietly spoke to one of the police officers.

The **dénouement** of the incident was that the officers examined the gun replica carefully, handed it to the principal, saluted Mr. Scintillating Social Studies (who saluted back), and **chortled** in amusement while getting into their car. The students, however, talked about the near-arrest for days.

"This calls for a haiku, and I know just the person to help me write one," said Jesse Jocose to himself as he **sauntered** to his homeroom, eager to **impart** the news to his friends.

It was William Waggish, though, who wrote the haiku to **commemorate** the excitement even though he only had heard about it second-hand from his friend Jesse. He entitled his poem "Mr. Punctilious Principal to the Rescue."

> A fake gun of **yore**
> **Effects** near-arrest, but lo,
> Principal saves day.

William and Jesse stood up among all their **peers** and recited the poem in **unison** at lunch at the top of their voices. There were seven teachers in the room at the time. Four of them and Dean Dread immediately rose on their toes, emitted **ebony** smoke and silver sparks from their ears and **proboscises**, raised their arms in the air, and wind-milled them. Then, two teachers **plummeted** to their knees, and they kneeled there for fewer than thirty seconds, blinking their eyes and muttering. Each one muttered something **inaudible** under his or her breath.

The students gasped in shock as Mr. Punctilious Principal **scurried** into the cafeteria, and then he sent everyone to his or her next class.

"I'm not finished with my lunch," **remonstrated** Isabelle Ingenuous.

"It's not fair," whined Pauline Puerile who had eaten only a bite of her sandwich.

"*Life* is not fair," **reiterated** Ms. Amicable Artist who had overheard Pauline's comment.

"What do you want to bet they call in Mr. Adept Fixit," **conjectured** Sam Sagacious.

As the crowd hastily exited the cafeteria, they, indeed, saw Mr. Adept Fixit **scurry** into the cafeteria, toolbox in hand and a worried look on his **weathered visage**.

"This is getting more and more peculiar," said Sam to his pals Jesse and William. "We must get to the bottom of this mystery. Some of our teachers are truly **atypical**," he concluded.

"What middle-school teacher is a normal adult?" asked Jesse Jocose. "Who ever would want to teach a bunch of **rampant**, living hormones for a career? They're all **eccentric**, if you ask me," Jesse finished.

"Some of them more than others," **persevered** Sam for whom solving this mystery was a serious **endeavor**.

As the end of the year approached, Mr. Scintillating Social Studies, Ms. Amicable Artist, Mr. Melodious Music, and Mr. Punctilious Principal (of all people) arranged a field trip to an amusement park as an end-of-the-year **diversion** for the eighth-graders. They proposed the treat as a reward for not having a single food fight the entire year and for exhibiting exemplary behavior in general after Orson had left HHMS. Danny and Dalbert had turned their **maliciousness** into trying to compose haiku with **superlative** vocabulary in order to affect their teachers.

Everyone was **elated** about the field trip. After all, all their trips had been cancelled in the seventh grade due to a **colossal** food fight started by none other than William Waggish who should have known better.

"Your field trip needs to be **correlated** to an **academic** subject," said Ms. Grammar Grouch to the principal. "Otherwise, it is forbidden by the school board."

"It is," piped up Ms. Witty Writing Wizard, the seventh-grade English teacher who had overheard the conversation. "Going to an amusement park provides **a plethora of** ideas for writing. We should have taken them earlier."

The day of the field trip dawned brightly. Five large, shiny, yellow school busses lined the side of the school. Eighth-graders **animatedly clambered** on them as they talked non-stop about the rides they planned to take. The **intrepid** friends all had signed up for the same bus. They wanted to plot and plan how to **flummox** their teachers into revealing their true nature, whatever it was. The group spent the entire ride writing and **compiling** haiku and planning to try to get, in the same area, all the teachers whom the poems affected.

"Let's call this 'Operation **Stealth**,'" volunteered Vivian. "Does everyone have his or her **fabricated** excuse ready?"

"Please include me," said a familiar voice. It was John **Jabbering**, a nice enough fellow whose problem was that he was too **loquacious**. His tall, lanky body with straw-like, limp hair was a familiar sight to the friends.

"Me, too, please," spoke a boy who sat nearby. "You're going to need a 'detail man' to coordinate your excuses, and that's my **forte**," insisted Mark **Meticulous**, his round glasses bobbing on his round face in **glee** at being included in the group.

The group accomplished its **objective** on the **tedious** bus ride to the amusement park. Once there, they forgot all about their **clandestine** plans as they swooped and swirled on the rides, **devoured** mounds of junk food, gossiped, laughed, and enjoyed a day of freedom with **peers**. As the allotted time at the park approached, the students, **laden** with purchases, slowly **meandered** towards the parking lot where the busses had parked.

There, in the spaces where five yellow school **conveyances** marked with their county's name were supposed to be waiting, was nothing! Mr. Punctilious Principal, who had driven separately in his van in case a student had become ill or wasn't **punctual** for the return trip, took out his cell phone and made a frantic call.

"They're where?" he shouted in a **wrathful** tone with a **soupçon (French word used in English meaning a suspicion or hint of panic)**. "Why didn't the rest remain? I see. One hour, you say? It's pushing their limits, you know. You'd better call Mr. Adept Fixit." With that **baffling** remark, he hung up.

Sam Sagacious was intrigued by hearing the Principal's end of the conversation.

"I wonder what he meant by that," Sam said, *sotto voce* to his friends among whom he stood.

"Let's wait and watch the teachers," suggested Isabelle. "Hey, Alessandra, tell us another story about your "abuela" and your waggish younger "primos" in Puerto Rico. Maybe that will take our minds off of standing here **sweltering** like hairy dogs in the **sultry** sun with no breeze to **mitigate** the heat."

"Yes, I just love hearing about Puerto Rico," sighed Olivia whose usual **otiose**, **indolent** nature did not apply to learning Spanish.

"I might be able to help," offered Felicia Fey.

"No, Felicia," said the rest of the group with **alacrity**.

Read-aloud passage

Felicia didn't listen to her friends. She muttered something under her breath, waved her hands (despite the fact that Isabelle and Vivian tried to hold them down) and "poof." A small, cool breeze

wafted by and rustled their **tresses**. A few birds flew by upside down. A white cloud turned slightly **chartreuse**.

"At least its effects weren't too **egregious**," said Vivian Virtuous, her ebony curls bobbing as she **gawked** upwards. "Birds flying upside down for a few moments never hurt anything, and no one saw the cloud but us."

"Way to go, Felicia," said Mark **Meticulous**. "The **zephyr** feels good."

"Don't encourage her, Mark," **asserted** Pauline Puerile. "She'll get into trouble when one of her spells doesn't go so well and affects a teacher."

Slightly less than an hour later, at 6 p.m., the busses pulled into the parking lot. As the students and teachers boarded them, Sam noticed that Ms. Stern Science, Mr. Math Martinet, and Ms. Grammar Grouch were moving more and more **lethargically**. Their faces were **inert** as if frozen. Unfortunately, each of the teachers boarded a different bus, so Jesse and William couldn't try a haiku on them. Ms. Grammar Grouch got on the bus with the intrepid friends, told the students in a slow, **monotone** voice to sit down, perched herself **gracelessly** in a front seat, and motioned slowly to Mr. Scintillating Social Studies (who also was on the same bus) to take over with the students. The busses took off for Horribly Hard Middle School.

Vivian Vivacious and Beth Bibliophilic took books out of their book bags that they had **secreted** under the seats and **commenced** to read. Vivian read <u>Their Eyes Were Watching God</u> by the **eminent** Florida author Zora Neale Hurston, and Beth read <u>David Copperfield</u> by the **illustrious** British author Charles Dickens. Most of the students dozed or quietly chatted.

"Let's do it," whispered Jesse Jocose to William and Sam.

"It's now or never," agreed William. "Wake up, girls. Put down those books. Get out the haiku we wrote and get ready to recite at my signal."

Ms. Grammar Grouch sat unsuspecting in her seat. Mr. Scintillating Social Studies continued to chat **affably** with a nearby student, unaware that a large group of students were about to **wreak havoc**.

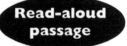

"Now," said William.

At his signal, a dozen students rose to their feet and shouted the following poem at the top of their voices:

Read-aloud passage

> Sparks, smoke **emanate**
> From their **orifices** as
> If they are on fire.

The bus driver ignored them.

Mr. Scintillating Social Studies commented, "**Incomparable** use of vocabulary, students," and laughed good-naturedly.

Ms. Grammar Grouch, on the other hand, reacted violently. Smoke and sparks did, as usual, **emanate** from all her **orifices**. She twitched, fluttered her eyes three times, threw her arms in the air, and then froze, **rigid** as a marble statue, eyes open, arms raised in the air. There she sat in that position, immobile.

"She's just having one of her spells," **placated** Mr. Scintillating Social Studies as he yanked out his cell phone and dialed frantically.

The bus pulled over next to the principal's van, and the two men carried the **inflexible** Ms. Grammar Grouch (whose arms still stuck straight up) from the bus to the van and laid her **transversely** across the back seat. They slammed the door shut, and Mr. Punctilious Principal **vaulted** into the driver's seat and sped off.

"That was interesting," said Sam Sagacious.

"That's a gross **understatement**," **rejoined** Isabelle Ingenuous.

"OK, guys," said Sam. "Now we go to the next step of 'Operation Stealth.' Can everyone sneak out Thursday night? Do you have your excuses ready for maximum **credibility**? Does everyone know what **comestibles** to bring so we don't starve or get caught carrying too much food in our lunch bags?"

"I will check everyone's excuse and coordinate who is supposed to be staying overnight with whom, so there should be no **glitches**," said Mark **Meticulous** with pride.

The friends spent the remainder of the long, **tedious** ride back to school **solidifying** their plans. Mark and Sam took **copious** notes.

The following Thursday afternoon when school let out, Isabelle, Felicia, Olivia, Pauline, Vivian, Alessandra, William, Jesse, Sam, Dalbert, and the newest members of the group, John **Jabbering** and Mark **Meticulous**, hid, one-by-one, in a small, stuffy, seldom-used book room in the eighth-grade wing of the school. Beth Bibliophilic, a **timorous** girl, **opted** out of the adventure. The group had decided to ask Dalbert Devious to join them because he knew how to pick

Read-aloud passage

locks. Dalbert was **ecstatic** to be included. Dalbert, being devious, had no problem giving his parents a **bogus pretext** for where he was spending the night.

Isabelle had convinced their beloved, seventh-grade English teacher, Ms. **Witty** Writing Wizard (for whom she now worked as an aide), that she needed to get into a book room but wasn't sure which one.

"She didn't know which book room either, so she gave me her master key that opens all the doors. I went to the book room, took out a book as my excuse, and left a thin book to block the door slightly **ajar**," she told her **cohorts** in stealth, "but it proved **redundant**. When I went back to her room, Ms. Witty Writing Wizard forgot about the key, so I still have it.

"I've never done anything like this before. I know it's for a good motive, but I'm nervous," she whispered to her assembled friends with **trepidation**. "It was the scariest thing I ever did," she added with a **quiver** that made the **omnipresent** plastic butterflies in her hair nod in agreement.

The group of twelve remained silent as they listened to someone open most of the classroom doors in the hallway. They **lingered mutely** until that person's footsteps echoed down the hall, and a door closed. Soon, there were no more sounds outside the book room, and even Mr. Adept Fixit had left the school.

They **warily** exited the book room, checking to make sure the coast was clear. One by one, they checked all the classrooms in the hallway. To their **utter incredulity**, they found, in most rooms, an **immobile** teacher, standing like a statue in the middle of the room. Ms. Stern Science didn't blink an eye when they touched her or said a haiku. Mr. Math Martinet remained rigid and unresponsive to every attempt to rouse him. Ms. Grammar Grouch stood like a silent **sentinel** in the middle of her room, totally **oblivious** to the twelve students who surrounded her, recited haiku, and waved their hands in her **static visage**.

"This is really strange," said Sam Sagacious as he wrote in his notebook. I **surmise** that these teachers are not human. I think that they are robots."

"Let's check for the controls," said William.

"Where do we begin?" asked Isabelle. "I don't want to undress a teacher, even if she is a robot, to find out."

"We'll look for a panel on the upper chest first. Have you noticed that all the teachers on whom the poems worked are always dressed in high-necked blouses or shirts and ties?" pointed out Sam.

The boys, since the chosen victim was a male teacher, loosened the teacher's **cravat** and unbuttoned his shirt halfway. Sure enough, there was a panel.

"Wow! These teachers truly are robots," **affirmed** Jesse and Alessandra in **unison**.

"Let's open the panel and see what's inside," suggested Sam.

Dalbert took out one of his **diverse**, little tools and pried open the panel on the teacher's chest. Everyone twisted his or her head to peer inside. Wires branched out from switches and vanished into the **crevices** of his body. Little green lights blinked slowly along the wires. There was no question. The teacher was a robot.

"'Tubular,'" said Jesse. "Our teachers are robots!"

"Not all of them, I think," argued Sam. "I think some of them are human. Neither Ms. Witty Writing Wizard, nor Mr. Scintillating Social Studies, nor Ms. Amicable Artist, nor Mr. Melodious Music ever were affected by the poems."

"Oh, my gosh," **interjected** Alessandra, "they are all the creative teachers—writing, new methods of studying history, art, music."

"You're right!" agreed William.

"They probably couldn't make robots creative and **innovative**," added Vivian.

"Wait a minute. What about Principal Punctilious?" **queried** William. "He didn't react to the poems either."

"It's a certainty that he's human as well," agreed Sam. They would need a human in charge to make all the decisions and to **assess** any situation that arose, like our field trip. Mr. Adept Fixit has to be human as well."

"Yes, I've never seen him react to any of our poems," said Jesse.

"I **deduce** that it's Mr. Adept Fixit who turns the robots on and off," offered Sam.

"Well, we'll find out in the morning, won't we?" said Isabelle. "Now, let's try to get a little sleep."

"I set the alarm clock to wake us up on time," said Mark Meticulous who was the detail guy.

Alessandra suggested, "Let's lie down on the carpet in the teachers' lounge with books for pillows and get some shut-eye. At least it's larger than that tiny book room, and the carpet, even though it is **sullied**, is better than the hard, **grubby** floor."

"Good idea, girlfriend," said Felicia Fey. "Does anyone want me to try to soften those books or clean the carpet a bit?"

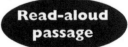

"No, Felicia," eleven voices shouted together.

The group of friends lay on the carpet, heads **bolstered** on books, and slept **fitfully** until 5 a.m. when Mark's alarm rang with a **cacophonous** sound.

The twelve students leapt up, went to do their morning **ablutions** in the boys' and girls' bathrooms respectively, scattered, each **secreting** himself or herself in a different classroom, and lay in wait to see what would happen.

An hour later footsteps **resonated** down the hall. Mr. Adept Fixit entered each classroom in turn. The students observed from their hiding spots as he opened the panel(s) on each robot teacher, flipped a switch, closed the panel, and **lingered** fewer than ten seconds for the teacher to come to life.

As he or she awoke, each robot said graciously, "Thank you, Mr. Fixit. Good morning. Have a nice day," in a **monotone** voice and proceeded to go to the blackboard to write the day's date and lesson.

As the school became alive with a **myriad** of students, the **intrepid** twelve **mingled** with the crowd and went to their homeroom as if they, too, had just arrived at school by foot, car, or bus. Like a bunch of **conspirators** in a spy novel, they had big, **covert** plans for the upcoming eighth-grade awards ceremony.

News of the truth about the robot teachers spread like mosquitoes in **stagnant** water among the students. Not one eighth grader "ratted" the **appalling** truth of the bizarre teachers to anyone not in his or her class. For once, everyone kept a secret.

The last few weeks of school dragged by like a slow-moving train. Everyone waited anxiously for the end-of-year awards ceremony. Every few days, someone would try out a haiku on the robot teachers. Superlative vocabulary in the poems **enhanced** the effects on the robots. The eighth-graders' **implausible**, **exemplary** behavior worried the principal. He knew they were up to something but had no clue what the kids were planning.

William Waggish had the honor of composing the ***coup de grace***. Every eighth-grader memorized the haiku, and they were more than ready.

Finally, the evening of the awards ceremony arrived. The administration and teachers sat on the stage, and parents and students filled the cafeteria to **capacity** with the **latter** spilling out into the hallway. All the eighth-graders were poised for the signal, and even Beth Bibliophilic laid down her **tome**, The Hunchback of Notre Dame, as she watched William with **rapt** attention.

William gave a **clandestine** sign to Isabelle, Felicia, Olivia, Pauline, Vivian, Alessandra, Jesse, Sam, Dalbert, John, and Mark. Then, just as Mr. Punctilious Principal had finished his welcoming speech, the twelve stood up. This was the signal. Every eighth-grader in the room recited the following haiku entitled "*Coup de Grace*" in his or her loudest voice.

Why does the school board
Use **egregious** robots when
Good teachers **abound**?

The robot teachers on stage spluttered. Sparks and smoke billowed from every **orifice**. They threw their arms into the air, opened their mouths, and stared out at the audience without blinking or **uttering** a sound.

The eighth-graders, led by the intrepid twelve, quickly followed this poem by a second haiku. They entitled it "We Want Human Teachers," and then they shouted it at the top of their voices in perfect unison.

"We **merit** real profs.
Creativity will die
Without humanness."

No fewer than twelve robot teachers sparked and smoked once more, emitted a huge dying sigh, and fell flat on their faces. The cafeteria was totally silent for a moment, and then all **perdition** broke loose. Parents protested loudly and **vociferously**.

"We want those abominable fake teachers replaced with real people as soon as you can do it," they insisted.

Students smiled and gave each other "high fives" and said, "We did it!"

As the human teachers clapped enthusiastically, too, they joined in the "high fives" with their students, and they patted each other on the back.

Ms. Amicable Artist murmured to Mr. Melodious Music, "Thank heavens, I couldn't take much more of those unfeeling **automatons**."

After a quick phone call, during which he was heard to say, "The jig is up," Mr. Punctilious Principal banged the podium for the **pandemonium** and **ruckus** to die down.

Finally, as the **din** turned to silence, and all eyes glared at the principal with dislike, the truth emerged. Beth even laid down her book, Little Women, and paid attention.

"First," he said, "I know that this is no excuse, but the human teachers and I fought the school board's

Final Exam

decision to save money by replacing real teachers with  robots. They used Horribly Hard Middle School as an experiment. Frankly, I am surprised that the robots lasted this long before our clever students' brains figured out the secret. I think the school board's little experiment is over. I, for one, am relieved and delighted. Thank you, students, for uncovering the truth. Students, keep ever **vigilant** because you never know what money-saving strategy they will try next."

When Mr. Punctilious Principal finished and sat down, a cheer arose from the assembled eighth-graders. The long nightmare of HHMS was over, and the mystery of the bizarre teachers was solved.

There were only two questions remaining. Why did the robot teachers react to the poems, and why did their reactions get even more intensified when the students incorporated great vocabulary in their poems?

"I've got it!" Sam exclaimed when they exited the cafeteria among the other students. "You see, the teachers who were creative and individualistic were human. They had to be. Robots cannot be pro-grammed to be individualistic or creative. They just react to the program in them.

"Ms. Amicable Artist, who taught art; Mr. Melodious Music, who taught music; Ms. Witty Writing Wizard, who taught creative writing; and Mr. Scintillating Social Studies, who came up with all kinds of weird ways to present history, all taught creative subjects or taught in a creative manner. All the robot teachers taught us in a rote manner by using the book exactly as written, by making us copy notes, or by giving us ditto sheets. They couldn't be creative at all," Sam concluded.

"Then why did the **superlative** vocabulary enhance their reactions to the poems?" asked Isabelle.

"Well," suggested Jesse, "I think that using super vocabulary is like being creative. It takes thought."

"I think you're right," said Sam. "The robots were obviously programmed only with the basic vocabulary of middle-school students. When we added those big, juicy vocabulary words to our poems, they only confused the robots more since those words 'did not compute.'"

"I think we've solved the entire mystery," concluded William Waggish with an air of relief and excitement. "I wonder what next year in high school will be like..." **Final Exam**

CHAPTER 6

125 Caught'yas for Sixth Grade

Introduction to the Sixth-Grade Story
125 Caught'ya Sentences for Grade Six

→ Almost Midterm Caught'ya Test and Key
→ Caught'ya Final Exam and Key
→ Twenty-Five Ideas for Writing Assignments

The first section is to be read out loud to your students to set the scene for the Caught'ya story that follows. You might want to read this section more than once in order to place the characters' names and the setting firmly in your students' minds. A copy of the entire uninterrupted Caught'ya story can be found in **Chapter 5**. You may wish to print out a copy or two of the sixth-grade part of the story to have in your classroom for any student who joins the class after the first week of school.

After the introduction, you will find 125 Caught'yas. Each Caught'ya consists of two to four sentences of the story, a vocabulary word or five, and a plethora of errors. There is a suggested writing assignment every five Caught'yas or so. A midterm and a final exam have been included in the middle and at the end of the Caught'yas. Finally, there are sections where you will be instructed to read a page or two to the class and give your students a break from the Caught'yas while continuing the story.

Please note that words in bold type are vocabulary words that may be repeated in the subsequent Caught'yas. It is a good idea to go over their meanings and to use them in your daily parlance and in vocabulary games so that your students will retain their meanings and become comfortable with them. All vocabulary words used in the Caught'yas that follow are listed (by Caught'ya number) in **Chapter 4** of this book. Please note that all poems in the sixth-grade story are written correctly below the corrected Caught'ya. You will need to copy them on the board. Please note that some of the Caught'yas are long. You may want to do them orally.

Introduction to the Sixth-Grade Story

As the August morning sun chased the shadows from the roofs of houses and painted the sky gold, there was an **eerie** silence at Horribly Hard Middle School. In the dawning light, you could not see into the classrooms because of the dark curtains at every window. No early teacher rushed out of a car in the parking lot to set up a lab or to get an early start on preparation for the first day of school. Horribly Hard Middle School was like a spooky mansion: closed, dark, and abandoned.

In contrast, across town, as the sun rose a bit higher in the sky, Marvelously Magic Magnet Middle School (known popularly as MMMMS) burst with energy and noise. Coffee perked in the teachers' lounge. Cars roared into the parking lot, parked, and spilled out teachers of different sizes, shapes, and complexions. Boxes, books, bags, and piles of "stuff" filled their arms as they walked into the school early to be ready for the first day of classes for the year.

Finally, two cars drove up to the **dormant** and silent Horribly Hard Middle School; one a new mauve Lexus sedan and the other an old blue Ford pick-up truck. A middle-aged man stepped out of each. The man who exited the Lexus wore a suit and tie and carried a battered briefcase. His face mirrored anxiety. The owner of the pick-up climbed out of his truck and lifted a large black tool case out of the bed of his truck. He **sported** a denim shirt and overalls, a red handkerchief in his upper pocket, a wrench hanging out of his lower pocket, and an air of excitement and purpose.

The two men nodded solemnly to each other as they **trekked** in different directions, the suited one toward the school office and the man in overalls toward the sixth-grade wing and the Custodian's office. No other human soul could be seen in the dim light of early morning.

Slowly, one after the other, classroom lights came on in HHMS. Soon the school was **ablaze** with light, and all classrooms were lit, but apart from Mr. **Adept** Fixit, the custodian, rushing from room to room to open the doors and turn on the lights, no sounds of people could be heard on the campus. If you listened carefully in the main office near the door to the principal's room, you could hear the faint click of computer keys as Mr. **Punctilious** Principal, a man who was always concerned with correct procedure, checked and rechecked the procedures which would be followed that first day as well as the list of students who would enter the **portals** of the HHMS in about an hour.

Half an hour later several more cars pulled up in front of the still silent Horribly Hard Middle School. A lady, dressed in a long pink skirt and a **blousy** white shirt spattered with paint, hurried towards one of the still-dark classrooms with rolls of paper under her arm and a **myriad** of paint brushes in her mouth and hands. A man **ambled** toward a nearby dark classroom. He was burdened with various-sized instrument cases. His purple tie, decorated with yellow musical notes, was **askew**, and his glasses perched unevenly on his large nose.

Meanwhile, in a house not far from Horribly Hard Middle School, a **gaggle** of sixth-graders had gathered to gossip about the upcoming first day of school. They stood in the **foyer** of Isabelle's house, waiting for Olivia **Otiose** whose lazy nature always made her late to everything. Isabelle **Ingenuous**, always animated, twirled in nervousness and an excess of energy. Pauline **Puerile** whined in a babyish manner about Olivia's tardiness. Felicia **Fey**, always acting in a bizarre manner, muttered words of a spell, parts of which she could not remember, under her breath to encourage her friend Olivia **Otiose** to hurry. Olivia **Otiose** did not appear, but Felicia's fingernails turned a putrid green. William **Waggish** made a tasteless but funny joke that **evoked titters** from the gathered friends. The last member of the troop, Sam **Sagacious**, simply stood wisely and silently with his backpack in his hand, waiting for the **clamor** to die down.

Isabelle **Ingenuous** danced out the open door, swiftly followed by her friends, with Pauline **Puerile** taking up the rear as she picked up her teddy bear that had fallen from her backpack and tucked it into the front pouch. Another girl joined them as they walked down the steps of Isabelle's house onto the sidewalk. Olivia **Otiose** had arrived, hair half combed and wrinkled blouse hanging out of her jeans. The group was ready but **reluctant** to face their first day at their new middle school: Horribly Hard Middle School.

A **myriad** of thoughts echoed and **rebounded** in each student's mind as the six sixth-graders **trudged** to their new school, a mile away, as if walking the plank of a pirate ship to their doom.

What would the new school be like? Would the new teachers be mean and hard? Were they going to have too much homework? Were the big eighth graders going to **harass** them? Would they be able to remember the combinations of those shiny new locks in their backpacks? Were they dressed appropriately? Were the teachers nice? Would middle school be much different from elementary school? How would they find all their classes? Would their friends be in their classes? Would they get lost? Was the dean mean?

These questions and many more circled around in the six friends' heads as they silently **ambled** towards the place where they would find all the answers. All too soon, the brick walls of Horribly Hard Middle School **loomed** in front of them.

Brown-faced with dark, expressive eyes, William **Waggish** recited a silly limerick to break the tension. (He always was composing poetry to try to **emulate** his hero, Langston Hughes.) The friends' steps matched the **cadence** of the hopeful poem.

> There is a bizarre middle school
> Where teachers are easy to fool.
> They fall for our jokes
> And don't call our folks
> Even when we break every rule.

B – Sentences for the Board	C – Corrected version of the CY
1. tedious nestled verdant Paragraph – new topic Types of Sentences – simple; compound Commas – city, state (appositive); 2 adj. where 2nd is not age, color, or linked; participle; no comma after "brick" as it is linked to noun; compound sen. Homophones – their/there/they're Other Skills – hyphen in 2 words serving as 1 adj.; go over irregular verbs "sit" (intransitive = no object) and "set" (transitive = takes object) Literary Devices – simile; vivid-verb description	**B -** horribly hard middle school did not look much different from their elementary school which was nearby in their town of **tedious** florida **(NOTE: Use your state)**. a big one-story brick building set **nestled** among large trees and a **verdant** lawn and a small city of white portables dotted the field behind the school like white lily pads in a green pond **C -** Horribly Hard Middle School did not look much different from their elementary school which was nearby in their town of **Tedious**, Florida **(NOTE: Use your state)**. A big, one-story brick building sat **nestled** among large trees and a **verdant** lawn, and a small city of white portables dotted the field behind the school like white lily pads in a green pond.
2. shrilled ingenuous auburn Paragraph – new speaker Types of Sentences – complex; simple Punctuation – quotes around what is said out loud; ! for emphasis Commas – 2 adj. where 2nd is not age, color, or linked to noun; list; modifier before noun Homophones – knew/new Other Skills – compound word (outfit); hyphen in 2 words acting as one Literary Devices – alliteration; description within action	**B -** look **shrilled** isabelle **ingenuous** in her high voice as she nervously twirled the purple plastic butterfly that was perched in her wild curly **auburn** hair. always upbeat isabelle was dressed in her knew outfit of purple shorts and bright green top **C -** "Look!" **shrilled** Isabelle **Ingenuous** in her high voice as she nervously twirled the purple, plastic butterfly that was perched in her wild, curly **auburn** hair. Always upbeat, Isabelle was dressed in her new outfit of purple shorts and bright-green top.

3. insipid   waggish

No Paragraph then Paragraph – same speaker; change speaker

Types of Sentences – compound; simple

Punctuation – 2 quotes; commas and periods **always** go inside quotes

Commas – compound sen.; adjective list; quote; unnecessary "who" clause (non-restrictive modifier);
2 adj. when 2nd is not age, color, or linked

Other Skills – use of "who" when referring to a person and as subject

Literary Devices – alliteration; putting description into action

B - all the lights are on and there is a teacher gazing out the window of each classroom isabelle ingenuous continued. i wish we were going to marvelously magic magnet middle school instead of this old ordinary **insipid** one groaned william **waggish** whom was not his usual teasing cheerful self

C - "All the lights are on, and there is a teacher gazing out the window of each classroom," Isabelle Ingenuous continued.

"I wish we were going to Marvelously Magic Magnet Middle School instead of this old, ordinary, **insipid** one," groaned William **Waggish**, who was not his usual teasing, cheerful self.

4. sagacious   otiose

2 Paragraphs – 2 speakers

Types of Sentences – simple; simple

Punctuation – quotes around what is said out loud; **!** for emphasis; **,** and **.** **always** go inside quotes

Commas – introductory word; "who" clause that is not necessary; quote; introductory word; quote; comma before "who" (unnecessary clause)

Homophones – their/there/they're

Other Skills – use "who" as subject to refer to people; never begin a sentence with a FANBOYS (coordinating conjunction); **'** in a contraction

Literary Devices – alliteration

B - yeah sighed sam **sagacious** who was usually reserved behind his horn-rimmed glasses i hear the teachers their are great. and yes i hear they dont give much homework either added olivia **otiose** who hated homework with a passion

C -   "Yeah," sighed Sam **Sagacious**, who was usually reserved behind his horn-rimmed glasses, "I hear the teachers there are great!"

　　　"Yes, I hear they don't give much homework either," added Olivia **Otiose**, who hated homework with a passion.

NOTE: My students never knew which form of "their/there/they're" I would use and got angry when I spelled it correctly. Mix them up so that your students have to think. I told students that "their" must be followed by something that is owned; they could substitute "here" for "there;" and forbade the use of "they're" or, for that matter, "it's" in the classroom for the year.

5. retorted   fey   meager   awry

NOTE: Do not use the first definition of "fey" which is "to be fated to die soon." I used "fey" to mean "enchanted one" or "enchanter," meaning that Felicia has some magic powers.

Paragraph – new speaker

Types of Sentences – compound; compound/complex

Punctuation – quotes around what is said out loud; commas and periods always go inside quotation marks

Commas – introductory word; compound sentence; quote; unnecessary clause before "whose"; subordinate clause at beginning; compound part of compound/complex sentence; 2 adj.

Homophones – their/there/they're

Other Skills – contraction; between (2) vs. among (2+); point out use of subjunctive ("If I were..."); abbreviation (Ms.)

Literary Device – alliteration

B - well we don't have enough magic in us so we cant go to MMMMS **retorted** felicia **fey** whose **meager** magic always went **awry**. if i were better at magic i would be going there with all the neat teachers and cool classes but i failed the entry test when i accidentally gave ms vice principal a big juicy zit right between her eyes

C - "Well, we don't have enough magic in us, so we can't go to MMMMS," **retorted** Felicia **Fey**, whose **meager** magic always went **awry**. "If I were better at magic, I would be going there with all the neat teachers and cool classes, but I failed the entry test when I accidentally gave Ms. Vice Principal a big, juicy zit right between her eyes."

Writing Idea #1: Narrative.
Write a narrative story about a time you went to a strange place. It could be a school, a home, or someplace on a trip. What happened? Did you encounter any bizarre people? You may write a fictional or a personal narrative.

B – Sentences for the Board	**C** – Corrected version of the CY
6. mane portal Paragraph – new speaker Types of Sentences – complex; simple Punctuation – quotes around what is said out loud; **,** and **.** always go inside " Commas – quote; quote Homophones – hair/hare Other Skills – use of italics for emphasis; spelling of "friend"; run-on sentence; contraction	**B -** at least you *have* some magic even if it always screws up isabelle ingenuous reminded her freind as she twirled the purple butterfly that perched in her **mane** of auburn hare and the rest of us cant even open a classroom **portal** she concluded **C -** "At least you *have* some magic, even if it always screws up," Isabelle Ingenuous reminded her friend as she twirled the purple butterfly that perched in her **mane** of auburn hair. "The rest of us can't even open a classroom **portal**," she concluded.
7. sextet monotone Paragraph – new time and subject Types of Sentences – simple; simple Punctuation – quotes around what is said out loud; **,** and **.** always go inside " Commas – introductory adverb; 2 prepositional phrases at beginning; list; no comma after "group" as not a compound sentence (no subject); adj. list; quote	**B -** suddenly right in front of this **sextet** stood a tall man who was dressed all in black with a shiny, new, black hat perched on his slick black hair. he peered down at the group and boomed in a loud **monotone** voice welcome to horribly hard middle school **C -** Suddenly, right in front of this **sextet**, stood a tall man who was dressed all in black with a shiny, new, black hat perched on his slick black hair. He peered down at the group and boomed in a loud, **monotone** voice, "Welcome to Horribly Hard Middle School."

B – Sentences for the Board	C – Corrected version of the CY
8. dread puerile commenced snivel 2 Paragraphs – each is about a different person Types of Sentences – compound; compound Punctuation – ( ) around narrator aside; use of quotes around made-up phrase Commas – compound sen.; compound sen. Homophones – hair/hare Other Skills – avoidance of quotes by use of "that"; no capital letter in "the dean" as is a general title; parallel construction (that...that); singular possessive; spelling of friend ("ie" rule) Literary Devices – alliteration	**B -** the frightening man then announced that he was the dean of the school and his name was dean **dread**. pauline **puerile commenced** to **snivel** (she was such a baby and felicia fey muttered a "cheer-up spell" but only succeeded in frizzing her friends hare **C -** The frightening man then announced that he was the dean of the school and that his name was Dean **Dread**. Pauline **Puerile commenced** to **snivel** (she was such a baby), and Felicia Fey muttered a "cheer-up spell" but only succeeded in frizzing her friend's hair.
9. somber Paragraph – new subject Types of Sentences – simple; simple Punctuation – quotes around made-up word Commas – extra info about a noun (appositive); appositive; intro. adverb of place Homophones – to/too/two; new/knew Other Skills – "friends" plural not possessive; spell of "friends" ("ie" rule); use of whom as object of "knew"; hyphen between 2 wds. acting as one Literary Devices – alliteration	**B -** dean dread a disturbing figure in his **somber** suit and tie directed the group to go too the cafetorium a combination of cafeteria and auditorium. there the freinds found other sixth graders who they already new from elementary school **C -** Dean Dread, a disturbing figure in his **somber** suit and tie, directed the group to go to the "cafetorium," a combination of cafeteria and auditorium. There, the friends found other sixth-graders whom they already knew from elementary school.

10. *sotto voce*

Paragraph – new speaker

Types of Sentences – simple; simple

Punctuation – quotes around what is said out loud; **!** for emphasis

Commas – quote

Other Skills – keep in past tense; use of italics for Latin word; contraction; negative...nor; use of subject vs. object pronoun + correct pronoun order

Literary Devices – alliteration

B - what a bizarre dean whispers sam sagacious *sotto voce* to william waggish. me and you wouldnt want to cross him or meet him in a dark alley

C - "What a bizarre dean!" whispered Sam Sagacious *sotto voce* to William Waggish. "You and I wouldn't want to cross him nor meet him in a dark alley."

NOTE: After this point the literary device of alliteration as used in the names of the characters will no longer be listed in the skills.

Writing Idea #2: Descriptive Essay.

Write an essay to describe a person who scared you at some time in your life. Make sure that you include this person's psychological as well as physical traits, and explain why you found him/her scary. Try to use strong, vivid verbs.

---

11. mausoleum surreptitiously surveyed

2 Paragraphs – new speakers

Types of Sentences – complex; complex

Punctuation – quotes around what is said out loud; **?** for question; **,** and **.** always go inside **"**

Commas – direct address; interjection; direct address; quote

Homophones – hear/here

Other Skills – "no one" is 2 words; spell of "weird" ("i" before "e" except after "c," and neighbor and weigh are weird)

B - from what **mausoleum** did he crawl out sam murmured william waggish **surreptitiously** so no one else could here. hey william look at the other weird teachers standing against the wall whispered always observant sam sagacious as he **surveyed** the room

C -   "From what **mausoleum** did he crawl out, Sam?" murmured William Waggish **surreptitiously** so no one else could hear.
   "Hey, William, look at the other weird teachers standing against the wall," whispered always observant Sam Sagacious as he **surveyed** the room.

B – Sentences for the Board	C – Corrected version of the CY
12. uttered loquacious 2 Paragraphs – subject change; new speaker Types of Sentences – complex; simple Punctuation – " around what is said out loud; , and . always go inside " Commas – subordinate clause (adverb) at beginning of sentence (A WHITE BUS word/subject/verb); interrupter ("eh"); direct address; quote Homophones – to/too/two Other Skills – use of fragment for emphasis; write out numbers to 120 Literary Devices – metaphor	**B -** as sam **uttered** this last statement dean dread suddenly appeared and loomed menacingly over the too boys. **loquacious** ones eh you 2 come here the dean ordered. his voice had the flatness of a cockroach . crunching under a shoe **C -** As Sam **uttered** this last statement, Dean Dread suddenly appeared and loomed menacingly over the two boys. "**Loquacious** ones, eh? You two, come here," the dean ordered. His voice had the flatness of a cockroach crunching under a shoe.
13. ushered tittered Paragraph – new action and speaker (narrator) Types of Sentences – simple; simple Punctuation – quotes around made-up word: , and . always go inside " (100% rule) Commas – 2 adj. and 2nd is not age, color, or linked; interrupter Other Skills – comparison (ham-sized); hyphen in 2 words acting as 1	**B -** dean dread put one huge ham sized hand on the back of each boy and **ushered** them to the front of the "cafetorium." all the other new sixth graders of course **tittered** at the sight of william and sam being caught talking **C -** Dean Dread put one huge, ham-sized hand on the back of each boy and **ushered** them to the front of the "cafetorium." All the other new sixth-graders, of course, **tittered** at the sight of William and Sam being caught talking.

B – Sentences for the Board	C – Corrected version of the CY
14. mortified jocose quell proximity 2 Paragraphs – new speakers (2nd is narrator) Types of Sentences – complex; compound/complex Punctuation – " around what is said out loud; **,** and **.** always go inside " Commas – direct address; keep in past tense; quote; no comma as subordinate clause at end; extra info about noun (unnecessary appositive); sub. clause at beginning; compound sen. Homophones – quiet/quite; aisle/isle	**B -** quiet students says dean dread in a deadly tone of voice as he placed william waggish and the **mortified** sam sagacious in the second row next to jesse **jocose** another talker. when dean dread said this he nodded his head and teachers lined up in the aisles to **quell** the noise with **proximity** control **C -** "Quiet, students," said Dean Dread in a deadly tone of voice as he placed William Waggish and the **mortified** Sam Sagacious in the second row next to Jesse **Jocose**, another talker. When Dean Dread said this, he nodded his head, and teachers lined up in the aisles to **quell** the noise with **proximity** control.
15. distraught garbed No Paragraph – same topic Types of Sentences – complex; compound Commas – 2 adj.; compound sentence; no comma before "as" (sub. clause at end); always a **,** around "too" when it means "also" Homophones – their/there/they're; new/knew Other Skills – use of passive voice ("were garbed" instead of "wore") to be avoided if possible; hyphen between 2 wds. acting as 1	**B -** the new sixth graders squirmed in fear and became **distraught** as they got a closer look at there knew teachers. only a few of them had genuine welcoming smiles on their faces and most were **garbed** in grey or black too. **C -** The new sixth-graders squirmed in fear and became **distraught** as they got a closer look at their new teachers. Only a few of them had genuine, welcoming smiles on their faces, and most were **garbed** in grey or black, too.

Writing Idea #3: Paragraph Writing.
Write a strong-verb paragraph to explain why you think the teachers scared the new sixth-graders.

---

16. formidable   somber

Paragraph – slightly different topic

Types of Sentences – complex; compound

Commas – intro adverb; compound sentence

Homophones – to/too/two; new/knew

Other Skills – among (more than 2) vs. between (2); contractions; "had had" pluperfect tense; use "like" only if nouns are compared

B - among the teachers only a few didnt look too mean or to **formidable** they just didnt look like the friendly teachers the kids had had in elementary school and most of them dressed in **somber** clothes that looked like they were stiff and uncomfortable

C -   Among the teachers, only a few didn't look too mean or **formidable**. They just didn't look like the friendly teachers the kids had had in elementary school, and most of them dressed in **somber** clothes that looked as if they were stiff and uncomfortable.

---

17. perceptive   blousy   tresses

Paragraph – new topic

Types of Sentences – simple; compound

Commas – unnecessary "who" clause; no **,** after "blousy," "long," or "thick" as 2ⁿᵈ adj. is color; compound sentence

Other Skills – use of "who" to refer to people and as subject; "than" for comparison; singular possessive; hyphen between 2 wds. acting as 1

B - olivia otiose who was more **perceptive** then most sixth graders but lazy when it came to work saw that one teachers smile was genuine. this teacher wore a **blousy** white shirt and a long pink skirt and she had stuck a pink flower in her thick blonde **tresses**

C -   Olivia Otiose, who was more **perceptive** than most sixth-graders but lazy when it came to work, saw that one teacher's smile was genuine. This teacher wore a **blousy** white shirt and a long pink skirt, and she had stuck a pink flower in her thick blonde **tresses**.

B – Sentences for the Board	C – Corrected version of the CY
18. quailed 2 Paragraphs – new speakers (2nd is narrator) Types of Sentences – simple; simple (compound subject) Punctuation – " around what is said out loud; , and . always go inside " Commas – direct address; quote; note no , after "friend" as Isabelle could have many friends, so appositive is necessary Homophones – their/there/they're; to/too/two Other Skills – spelling ("ie" rule); write out numbers to 120; never use "that" to refer to people; who (subject) vs. whom (object)	**B -** felicia that must be the art teacher isabelle ingenuous dared to whisper to her freind felicia fey. dean dread and 2 teachers glared at the two girls that **quailed** under there gaze **C -** "Felicia, that must be the art teacher," Isabelle Ingenuous dared to whisper to her friend Felicia Fey. Dean Dread and two teachers glared at the two girls who **quailed** under their gaze.
19. sentries glowering Paragraph – new action Types of Sentences – simple; compound Commas – participial phrase; compound sentence Homophones – aisle/isle; principal/principle; their/there/they're Literary Devices – simile	**B -** all the teachers still stood in the aisles like **sentries** most of them **glowering** at the kids as if daring them to speak. the principal stood up on the stage and dean dread joined him their **C -** All the teachers still stood in the aisles like **sentries**, most of them **glowering** at the kids as if daring them to speak. The principal stood up on the stage, and Dean Dread joined him there.

20. punctilious   mete

Paragraph – new speaker

Types of Sentences – simple; compound/complex

Punctuation – " around what is said out loud; . and , always go inside "

Commas – direct address; extra info about noun (appositive); quote; compound sen.; quote; 2 adj.: never a , before A WHITE BUS word (sub. conjunction)

Homophones – principal/principle; your/you're; right/rite

Other Skills – note difference between common and proper nouns; 2 singular possessives; abbreviation; use of "who" as subject

Literary Devices – metaphor

B - children i am the schools principal the captain of your ship said the principle. my name is mr **punctilious** principal and this is dean dread who will **mete** out any discipline for misbehaving students he continued as he put a hand on the deans broad right shoulder

C -   "Children, I am the school's principal, the captain of your ship," said the principal. My name is Mr. **Punctilious** Principal, and this is Dean Dread who will **mete** out any discipline for misbehaving students," he continued as he put a hand on the dean's broad, right shoulder.

NOTES: After this point, "quotes around what is said out loud" will no longer be pointed out in the skill list, nor will "commas and periods always go inside quotation marks." I suggest that you point these punctuation skills out to your students each time they appear.

If you have required that your students write the complete date above each Caught'ya, all the comma rules, except in the greeting and closing of a letter which you can cover in Writing Idea #4, have been covered in the first 20 Caught'yas. If you wish to do a review at this point, the comma rules are listed in the *Grammar, Usage, and Mechanics Guide*.

Writing Idea #4: Expository Essay in a Letter.

Every middle school has discipline problems. Think about discipline problems you already have experienced at your school. Pick one problem that bugs you. Think of some solutions to this problem. Now, write a letter to your principal to propose your solutions. Be sure to state the problem in your first paragraph of your letter. Use the correct headings, greeting, and closing for a business letter.

→   Teachers, when you teach the headings of a letter in order for your students to be able to complete Writing Assignment #4, you might want to make certain that your students understand how to write the postal code for your state and the states where they have relatives. (Florida, for example, is FL.) You can find a list in the *Grammar, Usage, and Mechanics Guide.*

---

21. subvocalize   utterance

Paragraph – new action

Types of Sentences – simple; simple; compound

Punctuation – put " around short works like poems, articles, and songs, and ___ or *italicize* titles of long works like books, newspapers, and albums; hyphen in 2 wds. acting as one

Commas – compound sen; extra info about noun (appositive); extra info; compound sen; unnecessary "who" clause (a non-restrictive modifier)

Homophones – breath/breathe; heard/herd; its/it's (I forbid use of the latter and make students write out "it is")

Other Skills – teach verb "choose/chose"; keep in past tense; go over irregular verbs "sit" (no object) and "set" (takes object)

B - william waggish always playfully humorous choose that moment to **subvocalize** a limerick under his breath his favorite way to deal with tension. he entitled it the mean dean. several people heard its **utterance** and jesse jocose who set nearby snorted in laughter

C -   William Waggish, always playfully humorous, chose that moment to **subvocalize** a limerick under his breath, his favorite way to deal with tension. He entitled it "The Mean Dean." Several people heard its **utterance**, and Jesse Jocose, who sat nearby, snorted in laughter.

> There was an old dean from Salt Lick
> (Kentucky)
> Who made all the kids very sick.
> One look at his face
> And students would race,
> Well-aided by steps that were quick.

NOTE: Now that students have encountered compound sentences a few times, it might be a good idea to have them memorize the FANBOYS (coordinating conjunctions—for, and, nor, but, or, yet, so). Students enjoy chanting them over and over with different body movements that I call out. For example, recite while clapping hands over the head, then in front, then between legs, then do an "Egyptian" or a "shower," etc. Students recite the FANBOYS every time one appears in a Caught'ya.

Students love this and memorize the conjunctions quickly. Once conjunctions are memorized, students easily can learn never to put a comma before FANBOYS unless in a list or a compound sentence. Students also can be told never to capitalize one in a title or begin a sentence with one until they get their driver's license. This will give them time to mature their writing so that every other sentence doesn't begin with "and" or "so."

I actually have given a special "FANBOYS Driver's License" to an outstanding writer, giving that student permission to judiciously use conjunctions for effect at the beginning of a sentence.

---

22. uttered   wisps

No Paragraph – same topic

Types of Sentences – complex; compound

Commas – subordinate clause at beginning

Other Skills – use of semicolons in a series of independent clauses (complete sentences); between (2) vs. among (3 or more)

Literary Devices – use of vivid verbs

B - as william waggish **uttered** the last word of his limerick the teacher nearest him twitched and nodded his head. his eyelids fluttered his tongue protruded between his closed lips and **wisps** of smoke curled from his ears

C - As William Waggish **uttered** the last word of his limerick, the teacher nearest him twitched and nodded his head. His eyelids fluttered; his tongue protruded between his closed lips; and **wisps** of smoke curled from his ears.

NOTE: With Caught'ya #22, you might want to teach the four reasons for using semicolons (series of independent clauses (as in this Caught'ya), instead of a coordinating conjunction in a compound sentence, when there are too many commas in a compound sentence, and, in a list, to avoid confusion because there are too many commas). This may avoid future abuse of the semicolon. See the *Grammar, Usage, and Mechanics Guide*.

23. muffle glowered swiveled Paragraph – new action Types of Sentences – simple (compound verb); compound Commas – no **,** before "and" (not a compound sen.—no subject); compound sen. Homophones – their/there/they're	**B -** jesse jocose pointed to that teacher with his one hand and held the other over his mouth to **muffle** his giggles. the other teachers turned and **glowered** at him as students **swiveled** theyre heads in the direction jesse pointed **C -** Jesse Jocose pointed to that teacher with his one hand and held the other over his mouth to **muffle** his giggles. The other teachers turned and **glowered** at him as students **swiveled** their heads in the direction Jesse pointed.
24. phenomenon colleague Paragraph – new topic Types of Sentences – simple; simple Commas – adj. list; interrupter; pause before simile; 2 adj. Other Skills – use of hyphen in 3 wds. used as one adj. (1st is modeled); run-on sen.; spelling confusion (breath and breathe) Literary Devices – description within action; simile	**B -** only the teacher with the pink flower in her hair and the paint on her shirt smiled at the strange **phenomenon** of her eye-fluttering ear smoking tongue sticking out **colleague** and she somehow was different like a cool glacier breeze in a hot classroom **C -** Only the teacher with the pink flower in her hair and the paint on her shirt smiled at the strange **phenomenon** of her eye-fluttering, ear-smoking, tongue-sticking-out **colleague**. She, somehow, was different, like a cool glacier breeze in a hot classroom.

B – Sentences for the Board	C – Corrected version of the CY
25. incident paid heed 2 Paragraphs – time change; new speaker Types of Sentences – complex; simple Commas – intro phrase; verb list; no **,** before A WHITE BUS word (sub. conjunction); quote; no **,** after "friends" (necessary appositive); **,** around "too" if means "also" Homophones – quiet/quite; to/too/two Other Skills – collective noun (everyone) is singular = sing. pronoun (antecedent/pronoun agreement); abbreviation; subject pronouns ("me" is object pronoun); "ie" spell rule; elicit a list of collective nouns	**B -** after that **incident** everyone quieted down turned his or her face towards the stage and **paid heed** to mr punctilious principal as he instructed students on where to go and what to do next. i hope me and my friends are in the same homeroom whispered isabelle ingenuous too her too freinds olivia otiose and pauline puerile **C -** After that **incident**, everyone quieted down, turned his or her face towards the stage, and **paid heed** to Mr. Punctilious Principal as he instructed students on where to go and what to do next. "I hope my friends and I are in the same homeroom, too," whispered Isabelle Ingenuous to her two friends Olivia Otiose and Pauline Puerile.
26. striplings Paragraph – time change Types of Sentences – simple; simple Commas – intro adverb; verb list Other Skills – run-on sen.; hyphen (2 wds. used as 1 adj.); "then" as adverb; do not end a sen. with a preposition	**B -** finally the assembly was over and teachers filed out directed the **striplings** to the homeroom lists on the walls of the sixth grade hall and then pointed the various classrooms out **C -** Finally, the assembly was over. Teachers filed out, directed the **striplings** to the homeroom lists on the walls of the sixth-grade hall, and then pointed out the various classrooms.

Writing Idea #5: Argumentative Essay in a Letter.
Write an argumentative essay in the form of a letter to your teacher to explain your views on assemblies. Do you think you should have assemblies at your school? What do you think? Explain why. Be sure to use the correct headings, greeting, and closing for a business letter.

---

27. intrepid   stern   martinet

No Paragraph – same topic

Types of Sentences – simple; simple

Commas – no **,** after "group" (necessary "who/adjective" clause); unnecessary appositive (already identified); unnecessary "who" clause

Homophones – their/there/they're

Other Skills – do not begin a sen. with FANBOYS; antecedent/pronoun agreement (group is a collective noun and thus sing.); abbreviation; review other collective nouns like "class"; do not split verbs; hyphen in 2 wds. acting as one.

B - the **intrepid** group who had begun their first day of school together found themselves in the same homeroom. there teacher was a very **stern** looking man mr math **martinet** who promptly announced that he was also their math teacher

C - The **intrepid** group who had begun the first day of school together found themselves in the same homeroom. Their teacher was a very **stern**-looking man, Mr. Math **Martinet**, who promptly announced that he also was their math teacher.

**28. shenanigans   confiscated
querulous   articulated
puerile**

Paragraph – no paragraph (same topic) then ¶ for new speaker

Types of Sentences – compound/ complex; simple

Commas – always put **,** around "too" if meaning is "also"; compound sentence; appositive; verb list; no comma before A WHITE BUS word (subordinating conjunction); intro word; direct address; quote

Other Skills – discuss use of "who" (subject) and "whom" (object); contraction; do not split verbs; do not end a sen. with a preposition; vocab lesson

B - he told the students too that he would tolerate no **shenanigans** and then he **confiscated** a headset from quincy **querulous** a student in the back of the room who made faces as his headset was taken opened his mouth as if to argue and then thought better of it. hey pauline thats the teacher who stuck his tongue out **articulated** felicia fey to her **puerile** friend who was silently crying

C - He told the students, too, that he would tolerate no **shenanigans**, and then he **confiscated** a headset from Quincy **Querulous**, a student in the back of the room who made faces as his headset was taken, opened his mouth as if to argue, and then thought better of it.

"Hey, Pauline, that's the teacher who stuck out his tongue," **articulated** Felicia Fey to her **puerile** friend who was crying silently.

NOTE: I know this is early in the year, but it is important that your students learn the eight parts of speech. It is a good idea to put an acronym for the eight parts of speech somewhere on a wall in your classroom. I used NIPPAVAC or PAVPANIC.

The second week of school, I challenged my students to figure out the acronym. It usually took a week or so until some bright student figured it out (or heard it from a sibling who had been in my class in a previous year).

Once the acronym is identified, you and your students can chant the parts of speech until you and they memorize them: Noun, Interjection, Preposition, Pronoun, Adverb, Verb, Adjective, Conjunction (NIPPAVAC). Once your students memorize the parts of speech, you can begin asking them to point them out in subsequent Caught'yas. I suggest that you do this, one part of speech at a time, all year long.

**29. inimitable   malevolent
     wrathful   wrath   stifled**

Paragraph – new topic

Types of Sentences – simple;
compound

Punctuation – put " around short
works and ____ or *italicize* long
works; . and , always go inside "

Commas – participial phrase;
appositive; compound sen.; "too"
means "also"; 2 adj.

Homophones – one/won

Other Skills – run-on sen.;
abbreviation; sing. poss.; always put ,
around "too" if means "also"; vocab
lesson

B - william waggish worried about
pauline whispered another of his
inimitable limericks this one about a
malevolent math teacher entitled
wrathful math and faint curls of
smoke wisped from mr math
martinets ears and his eyelids
fluttered too

C -   William Waggish, worried
about Pauline, whispered another of
his **inimitable** limericks, this one
about a **malevolent** math teacher
entitled "**Wrathful** Math." Faint
curls of smoke wisped from Mr. Math
Martinet's ears, and his eyelids
fluttered, too.

> The nasty, male teacher of math
> Was utterly filled with such **wrath**.
> He yelled at the boys
> And **stifled** their joys.
> He took a malevolent path.

Writing Idea #6: Poetry.
Write a limerick. Keep it funny but clean. Remember to follow the
syllable pattern and rhyme scheme. The last line must conclude the
poem.

	Syllable pattern	Rhyme scheme
Line 1	8	A
Line 2	8	A
Line 3	5	B
Line 4	5	B
Line 5	8	A

B – Sentences for the Board	C – Corrected version of the CY
30. peer demise uncompromising Paragraph – new action Types of Sentences – complex; simple Commas – intro phrase; 2 adj. Homophones – their/there/they're Other Skills – plural poss.; sing. poss.; antecedent/pronoun agreement ("class" is a collective, sing. noun); review collective nouns; keep in past tense Literary device – homily (hear a pin drop)	**B -** at this you could have heard a pin drop as the students mouths gaped open at their **peers** boldness and there teachers antics. the class waits for williams painful **demise** at the hands of their stern **uncompromising** teacher **C -** At this, you could have heard a pin drop as the students' mouths gaped open at their **peer**'s boldness and their teacher's antics. The class waited for William's painful **demise** at the hands of the stern, **uncompromising** teacher.
31. resumed emitting Paragraph – new idea Types of Sentences – simple; fragment; complex Punctuation – use of ! for emphasis Commas – sub. clause at beginning; no , before A WHITE BUS word Other Skills – deliberate use of fragment; fewer (can count) vs. less (can't count); abbreviation; correlative conjunctions (neither...nor); passive vs. active voice Literary Devices – use of fragment for emphasis	**B -** nothing happened. absolutely nothing after fewer than three seconds mr math martinet **resumed** his announcements as if he neither had been interrupted or had wisps of smoke **emitting** from his ears **C -** Nothing happened! Absolutely nothing! After fewer than three seconds, Mr. Math Martinet **resumed** his announcements as if he neither had been interrupted nor had wisps of smoke **emitting** from his ears.

NOTE: Now that your students know the coordinating conjunctions by chanting the FANBOYS, it is time for them to begin learning A WHITE BUS words, the subordinating conjunctions. Take the mnemonic device A WHITE BUS to help students learn them.

A   after, although, as

W   when, while, where
H   how
I   if
T   than
E   even though

B   because, before
U   until, unless
S   since, so that

Students enjoy chanting and chanting these in a sing-song voice every time one appears in a Caught'ya. I add "hey" at the end as we kick up a foot. Once they memorize the subordinating conjunctions, students can be taught that they *never, never* (well, almost never) put a comma before one and that if A WHITE BUS word is combined with a subject and a verb, it is a subordinate clause which is almost always used as an adverb. In this way, they can learn to begin a sentence with "because" and have a chance to complete the sentence.

Tread carefully, though. I have had students in tears as I made a liar out of their beloved fourth-grade teacher who had told them *never* begin a sentence with "because." I informed my kids that, now that they are in middle school, it is OK, just as they can't begin a sentence with any FANBOYS until they get a driver's license.

B – Sentences for the Board	C – Corrected version of the CY
32. pandemonium No Paragraph – same topic; Paragraph – new topic Types of Sentences – complex; complex Commas – sub. clause at beginning of both sentences Homophones – their/there/they're Other Skills – plural poss.; antecedent/pronoun agreement ("everyone" is a sing. collective noun); review collective nouns	**B -** after he went over the school rules mr math martinet handed out a schedule and a map of the school to everyone. as soon as the students schedules were in theyre hands **pandemonium** broke out as everyone tried to see who was in their classes **C -** After he went over the school rules, Mr. Math Martinet handed out a schedule and a map of the school to everyone. As soon as the students' schedules were in their hands, **pandemonium** broke out as everyone tried to see who was in his or her classes.
33. intrepid amicable melodious No Paragraph – same topic Types of Sentences – simple; compound Commas – noun list; noun list; compound sen. Homophones – to/two/too Other Skills – use of colon in a list; do not capitalize subjects (except names of languages); abbreviations	**B -** the **intrepid** six compared notes and found that they shared some of the same classes math english and science. pauline isabelle jesse william and felicia had art with ms **amicable** artist and the other two had music with mr **melodious** music **C -** The **intrepid** six compared notes and found that they shared some of the same classes: math, English, and science. Pauline, Isabelle, Jesse, William, and Felicia had art with Ms. **Amicable** Artist, and the other two had music with Mr. **Melodious** Music.

34. pealed Paragraph – subject change Types of Sentences – simple; complex Commas – participial phrase; sub. clause at beginning Other Skills – review A WHITE BUS words; subject/verb agreement (group was); discuss passive vs. active voice; good (adj.) vs. well (adverb)	**B -** the bell **pealed** signaling the end of homeroom. although the group were going to the same place pauline puerile got lost. things were not going good for her **C -** The bell **pealed**, signaling the end of homeroom. Although the group was going to the same place, Pauline Puerile got lost. Things were not going well for her.
35. daunted No Paragraph – support for topic sentence in CY #34 Types of Sentences – simple; simple; complex Commas – 3 intro wds. (transitions); compound sen. Other Skills – teach about simple transitions; run-on sen.; "ie" spell rule; hyphen in 2 wds. acting as 1; keep in past tense Literary Devices – vivid verbs	**B -** first she became separated from her freinds and then she turned her map upside down and next the size of the eighth graders **daunted** her and finally she gets lost **C -** First, she became separated from her friends. Then, she turned her map upside down. Next, the size of the eighth-graders **daunted** her, and finally, she got lost.

NOTE: To teach the simple transitions to students, I found it very effective to sing them to a simple tune. I liked to use the song "She'll Be Coming 'Round the Mountain" and sing the following words:

Topic sentence, first, next, then,
Finally and a conclusion.
Topic sentence, first, next, then, finally-y
And end with a conclusion.

Writing Idea #7: Expository/Expressive Essay.
Teachers try to set the tone for the year in the first days of school. This is an important time for students as well. Write an expressive essay explaining why it is important for students to get off "on the right foot" the first few days of school.

36. titanic

No Paragraph – conclusion to paragraph; Paragraph – new topic

Types of Sentences – complex; double compound with compound subject

Commas – 2 sub. clauses at beginning; 2 adj.; intro adverb; compound sen.

Homophones – right/rite; their/there/they're

Other Skills – review FANBOYS and A WHITE BUS words; plural poss.; hyphen in 2 wds. acting as 1

B - as pauline puerile stood in the crowded hallway blubbering while others laughed and pointed fingers at her a kind **titanic** eighth grader took pity on her and pointed her in the right direction. meanwhile isabelle ingenuous and felicia fey found the girls bathroom but theyre were too many eighth graders for comfort in there so they left hurriedly

C - As Pauline Puerile stood in the crowded hallway blubbering while others laughed and pointed fingers at her, a kind, **titanic** eighth-grader took pity on her and pointed her in the right direction.

Meanwhile, Isabelle Ingenuous and Felicia Fey found the girls' bathroom, but there were too many eighth-graders for comfort in there, so they left hurriedly.

37. petite

No Paragraph – same topic

Types of Sentences – simple (compound subject); simple; compound

Commas – interrupter; participial phrase (before entering); unnecessary "who" clause; intro phrase

Homophones – to/too/two; hair/hare

Other Skills – use of ( ) for narrator aside; write out numbers to 120; further (not distance) vs. farther (distance); use of ; in a compound sen. instead of FANBOYS; who (subject) vs. whom (object)

B - felicia and isabelle found their first class (which thankfully was only 10 steps further. before entering the classroom felicia fey who should have known better tried too fix her flyaway hair with a **petite** spell. as usual it backfired this time it turned her hair purple

C - Felicia and Isabelle found their first class (which, thankfully, was only ten steps farther). Before entering the classroom, Felicia Fey, who should have known better, tried to fix her flyaway hair with a **petite** spell. As usual, it backfired; this time it turned her hair purple.

NOTE: You might want to review the four reasons for using semicolons (series of independent clauses, instead of a coordinating conjunction in a compound sentence (as in Caught'ya #37), when there are too many commas in a compound sentence, and, in a list, to avoid confusion because there are too many commas). This may avoid future abuse of the semicolon. See the *Grammar, Usage, and Mechanics Guide*.

38. jocose   wrath   jocularity

Paragraph – new subject

Types of Sentences – simple; simple

Commas – intro adverb; appositive; put **,** around "too" if it means "also"

Homophones – to/too/two; their/ there/they're

Other Skills – keep in past tense; "ie" spell rule; never use "that" to refer to people

B - at the same time william waggish finds a new friend jesse **jocose** the boy that had experienced the **wrath** of dean dread too. the too of them discovered there love for **jocularity** and limericks

C -   At the same time, William Waggish found a new friend, Jesse **Jocose**, the boy who had experienced the **wrath** of Dean Dread, too. The two of them discovered their love for **jocularity** and limericks.

B – Sentences for the Board	C – Corrected version of the CY

39. appropriate   encountered

No Paragraph – same topic

Types of Sentences – complex

Punctuation – put " around short works

Commas – interrupter; sub. clause at beginning; no **,** before A WHITE BUS word (even though); compound sen.

Other Skills – use "like" to compare nouns; capitalize names of languages; sing. poss.; "ie" spell rule

B - since like williams other friends they were headed for english class they composed an **appropriate** poem and entitled it awful teacher even though they had not yet **encountered** the teacher

C - Since, like William's other friends, they were headed for English class, they composed an **appropriate** poem and entitled it "Awful Teacher" even though they had not yet **encountered** the teacher.

An English teacher from Slade   (Kentucky)
Confused the verbs "lay" and "laid."
She did not know squat
And was put on the spot,
So she quit and didn't get paid.

NOTE: Since "lay" and "laid" are referred to in the limerick, you might want to teach the irregular verbs "lie" and "lay." "Lie" is intransitive and "lay" is transitive and takes an object. The difficulty lies (ha) in "lay" which is the present tense of the transitive verb and the past tense of the intransitive one—"I lay down a few minutes ago," but "I lay the pen down right now." Since "laid" is always transitive, I told students that "something has to get laid." When they stopped snickering, I made my point: "Some*thing*, an object, has to be placed after using the word 'laid,'" and then I gave them lots of examples. Just so you know, in all the years I taught "lie" and "lay" this way, I never had a parent complain. Once, I even had a parent witness my explanation. She doubled over in laughter and said that *she* would never make that mistake again either.

40. proboscis

Paragraph – new subject

Types of Sentences – simple; compound

Commas – participial phrase (standing); appositive; compound sen.

Homophones – their/there/they're; new/knew; heard/herd

Other Skills – capitalize names of languages and specific types of poetry; abbreviation; verbs rise (intransitive = no object) and raise (transitive = takes object)

Literary Devices – vivid verbs

B - standing at her door there new english teacher ms grammar grouch heard the limerick. her eyes fluttered and she stuck out her tongue while curls of smoke wisped from her **proboscis** and rose to the ceiling

C -   Standing at her door, their new English teacher, Ms. Grammar Grouch, heard the limerick. Her eyelids fluttered, and she stuck out her tongue while curls of smoke wisped from her **proboscis** and rose to the ceiling.

Writing Idea #8: Summary and Prediction.
Write a summary of what has happened in the story so far. At the end of your summary, write what you predict is going to happen in the rest of the story.

41. eerie

2 Paragraphs – new speakers (2nd is narrator)

Types of Sentences – simple; simple; compound; simple

Commas – interjection; direct address; quote; participial phrase (pleased...); compound sen.

Homophones – their/there/they're

Other Skills – affect vs. effect; subject pronouns ("me" is object pronoun); do not begin a sen. with FANBOYS; this/that/these/those (demonstrative   pronouns); keep in past tense; further vs. farther (distance)

B - hey jesse look at that giggled william waggish pleased with their poetic efforts and their effect on the teachers. these teachers are **eerie**. maybe me and my friends are wrong and this year will be fun after all. and sam sagacious just makes a further notation in his pocket notebook

C -   "Hey, Jesse, look at that," giggled William Waggish, pleased with their poetic efforts and their effect on the teachers. "These teachers are **eerie**! Maybe my friends and I are wrong, and this year will be fun after all."

    Sam Sagacious just made a further notation in his pocket notebook.

NOTE: This is an appropriate point at which you may want to introduce the seven types of pronouns. (See *Grammar, Usage, and Mechanics Guide*.) Then, as you encounter examples of each in subsequent Caught'yas, you can point them out to your students.

42. queried

2 Paragraphs – new speaker; new topic

Types of Sentences – complex; simple

Punctuation – need for **?** to denote question

Commas – no **,** before A WHITE BUS word; quote

Other Skills – spell rule of consonant/vowel/consonant (CVC) = double last consonant before suffix (stepped)

B - jesse jocose **queried** with a grin as they stepped into the room of the slightly smoking teacher i wonder what makes them do that. just then they spied felicia fey in her newly purpled hair

C -   Jesse Jocose **queried** with a grin as they stepped into the room of the slightly smoking teacher, "I wonder what makes them do that?"

    Just then they spied Felicia Fey in her newly purpled hair.

43. differentiate   consternation

2 Paragraphs – new speakers (2nd is narrator)

Types of Sentences – simple; compound

Punctuation – " around words that are referred to

Commas – interjection; direct address; quote; compound sen.; interrupter

Other Skills – use of *italics* for emphasis; between (2) vs. among (3 or more); review verbs "lie" and "lay"

B - oh oh william I bet the teachers are not going to find *that* amusing said jesse jocose. ms grammar grouch *could* **differentiate** between the verbs "lay" and laid and much to the **consternation** of olivia otiose she loaded the class with a list of vocabulary words to learn

C - "Uh oh, William, I bet the teachers are not going to find *that* amusing," said Jesse Jocose.

    Ms. Grammar Grouch *could* **differentiate** between the verbs "lay" and "laid," and, much to the **consternation** of Olivia Otiose, she loaded the class with a list of vocabulary words to learn.

NOTE: At this point a review (or lesson) on the common irregular verbs which students often confuse might be appropriate. Be sure to include lie/lay, rise/raise, sit/set. In that list, the problem lies in which is intransitive (the first) and which is transitive and takes an object (the second).

44. amiable   terse

No Paragraph – continuation

Types of Sentences – simple; simple; simple

Commas – intro phrase (transition); no **,** before "and" (not a list or a compound sen.—no subject)

Other Skills – use of "nor" with negative; sing. poss.

B - in addition ms grammar grouch did not permit any student to end a sentence with a preposition nor to split a verb. she was a true grammar grouch. she also was not very **amiable** and was going to send felicia fey to the dean with a **terse** note to call felicias parents about her coming to school with purple hair

C - In addition, Ms. Grammar Grouch did not permit any student to end a sentence with a preposition nor to split a verb. She was a true Grammar Grouch. She also was not very **amiable** and was going to send Felicia Fey to the dean with a **terse** note to call Felicia's parents about her coming to school with purple hair.

45. blurted   coiffure   tittered

2 Paragraphs – 2 new speakers (2nd is narrator)

Types of Sentences – simple; complex; simple

Punctuation – put " around short works

Commas – direct address; no , before "as" (A WHITE BUS word = sub. clause at end); appositive (only one *new* friend)

Homophones – its/it's

Other Skills – sing. poss.; "ie" spell rule

Literary Devices – repetition for effect

B - wait, ms grouch i can fix it. its fixable **blurted** felicia as she muttered another spell which turned her hair back to its normal color but put a purple streak in ms grouchs **coiffure**. jesse jocose composed a limerick on the spot that he entitled my new friend felicia and sent it in a note to william waggish who whispered it to felicia who **tittered**

C -   "Wait, Ms. Grouch, I can fix it. It's fixable," **blurted** Felicia as she muttered another spell which turned her hair back to its normal color but put a purple streak in Ms. Grouch's **coiffure**.

    Jesse Jocose composed a limerick on the spot that he entitled "My New Friend, Felicia" and sent it in a note to William Waggish who whispered it to Felicia who **tittered**.

There was a young lady from Day   (Florida)
Whose nature was quirkily fey.
She purpled her hair,
But she didn't care
And merrily did things her way.

NOTE: I never understood why "it's" and "its" are difficult words for students to differentiate when they write. But, the truth is that they constantly confuse them in their writing. I solved the problem by forbidding the use of "it's." Students had to write out "it is" instead, leaving "its" to its proper use as a possessive pronoun.

    Another trick is to request students to try to use "his" every time they want to use "its" or "it's." Of course, "his" does not work if you wish to say "it is..."

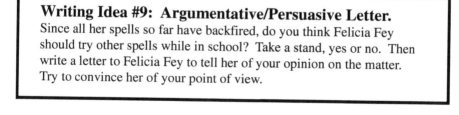

Writing Idea #9: Argumentative/Persuasive Letter.
Since all her spells so far have backfired, do you think Felicia Fey should try other spells while in school? Take a stand, yes or no. Then write a letter to Felicia Fey to tell her of your opinion on the matter. Try to convince her of your point of view.

46. juncture   emitted

Paragraph – new action

Types of Sentences – simple; simple (no 2nd subject)

Commas – intro adverb; verb list; verb list; quote; quote

Other Skills – CVC = double 2nd consonant when adding a suffix (stopped, occurred); fewer (can count) vs. less (can't count); write out #s

B - at this **juncture** ms grammar grouch stuck out her tongue fluttered her eyelids and **emitted** smoke from her ears. she stopped teaching froze for fewer than 3 seconds mumbled that is unanswerable and then resumed her grammar lecture as if nothing had occurred

C -   At this **juncture**, Ms. Grammar Grouch stuck out her tongue, fluttered her eyelids, and **emitted** smoke from her ears. She stopped teaching, froze for fewer than three seconds, mumbled, "That is unanswerable," and then resumed her grammar lecture as if nothing had occurred.

47. penned   furtive   micturated

2 Paragraphs – 2 new speakers

Types of Sentences – simple; compound/complex

Commas – quote; quote; no , before "as" (A WHITE BUS); verb list; compound part of sen.

Homophones – peal/peel

Other Skills – "ie" spell rule; contraction; subject pronouns; put noun first (Felicia and she); plural poss.; add "ly" to adj. to form adverb (quickly)

B - weirder and weirder **penned** william to jesse in another **furtive** note. i dont think i like that teacher very much said isabelle to her freinds as they exited the room at the peal of the bell and her and felicia dashed into the ladies room **micturated** quick washed their hands in the filthy sink and ran out to join their friends

C -   "Weirder and weirder," **penned** William to Jesse in another **furtive** note.

"I don't think I like that teacher very much," said Isabelle to her friends as they exited the room at the peal of the bell, and Felicia and she dashed into the ladies' room, **micturated** quickly, washed their hands in the filthy sink, and ran out to join their friends.

48. loathed latter Paragraph – new speaker Types of Sentences – simple; simple Commas – quote; no **,** before FANBOYS as not compound sen. or list Other Skills – comparisons (good/better/best); "ie" spell rule	**B -** i wonder if the science teacher will be any gooder. we already know what the math teacher is like said sam sagacious who liked the vocabulary lesson of ms grammar grouch but **loathed** the way the **latter** had wanted to send his friend to dean dread **C -** "I wonder if the science teacher will be any better. We already know what the math teacher is like," said Sam Sagacious who liked the vocabulary lesson of Ms. Grammar Grouch but **loathed** the way the **latter** had wanted to send his friend to Dean Dread.
49. perceive Paragraph – new speaker Types of Sentences – simple; simple Commas – intro word; quote Homophones – who's/whose; hair/hare Other Skills – comparatives (bad/worse/worst); "ie" spell rule; "until" has one "l" (check student papers); further vs. farther (distance); contraction	**B -** well She couldn't be worser said felicia fey whos Narrow Escape had Scared them all farther. I hope She doesnt **perceive** that purple Streak in her hair until she gets Home **C -** "Well, she couldn't be worse," said Felicia Fey whose narrow escape had scared them all further. "I hope she doesn't **perceive** that purple streak in her hair until she gets home."

NOTE: Many students are profligate with capital letters and, when they write, capitalize many words that should not be capitalized. If this is a problem with your students, I highly recommend that, intermittently all year long, you put in a few extraneous capital letters in the Caught'ya as I did in this last one.

**50. countered   unison   infamous
    livid**

Paragraph – place and subject change

Types of Sentences – simple;
complex

Punctuation – " around colloquial
phrase (high five); " around short
works; . and , always go inside "

Commas – no , before A WHITE
BUS word; extra info about noun;
compound sen. in poem

Other Skills – contraction; never use
"that" to refer to people; friends; do
not split infinitives (Star Trek was
wrong—"to boldly go" should be "to
go boldly"); sing. poss.

B - shes the one who deserved it
countered felicias freinds william
waggish and pauline puerile in
unison. they shared a high five as
william proceeded to happily recite
another one of his **infamous** limericks
this one entitled frigid english

C -   "She's the one who deserved it,"
countered Felicia's friends William
Waggish and Pauline Puerile in
unison. They shared a "high five" as
William proceeded to recite happily
another one of his **infamous**
limericks, this one entitled "Frigid
English."

> Our grammar teacher is rigid.
> On English rules, she's quite frigid.
> She never splits verbs
> And teaches hard words,
> And errors make her quite **livid**.

Writing Idea #10: Problem/Solution Expository Essay.

William and Jesse use humor as a solution to adjusting to middle school
and their new teachers. Think of some things that could have made your
transition to middle school much easier. Now, write an essay to propose
your solutions that would help future sixth-graders in their adjustment to
middle school. Write your essay in the form of a letter addressed to the
teachers of your middle school.

51. nostrils   anomalies

Paragraph – action change

Types of Sentences – simple; simple

Commas – intro adverb; verb list

Homophones – to/too/two; their/there/they're

Other Skills – keep in past tense; write out numbers to 120; between (2) vs. among (3+); fewer (can count) vs. less (can't count)

Literary Devices – vivid verbs

B - nearby too teachers in unison flutter their eyelids stuck out theyre tongues between closed lips froze in place for less than 3 seconds and emitted wisps of smoke from there **nostrils**. sam sagacious noted the **anomalies** in there reactions

C -   Nearby, two teachers in unison fluttered their eyelids, stuck out their tongues between closed lips, froze in place for fewer than three seconds, and emitted wisps of smoke from their **nostrils**. Sam Sagacious noted the **anomalies** in their reactions.

Midterm Caught'ya Test follows on next page.

Remember, you can adapt the test to fit the needs of your students and then print copies from the CD included with this book.

If you choose not to use this test, you will need to read the passage in Part 1 of the Teacher's Key to your students so that they don't lose the thread of the story.

If you give the test, read the corrected version of the test (the key) aloud several times to your students when they have the test in front of them. This way, they can "hear" the punctuation. You might want to go over any words of which they do not know the meaning since this is a grammar test, not a vocabulary quiz.

Some teachers like to let students mark up the xeroxed test and then write the corrected version on their own. Others simply let students write in the corrections on the xerox and leave it at that. Personally, I prefer the first method as it makes students think and be more careful, but if time is a factor, the second option would be more appropriate.

This test is a review of most of the skills your students have learned in previous Caught'yas. There are three parts of the test, but not all three must be used. If you feel, for example, that your students are not ready to handle Part 3, skip it.

I usually liked to give a midterm around December to check that my students were learning. I also gave one or two Caught'yas as a "quickie quiz" about once every three weeks or so to make sure students paid attention when we went over the daily Caught'ya and didn't cheat when marking the number of errors missed.

Almost Midterm Caught'ya Test

Directions for Part 1:

Students, correct the following long Caught'ya. This test will show how carefully you listen when your teacher goes over the Caught'yas. You will lose two points per error, so **be very careful** and be sure to check your work when finished. Ask your teacher for meanings of words you do not know. This is not a vocabulary test. Follow your teacher's directions on how to do the test and read it again to yourself to help with punctuation.

Hint: There are five paragraphs. All periods are correct. Do not change any of them. Twice, the first quotation mark has been left in to help you. There are six spelling errors and one missing hyphen. Some words will need to be changed.

bizarre sam sagacious muttered to himself as he took notes. the rest of the day went pretty much the same. the teachers for the most part were **clad** in somber colors and they had no sense of humor. unfortunately in science class the freinds found there old **nemesis** orson **odious**. as they entered the room orson was "holding court in the back between many of the popular kids. ah guys look at the weird ones who just entered science class orson said **maliciously**. theres the witch that cant do a spell right the four eyed wise guy who knows it all the free spirit that even wears stupid plastic butterflies in her hair the crybaby the lazy one who never has her homework and the 2 that think there funny. what losers he stated and he chucked too his audience and encouraged them to laugh. im sorry my parents made my buds and me late this morning and me and my buds missed too of the "geeks getting caught by the dean **expounded** odious orson as he concluded his **verbal** attack. the intrepid 6 and jocose jesse heads down slunk into seats in the front of the room just as the science teacher entered and closed the door behind him. when the class saw their teacher silence **reigned** even from the back of the room where orsons gang sat.

Directions for Part 2:

First, number the eleven sentences on your corrected copy of the test so you don't lose track of the numbers. Then, use your corrected version of the test to identify the types of sentences of each of the eleven sentences in this exam—simple, compound, complex, or compound/complex.

Hint: Four are simple. Two are compound. Four are complex. One is compound/complex.

1. _____

2. _____

3. _____

4. _____

5. _____

6. _____

7. _____

8. _____

9. _____

10. _____

11. _____

Directions for Part 3:

First, invent an imaginary obnoxious person who joins your English class. Next, give that imaginary person a name. Then, think of two or three things (actions) that this odious person might do that would make class miserable for you and your classmates. Finally, write down your ideas.

Now, write an essay explaining why the things that this odious person does would disrupt the class and make life miserable for everyone.

Almost Midterm Caught'ya Test KEY

Part I:

"**Bizarre**," Sam Sagacious muttered to himself as he took notes.

The rest of the day went pretty much the same. The teachers, for the most part, were **clad** in somber colors, and they had no sense of humor. Unfortunately, in science class, the friends found their old **nemesis**, Orson **Odious**. As they entered the room, Orson was "holding court" in the back among many of the popular kids.

"Ah, guys, look at the weird ones who just entered science class," Orson said **maliciously**. "There's the witch who can't do a spell right, the four-eyed wise guy who knows it all, the free spirit who even wears stupid, plastic butterflies in her hair, the crybaby, the lazy one who never has her homework, and the two who think they're funny. What losers," he stated, and he chuckled to his audience and encouraged them to laugh.

"I'm sorry my parents made my buds and me late this morning, and my buds and I missed two of the "geeks" getting caught by the dean," **expounded** Orson Odious as he concluded his **verbal** attack.

The intrepid six and Jesse Jocose, heads down, slunk into seats in the front of the room just as the science teacher entered and closed the door behind him. When the class saw the teacher, silence **reigned**, even from the back of the room where Orson's gang sat.

Part 2:

1. complex
2. simple
3. compound
4. simple
5. complex
6. simple
7. simple
8. compound
9. compound/complex
10. complex
11. complex

52. stern   monotone
a plethora of   a dearth of

Paragraph – new speaker

Types of Sentences – simple;
compound

Commas – quote; noun list;
compound sen.

Other Skills – science; "a lot" is 2
wds.; good (adjective) vs. well
(adverb)

B - i am ms **stern** science the teacher
said in a **monotone** voice. i believe
in a lot of hard tests **a plethora of**
homework and **a dearth of** student
talking in my class but i also expect
students to do good

C -   "I am Ms. **Stern** Science," the
teacher said in a **monotone** voice.
"I believe in a lot of hard tests, **a
plethora of** homework, and **a dearth
of** student talking in my class, but I
also expect students to do well."

TWO NOTES:
1) It is a good idea to stress the use of "a plethora of" and "a dearth of" as
students like using these phrases. Besides, they always spell "a lot of"
incorrectly anyway...

2) Now that the year is half over and your students have memorized the
coordinating and subordinating conjunctions, it is time to memorize the
prepositions. They are listed in the *Grammar, Usage, and Mechanics Guide*.

Students learn them painlessly if you chant only four new ones a day
(adding four each day until you cover the entire list). Middle-school
students love to chant these with a different gesture (like "the Egyptian" or
raising an arm, etc.) with each set of four prepositions. When all have been
added to the chant, you and your class (although *you* will never remember
the gestures, *they* will) can chant and move to the prepositions each time
one appears in a Caught'ya (which is most of them) until your students tire
of the exercise.

Once memorized, students can learn not to capitalize them in a title,
that when you combine one with a noun, you have an adjective or adverb in
a prepositional phrase, and that when you put two prepositional phrases
together at the beginning of a sentence, you must have a comma after them.

B – Sentences for the Board	C – Corrected version of the CY
53. slumped woe Paragraph – new speaker Types of Sentences – simple; simple; simple Commas – intro phrase; interjection; intro word Other Skills – further vs. farther (distance); run-on sen.; bad (adj.) vs. badly (adv.)	**B -** at this olivia otiose **slumped** in her desk in **woe**. oh no she whined as she sank farther into her seat and this year is starting out bad **C -** At this, Olivia Otiose **slumped** in her desk in **woe**. "Oh, no," she whined as she sank farther into her seat. "This year is starting out badly."
54. ominous pontificate 2 Paragraphs – new speakers (2nd is narrator) Types of Sentences – compound/complex; compound Commas – compound sen.; 2 adj.; 2 adj. where 2nd is not age, color, or linked; quote; compound sen. Homophones – heard/herd; their/there/they're Other Skills – abbreviation; **science**; hyphen in 2 wds. acting as 1 adj.; do not split verb Literary Devices – simile	**B -** ms stern science stared at olivia otiose with his bird like beady eyes and she said in a low **ominous** tone there will always be silence in this classroom when i **pontificate**. olivia otiose thought she heard a snicker from orson odious in the back but the teacher did not catch it **C -** Ms. Stern Science stared at Olivia Otiose with her bird-like, beady eyes, and she said in a low, **ominous** tone, "There always will be silence in this classroom when I **pontificate**." Olivia Otiose thought she heard a snicker from Orson Odious in the back, but the teacher did not catch it.

NOTES: It is almost halfway through the year. You might want to review the eight parts of speech (if you have not been doing so all along) and ask students to point them out in the Caught'yas.

    Many Caught'yas in this story use the basic abbreviations. The postal code abbreviations for the states, however, are not addressed. You may wish to conduct a lesson in the use of these codes (see *Grammar, Usage, and Mechanics Guide*).

55. elude   wretched   commenced

Paragraph – place change

Types of Sentences – complex; compound

Punctuation – put " around short works and ____ or *italicize* long works; **,** and **.** always go inside "; semicolon in series of indep. clauses

Commas – sub. clause at beginning; extra info about a noun; compound sen.; 2 adj.

Homophones – new/gnu/knew

Other Skills – write out #s to 120; friends; who (subject) vs. whom (object); plural poss.

B - as the 7 friends left the room they tried to **elude** orson odious who knew all the tricks of making other students lives **wretched** without getting caught by the teachers himself. william waggish and his new friend jesse jocose **commenced** composing another limerick this one about the stern science teacher and they entitled it crude science

C -   As the seven friends left the room, they tried to **elude** Orson Odious who knew all the tricks of making other students' lives **wretched** without getting caught by the teachers himself. William Waggish and his new friend Jesse Jocose **commenced** composing another limerick, this one about the stern science teacher, and they entitled it "Crude, Rude Science."

> Our old science teacher is rude.
> She also is horribly crude.
> She picks at her nose;
> She sports ugly toes;
> And always is in a bad mood.

Writing Idea #11: Expository/Argumentative Essay.

Think of the class you like the least. Think what it is about that class that makes it your least favorite. Please make up names to protect the guilty. (You also may make things up if you run out of true things to dislike about that class or like all your classes.) Now, write an essay to explain why that class is your least favorite. Again, please do not use real names of real people. You do not want to hurt someone's feelings. Make up names.

---

56. unsightly

Paragraph – new action

Types of Sentences – simple
(compound subject); simple

Commas – participial phrase; no ,
after "toad" as there are many who fit
that description (restrictive modifier)

Homophones – to/too/two; their/there/
they're

Other Skills – friends; sing. poss.

Literary Devices – metaphor (toad)

B - isabelle ingenuous and her friends
laughed imagining their teachers
unsightly toes. they forgot about
the toad orson odious and all that he
liked too do too make theyre lives
miserable

C -   Isabelle Ingenuous and her
friends laughed, imagining their
teacher's **unsightly** toes. They forgot
about the toad Orson Odious and all
that he liked to do to make their lives
miserable.

**NOTE: If your students have progressed enough to understand, now would
be a good time to point out the difference between a clause (has a subject
and a verb) and a phrase (a group of words, serving as one part of speech,
that lack either a subject or a verb or both). A sentence, for example, is an
"independent clause" since it has a subject and a verb and can stand on its
own.**

57. portal   proboscis

2 Paragraphs – place change; new
speaker

Types of Sentences – simple
(compound predicate); simple

Commas – 2 prep. phrases at
beginning; verb list; quote

Other Skills – hyphenated noun;
fewer (can count) vs. less (can't
count); write out #s to 120; weirder;
who (subject) vs. whom (object)

Literary Devices – simile

B - by her desk near the **portal** of the
room ms stern science stuck out her
tongue smoked slightly from her
proboscis fluttered her eyes like a
blinking lizard and froze mid-step for
less than 3 seconds. stranger and
weirder murmured sam sagacious
whom noticed these things

C -   By her desk near the **portal** of
the room, Ms. Stern Science stuck out
her tongue, smoked slightly from her
proboscis, fluttered her eyes like a
blinking lizard, and froze mid-step for
fewer than three seconds.
     "Stranger and weirder,"
murmured Sam Sagacious who
noticed these things.

B – Sentences for the Board	C – Corrected version of the CY
58. boisterous pandemonium **rumor-monger purportedly** Paragraph – time, place, and subject change Types of Sentences – simple; compound Commas – compound sen. Homophones – to/too/two Other Skills – keep in past tense; hyphen between 2 wds. acting as 1 adj.; between (2) vs. among (3+); write out #s to 120; hyphenated noun	**B -** lunch is the usual **boisterous pandemonium** typical of a middle school lunchroom. a fight broke out among 2 girls over something a **rumor-monger** had reported that the other had **purportedly** said and both were suspended on the spot **C -** Lunch was the usual **boisterous pandemonium** typical of a middle-school lunchroom. A fight broke out between two girls over something a **rumor-monger** had reported that the other had **purportedly** said, and both were suspended on the spot.
59. peers forebodingly No Paragraph then ¶ – same topic; new time and topic Types of Sentences – simple; complex Commas – pause before adverbial phrase; intro phrase (optional); participle; no **,** before A WHITE BUS word Homophones – their/there/they're Other Skills – plural poss.; hyphen in 2 wds. acting as 1 adj.; accept vs. except Literary Devices – metaphor (ham-sized)	**B -** dean dread called theyre parents from the lunchroom right in front of the girls **peers**. after that incident dean dread stood on the stage with his ham sized hands on his hips glaring **forebodingly** at the students as if he dared them to try anything else accept talking and eating **C -** Dean Dread called their parents from the lunchroom, right in front of the girls' **peers**. After that incident, Dean Dread stood on the stage with his ham-sized hands on his hips, glaring **forebodingly** at the students as if he dared them to try anything else except talking and eating.

60. compatriot

Paragraph – new speaker

Types of Sentences – simple; simple (compound verb)

Punctuation – " around short works; , and . always go inside "

Commas – direct address; quote; verb list; no , before "green" as is color

Homophones – its/it's

Literary Devices – simile

B - its amazing he lets us talk at all sam said william waggish to his **compatriot** at the table. he also composed another limerick for the occasion entitled it mean green dean and caused everyone at his table to hoot with laughter like a bunch of hyenas

C - "It's amazing he lets us talk at all, Sam," said William Waggish to his **compatriot** at the table. He also composed another limerick for the occasion, entitled it "Mean Green Dean," and caused everyone at his table to hoot with laughter like a bunch of hyenas.

> The dean of students is mean.
> His face in anger turns bright green.
> He maintains his right
> To stop any fight
> And suspend those who are obscene.

NOTE: I suggest that you continue to ban the use of "it's" in your classroom. You can go over the difference *ad nauseum,* but until the lightbulb shines, students will persist in confusing these two homophones.

Writing Idea #12: Vivid Verb Paragraph Writing.
Write a strong-verb paragraph of six to eight sentences with the topic sentence: _____ Middle School's lunchroom is wild during sixth-grade lunch. Be sure to follow all the guidelines of what to include in your paragraph.

B – Sentences for the Board	C – Corrected version of the CY
61. malevolent visage marred pursed No Paragraph – same topic Types of Sentences – simple (students won't believe it) Commas – long intro phrase; participle (and repetition) Homophones – their/there/they're Other Skills – between (2) vs. among (3+)	**B -** after a brief flutter of his eyelids and one wisp of smoke curling from his left ear dean dread turned to stare at their table with a **malevolent** expression on his **visage marred** only by his tongue that still stuck out between his **pursed** lips **C -** After a brief flutter of his eyelids and one wisp of smoke curling from his left ear, Dean Dread turned to stare at their table with a **malevolent** expression on his **visage, marred** only by his tongue that still stuck out between his **pursed** lips.
62. amicable Paragraph – new subject Types of Sentences – simple; simple (compound predicate) Commas – intro phrase; appositive Homophones – their/there/they're Other Skills – subject/verb agreement (art and music were); abbreviation; "a lot" is 2 wds.; use "an" before a vowel; further vs. farther (distance); good (adj. vs. well (adverb)	**B -** art and music was the only relief for the rest of the week. in art, the teacher ms **amicable** artist smiled alot and promised the class that they would release butterflies on earth day and celebrate the event farther with an art project of there own choosing as good **C -** Art and music were the only relief for the rest of the week. In art, the teacher, Ms. **Amicable** Artist, smiled a lot and promised the class that they would release butterflies on Earth Day and celebrate the event further with an art project of their own choosing as well.

63. opted No Paragraph then ¶ – continuation; new speaker Types of Sentences – simple (compound subject); simple Commas – noun list; unnecessary "who" clause (as opposed to the necessary one in the 2nd sen.); direct address; quote Other Skills – who (subject) vs. whom (object)	**B -** pauline isabelle jesse william and felicia who had **opted** to take art were delighted. this teacher seems almost human girlfriend whispered isabelle to felicia who nodded in agreement **C -** Pauline, Isabelle, Jesse, William, and Felicia, who had **opted** to take art, were delighted. "This teacher seems almost human, girlfriend," whispered Isabelle to Felicia who nodded in agreement.

64. commenced   Impressionist   touts
 	
2 Paragraphs – speaker change (narrator); subject change
 	
Types of Sentences – simple (compound predicate); compound
 	
Punctuation – " around short works
 	
Commas – long intro phrase; compound sen.
 	
Homophones – to/two/too; piece/peace
 	
Other Skills – abbreviation; write out #s to 120; proper noun
	B - with only a small frown at isabelle ms amicable artist quietly moved by the 2 girls and **commenced** a lecture about the **Impressionist** artists. william waggish took out a pencil and a peace of paper and he composed another limerick entitled art
	
	C - With only a small frown at Isabelle, Ms. Amicable Artist quietly moved by the two girls and **commenced** a lecture about the **Impressionist** artists.
	
	   William Waggish took out a pencil and a piece of paper, and he composed another limerick entitled "Art."
	
	      We have a bizarre art teacher
	      Who **touts** painters like a preacher.
	      Cassat and Van Go
	      And Monet, now we know,
	      Are the ones who really reach her.

65. periodically ambled perused

Paragraph – new action

Types of Sentences – simple; simple

Commas – participial phrase; verb list; direct address; pause before "not"

Homophones – its/it's

Other Skills – quote within a quote; sing. poss.; use hyphens to indicate spelling of word

B - ms amicable artist still lecturing and **periodically** showing pictures from a stack in her hand **ambled** over to william confiscated the paper swiftly **perused** its contents smiled and said you spelled van goghs name incorrectly william. its spelled g-o-g-h not go

C - Ms. Amicable Artist, still lecturing and **periodically** showing pictures from a stack in her hand, **ambled** over to William, confiscated the paper, swiftly **perused** its contents, smiled, and said, "You spelled Van Gogh's name incorrectly, William. It is spelled 'G-o-g-h,' not 'G-o.'"

NOTE: You will need a large print of a painting. You can buy poster-sized reproductions at local art galleries for less than $20, but your art teacher probably has a few on hand. My students *loved* Van Gogh's art.

Writing Idea #13: Critique or Evaluative Writing.
Your teacher will show you a picture. Write a critique of that painting. Be sure to include a description of the painting, your perception of the artist's purpose and audience, an analysis of the colors and subject used, and finally, why you do or do not like the painting.

B – Sentences for the Board	C – Corrected version of the CY

66. hued   coiffure   spiel   rapt

2 Paragraphs – talking about 2 different persons

Types of Sentences – complex; simple (compound sub.)

Commas – no , before A WHITE BUS word; verb list

Other Skills – except/accept; hyphen in 2 wds. used as 1 adj.; sing. poss.; capitalize names of countries; sing. poss.

B - nothing else happened accept that the pink **hued** flower in her **coiffure** fell onto williams desk as she nodded her head at him handed back williams paper and continued her **spiel** on the impressionists. william waggish corrected the spelling of the dutch painters name and paid **rapt** attention for the rest of the period

C -   Nothing else happened except that the pink-**hued** flower in her **coiffure** fell onto William's desk as she nodded her head at him, handed back William's paper, and continued her **spiel** on the Impressionists.

William Waggish corrected the spelling of the Dutch painter's name and paid **rapt** attention for the rest of the period.

---

67. mused

Paragraph – new speaker

Types of Sentences – simple; complex

Punctuation – continued quote

Commas – interjection; quote; no , before A WHITE BUS word

Other Skills – affect vs. effect

B - hey **mused** william waggish to himself maybe the limerick has to be said out loud for it to effect the teachers. i must tell sam as he would want to make a note

C -   "Hey," **mused** William Waggish to himself, "maybe the limerick has to be said out loud for it to affect the teachers. I must tell Sam as he would want to make a note."

68. melodious   neophyte

Paragraph – new place

Types of Sentences – compound; simple (no subject)

Commas – intro phrase of time; compound sen.; 2 adj.

Homophones – their/there/they're; new/knew/gnu

Other Skills – keep in past tense; hyphen between 2 wds. acting as 1

B - meanwhile in music mr **melodious** music tells his class all about band and he let the untried **neophyte** sixth graders choose there instruments. sam sagacious played the guitar at home but wanted to take up a gnu challenge

C -   Meanwhile in music, Mr. **Melodious** Music told his class all about band, and he let the untried, **neophyte** sixth-graders choose their instruments. Sam Sagacious played the guitar at home but wanted to take up a new challenge.

NOTE: At this juncture in the school year, sixth-graders "should" be ready to learn the three questions an adjective could answer and the five questions an adverb could answer. See the *Grammar, Usage, and Mechanics Guide*. I liked to teach this and then post the questions on the wall somewhere for reference.

69. arduous

No Paragraph – continuation

Types of Sentences – simple; simple

Commas – appositive; 2 unnecessary "who" clauses

Homophones – to/too/two

Other Skills – use "an" if noun begins with a vowel; who (subject) vs. whom (object); sing. poss.; use "that" with objects

B - he chose the oboe an **arduous** instrument too learn to play. olivia otiose who had not signed up for any exploratory class and whom had been randomly assigned to band by the schools computer wanted the instrument that was the easiest to play

C - He chose the oboe, an **arduous** instrument to learn to play. Olivia Otiose, who had not signed up for any exploratory class and who had been randomly assigned to band by the school's computer, wanted the instrument that was the easiest to play.

70. compel

No Paragraph then ¶ – continuation; new speaker

Types of Sentences – simple (no subject); compound/complex

Punctuation – " around vernacular

Commas – quote; sub. clause at beginning; compound sen.

Other Skills – note passive voice (not good writing) vs. active (good)

B - she wanted to play the triangle but was given a clarinet. bummer she said. if i have to learn to play this instrument i will be forced to carry this home every day and my mother will **compel** me to practice

C - She wanted to play the triangle but was given a clarinet.
        "'Bummer,'" she said. "If I have to learn to play this instrument, I will be forced to carry this home every day, and my mother will **compel** me to practice."

Writing Idea #14: Persuasive/Argumentative Essay.

Think of a time when an adult made you do something you didn't want to do (like play the clarinet or take piano lessons) because they thought it would be "good for you." Write an essay to convince that person that you should be let "off the hook." Be sure to address your arguments to that person using direct address. For example, "Mom, I really don't think I should have to do the dishes every night."

---

71. plodded

Paragraph – new scene

Types of Sentences – simple; compound/complex

Punctuation – use ( ) around narrator aside

Commas – intro adverb (optional); participial phrase; compound sen.; no **,** before A WHITE BUS word

Other Skills – write out #s to 120; friends; no caps on "science" and "math" as they are adjectives; do not split verbs

B - that day the 6 friends jesse jocose took a bus to school **plodded** home piled with science and math homework. olivia otiose was not pleased so she did none of it and lied to her mother when her mother asked if she had ever been assigned any

C -   That day, the six friends (Jesse Jocose took a bus to school) **plodded** home, piled with science and math homework. Olivia Otiose was not pleased, so she did none of it and lied to her mother when her mother asked if she ever had been assigned any.

NOTE: This is a good point to review the subordinating and coordinating conjunctions, prepositions, and "dead verbs."

72. invariable

No Paragraph then ¶ – concluding sen. to ¶; new topic and time

Types of Sentences – simple; complex

Commas – sub. clause at beginning; 2 adj.

Homophones – new/knew/gnu; week/ weak; passed/past

Other Skills – sing. poss.; gerund; use "an" before vowel

B - olivia's lying about homework was nothing knew. months passed in a similar **invariable** manner

C - Olivia's lying about homework was nothing new.
    Months passed in a similar, **invariable** manner.

NOTES: I see no reason to teach students about gerunds (verbs acting as nouns) since they will use them naturally, and there are no commas involved. Why confuse the issue? I include them just in case...
    If your students still are confusing plurals and possessives (as in putting apostrophes in plural nouns), you might want to start putting apostrophes in future Caught'yas whenever a word ends in "s." In this way, students will have to think about whether to use that apostrophe. I have put in extraneous apostrophes in the "B" sentence in the next two Caught'yas for illustration.

B – Sentences for the Board	C – Corrected version of the CY
73. comely pulchritudinous **amorous dapper** No Paragraph – continuation Types of Sentences – simple (compound predicate); simple (cp) Commas – verb list; 2 adj. where 2nd is not age, color, or linked; long intro phrase Homophones – their/there/they're Other Skills – write out #s to 120; who (subject) vs. whom (object); CVC = double last consonant when add suffix (bussed) Literary device – use of vivid verbs; vocab lesson	**B -** the 6 walked to school met up with their friend's who bussed to school suffered through classes' with their bizarre teacher's and tried to avoid orson odious and his popular pal's the **comely** petra **pulchritudinous** lovely alessandra **amorous** and handsome danny **dapper**. accept in art and music the nasty annoying teachers' gave tons of homework **C -** The six walked to school, met up with their friends who bussed to school, suffered through classes with their bizarre teachers, and tried to avoid Orson Odious and his popular pals, the **comely** Petra **Pulchritudinous**, lovely Alessandra **Amorous**, and handsome Danny **Dapper**. Except in art and music, the nasty, annoying teachers gave tons of homework.
74. afoot atrocious hilarious Paragraph – new subject Types of Sentences – complex; simple Commas – sub. clause at beginning Homophones – new/knew/gnu; their/there/they're Other Skills – affect vs. effect; "ie" spell rule and neighbor and weigh are weird; sing. poss.	**B -** while middle school is alway's a wierd place they new that something strange was **afoot** at horribly hard middle school. sam kept note's on the effect's that william's and jesses' **atrocious** but **hilarious** limerick's had on there teachers' **C -** While middle school is always a weird place, they knew that something strange was **afoot** at Horribly Hard Middle School. Sam kept notes on the effects that William's and Jesse's **atrocious** but **hilarious** limericks had on their teachers.

75. evoked   infamous   monotone

2 Paragraphs – new topics

Types of Sentences – simple; simple

Punctuation – put " around short works and _____ or *italicize* long works; **,** and **.** always go inside "; semicolon in series of indep. clauses

Commas – appositive; appositive; long intro phrase; quote

Homophones – their/there/they're

Other Skills – do not capitalize social studies as adj.; abbreviation; plural poss.; fewer (can be counted) vs. less (can't); write out #s to 120

Literary Device – alliteration

B - one of their best a wicked limerick about the social studies teacher ms grumpy geography **evoked** more than smoke from her ears and fluttering eyes. in addition to the teachers usual reactions to hearing one of their **infamous** verses ms grumpy geography repeated over and over in a **monotone** voice for more than too seconds but less than 3 you must read the book great geography. you must read the book great geography

C -   One of their best, a wicked limerick about the social studies teacher, Ms. Grumpy Geography, **evoked** more than smoke from her ears and fluttering eyes.

In addition to the teachers' usual reactions to hearing one of their **infamous** verses, Ms. Grumpy Geography repeated over and over in a **monotone** voice for more than two seconds but fewer than three, "You must read the book <u>Great Geography</u>. You must read the book <u>Great Geography</u>."

There is a teacher from Noodle   (Texas)
Whose hair looks like a French poodle.
She paints her nails green;
She taps on the screen;
Her face looks like pale apple strudel.
                    **(Pronounce "apple"
                    as one syllable.)**

Writing Idea #15: Expository/Argumentative Essay.
Think of a book you have read and liked. It could be a book you read recently or a long time ago. Think of the reasons why you liked that book. Now, write an essay to explain why you think a friend would also enjoy that book. Be careful—this is NOT a summary.

76. *apropos* (pronounced ahh-proh-poh with a short "A" and long "Os")

Paragraph – new subject

Types of Sentences – compound; compound

Commas – intro phrase (optional); compound sen.; compound sen.

Homophones – their/there/they're; its/it's

Other Skills – do not use "would" to denote past tense; neither...nor; "no one" is 2 wds.

Literary Devices – use *italics* for Latin wds.

B - as usual sam sagacious would take notes *apropos* of the incident but neither he or anyone else could draw any conclusions. there was just something different about there school but noone could put a finger on what its difference was

C -   As usual, Sam Sagacious took notes *apropos* of the incident, but neither he nor anyone else could draw any conclusions. There was just something different about their school, but no one could put a finger on what its difference was.

NOTE: I suggest again that you continue to insist that your students write out "it is" instead of using the contraction "it's." It is the only way they will learn the difference between the possessive pronoun and the contraction.

77. indolent

Paragraph – new topic

Types of Sentences – simple; compound

Punctuation – use " around colloquial wds.; , and . always go inside "

Commas – compound sen.; 2 adj.

Other Skills – good (adjective) vs. well (adverb)

B - art continued to be awesome. band was challenging and even lazy **indolent** olivia otiose was getting into playing her clarinet good

C -   Art continued to be "awesome." Band was challenging, and even lazy, **indolent** Olivia Otiose was getting into playing her clarinet well.

B – Sentences for the Board	C – Corrected version of the CY
78. innovative Paragraph – new topic Types of Sentences – simple; simple Commas – intro adverb (optional) Homophones – to/too/two; their/there/they're Other Skills – do not split infinitive; parallel construction (pronoun noun...pronoun noun); confusion of adverb "well" and adj. "good"	**B -** then there was this **innovative** teacher who visited there english class from time to time to teach creative writing. her humor and enthusiastic inspired students to write good **C -** Then, there was this **innovative** teacher who visited their English class from time to time to teach creative writing. Her humor and her enthusiasm inspired students to write well.

NOTE: *Star Trek* was wrong. **"To boldly go where..."** should be **"To go boldly."** Infinitives should never be split.

79. apathetic superlative noxious No Paragraph – still explaining about English teacher Types of Sentences – simple; simple Commas – intro phrase (transition) Homophones – won/one Other Skills – use "an" only if noun begins with vowel; use of dash when clarifying	**B -** usually **apathetic** olivia otiose wrote a personal narrative that won a prize. in addition william waggish even abandoned his favorite form of writing—the limerick and composed a **superlative** argumentative essay defending his position that school uniforms were an **noxious** idea **C -** Usually **apathetic** Olivia Otiose wrote a personal narrative that won a prize. In addition, William Waggish even abandoned his favorite form of writing—the limerick—and composed a **superlative** argumentative essay defending his position that school uniforms were a **noxious** idea.

B – Sentences for the Board	C – Corrected version of the CY
80. insufferable taunts pugnacious Paragraph – new time and place Types of Sentences – simple; simple (compound predicate) Commas – 2 intro adverbs Other Skills – keep in past tense; parallel construction (to...to)	**B -** one day in science orson odious was particularly **insufferable**. his **taunts** provoke the usually cheerful jesse jocose to become **pugnacious** and swing at him in fury **C -** One day in science, Orson Odious was particularly **insufferable**. His **taunts** provoked the usually cheerful Jesse Jocose to become **pugnacious** and to swing at him in fury.
81. countered visage fray rapscallions No Paragraph then ¶ – same topic; new speaker Types of Sentences – simple; compound; simple Commas – compound sen.; direct address and quote; interrupted quote Homophones – to/too/two Other Skills – sing. poss.; fri**e**nd; abbreviation; CVC = double last consonant when adding suffix (stepped); write out #s to 120	**B -** orson **countered** with a blow too jesses **visage**. william jumped into the **fray** to support his freind and then ms stern science steped into the act. you 3 **rapscallions** she said in a loud voice go to the deans office immediately **C -** Orson **countered** with a blow to Jesse's **visage**. William jumped into the **fray** to support his friend, and then Ms. Stern Science stepped into the act. "You three **rapscallions**," she said in a loud voice, "go to the dean's office immediately.

NOTE: No end " as will be continued in CY #82.

Writing Idea #16: Narrative/Expressive Essay.
Did you ever witness a fight? What happened? What was the effect of the fight? What can be the bad results of a fight? Write a narrative about a fight you have witnessed (or imagined in your head). Do not use names of real people. Be sure to include a description of the fight, its probable cause, and its effect on the participants (suspension, lost friendship, etc.).

82. goaded

No Paragraph then ¶ – continuation of quote; new speaker (narrator)

Types of Sentences – imperative; complex

Punctuation – no " at beginning as a continuation; " around sarcasm; , and . always go inside "

Commas – direct address; verb list; quote; participial phrase; noun list

Other Skills – review collective nouns (group); sing. poss.

Literary Devices – humor

B - isabelle take this note and go see that they arrive in the appropriate place and get a return note from the dean she concluded punching the call button to inform the office that dean dread had some customers. as the group walked to the deans office orson **goaded** and teased jesse william and isabelle

C - "Isabelle, take this note, go see that they arrive in the appropriate place, and get a return note from the dean," she concluded, punching the call button to inform the office that Dean Dread had some "customers."

As the group walked to the dean's office, Orson **goaded** and teased Jesse, William, and Isabelle.

---

83. jeered   quiescent   exacerbate

2 Paragraphs – new speakers (2ⁿᵈ is narrator)

Types of Sentences – simple; compound

Commas – quote; compound sen.

Homophones – your/you're

Other Skills – write out #s to 120; keep in past tense

B - your nothing but unpopular little geeks he **jeered**. the 3 remain **quiescent** at this insult for they dared not **exacerbate** the situation

C - "You're nothing but unpopular little geeks," he **jeered**.

The three remained **quiescent** at this insult, for they dared not **exacerbate** the situation.

NOTE: As with "it's," I forbade my students to write the contraction "you're." I insisted that they write out "you are" instead. This helped them learn the difference between the homophones.

B – Sentences for the Board	C – Corrected version of the CY
84. loathes pacifistic 2 Paragraphs – new speakers Types of Sentences – simple; complex Punctuation – continued quote Commas – quote; quote; no **,** before A WHITE BUS word Homophones – your/you're; to/too/ two Other Skills – contraction; bad (adj.) vs. badly (adv.)	**B -** everyone **loathes** your stupid poems he continued they are written bad. now youve gone to far growled the usually **pacifistic** william waggish as he rushed in on his tormentor **C -** "Everyone **loathes** your stupid poems," he continued. "They are written badly." "Now you've gone too far," growled the usually **pacifistic** William Waggish as he rushed in on his tormentor.
85. orchestrated obstreperous Paragraph – new action Types of Sentences – complex; compound; simple Commas – sub. clause at beginning; clarification; compound sen.; noun list Other Skills – compound word; write out #s; keep story in past tense; use "an" with vowel; go over "sit" (no object) and "set" (takes object)	**B -** as if they had **orchestrated** it beforehand the 3 friends jump on orson all at the same time. orson fell to the ground and jesse william and isabelle set on him and called him an **obstreperous** jerk. orson odious was shocked into silence **C -** As if they had **orchestrated** it beforehand, the three friends jumped on Orson, all at the same time. Orson fell to the ground, and Jesse, William, and Isabelle sat on him and called him an **obstreperous** jerk. Orson Odious was shocked into silence.

86. ushered   miscreants

Paragraph – new person appears

Types of Sentences – simple (compound verb); compound

Commas – intro adverb; 2 adj.; compound sen.; interrupter

Other Skills – write out #s; do not split verbs

Literary Devices – simile

B - at that moment dean dread appeared suddenly like a huge swooping bat and **ushered** all four **miscreants** into his office. orson odious tried to blame the 3 for the entire incident but ms stern science had luckily seen him take a swing at jesse jocose

C -   At that moment, Dean Dread appeared suddenly, like a huge, swooping bat, and **ushered** all four **miscreants** into his office. Orson Odious tried to blame the three for the entire incident, but luckily Ms. Stern Science had seen him take a swing at Jesse Jocose.

87. miscreants

Paragraph – new topic

Types of Sentences – compound; simple

Commas – compound sen.

Homophones – their/there/they're

Other Skills – do not use "would" to denote past tense—it is conditional; review collective nouns; sing. poss.; write out #s

B - dean dread would call everyones parents to come get there **miscreants** and then he would suspend all 4 of them for 2 days. william waggish didn't even have time to compose a limerick appropriate for the occasion

C -   Dean Dread called everyone's parents to come get their **miscreants**, and then he suspended all four of them for two days. William Waggish didn't even have time to compose a limerick appropriate for the occasion.

Writing Idea #17: Vivid Verb Paragraph Writing.

Write a strong-verb paragraph of six to eight sentences using the topic sentence: The child was a miscreant. Include at least two similes in your paragraph. Use a checklist to make sure that you included all the required elements of a paragraph.

B – Sentences for the Board	C – Corrected version of the CY

88. docile   bibliophilic   secreted

Paragraph – new time

Types of Sentences – compound/ complex; simple

Punctuation – _____ or *italicize* titles of long works

Commas – sub. clause at beginning; compound part; interrupter

Other Skills – comparatives (good/ better/best); "a while" is 2 wds.; who (subject) vs. whom (object); use of pluperfect tense; write out #s

Literary Devices – literary reference

B - when the suspension had ended and all were back in school things got gooder for a while. orson odious remained unusually **docile**. he did however start targeting a girl named beth **bibliophilic** who had read harry potter more than 4 times and whom always **secreted** a book on her knees under her desk

C -   When the suspension had ended, and all were back in school, things got better for a while. Orson Odious remained unusually **docile**. He did, however, start targeting a girl named Beth **Bibliophilic** who had read <u>Harry Potter</u> more than four times and who always **secreted** a book on her knees under her desk.

---

89. meticulous   elated

Paragraph – new subject

Types of Sentences – simple; simple (compound subject)

Commas – appositive; interrupter

Other Skills – never use "that" to refer to people; write out #s; relative pronouns

B - orson also picked on a boy named mark **meticulous** a perfectionist that always rewrote his papers many times. these 2 of course were not **elated** with this turn of events

C -   Orson also picked on a boy named Mark **Meticulous**, a perfectionist who always rewrote his papers many times. These two, of course, were not **elated** with this turn of events.

90. warrant   scoffed

No Paragraph then ¶ – same topic; new speaker

Types of Sentences – complex; simple

Commas – interrupter; quote

Other Skills – pronouns unclear—need noun; keep in past tense; CVC = double 2ⁿᵈ consonant when adding suffix; use of subjunctive ("as if they were"); never use "that" to refer to people; "ie" spell rule and n**ei**ghbor and w**ei**gh are w**ei**rd; sit (intransitive) vs. set (transitive); contraction

B - they to be sure prefer it when orson odious had ignored them as if they werent there. weirdos that set on people dont **warrant** my attention orson **scoffed**

C - Beth Bibliophilic and Mark Meticulous, to be sure, preferred it when Orson Odious had ignored them as if they weren't there.

"Weirdos who sit on people don't **warrant** my attention," Orson **scoffed**.

NOTE: Tell students that, in one place, the word "they" needs to be changed to two nouns.

---

91. retorted   daunt   mutual nurturing

2 Paragraphs – new speakers (2ⁿᵈ is narrator)

Types of Sentences – simple; simple

Commas – quote; appositive; 2 intro prep. phrases

Homophones – their/there/they're; to/too/two

Other Skills – never use "that" to refer to people; CVC = double last consonant when adding a suffix (expelled); who (subject) vs. whom (object); parallel construction (in...in); use dash for elaboration

 B - bullies that taunt my friends deserve to be expelled **retorted** isabelle ingenuous the free spirit who even dean dread did not **daunt**. then in art and music ms amicable artist and mr melodious music joined there classes too present a **mutual** art/music project **nurturing** and releasing butterflies

C -   "Bullies who taunt my friends deserve to be expelled," **retorted** Isabelle Ingenuous, the free spirit whom even Dean Dread did not **daunt**.

Then in art and in music, Ms. Amicable Artist and Mr. Melodious Music joined their classes to present a **mutual** art/music project—**nurturing** and releasing butterflies.

NOTE: Your students have heard the word "pronoun" many times in previous Caught'yas. They may be ready to learn the seven different kinds of pronouns. If they can learn these (especially the subject, object, and possessive pronouns), they will have a better chance to use them and spell them ("its" in particular) correctly. See "Pronouns" in the *Grammar, Usage, and Mechanics Guide*.

92. widespread   species

Paragraph – new speaker

Types of Sentences – compound; simple (compound verb)

Commas – compound sen.; quote

Homophones – your/you're

Other Skills – irregular verbs rise (no object) vs. raise (takes object); plural of nouns ending in "y"; compound word (widespread); abbreviation

B - we have ordered youre kits and you will rise painted lady butterflies said ms amicable artist. painted lady butterflies are probably the most **widespread** butterfly **species** and are found all over the world she said

C - "We have ordered your kits, and you will raise Painted Lady butterflies," said Ms. Amicable Artist. "Painted Lady butterflies are probably the most **widespread** butterfly **species** and are found all over the world," she said.

NOTE: This is a good place for a review of transitive vs. intransitive verbs. You might want to review the most often confused ones: lie/lay; rise/raise; sit/set, etc. It is also a good place for a final review of "your" vs. "you're."

Writing Idea #18: Descriptive Writing.
Find a picture of a Painted Lady butterfly or some other species of butterfly you think is pretty. Write a vivid verb description of that butterfly. Then write a story about that butterfly if it were real and you found it always hovered near you for some reason as if it liked only you. Include your description of the butterfly in your story. Try to fit your description into the action of your story.

NOTE: Since it has so many words ending in an "s," this is an appropriate Caught'ya to play with plurals and possessives again in order to make students think twice before using an apostrophe. I have put in extraneous apostrophes. Take them out if you think this is too much for your students.

93. habitat

No Paragraph – continuation

Types of Sentences – compound; compound/complex

Punctuation – use colon in a long list but never after a verb

Commas – compound sen.; noun list; sub. clause at beginning; quote; quote and compound/complex sen.

Homophones – their/there/they're

Other Skills – demonstrative pronouns

B - they particularly like living in mountain's and flowery meadow's and they love the following flower's aster cosmos' thistle and buttonbush. after we release the butterflie's on earth day art student's will paint an appropriate **habitat** with there butterfly in it she lectured and music students' will compose a short tune

C - "They particularly like living in mountains and flowery meadows, and they love the following flowers: aster, cosmos, thistle, and buttonbush. After we release the butterflies on Earth Day, art students will paint an appropriate **habitat** with their butterfly in it," she lectured, "and music students will compose a short tune."

94. larvae   chrysalis   metamorphosis

Paragraph – new speaker

Types of Sentences – simple

Punctuation – ( ) around speaker aside

Commas – transition; quote

Other Skills – rise (no object) vs. raise (takes object); antecedent/ pronoun agreement ("each student" is singular and needs a sing. pronoun); abbreviation; use "an" before a vowel

B - each student will rise their own butterfly from an caterpillar which is the **larvae** to the **chrysalis** in which the caterpillar **metamorphosis** will occur and finally into a painted lady butterfly mr melodious music concluded

C - "Each student will raise his or her own butterfly from a caterpillar (which is the **larvae**) to the **chrysalis** (in which the caterpillar **metamorphosis** will occur) and, finally, into a Painted Lady butterfly," Mr. Melodious Music concluded.

95. stupendous exhilaration oozed	**B -** this will be **stupendous** felicia fey informed her pals. than in her **exhilaration** she accidentally waved her hands the wrong way enacting a spell and a white maggot **oozed** out of sams left ear
Paragraph – new speaker	
Types of Sentences – simple; compound	
Punctuation – ( ) around narrator aside	**C -** "This will be **stupendous**," Felicia Fey informed her pals. Then, in her **exhilaration**, she accidentally waved her hands the wrong way, enacting a spell, and a white maggot **oozed** out of Sam's left ear.
Commas – quote; intro adverb (optional); 2 intro adverbs; participial phrase; compound sen.	
Homophones – its/it's	
Other Skills – then (adverb) vs. than (comparative); sing. poss.	
Literary Devices – vivid verbs	

96. shrilled	**B -** eewww thats gross felicia **shrilled** isabelle and pauline in unison. sam sagacious and the other boys collected the discusting maggot felicias spell had produced and admired its properties
2 Paragraphs – new speakers	
Types of Sentences – simple (compound subject); simple (compound subject and verb)	
Commas – interjection; direct address; quote.	**C -** "EEWWW, that's gross, Felicia," **shrilled** Isabelle and Pauline in unison.
Homophones – its/it's	Sam Sagacious and the other boys collected the disgusting maggot Felicia's spell had produced and admired its properties.
Other Skills – use caps to denote yelling; contraction; plural rule with nouns ending in "y"; spelling of "disgusting;" sing. poss.	

Writing Idea #19: Expository/Explanatory Essay.

Think of something that completely "grossed you out." Think of two to three reasons why this disgusted you. Now write an essay to explain why you were "grossed out." Be sure to include the event in your first paragraph. You may make up something if you can't think of a real event.

97. concur No Paragraph – continuation Types of Sentences – simple; simple; simple Punctuation – use **?**; **?** and **!** go outside **"** if a word or phrase only Homophones – their/there/they're; double meaning of present (noun and verb) Other Skills – CVC = double 2nd consonant when add suffix; sing. poss.; contraction Literary Devices – word irony (present)	**B -** they ploted to leave it on some unsuspecting teachers desk. which teacher deserved their present. they couldnt **concur** **C -** They plotted to leave it on some unsuspecting teacher's desk. Which teacher deserved their "present"? They couldn't **concur**.
98. adamant retched animated 2 Paragraphs – new speakers Types of Sentences – compound; compound; simple quote Commas – compound sen.; quote; compound sen.; direct address; quote; extra info in a participial phrase Homophones – their/there/they're; to/too/two Other Skills – go over possessive pronouns; write out numbers; plural rule with noun ending in "y"; contraction; rise vs. raise (takes object)	**B -** it came out of my ear so i get to decide insisted an **adamant** sam the three girls almost **retched** in disgust but they quickly turned there thoughts too butterflies. oh you guys i cant wait until the caterpillars arrive said isabelle her face **animated** by the thought of raising a butterfly **C -** "It came out of my ear, so I get to decide," insisted an **adamant** Sam. The three girls almost **retched** in disgust, but they quickly turned their thoughts to butterflies. "Oh, you guys, I can't wait until the caterpillars arrive," said Isabelle, her face **animated** by the thought of raising a butterfly.

99. problematical horrendous 2 Paragraphs – new time; new speaker Types of Sentences – compound; simple Commas – intro adverb (optional); 2 intro adverbs; compound sen.; intro word; direct address; quote	**B -** then on a day that had been particularly **problematical** the group arrived in art and music and they breathed a sigh of relief. boy pauline this has been a **horrendous** day said isabelle ingenuous **C -** Then, on a day that had been particularly **problematical**, the group arrived in art and music, and they breathed a sigh of relief. "Boy, Pauline, this has been a **horrendous** day," said Isabelle Ingenuous.

**100. spectacles   puckishly
      stripling   barbs**
 	
2 Paragraphs – new speakers
 	
Types of Sentences – complex; compound; simple
 	
Commas – interjection; compound sen.; quote; direct address; quote
 	
Other Skills – keep in past tense; elaboration; CVC = double 2nd consonant when adding suffix (nodded); vocab lesson
	B - pauline puerile just nods in agreement as she didnt trust herself not to cry. yeah orson odious forgot his truce and he insulted sam about his **spectacles** groaned jesse jocose. we must make up a limerick about him william he grined **puckishly**
	
	C - Pauline Puerile just nodded in agreement as she didn't trust herself not to cry.
	    "Yeah, Orson Odious forgot his truce, and he insulted Sam about his **spectacles**," groaned Jesse Jocose. "We must make up a limerick about him, William," he grinned **puckishly**.
	
	A nasty young **stripling** from Toast
	                    (North Carolina)
	Was meaner and crueler than most.
	His **barbs** were so cruel
	That we hated school
	Where he made his nastiest boasts.

101. doggerel

Paragraph – new topic

Types of Sentences – simple (compound subject); simple

Commas – unnecessary "who" clause; extra info

Homophones – their/there/they're

Other Skills – abbreviation; who (subject) vs. whom (object); CVC = double 2nd consonant when adding suffix

B - ms grammar grouch and mr math martinet whom were passing by the group just as jesse jocose recited his **doggerel** stoped dead in their tracks one foot raised as if to take another step. there eyelids fluttered wildly

C -   Ms. Grammar Grouch and Mr. Math Martinet, who were passing by the group just as Jesse Jocose recited his **doggerel**, stopped dead in their tracks, one foot raised as if to take another step. Their eyelids fluttered wildly.

Writing Idea #20: Summary and Prediction.
Write a summary of the story so far. Then write what you predict will happen.

---

102. protruded

No Paragraph – continuation

Types of Sentences – simple; compound; complex

Commas – participle

Homophones – their/there/they're

Literary Device – simile

B - there lips clamped shut but theyre tongues still **protruded** like pink taffy. wisps of smoke curled from there ears as they stood their unmoving

C - Their lips clamped shut with their tongues still **protruded** like pink taffy. Wisps of smoke curled from their ears as they stood there, unmoving.

NOTE: Tell students to be careful as all forms of their/there/they're are spelled wrong in this Caught'ya.

B – Sentences for the Board	C – Corrected version of the CY
103. manifesting gargoyles No Paragraph – same topic Types of Sentences – simple; compound Commas – participial phrase; 2 adj. Homophones – their/there/they're Other Skills – fewer (can count) vs. less (can't); write out #s; contraction; use of **;** in a compound sen. Literary Devices – simile	**B -** their they froze **manifesting** their bizarre behavior for less than 3 seconds. it wasnt a pretty sight they looked like ugly stone **gargoyles** **C -** There they froze, **manifesting** their bizarre behavior for fewer than three seconds. It wasn't a pretty sight; they looked like ugly, stone **gargoyles**!

NOTE: You might want to review the four reasons for using semicolons. See the *Grammar, Usage, and Mechanics Guide*.

**104. omnipresent   interlude
      proboscis**
 	
2 Paragraphs – new speakers (2nd is narrator)
 	
Types of Sentences – complex; simple
 	
Commas – quote; no **,** before A WHITE BUS word; intro adverb; 2 adj.
 	
Other Skills – do not split infinitives; use hyphen in 2 wds. acting as 1 adj.
 	
Literary Devices – simile; literary reference
	B - stranger and stranger murmured sam as he made a note in his **omnipresent** notebook. during the peculiar **interlude** william dared to gently touch mr math martinet on the tip of his large pinocchio like **proboscis**
	
	C - "Stranger and stranger," murmured Sam as he made a note in his **omnipresent** notebook.
	        During the peculiar **interlude**, William gently dared to touch Mr. Math Martinet on the tip of his large, Pinocchio-like **proboscis**.

105. latter untoward No Paragraph – continuation Types of Sentences – simple; complex	**B -** the **latter** did not even notice. william waggish quickly withdrew before both teachers resumed walking as if nothing **untoward** had occurred **C -** The **latter** did not even notice. William Waggish quickly withdrew before both teachers resumed walking as if nothing **untoward** had occurred.

106. regale   bellowed

2 Paragraphs – new topic; new speaker

Types of Sentences – complex; simple

Punctuation – use of **!** when shouting and for emphasis

Commas – sub. clause at beginning

Homophones – their/there/they're

Other Skills – comparatives; keep in past tense; review collective nouns (crew)

B - as william and jesse continued to **regale** the rest with their account of theyre horrendous day the crew sees a big box being delivered to the art room. caterpillars **bellowed** felicia fey in her loud voice

C -   As William and Jesse continued to **regale** the rest with their account of their horrendous day, the crew saw a big box being delivered to the art room!
        "Caterpillars!" **bellowed** Felicia Fey in her loudest voice.

Writing Idea #21: Narrative or Expressive Essay.

William and Jesse regaled their friends with the tale of their horrendous day. Have you ever had a day like that? Regale your teacher with a story about the worst day you ever had. You may include fiction.

---

107. articulated   awe   replica   tresses

Paragraph – new speaker

Types of Sentences – simple; compound/complex

Punctuation – use **!** for emphasis

Commas – intro phrase; compound sen.

Other Skills – fragment for emphasis; plural with nouns that end in "y"; CVC = double 2ⁿᵈ consonant when adding suffix

B - future butterflies **articulated** isabelle ingenuous with **awe** in her tone. as usual she wore a plastic **replica** of one in her auburn **tresses** and it bobed as she spoke

C -   "Future butterflies!" **articulated** Isabelle Ingenuous with **awe** in her tone. As usual, she wore a plastic **replica** of one in her auburn **tresses**, and it bobbed as she spoke.

108. oblivious barbs jabs 2 Paragraphs – new time; new action Types of Sentences – compound; simple Punctuation – use **!** for emphasis Commas – phrase list; intro adverb Homophones – past/passed Other Skills – sing. and plural poss.; antecedent/pronoun agreement (collective nouns are singular and need sing. pronouns) Literary Devices – personification of homework	**B -** the rest of the day past and the group remained **oblivious** to orsons verbal **barbs** and **jabs** their teachers love affair with homework and the usual battle to walk in the crowded halls with the bigger students. finally it was time for art and music **C -** The rest of the day passed, and the group remained **oblivious** to Orson's verbal **barbs** and **jabs**, the teachers' love affair with homework, and the usual battle to walk in the crowded halls with the bigger students. Finally, it was time for art and music!
109. crammed massive No Paragraph – same topic Types of Sentences – complex (compound subject); simple Commas – no comma before A WHITE BUS word; 2 adj. Homophones – their/there/they're Other Skills – abbreviation; spelling of "themselves"; fewer (can count) vs. less (can't); go over irregular verbs "sit" and "set" (takes object) Literary Devices – personification of box; vivid verbs	**B -** ms amicable artist and mr melodious music stood in the front of the art room as their students **crammed** theirselves into a room made for many less bodies. a **massive** opened box set on the front table **C -** Ms. Amicable Artist and Mr. Melodious Music stood in the front of the art room as their students **crammed** themselves into a room made for many fewer bodies. A **massive**, opened box sat on the front table.

110. approximately

Paragraph – new speaker

Types of Sentences – simple; compound

Commas – quote; compound sen.; extra info

Homophones – quiet/quite/quit; week/weak

Other Skills – this/that/these/those; hyphens in 3 words used as 1 and #s of 2 or more words; write out #s; plural of nouns ending in "y"

Literary Devices – building anticipation

B - these are the caterpillars said ms amicable artist in a quite voice. the caterpillar to butterfly life cycle is **approximately** twenty one days so 3 weeks from now on earth day we will release butterflies

C - "These are the caterpillars," said Ms. Amicable Artist in a quiet voice. "The caterpillar-to-butterfly life cycle is **approximately** twenty-one days, so three weeks from now, on Earth Day, we will release butterflies."

111. reproached

No Paragraph then 2 ¶s – same speaker; narrator; new speaker

Types of Sentences – simple; complex; simple

Commas – intro word (transition); direct address; quote

Other Skills – confusion of "choose" (present) with "chose" (past); re**cei**ve

B - she added first you will choose a partner. murmurs erupted from the students as they searched for partners. silence students you may choose partners after you recieve all the instructions ms amicable artist gently **reproached** the kids

C - She added, "First, you will choose a partner."
     Murmurs erupted from the students as they searched for partners.
     "Silence, students, you may choose partners after you receive all the instructions," Ms. Amicable Artist gently **reproached** the kids.

Writing Idea #22: Dialogue/Conversation.

Listen in class or in the lunchroom to your peers and your teachers. Write down conversations, and show your notes to your English teacher. Then, write out a dialogue or a conversation you overheard. It will not be exact as you couldn't possibly write down everything you heard. You know the gist of the conversation. Make up the exact words. Be sure to indent with each new speaker no matter how short the quote.

112. discourse

No Paragraph then ¶ – same speaker; new speaker

Types of Sentences – complex; simple; simple

Punctuation – continued quote = no caps

Commas – transition; quote; 2 adj.; quote; participial phrase; continued quote

Homophones – pair/pare/pear

Other Skills – "ie" spell rule; this/that/these/those; write out #s; sing. poss.

B - next each pear of you will recieve one of these cups she continued as mr melodious music held up several small covered cups in his hand. mr melodious music continued ms amicable artists **discourse**. each one of these he said indicating the covered cups contains 4 to 5 caterpillars

C - "Next, each pair of you will receive one of these cups," she continued as Mr. Melodious Music held up several small, covered cups in his hand.

　　Mr. Melodious Music continued Ms. Amicable Artist's **discourse**. "Each one of these," he said, indicating the covered cups, "contains four to five caterpillars.

NOTE: End quote is not needed since next CY continues his speech in the same paragraph.

113. metamorphose chrysalises No Paragraph – same speaker Types of Sentences – complex; simple; simple (imperative) Commas – sub. clause at beginning; quote Homophones – pair/pare/pear; their/there/they're Other Skills – between/among = 2 vs. 3 or more; write out #s; no " because quote is continued from last CY; spell rule—add "es" after "s"	**B -** because not all of the caterpillars will live each pear of students will have among 3 to 5 butterflies to release. the caterpillar cup has all the food the caterpillars need to **metamorphose**. finally keep the lid on the cup until the caterpillars form theyr **chrysalises** he warned the students **C -** Because not all of the caterpillars will live, each pair of students will have between three to five butterflies to release. The caterpillar cup has all the food the caterpillars need to **metamorphose**. Finally, keep the lid on the cup until the caterpillars form their **chrysalises**," he warned the students.
114. marveled No Paragraph then ¶ – conclusion of ¶; new speaker Types of Sentences – simple; simple Commas – quote; quote Other Skills – gerund as subject; do not split verb; write out numbers; who (subject) vs. whom (object); plural of nouns ending in "y"	**B -** completing the chrysalis will only take about ten days he concluded. awesome **marveled** isabelle ingenuous whom adored butterflies **C -** "Completing the chrysalis will take only about ten days," he concluded. "Awesome," **marveled** Isabelle Ingenuous who adored butterflies.

115. *caveat* **refrain**

Paragraph – new topic (the warning)

Types of Sentences – complex; compound with **;**

Commas – quote; intro adverb (optional)

Homophones – your/you're

Other Skills – abbreviation; use *italics* for Latin words; do not split infinitives; use of **;** in compound sen.

B - ms amicable artist resumed the lecture with a ***caveat*** handle your cups as little and as gently as possible so that you do not disturb the caterpillars. occasionally you may open the lid to peer inside carefully but **refrain** from touching the caterpillars it will stop them from changing

C - Ms. Amicable Artist resumed the lecture with a ***caveat***. "Handle your cups as little and as gently as possible so that you do not disturb the caterpillars. Occasionally, you may open the lid to peer inside carefully, but **refrain** from touching the caterpillars; it will stop them from changing."

NOTE: You might want to give a final review of the four uses of the semicolon. See the *Grammar, Usage, and Mechanics Guide*.

116. reigned mesmerized clamor

Paragraph – new topic

Types of Sentences – complex; compound

Commas – sub. clause at beginning; intro adverb (optional); compound sen.

Homophones –their/there/they're; its/it's

Other Skills – write out numbers to 120; review cardinal and ordinal numbers; re**i**gned ("ei" before "gn" as in "foreign"); antecedent/pronoun agreement (review collective nouns); hyphen between 2 wds. acting as 1

B - even though there were 60 6th graders in the overcrowded room, silence **reigned**. suddenly one student coughed and the **mesmerized** crowd resumed their usual **clamor**

C - Even though there were sixty sixth-graders in the overcrowded room, silence **reigned**. Suddenly, one student coughed, and the **mesmerized** crowd resumed its usual **clamor**.

Writing Idea #23: Expository/Informational/Cause-and-Effect Essay.

What do you think causes a learning unit to be exciting? Think of a unit one of your teachers conducted that you liked. It can be in any subject. Now write an essay to explain why you think this unit appealed to you.

---

117. puled   petulant   querulous   peevishly

2 Paragraphs – 2 speakers

Types of Sentences – simple; simple; simple

Punctuation – use of **!** to denote tone of voice; use **?** inside **"** in a full quote

Homophones – week/weak

Other Skills – contractions; write out #s; sing. poss.; don't split verbs

Literary Devices – alliteration; vivid verbs; vocab lesson

B - i cant wait 3 weeks **puled** pauline puerile in a **petulant** tone. a boy named quincy **querulous** echoed paulines whine. why cant we speed up the things he asked **peevishly**

C -   "I can't wait three weeks!" **puled** Pauline Puerile in a **petulant** tone.

A boy named Quincy **Querulous** echoed Pauline's whine. "Why can't we speed up the things?" he asked **peevishly**.

---

118. mollified

2 Paragraphs – new speakers (2nd is narrator)

Types of Sentences – simple; simple; simple

Commas – quote; intro adverb; participial phrase

Homophones – its/it's; pair/pare/pear

Other Skills – write out numbers; antecedent/pronoun agreement (review collective noun "pair"); keep in past tense; spell rule—add "es" after "s"

Literary Devices – personification of nature; repetition of sen. for effect

B - nature takes its own time **mollified** sam sagacious. nature did take its own time. in 3 weeks each pear of students opens their box revealing several chrysalises on the sides and little green balls on the bottom

C -   "Nature takes its own time," **mollified** Sam Sagacious.

Nature did take its own time. In three weeks, each pair of students opened a box, revealing several chrysalises on the sides and little green balls on the bottom.

---

119. querulous   peers   adept

2 Paragraphs – new speakers

Types of Sentences – simple; simple (really) run-on (make several sen.)

Punctuation – use of **!** for effect; ( ) around narrator aside

Commas – no **,** before "green" (color); direct address; quote

Homophones – their/there/they're

Other Skills – use of caps for emphasis; who (subject) vs. whom (object); do not split verbs

B - eewww what are those little green balls asked pauline puerile who was totally grossed out. there caterpillar poop you dummy piped up quincy **querulous** who had actually done his homework and he liked to insult his **peers** almost as much as orson odious but wasn't as **adept** at it

C -   "EEWWW! What are those little green balls?" asked Pauline Puerile who was totally grossed out.

"They are caterpillar poop, you dummy," piped up Quincy **Querulous** who actually had done his homework. (He liked to insult his **peers** almost as much as Orson Odious but wasn't as **adept** at it.)

NOTE: Take a day or two break from the Caught'yas (it's the end of the year anyway) and read the following to your students several times. Write on the board, go over, require students to put them in their vocabulary notebooks, and play with any vocabulary in the passage. I did not want to cut the story short, but it is too long to fit into 125 Caught'yas, two sentences at a time. The following, read out loud, will continue the story up to the last six Caught'yas and the final exam.

Passage to be read out loud to students

After the teachers sent Quincy Querulous out of the room for his **insensitive** remark, the rest of the class **warily** removed the small pieces of paper to which the chrysalis had **adhered**. They then taped them to the inside wall of one of the butterfly **abodes** that the art class had constructed. They also placed twigs inside the abode. Pauline Puerile, of course, dropped a chrysalis and cried with **consternation**.

In science, Orson Odious, who took P.E. instead of art or music, yanked the plastic butterfly from Isabelle's hair, put it in his **unruly**, uncombed mop, flapped his arms, and pretended to fly around the room like a butterfly to make fun of the students who were excited about the project. In reality, the **obnoxious** pest was jealous.

In art, each student drew a picture of his or her chrysalis, and in music, they played a **pastoral** piece with a **lilting** melody that gave the airy feeling of a butterfly in flight. Even Olivia Otiose practiced her part **assiduously** and played it beautifully. Everyone was anxious for the final metamorphosis to take place.

A little more than a week later, William Waggish arrived in art. To his amazement, he spied lovely Painted Lady butterflies in the butterfly **abode**. They clung to the side. Their wings looked as if they had been painted with black, brown, and orange paint with spots of white, red, and blue thrown in. They were lovely! They perched on the twigs and pumped their **frangible** wings to unfurl them.

"Oh, look, guys," William Waggish gleefully **whooped** to his classmates, "the butterflies are emerging!"

As the class supplied the newly formed insects with food (sugar water), they impatiently waited for Earth Day which was two days **hence**, at the end of April.

120. balmy

Paragraph – new time

Types of Sentences – simple; simple; compound

Commas – extra information about class; compound sen.

Homophones – their/there/they're

Other Skills – hyphen in 2 wds. acting as 1 adj; use "that" to refer to things

B - finally earth day arrived. the entire sixth grade class orson odious included gathered around the butterfly houses that were on tables in the middle of the P.E. field. the weather was **balmy** and there was a slight breeze

C - Finally Earth Day arrived. The entire sixth-grade class, Orson Odious included, gathered around the butterfly houses that were on tables in the middle of the P.E. field. The weather was **balmy**, and there was a slight breeze.

Writing Idea #24: Expository/Explanatory/Expressive Essay.

What is your favorite holiday? Think of why this holiday is your favorite. Now write an essay to explain to your reader the reasons why you like this holiday so much.

---

121. aggressive   banished

Paragraph – new topic

Types of Sentences – compound/complex

Commas – compound sen.; unnecessary "who" clause (adjective)

Homophones – their/there/they're

Other Skills – collective noun (crowd); abbreviation; who (subject) vs. whom (object); plural rules with nouns ending in "y"; further vs. farther (distance)

B - orson odious pushed and pinched his way to the front of the crowd and ms amicable artist whom did not feel amicable towards **aggressive** bullies **banished** him farther back because dean dread was their

C - Orson Odious pushed and pinched his way to the front of the crowd, and Ms. Amicable Artist, who did not feel amicable towards **aggressive** bullies, **banished** him farther back because Dean Dread was there.

122. vicarious	**B -** she then asked isabelle and william to come forward. pauline whined in disappointment and felicia danced in a circle of **vicarious** joy for her friends. too brown moths flew out of ms grammar grouchs hare
Paragraph – new action	
Types of Sentences – simple; compound; simple	
Commas – compound sen.	
Homophones – to/too/two; hair/hare	**C -** Ms. Amicable Artist then asked Isabelle and William to come forward. Pauline whined in disappointment, and Felicia danced in a circle of **vicarious** joy for her friends. Two brown moths flew out of Ms. Grammar Grouch's hair.
Other Skills – pronoun unclear (need noun); abbreviation; then vs. than; sing. poss.	

123. flabbergasted diligent	**B -** mr melodious music called upon sam sagacious and much to her surprise a **flabbergasted** olivia otiose. you sam are a talented and **diligent** student he said
Paragraph – new person and speaker	
Types of Sentences – simple; simple	
Commas – narrator aside; direct address; quote	**C -** Mr. Melodious Music called upon Sam Sagacious and, much to her surprise, a **flabbergasted** Olivia Otiose. "You, Sam, are a talented and **diligent** student," he said.
Other Skills – abbreviation	

124. noxious   deem   abodes

2 Paragraphs – new speakers (1ˢᵗ is narrator)

Types of Sentences – simple; complex

Commas – direct address; always surround "too" with **,** if it means "also"; quote; no **,** before A WHITE BUS word

Homophones – to/too/two

Other Skills – abbreviation

B - orson odious made **noxious** faces from the last row of students. you olivia otiose have improved so much that i **deem** that you too deserve this honor mr melodious music stated as he beckoned with his finger for the too students too come up close too the butterfly **abodes**

C -   Orson Odious made **noxious** faces from the last row of students.
    "You, Olivia Otiose, have improved so much that I **deem** that you, too, deserve this honor," Mr. Melodious Music stated as he beckoned with his finger for the two students to come up close to the butterfly **abodes**.

**125. simultaneously   unison
       hues   dispersed   diverse**

Paragraph – new action

Types of Sentences – simple (compound subject); complex

Punctuation – **,** and **.** always go inside **"**

Commas – intro adverb; 2 intro prep. phrases; noun list; quote; quote; sub. clause at beginning; adj. list

Other Skills – write out #

Literary Devices – metaphor (cloud of...); description within action; vocab lesson

B - then at a nod from the two teachers isabelle william sam and olivia **simultaneously** lifted the lid to a butterfly abode. as the crowd gasped ahhh in **unison** a fluttering cloud of brown black and orange **hues** rose from the boxes and **dispersed** in **diverse** directions

C -   Then, at a nod from the two teachers, Isabelle, William, Sam, and Olivia **simultaneously** lifted the lid to a butterfly abode. As the crowd gasped, "Ahhh," in **unison**, a fluttering cloud of brown, black, and orange **hues** rose from the boxes and **dispersed** in **diverse** directions.

Writing Idea #25: Summary.

Now that the sixth-grade part of the Caught'ya story of the bizarre school is almost complete, write a summary of it. Then write a paragraph predicting where you think the story will go from here.

NOTE: Now you have finished the daily Caught'yas for the year. If you have more time and wish to do more Caught'yas, you can put the following passage into Caught'ya form and use as many as you need (up to the ones in the final exam) to complete the year.

If, on the other hand, your students have "had it" or you have run out of time, take a day or two before the final exam and read the following to your students several times.

Write on the board, go over, require students to put them in their vocabulary notebooks, and play with any vocabulary in the passage. The following section, however you choose to address these extra sentences, will continue the story up to the final exam.

Passage to be read out loud to students

Orson Odious tried to catch one to crush it; thankfully, he failed. As the cloud of butterflies rose into the air and **dispersed** with the breeze, the sixth-graders craned their necks to watch their departure. This had been a truly **prodigious** experience for the **majority** of the sixth-graders. Even Orson Odious was impressed although he did not admit it.

The last six weeks of school sped by with **alacrity**. The band concert went well, and although she earned her usual "Ds" and "Fs" in the majority of her classes, Olivia Otiose and her clarinet wowed the audience. Sam Sagacious aced all the exams with ease, and Isabelle Ingenuous earned all "As" and "Bs" except for a "C" in math, the **bane** of her existence (besides Orson Odious). Her drawing of her butterfly astounded all at the **annual** art show. William Waggish and his new friend, Jesse Jocose, continued to compose **outlandish** limericks. Felicia Fey only let fly a few **inappropriate** spells that had minor, **insignificant** results, usually involving Ms. Grammar Grouch. Pauline Puerile still cried when frustrated, but even she **ameliorated** her grades. Thus, their sixth-grade year drew to a close.

One gorgeous morning at the end of May, the sextet **strolled** to school. They were unusually early. (Olivia Otiose, who had spent the night at Isabelle's house, actually was on time!) They reached the parking lot at the school just as the custodian, Mr. **Adept** Fixit, got out of his blue pick-up truck. Mr. Adept Fixit waved at the group of friends, grabbed a strange-looking tool from his truck, and **scurried** into the building. He had an **apprehensive** look on his face.

Caught'ya Final Exam follows on next page.

Remember, you can adapt the test to fit the needs of your students and then print copies from the CD included with this book.

Caught'ya Final Exam

Directions for Part 1:

Students, correct the following long Caught'ya. This test will show how carefully you listen when your teacher goes over Caught'yas. You will lose two points per error, so check your work. Ask your teacher for meanings of words if necessary. This is not a vocabulary test. Follow your teacher's directions, and read the test again to yourself to help with punctuation.

Hint: There are ten paragraphs. All periods are correct except one that needs to be changed to a question mark. Only change that one. There are spelling errors and three missing hyphens. Some words need to be changed.

the friends watched in amazement as mr adept fixit **bustled** from room to room with only 1 tool. as he exits each room the lights went on quickly and the blinds rose. from their **vantage** point on the sidewalk the freinds could see good the outlines of their teachers in the rooms. where did they come from asked sam. i see less than 3 cars in the parking lot and the teachers arent moving too. this is a mystery to be solved next year when we are in the seventh grade said william in a rare serious tone. yes william i **concur** said sam. their are neither enough time or enough clues and i only want to think about my summer and the book the mystery of the terrible teachers he agreed. yeah said isabelle as she nodded her head in **assent** and her plastic butterfly bobbed **in accord**. i dont like this whined pauline. everyone else heaved their shoulders in **exasperation**. was pauline going to grow up and was she ever going too stop her sniveling. i think i will wear all black next year in the seventh grade announced felicia that had not produced a single successful spell the entire sixth grade year. the freinds except sam of course promptly forgot about their strange teachers and concentrate on the end of year activities and there summer plans. on the last day of school (after all the students had left all was silent except for muffled sounds from the art and music rooms and the clack of computer keys in the main office

Directions for Part 2:

Use your corrected version to the test to identify the types of sentences of each of the fifteen sentences in this exam—simple, compound, complex, or compound/complex.

Hint: Seven of them are simple sentences. Three are compound. Three are complex, and two are compound/complex.

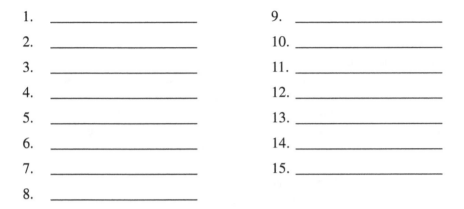

1. _____
2. _____
3. _____
4. _____
5. _____
6. _____
7. _____
8. _____

9. _____
10. _____
11. _____
12. _____
13. _____
14. _____
15. _____

Directions for Part 3:

As clearly as you can, write a paragraph or two explaining what you think is the answer to the mystery of Horribly Hard Middle School. Be sure to support your theory. Include a topic sentence and a concluding sentence for each paragraph. Use transitions and similes. Vary sentence structure. Most importantly, put passion and flair into your answer.

Caught'ya Final Exam KEY

Part 1:

The friends watched in amazement as Mr. Adept Fixit **bustled** from room to room with only one tool. As he exited each room, the lights went on quickly, and the blinds rose. From their **vantage** point on the sidewalk, the friends could see well the outlines of their teachers in the rooms.

"Where did they come from?" asked Sam. I see fewer than three cars in the parking lot, and the teachers aren't moving, too."

"This is a mystery to be solved next year when we are in the seventh grade," said William in a rare serious tone.

"Yes, William, I **concur**," said Sam. "There are neither enough time nor enough clues, and I only want to think about my summer and the book <u>The Mystery of the Terrible Teachers</u>," he agreed.

"Yeah," said Isabelle as she nodded her head in **assent**, and her plastic butterfly bobbed **in accord**.

"I don't like this," whined Pauline.

Everyone else heaved his or her shoulders in **exasperation**. Was Pauline going to grow up, and was she ever going to stop her sniveling?

"I think I will wear all black next year in the seventh grade," announced Felicia who had not produced a single successful spell the entire sixth-grade year.

The friends, except Sam, of course, promptly forgot about their strange teachers and concentrated on the end-of-year activities and their summer plans.

On the last day of school (after all the students had left), all was silent except for muffled sounds from the art and music rooms and the "clack" of computer keys in the main office.

Part 2:

1. complex
2. compound/complex
3. simple
4. simple
5. compound
6. complex
7. simple
8. compound
9. compound/complex
10. simple
11. simple
12. compound
13. simple (despite its length)
14. simple (no subject)
15. complex

CHAPTER 7

125 Caught'yas for Seventh Grade

Introduction to the Seventh-Grade Story
125 Caught'ya Sentences for Grade Seven

→ Almost Midterm Caught'ya Test and Key
→ Caught'ya Final Exam and Key
→ Twenty-Five Ideas for Writing Assignments

The first section of the story is to be read aloud to your students to set the scene for the Caught'ya story that follows. You might want to read this section more than once in order to place the characters' names and the setting firmly in your students' minds. A copy of the entire uninterrupted story can be found in **Chapter 5**. You may wish to print out a copy or two of the sixth- and seventh-grade part of the story to have in your classroom for any student who joins the class later in the year.

If the sixth-grade English teachers in your school are not using this book, you will need to read the sixth-grade part of the story to your students in order to keep them abreast of what happened to our intrepid heroes and heroines in the sixth grade.

After the introduction, you will find 125 Caught'yas. Each Caught'ya consists of two to four sentences of the story, a vocabulary word or five, and a plethora of errors. There is a suggested writing assignment every five Caught'yas or so. A midterm and a final exam have been included in the middle and at the end of the Caught'yas. Finally, there are sections where you will be instructed to read a page or two to the class to give your students a break and to expand the story.

A review of the vocabulary, particularly those used in the names, certainly can't hurt since many of the words are used in earlier parts of the story. You will find that the vocabulary words used in the Caught'yas that follow are listed (by Caught'ya number) in **Chapter 4** of this book.

Please note that words in bold type are vocabulary words that may be repeated in the subsequent Caught'yas. It is a good idea to go over their meanings and to use them daily so that your students will retain their meanings and become comfortable with them.

Introduction to the Seventh-Grade Story

As the August morning sun chased the shadows from the roofs of houses and painted the sky gold, once again there was an **eerie** silence at Horribly Hard Middle School. In the dawning light, you could not see into the classrooms because of the light-blocking curtains at every window. No early teacher rushed out of a car in the parking lot to set up a lab or to get an early start on preparation for the first day of school. Horribly Hard Middle School was like a spooky mansion: closed, dark, and abandoned.

In contrast, across town, as the sun rose a bit higher in the sky, Marvelously Magic Magnet Middle School (known popularly as MMMMS) burst with energy and noise. Coffee perked in the teachers' lounge. Cars roared into the parking lot, parked, and spilled out teachers of different sizes, shapes, and complexions. Boxes, books, bags, and piles of "stuff" filled their arms as they walked into the school early to be ready for the first day of classes for the year.

Finally, three cars drove up to the **dormant** and silent Horribly Hard Middle School—a new mauve Lexus sedan, an old blue Ford pick-up truck, and an old, battered, tan Subaru station wagon that had seen better days. A middle-aged man, Mr. **Punctilious** Principal, stepped out of the Lexus. Another middle-aged man, the custodian, Mr. **Adept** Fixit, exited the blue pick-up.

The man who exited the Lexus wore a suit and tie, and carried a battered briefcase. The owner of the Ford climbed out of his pick-up, walked to the back, and lifted a tool chest from the bed of his truck. He **sported** a denim shirt and overalls, a red handkerchief in his upper pocket, a wrench that hung out of his lower pocket, and a purposeful air.

The door of the Subaru creaked open and out fell construction paper and magazines, followed by a **harried**-looking woman. She was dressed in a long, loose pink dress with a pink flower in her thick blonde hair and a **myriad** of new paint brushes in her mouth. The two men nodded solemnly to each other and smiled at the woman as she gathered the stuff that had fallen from her car.

The men **trekked** in different directions, the suited one toward the school office and the man in overalls toward the custodian's office. The woman gathered her materials from the pavement and **ambled** slowly to a building set slightly off from the main part of the school. No other human soul could be seen in the dim light of early morning.

Slowly, one after the other, classroom lights came on in HHMS. Soon the school was **ablaze**, and all classrooms were lit, but apart from Mr. **Adept** Fixit, the custodian, rushing from room to room to open the doors and turn on the lights, no sounds of people could be heard on the campus. This was the first day of school?

If you listened carefully in the main office near the door to the principal's room, you could hear the faint click of computer keys as Mr. **Punctilious** Principal, a man who was always concerned with correct procedure, checked and rechecked the procedures which would be followed that first day of school as well as the list of students who would enter the **portals** of the HHMS in about an hour. If you **strolled** over to the art room, and listened very carefully, you could hear faint singing of an old Beatles tune and the rustling of paper.

Ten minutes later another car pulled up in front of the still silent Horribly Hard Middle School. A man in a **dapper** suit who was humming a Mozart sonata **ambled** toward a nearby dark classroom. He was burdened with various-sized instrument cases. He wore his favorite purple tie that was decorated with yellow musical notes. His tie was **askew**, and his glasses perched unevenly on his nose, ruining the effect of his handsome suit.

Before the man with the instrument cases could close the trunk of his car, a final **vehicle**, an ancient white Volvo sedan, **careened** into the lot and parked next to the **decrepit** tan Subaru. A pleasingly-plump middle-aged woman with curly grey hair jumped **animatedly** out of the Volvo and dashed up to the man who hummed the Mozart sonata.

She spoke briefly to him, gesturing with both hands. The man pointed to a building, nodded **genially** in farewell (since his arms were filled), turned around, shifted his burden of instrument cases, and walked in the opposite direction from where he had pointed.

The **stout** woman returned to her car, opened the trunk, and removed an obviously heavy box that was **brimful** with books. She heaved the box for better **leverage** and trudged slowly with her heavy burden in the direction the Mozart-humming man had indicated. The staff parking lot of Horribly Hard Middle School once again fell silent. Only five cars awaited their drivers.

On another side of the school, school busses arrived, one by one. Each **disgorged** a bunch of chattering students. Other students who had walked to school **ambled** slowly onto the school grounds to join the mobs being let off by the busses. Horribly Hard Middle School came alive with voices. A new school year was about to begin.

Meanwhile, in a house not far from Horribly Hard Middle School, a group of five **diverse** seventh-graders had gathered to gossip about the upcoming first day of school. They stood in the **foyer** of Isabelle **Ingenuous**'s house, waiting for Olivia **Otiose** whose **languid** (yet delightful) nature usually made her late to everything, even the first day of seventh grade.

B – Sentences for the Board	C – Corrected version of the CY
1. ingenuous animated excess puerile tardiness otiose Paragraph – new topic Types of Sentences – simple; simple Commas – participial phrase; list Verbs – use of strong verbs Other Skills – vocabulary; use "an" before a vowel Literary Devices – alliteration	**B -** isabelle **ingenuous** always **animated** twirled in nervousness and a **excess** of energy. pauline **puerile** whined in a babyish manner about the **tardiness** of olivia **otiose** about having to return to horribly hard middle school for another year and about the homework the teachers loved to pile on her **C -** Isabelle **Ingenuous**, always **animated**, twirled in nervousness and an **excess** of energy. Pauline **Puerile** whined in a babyish manner about the **tardiness** of Olivia **Otiose**, about having to return to Horribly Hard Middle School for another year, and about the homework the teachers loved to pile on her.

→ **Caution to teacher: Do not use the first definition of "fey" which is "to be fated to die soon." I used "fey" to mean "enchanted one" or "enchanter," meaning that Felicia has some magic powers.**

2. garbed fey awry Paragraph – new topic Types of Sentences – simple; simple; simple Commas – 2 "who" clauses Other Skills – who (subject) vs. whom (object); use "that" to describe objects Literary Devices – alliteration	**B -** another girl was **garbed** all in black. even her hair was dyed black. it was felicia **fey** who acted in a bizarre manner and whom was known for her spells that always went **awry** **C -** Another girl was **garbed** all in black. Even her hair was dyed black. It was Felicia **Fey**, who acted in a bizarre manner and who was known for her spells that always went **awry**.

B – Sentences for the Board	C – Corrected version of the CY
3. otiose ingenuous uttering No Paragraph – same topic Types of Sentences – simple; compound Commas – compound sen. Other Skills – singular possessive; "i" before "e" except after "c" spell rule Literary Devices – alliteration	**B -** felicia began to mutter words of a spell to encourage her friend olivia **otiose** to hurry. isabelle **ingenuous** put her hand over felicias mouth to stop her from **uttering** her spell and she warned her freind **C -** Felicia began to mutter words of a spell to encourage her friend Olivia **Otiose** to hurry. Isabelle **Ingenuous** put her hand over Felicia's mouth to stop her from **uttering** her spell, and she warned her friend.
4. putrid Paragraph – new person speaking Types of Sentences – simple; complex Punctuation – " around what is said out loud; **?** needed; . and , always go inside " Commas – direct address; quote; no **,** if second adj. is color, size, or linked to noun; no **,** if subordinate clause is at end; extra info Homophones – to/too/two; your/ you're; new/knew/gnu Other Skills – contraction Literary Devices – alliteration	**B -** you know it will backfire on you felicia warned isabelle ingenuous. you dont want to ruin youre new black hairdo or start the seventh grade with **putrid** purple streaks in your hair as you did in the sixth grade last year do you **C -** "You know it will backfire on you, Felicia," warned Isabelle Ingenuous. "You don't want to ruin your new black hairdo or start the seventh grade with **putrid** purple streaks in your hair as you did in the sixth grade last year, do you?"

5. waggish   lame   vapid

Paragraph – New topic

Types of Sentences – compound; simple

Commas – compound sen.; noun list

Homophones – their/there/they're

Other Skills – vocabulary; "i" before "e" except after "c," and ne**i**ghbor and we**i**gh are we**i**rd; "no one" is 2 words

Literary Devices – alliteration

B - william **waggish** made a tasteless but funny joke about girls and there wierd habits but no one listened. they were used to his **lame** limericks **vapid** jokes and strange sense of humor

C -   William **Waggish** made a tasteless but funny joke about girls and their weird habits, but no one listened. They were used to his **lame** limericks, **vapid** jokes, and strange sense of humor.

NOTE: My students never knew which form of "their/there/they're" I would use and got angry when I spelled it correctly. Mix them up so that your students have to think. I tell students that "their" must be followed by something that is owned; you can substitute "here" for "there;" and forbid the use of "they're" (or "it's") in the classroom for the year.

Writing Idea #1: Expository Essay in a Friendly Letter.
Write to your English teacher to introduce him or her to a few of your closest friends. Be sure to include personality traits that make each one unique. Explain why you like to hang around with these friends.

NOTE: All the nine comma rules, except those in a letter, will be included in the first twenty Caught'yas. To this end, you might want to point out the correct use of commas in the friendly letter.

When you teach the headings of a letter in order for your students to be able to complete Writing Assignment #1, you might want to make certain that your students understand how to write the postal code for your state and the states where they have relatives. (Florida, for example, is FL.) You can find a list in the *Grammar, Usage, and Mechanics Guide*.

B – Sentences for the Board	C – Corrected version of the CY

6. sagacious   clamor   erudite

No Paragraph (same topic)

Types of Sentences – simple (compound verb); compound

Commas – appositive (extra info about a noun); participial phrase; appositive; appositive; compound sen.

Homophones – die/dye; by/bye

Other Skills – "an" before a vowel; _____ or *italicize* titles of books, movies, newspapers; "no one" is 2 wds.; "ie" spell rule

Literary Devices – literary reference; alliteration

B - the last member of the troop sam **sagacious** simply stood wisely and silently waiting for the **clamor** to die down. a **erudite** young man sam held a book in his hand the count of monte cristo by alexander dumas and he read as he waited

C - The last member of the troop, Sam **Sagacious**, simply stood wisely and silently, waiting for the **clamor** to die down. An **erudite** young man, Sam held a book in his hand, <u>The Count of Monte Cristo</u> by Alexander Dumas, and he read as he waited.

7. waggish   regaled   aspiration   eloquent   articulate

Paragraph – new topic

Types of Sentences – compound/complex; compound

Punctuation – " around word said out loud; period at end of poem; hyphen in 2 wds. acting as one

Commas – subordinate clause at beginning; compound part of sen.; appositive; appositive (hero identified so unnecessary)

Homophones – no/know; knew/gnu/new; to/too/two

Other Skills – vocabulary; who (subject) vs. whom (object); use of colon (never after verb); capitalize first line of limericks; who's (who is) vs. whose

Literary Devices – alliteration; use of literary reference; simile (poem)

B - since his joke had fallen flat and no one had laughed william **waggish regaled** his freinds with a new limerick about girls whom wear black. brown faced with expressive dark pupils william composed mischievous poems to hide his real **aspiration** two be as **eloquent** and **articulate** a poet as his secret hero langston hughes

there once was a strange girl from mack
                              (Colorado)
who's hair and clothes were all black.
she looked like a crow,
and she should have said no
to trying a magical act

C -   Since his joke had fallen flat, and no one had laughed, William **Waggish regaled** his friends with a new limerick about girls who wear black. Brown-faced with expressive dark pupils, William composed mischievous poems to hide his real **aspiration**: to be as **eloquent** and **articulate** a poet as his secret hero, Langston Hughes.

There once was a strange girl from Mack
                              (Colorado)
Whose hair and clothes were all black.
She looked like a crow,
And she should have said "No"
To trying a magical act.

B – Sentences for the Board	C – Corrected version of the CY
8. sagacious fey deter Paragraph – new topic Types of Sentences – compound; compound Commas – 2 compound sentences Homophones – to/too/two Verbs – use of strong verbs; note active vs. passive voice Other Skills – contractions Literary Devices – alliteration	**B -** sam **sagacious** put his book in his backpack and he laughed. felicia **fey** threatened to zap william with a spell but that didnt **deter** him **C -** Sam **Sagacious** put his book in his backpack and laughed. Felicia **Fey** threatened to zap William with a spell, but that didn't **deter** him.
9. affront glowered No Paragraph – same topic (reaction to poem) Types of Sentences – compound/complex; simple; simple Commas – compound part of sen.; no comma before "because" since subordinate clause is at end; no comma before "Felicia" as appositive is necessary (which friend); verb list Homophones – to/too/two Other Skills – sing. poss.; contraction; then (adv.) vs. than (conjunc.)	**B -** isabelle ingenuous smiled at williams poem and the image of felicia as a crow but she dared not laugh because she didnt want too **affront** her friend felicia felicia **glowered** stuck out her tongue at william and than muttered something rude under her breath **C -** Isabelle Ingenuous smiled at William's poem and the image of Felicia as a crow, but she dared not laugh because she didn't want to **affront** her friend Felicia. Felicia **glowered**, stuck out her tongue at William, and then muttered something rude under her breath.

10. insipid Paragraph – new speaker Types of Sentences – simple question; simple question Punctuation – " around what is said out loud; . and , always go inside "; ? needed Commas – direct address; no , before "and" as not a compound sen. (no subject) Homophones – right/write/rite; for/four Verbs – accept vs. except Other Skills – contraction	**B -** william cant you write anything accept those **insipid** limericks she snapped. how about giving us a break and trying another form of poetry for a change **C -** "William, can't you write anything except those **insipid** limericks?" she snapped. "How about giving us a break and trying another form of poetry for a change?"

NOTE: After this point, the literary device of alliteration as used in the names of the characters will no longer be listed in the skills.

11. deftly ensued amicable **odious** Paragraph – new speaker Types of Sentences – simple; simple; compound Punctuation – " around what is said out loud; all , and . go inside "; abbreviation Commas – quote; compound sen.; quote Verbs – accept vs. except Other Skills – "an" before a vowel; contraction; hyphen between 2 wds. acting as one adj.; "ie" spell rule	**B -** isabelle ingenuous **deftly** changed the subject before a argument **ensued**. i dread going back to horribly hard middle school for another year she groaned. i dislike all the teachers except ms **amicable** artist and i dont want to be laughed at by orson **odious** and his stuck up freinds she concluded **C -** Isabelle Ingenuous **deftly** changed the subject before an argument **ensued**. "I dread going back to Horribly Hard Middle School for another year," she groaned. "I dislike all the teachers except Ms. **Amicable** Artist, and I don't want to be laughed at by Orson **Odious** and his stuck-up friends," she concluded.

Writing Idea #2: Personal Narrative.
Write about a time when you had to do something you dreaded. Be sure to explain what you dreaded, explain the reasons why you dreaded it, and tell the story of what happened. You may add elements of fiction if you wish to embellish your story.

---

12. concurred   fervor   queried

Paragraph – new speaker

Types of Sentences – compound; simple question; simple question

Punctuation – " around what is said out loud; . and , always go inside "; continued quote (no capital "B"); question marks

Commas – introductory word; direct address; quote; extra info

Verbs – affect (to influence) vs. effect (to cause)

Other Skills – contractions; further vs. farther (can be counted)

B - yes im with you isabelle **concurred** sam sagacious with **fervor** but we also need to curb william and his limericks. doesnt he know any other form of poetry. would other types of poetry have the same effect on the teachers he **queried** further always curious

C -   "Yes, I'm with you, Isabelle," **concurred** Sam Sagacious with **fervor**, "but we also need to curb William and his limericks. Doesn't he know any other form of poetry? Would other types of poetry have the same effect on the teachers?" he **queried** further, always curious.

13. otiose   chartreuse   abode

Paragraph – new topic

Types of Sentences – complex; simple; complex

Punctuation – " around what is said out loud; . and , always go inside "

Commas – interrupter; participial phrase; direct address; quote; quote; no , before "as" since subordinate clause after verb

Homophones – knew/new/gnu

Verbs – story in past tense so verb needs to be in past

Other Skills – use of transition; sing. poss.; capitalize the names of languages; "ie" spell rule

Literary Devices – use of foreign language for effect

B - finally olivia **otiose** arrives late as usual shrugging on her knew **chartreuse** backpack as she hurried up to the door of isabelles **abode**. hola amigos she said in spanish she had learned over the summer am i late she queried as she approached her friends

C -   Finally Olivia **Otiose** arrived, late as usual, shrugging on her new **chartreuse** backpack as she hurried up to the door of Isabelle's **abode**. "Hola, amigos," she said in Spanish she had learned over the summer, "Am I late?" she queried as she approached her friends.

NOTE: To teach the simple transitions to students, I found it very effective to sing them to a simple tune. I liked to use the song "She'll Be Coming 'Round the Mountain" and sing the following words:

> **Topic sentence, first, next, then,**
> **Finally and a conclusion.**
> **Topic sentence, first, next, then, finally-y**
> **And end with a conclusion.**

14. sniped   ineptitude

Paragraph – new speaker

Types of Sentences – simple question; complex

Punctuation – question marks; " around what is said out loud; . and , always go inside "

Commas – direct address; unnecessary "who" clause; no , before "as" since subordinate clause is after verb;

Other Skills – contraction; relative pronouns "who" (subject) vs. "whom" (object); sing. poss.

Literary Devices – sarcasm; use of strong verbs

B - arent you always olivia **sniped** felicia who still smarted from williams limerick about her magical **ineptitude**. are we ready to go face school for another year. she finished as she waltzed out the door and onto the sidewalk

C - "Aren't you always, Olivia?" **sniped** Felicia, who still smarted from William's limerick about her magical **ineptitude**. "Are we ready to go face school for another year?" she finished as she waltzed out the door and onto the sidewalk.

15. intrepid   abode   paucity   trekked

Paragraph – new action

Types of Sentences – complex; simple; simple

Commas – subordinate clause at beginning; no , before "as" since subordinate clause is at end

Homophones – their/there/they're

Other Skills – vocab.; compound word (backpack); "ie" spell rule; sing. poss.

B - as they slung there backpacks over their shoulders the **intrepid** freinds followed felicia out of isabelles **abode**. there was a **paucity** of talk as the group **trekked** the short walk to horribly hard middle school

C - As they slung their backpacks over their shoulders, the **intrepid** friends followed Felicia out of Isabelle's **abode**. There was a **paucity** of talk as the group **trekked** the short walk to Horribly Hard Middle School.

Writing Idea #3: Paragraph Writing.

Write a strong, vivid-verb paragraph using the topic sentence, "School is a drag." This paragraph must have a title, a topic sentence similar to the one given, five strong, vivid-verb sentences that explain why school is a drag, and a concluding sentence that may use a "dead" verb.

→ Teachers, see *Blowing Away the State Writing Assessment Test* (Kiester, 2000)

16. mutely

Paragraph – new place

Types of Sentences – simple; simple

Commas – 2 prepositional phrases at beginning of sen.

Homophones – their/there/they're; new/knew/gnu; to/too/two

Verbs – use of pluperfect

Other Skills – antecedent/pronoun agreement ("each" = one so can't use pl. poss. "their")

B - at the edge of the campus each wondered **mutely** what their new school year in the seventh grade would be like. all two soon they had reached there school

C -   At the edge of the campus, each wondered **mutely** what the new school year in the seventh grade would be like. All too soon, they had reached their school.

NOTE: I know this is early in the year, but it is important that your students learn the eight parts of speech. It is a good idea to put an acronym for the eight parts of speech somewhere on a wall in your classroom. I used NIPPAVAC or PAVPANIC.

The second week of school, I challenged my students to figure out the acronym.

Once the acronym is identified, you and your students can chant the parts of speech until you and they memorize them: Noun, Interjection, Preposition, Pronoun, Adverb, Verb, Adjective, Conjunction (NIPPAVAC). Once your students memorize the parts of speech, you can begin asking them to point them out in subsequent Caught'yas. I suggest that you do this, one part of speech at a time, all year long.

17. jocose

Paragraph – change of place

Types of Sentences – simple; simple

Commas – intro of 2 prepositional phrases; appositive (unnecessary)

Verbs – passive voice (were joined);

Other Skills – "ie" spell rule; who (subject) vs. whom (object); subject/pronoun agreement ("each" = one so can't use pl. poss. "their"; hyphen between 2 wds. acting as one adj.

B - at the school by the bus port they were joined by another freind jesse **jocose** who rode the school bus. each of them found their name on lists posted on the doors to the seventh grade wing of the school

C -   At the school by the bus port, they were joined by another friend, Jesse **Jocose**, who rode the school bus. Each of them found his or her name on lists posted on the doors to the seventh-grade wing of the school.

---

18. puerile   dejection

Paragraph – new speaker

Types of Sentences – simple; simple

Punctuation – " around what is said out loud; , and . always go inside "

Commas – interjection; introductory word; direct address; quote; commas around "too" when it means "also"

Homophones – its/it's; to/too/two

Other Skills – use "like" only to compare 2 nouns; hyphen in 2 wds. acting as 1

Literary Devices – foreshadowing

B - oh no guys its bad. it looks like many of our sixth-grade teachers followed us to the seventh grade too moaned pauline **puerile** in **dejection**

C -   "Oh, no, guys, it's bad. It looks as if many of our sixth-grade teachers followed us to the seventh grade, too." moaned Pauline **Puerile** in **dejection**.

NOTE: I never understood why "it's" and "its" are difficult words for students to differentiate when they write. But, the truth is that they constantly confuse them in their writing. I solved the problem by forbidding the use of "it's." Students had to write out "it is" instead, leaving "its" to its proper use as a possessive pronoun.

Another trick is to request students to try to use "his" every time they want to use "its" or "it's." Of course, "his" does not work if you wish to say "it is..."

B – Sentences for the Board	C – Corrected version of the CY
19. incessant predicted eerie 2 Paragraphs – 2 new speakers Types of Sentences – compound; simple Punctuation – " around what is said out loud; **,** and **.** always go inside " Commas – 2 adj. where second is not age, color, or related to noun (3 sets); compound sen.; quote; interjection; direct address; quote Homophones – our/are; see/sea Other Skills – "a lot" is 2 wds.; "an" before a vowel Literary Devices – foreshadowing	**B -** i see alot of homework in our future and i see william getting into trouble with his **incessant** stupid limericks **predicted** felicia fey in an **eerie** spooky voice. hey wait up people chirped a soft cheery tone **C -** "I see a lot of homework in our future, and I see William getting into trouble with his **incessant**, stupid limericks," **predicted** Felicia Fey in an **eerie**, spooky voice. "Hey, wait up, people," chirped a soft, cheery tone.
20. virtuous odious Paragraph – new speaker Types of Sentences – simple; complex; compound; complex Punctuation – " around what is said out loud; **,** and **.** always go inside "; use single quotes around a quote within a quote; use " around a letter Commas – quote; no **,** before "as" or "whenever" since sub. clause is at end; compound sen.; quote Homophones – its/it's (always write out "it is"); one/won Other Skills – "ie" spell rule; go over plural rules (see *Grammar, Usage, and Mechanics Guide*); who (subject) vs. whom (object–here object of preposition)	**B -** its vivian **virtuous** whispered isabelle to her freinds. i remember her from last year as she was in a few of my classes. she always did her work and she got straight as. she was the one on who orson **odious** picked whenever he could she finished **C -** "It's Vivian **Virtuous**," whispered Isabelle to her friends. "I remember her from last year as she was in a few of my classes. She always did her work, and she got straight 'As.' She was the one on whom Orson **Odious** picked whenever he could," she finished.

NOTES: After this point, "quotes around what is said out loud" will no longer be pointed out in the skill list, nor will "commas and periods always go inside quotation marks." I suggest that you point these punctuation skills out to your students each time they appear.

   If you have required that your students write the complete date above each Caught'ya, all the comma rules, except in the greeting and closing of a letter which you can cover in Writing Idea #1 and the comma required between a city and state, have been covered in the first 20 Caught'yas. You can review the comma rules listed in the *Grammar, Usage, and Mechanics Guide*.

Writing Idea #4: Expository Essay–Problem/Solution.

Every school has its problem students who annoy the teachers and pick on other students and get into trouble. Every school has a different way of dealing with these students, but not everything is effective. Explain some of the things the problem students do at your school. Then write an essay to propose some solutions to keep these problem students from being annoyances to everyone.

---

21. coiffed   ebony

Paragraph – new speaker

Types of Sentences –simple; simple

Punctuation – **?** in question

Commas – adjective series

Homophones – quit/quiet/quite

Other Skills – hyphen in 2 wds. acting as one adj.; _____ or *italicize* names of long works (see *Grammar, Usage, and Mechanics Guide* for rule)

Literary Devices – reference to literature

B - remember me murmured the girl with a quite voice and carefully **coiffed** intricately braided **ebony** hair. she clutched a huge hard back book in her hand entitled war and peace by leo tolstoy

C -   "Remember me?" murmured the girl with a quiet voice and carefully **coiffed**, intricately-braided, **ebony** hair. She clutched a huge hard-back book in her hand entitled War and Peace by Leo Tolstoy.

22. **odious   crony   dapper**

No Paragraph – same speaker

Types of Sentences – compound; simple

Punctuation – quote that will be continued in next ¶

Commas – compound sen.

Homophones – to/too/two

Verbs – irregular verbs lie/lay and sit/sat (see *Grammar, Usage, and Mechanics Guide*); transitive vs. intransitive verbs

Other Skills – "ie" spell rule; between (2) vs. among (3 or more)

B - i was in your sceince class last year and i set in the last row as far away from orson **odious** and his **crony** danny **dapper** as i could get. they used too lay in wait for me between classes

C - "I was in your science class last year, and I sat in the last row as far away from Orson **Odious** and his **crony** Danny **Dapper** as I could get. They used to lie in wait for me between classes.

NOTE: This Caught'ya and the next few are part of a quote where the speaker speaks more than one paragraph. The correct punctuation for this is to leave off the end quote in the first paragraph and put one in at the beginning of the next paragraph.

23. **malevolent**

Paragraph – different subject, same speaker

Types of Sentences – compound; simple

Punctuation – quote continued in next paragraph; quote within a quote

Commas – quote; compound sen.; put , around "too" if it means "also"; introductory adverb (optional)

Other Skills – hyphen in 2 wds. acting as one

B - orson always whispered **malevolent** things under his breath in my direction too she sighed and he called me a suck up. unfortunately the teacher never caught him doing it

C - "Orson always whispered **malevolent** things under his breath in my direction, too," she sighed, "and he called me a 'suck-up.' Unfortunately, the teacher never caught him doing it.

NOTE: You might want to begin to teach the irregular verbs "lie" and "lay." These will be repeated in subsequent Caught'yas. "Lie" is intransitive and "lay" is transitive and takes an object. The difficulty lies (ha) in "lay" which is the present tense of the transitive verb and the past tense of the intransitive one—"I lay down a few minutes ago," but "I lay the pen down right now." Since "laid" is always transitive, I told students that "something had to get laid."

When they stopped snickering, I made my point. "Some*thing*, an object, has to be placed after using the word 'laid,'" and then I gave them lots of examples.

24. coerced shenanigans Paragraph – new topic (now Danny's nastiness) Types of Sentences – complex (compound verb in main clause); simple Commas – interrupter; no , before "so that" (sub. conjunction—see *Grammar, Usage, and Mechanics Guide*) Homophones – to/too/two; know/no Other Skills – plural rule (if word ends in consonant + "y," change to "ies"	**B -** danny on the other hand threatened and **coerced** me into doing his homework so that he could go to partys. know adult ever caught on to his **shenanigans** either **C -** "Danny, on the other hand, threatened and **coerced** me into doing his homework so that he could go to parties. No adult ever caught on to his **shenanigans** either."

25. appropriate

Paragraph – new subject

Types of Sentences – complex (sub. clause at end); complex (sub. clause at beginning)

Commas – no **,** before "as" (sub. conj.)

Homophones – their/there/they're

Other Skills – write out #s to 120 (3 wds.); subject/pronoun agreement ("each" and "everyone" are singular); "ie" spell rule; hyphen between 2 wds. acting as 1

B - vivian virtuous joined the group of 7 seventh graders as each member searched for their correct homeroom. when everyone had found their **appropriate** classroom the friends found that they had different homerooms

C - Vivian Virtuous joined the group of seven seventh-graders as each member searched for the correct homeroom. When everyone had found his or her **appropriate** classroom, the friends found that they had different homerooms.

Writing Idea #5: Expository (Explanatory) Essay.

Write a letter to your homeroom teacher to explain to him or her some ideas on how to improve homeroom each morning. Make some concrete suggestions, and support your suggestions with examples or proof.

Be sure to use proper business-letter headings, greetings, and closings in your letter.

---

26. whimpered nemesis torment

2 Paragraphs – different speakers (narrator then Pauline)

Types of Sentences – complex; simple; simple; compound

Commas – sub. clause at beginning; quote; compound sen.

Homophones – its/it's; fair/fare

Other Skills – "not only...but"; go over ordinal #s (first, second, etc.)

Literary Devices – repetition for emphasis

B - when she arrived in her homeroom pauline puerile whined at the unfairness of it all. its not fair pauline **whimpered** to herself. its just not fair. not only do i have to go back to school, but my worst **nemesis** is in homeroom to **torment** me first thing every morning

C - When she arrived in her homeroom, Pauline Puerile whined at the unfairness of it all.

"It's not fair," Pauline **whimpered** to herself. "It's just not fair. Not only do I have to go back to school, but my worst **nemesis** is in homeroom to **torment** me first thing every morning."

NOTE: I suggest that you continue to ban the use of "it's" in your classroom. You can go over the difference *ad nauseum*, but until the lightbulb shines, students will persist in confusing these two homonyms.

27. odious maliciously lobbed 　　**wrath martinet** Paragraph – new subject Types of Sentences – simple (compound verb); compound Commas – unnecessary who clause; interrupter; compound sen.; appositive (extra info about a noun) Verbs – strong, vivid verbs; active vs. passive voice Other Skills – vocabulary; who (subject) vs. whom (object); sing. poss.; do not start a sentence with FANBOYS; abbreviation	**B -** orson **odious** whom indeed was in paulines homeroom grinned **maliciously** at her and **lobbed** a slimy spit wad in her direction. but pauline ducked and she incurred the **wrath** of the homeroom teacher mr math **martinet** **C -** Orson **Odious**, who, indeed, was in Pauline's homeroom, grinned **maliciously** at her and **lobbed** a slimy spit wad in her direction. Pauline ducked, and she incurred the **wrath** of the homeroom teacher, Mr. Math **Martinet**.

NOTE: Now that students have encountered compound sentences quite a few times, it might be a good idea to have them memorize the FANBOYS (coordinating conjunctions—for, and, nor, but, or, yet, so). Students enjoy chanting them over and over with different body movements that I call out. For example, recite while clapping hands over the head, then in front, then between legs, then do an "Egyptian" or a "shower," etc. Students should continue to recite the FANBOYS every time one appears in a subsequent Caught'ya.

　　Students love this and memorize the conjunctions quickly. Once the conjunctions are memorized, students easily can learn never to put a comma before FANBOYS unless in a list or a compound sentence. Students also can be told never to capitalize one in a title or begin a sentence with one until they get their driver's license. This will give them time to mature their writing so that every other sentence doesn't begin with "and" or "so."

　　I actually have given a special "FANBOYS Driver's License" to an outstanding writer, giving that student permission to judiciously use conjunctions for effect at the beginning of a sentence.

28. fidgeting sagacious ambled portal 2 Paragraphs – 2 speakers (2nd is narrator) Types of Sentences – simple (compound verb); complex Commas – direct address; quote; sub. clause at beginning Homophones – to/too/two; new/knew/gnu Other Skills – vocabulary; 2 sing. poss.; hyphen in 2 wds. acting as one Literary Devices – foreshadowing	**B** - stop **fidgeting** young lady and sit still he ordered pauline in a menacing tone of voice. sam **sagacious ambled** to his new homeroom a few doors down from paulines. as he entered the rooms **portal** he froze mid stride **C** - "Stop **fidgeting**, young lady, and sit still," he ordered Pauline in a menacing tone of voice. 　　Sam **Sagacious ambled** to his new homeroom a few doors down from Pauline's. As he entered the room's **portal**, he froze mid-stride.
29. comely demurely pulchritudinous Paragraph – new speaker Types of Sentences – complex (sub. clause at end); simple Commas – 2 interjections; no **,** before coordinating conj. (see *Grammar, Usage, and Mechanics Guide*); extra directional info Homophones – right/write/rite Other Skills – who (subject) vs. whom (object); use of intensifier (hastily); spell rule (consonant-vowel-consonant = double last consonant when adding a suffix as in **"grabbed"**) Literary Devices – building interest	**B** - oh my sam sagacious muttered in awe as he spied a **comely** girl who sat **demurely** in the third row of desks. sam hastily grabbed a seat in the fourth row write behind the **pulchritudinous** girl **C** - "Oh, my," Sam Sagacious muttered in awe as he spied a **comely** girl who sat **demurely** in the third row of desks. Sam hastily grabbed a seat in the fourth row, right behind the **pulchritudinous** girl.

NOTE: Now that your students know the coordinating conjunctions by chanting the FANBOYS, it is time for them to begin learning A WHITE BUS words, the subordinating conjunctions. Use the mnemonic device A WHITE BUS to help students learn them.

A   after, although, as

W   when, while, where
H   how
I   if
T   than
E   even though

B   because, before
U   until, unless
S   since, so that

    Students enjoy chanting and chanting these in a sing-song voice every time one appears in a Caught'ya. I added "hey" at the end as we kicked up a foot. Once they memorize the subordinating conjunctions, students can be taught that they *never, never* (well, almost never) put a comma before one and that if A WHITE BUS word is combined with a subject and a verb, it is a subordinate clause which is almost always used as an adverb. In this way, they can learn to begin a sentence with "because" and have a chance to complete the sentence.

NOTE: Since this is such a long Caught'ya, you might want to do part of it orally. Also note that this is a descriptive passage.

30. comely

Paragraph – new speaker (narrator) and new subject

Types of Sentences – simple; simple (compound verb); simple

Punctuation – " around word that has double meaning (double entendre)

Commas – 2 adj. where 2nd is not age, size, or linked to noun; no , bet. 2 adj. because 2nd one is color; extra info; interrupter

Verbs – verb tense switch; use of passive voice ("was struck dumb")

Other Skills – hyphen in 2 wds. acting as one; plural poss.

Literary Devices – double entendre; pun; description

B - the young **comely** lady wears a tight ribbed aqua top that barely meets the top of her equally tight jeans. her medium length black hair curled gently around her ears and flipped up in the back like birds tail feathers only softer. sam sagacious for once in his life was struck dumb

C -   The young, **comely** lady wore a tight, ribbed, aqua top that barely met the top of her equally-tight jeans. Her medium-length black hair curled gently around her ears and flipped up in the back like birds' tail-feathers, only softer. Sam Sagacious, for once in his life, was struck "dumb." **(pun–meaning for "dumb" = "silent, speechless")**

> # Writing Idea #6: Personal Narrative.
> Write about a time you were impressed by someone. It doesn't have to be "love"; it could be just a time someone did something that awed you. Tell about this person, and tell what happened when you encountered this person. Then in your story, explain why this person made an impression on you. Be sure to give details.

NOTE: There are extraneous capital letters in this Caught'ya.

31. pulchritudinous ebony tresses

Paragraph – new subject

Types of Sentences – compound; simple (compound verb)

Punctuation – " around double entendre

Commas – interrupter; compound sen.; extra directional info; 2 adj. where second is not age, size, color, or linked to noun; (no **,** before "ebony" as is a color)

Homophones – by/bye; knew/new/gnu; their/their/they're

Verbs – use of pluperfect

Other Skills – between (2) vs. among (3 or more); contraction; do not start a sentence with FANBOYS

Literary Devices – double entendre (vision)

B - sam by the way new that He had Seen this **pulchritudinous** Girl before between other Students but he couldnt place Her. and he Sat their in the fourth Row right behind the Vision and Breathed in the fresh shampoo Scent from her cute **ebony tresses**

C - Sam, by the way, knew that he had seen this **pulchritudinous** girl before among other students, but he couldn't place her. He sat there in the fourth row, right behind the "vision," and breathed in the fresh, shampoo scent from her cute **ebony tresses**.

NOTE: Many students are profligate with capital letters and, when they write, capitalize many words that should not be capitalized. If this is a problem with your students, I highly recommend that, intermittently all year long, you put a few extraneous capital letters in the Caught'ya as I did in this last one.

32. novel (meaning "new, original, different")

Paragraph – new speaker

Types of Sentences – simple; complex

Punctuation – " around made-up word and vernacular; " around single letters; " around thoughts; quote within a quote

Commas – quote; no **,** before A WHITE BUS word; modifier (participial phrase)

Homophones – to/too/two

Other Skills – contraction; intensifier (extremely); misplaced modifier ("busily writing") as the schedule is not writing

Literary Devices – play on words ("novel" meaning "new"); use of vernacular

B - this is a **novel** twist. shes extremely hott' with two 'ts sam thought too himself as he copied the daily schedule busily writing

C - "This is a **novel** twist. She's extremely 'hott' with two 'Ts,'" Sam thought to himself as, busily writing, he copied the daily schedule.

33. unison

2 Paragraphs – new time; new speaker

Types of Sentences – complex; simple (compound subject)

Commas – sub. clause at beginning; quote

Other Skills – write out #s to 120; "ie" spell rule; comparatives; pronoun use (subject pronoun needed)

B - as the day progressed the 8 freinds met periodically in the hall to compare gossip and the latest news flashes me and my friend think that orson odious is worser than ever this year proclaimed isabelle and vivian almost in **unison**

C -   As the day progressed, the eight friends met periodically in the hall to compare gossip and the latest news flashes.
      "My friend and I think that Orson Odious is worse than ever this year," proclaimed Isabelle and Vivian almost in **unison**.

NOTE: Your students have heard the word "pronoun" many times in previous Caught'yas. They may be ready to learn the seven different kinds of pronouns. If they can learn these (especially the subject, object, and possessive pronouns), they will have a better chance to use them and spell them ("its" in particular) correctly. See "Pronouns" in the *Grammar, Usage, and Mechanics Guide*.

34. dapper   abhorrent
      vindictive   grimace

Paragraph – new speaker (Isabelle alone)

Types of Sentences – simple; compound

Commas – compound sentence; quote

Other Skills – vocabulary; well (adverb) vs. good (adjective)

B - danny **dapper** is worse than ever as well. most of the girls think he is so handsome and good but i think he is **abhorrent** and **vindictive** added isabelle with a **grimace**

C -   "Danny **Dapper** is worse than ever as well. Most of the girls think he is so handsome and good, but I think he is **abhorrent** and **vindictive**," added Isabelle with a **grimace**.

**35. skirmish   nemesis
   obstreperous   carped**

2 Paragraphs – 2 new speakers

Types of Sentences – simple with
who clause; simple; simple

Commas – quote; appositive (more
info about a noun); no , after "pal" as
Orson could have several and
appositive is necessary; quote

Homophones – to/too/two; right/rite/
write; their/there/they're; it's/its

Verbs – use of pluperfect; do not split
verb

Other Skills – who vs. whom (relative
pronouns); poss. pronouns; use of
italics for emphasis

Literary Devices – use of vernacular
("too right")

B - to right said william whom had
already experienced a **skirmish** with
his arch **nemesis** the **obstreperous**
orson and his pal danny. there *both* in
my homeroom **carped** pauline
puerile. its unfair

C - "Too right," said William,
who already had experienced a
skirmish with his arch **nemesis**, the
obstreperous Orson, and his pal
Danny.
   "They're *both* in my
homeroom," **carped** Pauline Puerile.
"It's unfair."

**NOTE: This is an appropriate point to introduce the seven types of
pronouns. (See *Grammar, Usage, and Mechanics Guide*.) Then, as you
encounter examples of each in subsequent Caught'yas, you can point them
out to your students.**

Writing Idea #7: Persuasive (Argumentative) Essay.

Write a persuasive letter to convince someone who bugs you to stop. Be
sure to support your arguments. You may make up a character if you wish
and embellish your essay to make it more interesting.

NOTE: Warn students that the second sentence will need to be reworked. You might want to refer to the rule that one never should use "that" to refer to people nor end a sentence with a preposition if at all possible.

36. queried Paragraph – new speaker Types of Sentences – simple question; simple Punctuation – note placement of **?** and **!** in quotes; use of **!** for emphasis Homophones – new/knew/gnu Other Skills – capitalize names of languages; contraction; who vs. whom; never use "that" to refer to people; do not end sentence with a preposition; good (adj.) vs. well (adv.)	**B -** have you seen the new english teacher yet **queried** sam. shes one that even olivia otiose will work for. she does good **C -** "Have you seen the new English teacher yet?" **queried** Sam. "She's one for whom even Olivia Otiose will work! She does well."

**37. vernacular   concurred
    jocose   slang**
 	
2 Paragraphs – 2 speakers
 	
Types of Sentences – simple; simple
 	
Punctuation – quote within a quote
 	
Commas – quote; 2 interjections; direct address; unnecessary who clause
 	
Other Skills – vocabulary; contractions; who vs. whom; compound word
 	
Literary Devices – use of vernacular ("boss" and "tubular")
	B - shes boss william concluded in the current **vernacular**. oh yeah william shes tubular **concurred** jesse **jocose** who was not to be outdone in his knowledge of **slang**
	
	C - "She's 'boss,'" William concluded in the current **vernacular**.
	    "Oh, yeah, William, she's 'tubular,'" **concurred** Jesse **Jocose**, who was not to be outdone in his knowledge of **slang**.

38. reiterated

Paragraph – new speaker

Types of Sentences – simple; compound; compound

Commas – interjection; quote; interrupter; compound sen; compound sen.

Other Skills – contractions; abbreviation; use of a **;** in a compound sen.; review pronouns

Literary Devices – use of folksy language ("like"); metaphor

B - yeah shes not like ms grammar grouch at all **reiterated** felicia fey. shes like almost human and i think she has a touch of magic in her. she has such a way with words she almost paints pictures with them

C - "Yeah, she's not like Ms. Grammar Grouch at all," **reiterated** Felicia Fey. "She's, like, almost human, and I think she has a touch of magic in her. She has such a way with words; she almost paints pictures with them."

NOTE: With Caught'ya #38, you might want to teach the four reasons for using semicolons (series of independent clauses, instead of a coordinating conjunction in a compound sentence, as in this Caught'ya, when there are too many commas in a compound sentence, and, in a list, to avoid confusion because there are too many commas). This may avoid future abuse of the semicolon. See the *Grammar, Usage, and Mechanics Guide*.

39. taunted   somber

Paragraph – new subject introducing new speaker

Types of Sentences – simple; simple; simple; compound

Commas – introductory phrase; quote; direct address; compound sen.

Homophones – by/bye; right/write/ rite; their/there/they're; your/you're

Verbs – confusing "past" with verb "passed"

Other Skills – who vs. whom; never use "that" to refer to people; contractions; exception to the "ie" spell rule; double negative

Literary Devices – simile

B - at that moment orson odious past bye. theirs the girl that cant do anything right he **taunted**. your weird felicia. your **somber** outfit is ugly and your hair looks like a muddy broom. you dont got no class

C - At that moment, Orson Odious passed by. "There's the girl who can't do anything right," he **taunted**. "You're weird, Felicia. Your **somber** outfit is ugly, and your hair looks like a muddy broom. You don't have any class."

40. glowered   perilous

2 Paragraphs – 2 new speakers (1ˢᵗ is narrator)

Types of Sentences – compound/complex; simple; simple

Commas – compound sen.; direct address; interrupted quote; no **,** before A WHITE BUS word

Homophones – your/you're; counsel/council; its/it's; to/too/two

Verbs – do not use "would" for past tense (it is conditional)

Other Skills – plural poss.; CVC = double 2ⁿᵈ consonant before suffix ("stopped"); the "y" in "your" is not capitalized since it is an interrupted quote; contraction

B - felicia fey would **glower** at orson and would prepare to zap him with a spell but her friends warnings stoped her before she could mouth the first word. careful felicia counseled isabelle youre spells dont always work the way you want. its two **perilous** to try one

C -   Felicia Fey **glowered** at Orson and prepared to zap him with a spell, but her friend's warnings stopped her before she could mouth the first word.
    "Careful, Felicia," counseled Isabelle, "your spells don't always work the way you want. It's too **perilous** to try one."

Writing Idea #8: Personal/Imaginative Narrative.
Think of a time when a friend warned you not to do something, but you did it anyway. Write about what happened. You may embellish your story to make it more interesting.

---

41. comeuppance

Paragraph – new speaker

Types of Sentences – simple (compound verb); simple

Commas – no **,** before FANBOYS (not compound sen. or list); quote

Homophones – your/you're

Literary Devices – alliteration; foreshadowing

B - felicia held back and just stared in the direction of the rapidly retreating orson. youre going to get youre **comeuppance** some day she muttered

C -   Felicia held back and just stared in the direction of the rapidly retreating Orson. "You're going to get your **comeuppance** some day," she muttered.

NOTE: As with "it's," I forbade my students to write the contraction "you're." I insisted that they write out "you are" instead. This helped them learn the difference between the homophones.

42. enamored avail oblivious aloof Paragraph – new speaker (narrator) Types of Sentences – complex (sub. clause at end); simple; simple Commas – intro phrase; Homophones – past vs. passed; to/too/ two; presence/presents Other Skills – vocabulary; few (can count) vs. less; accept vs. except; use of dash for aside; use of intensifier (very) Literary Devices – narrator aside	**B -** after that the first few months of school past in the usual fashion accept that sam was **enamored** of the girl in his homeroom and kept trying two get her to notice him too no **avail**. she seemed **oblivious** of his presence and very **aloof** **C -** After that, the first few months of school passed in the usual fashion except that Sam was **enamored** of the girl in his homeroom and kept trying to get her to notice him—to no **avail**. She seemed **oblivious** of his presence and very **aloof**.
43. blithe No Paragraph – same subject Types of Sentences – simple; compound Homophones – to/too/two Verbs – verb tense shift Other Skills – run-on sen.; contraction; use "like" only to compare nouns	**B -** something was troubling her and she didnt seem to be two **blithe** and she always looked like something was wrong **C -** Something was troubling her. She didn't seem to be too **blithe**, and she always looked as if something was wrong.

44. a plethora of

Paragraph – topic change

Types of Sentences – simple; simple; simple

Punctuation – " around vernacular

Commas – extra info

Verbs – do not use "would" to denote past tense (it is conditional); rise (transitive) vs. raise (intransitive) (see *Grammar, Usage, and Mechanics Guide*); story in past tense

Other Skills – than (comparative) vs. then (adv.); fewer (can count) vs. less; write out #s to 120; hyphen in 2 wds. acting as 1

Literary Devices – use of student vernacular

B - teachers would assign **a plethora of** homework but less than at the end of the previous year. vivian virtuous would rise her hand no less then 3 times each period, even in science class. orson still calls her a suck up at every opportunity

C -   Teachers assigned **a plethora of** homework but less than at the end of the previous year. Vivian Virtuous raised her hand no fewer than three times each period, even in science class. Orson still called her a "suck-up" at every opportunity.

NOTE: At this point a review (or lesson) on the common irregular verbs which students often confuse might be appropriate. Be sure to include lie/ lay, rise/raise, sit/set. In that list, the problem lies in which is intransitive (the first) and which is transitive and takes an object (the second).

     It is a good idea to stress the use of "a plethora of" and "a dearth of" as students like using these phrases a lot. Besides, students never can spell "a lot" correctly anyway...

NOTE: Warn students that this is a run-on sentence.

45. bibliophilic   cad

Paragraph – new topic

Types of Sentences – simple;
compound

Punctuation – " around name of
special event

Commas – intro phrase (optional);
appositive; compound sen.

Homophones – won/one

Other Skills – run-on sen.; capitalize
specific event; fewer (can count) vs.
less; write out #s to 120

Literary Devices – use of
metaphorical insult

B - as usual beth **bibliophilic** won the
million minutes of reading contest
and orson the **cad** picked on her as
much as he could and he reduced her
to tears on more than one but less than
10 occasions

C -   As usual, Beth **Bibliophilic**
won the "Million Minutes of
Reading" contest. Orson, the **cad**,
picked on her as much as he could,
and he reduced her to tears on more
than one but fewer than ten occasions.

Writing Idea #9: Persuasive (Argumentative) Essay.

Beth Bibliophilic reads a plethora of books. She likes some more than
others. Think of a book you read that you really liked and convince a
friend to read that book. Include at least three arguments and support each
argument with evidence that will help convince your friend. Use direct
address. ("Hey, Bob,...")

**46. pulchritudinous   abounded
      atrocious**

Paragraph – topic change

Types of Sentences – simple (could
be made compound); simple

Punctuation – ( ) around narrator
aside

Commas – unnecessary appositive

Other Skills – plural poss.; do not
begin a sentence with FANBOYS

Literary Devices – narrator aside

B - petra **pulchritudinous** as
beautiful as ever spent as much time
as possible in the girls bathroom. and
gossip **abounded** in the halls and
students bathrooms which still
smelled **atrocious**

C -   Petra **Pulchritudinous**, as
beautiful as ever, spent as much time
as possible in the girls' bathroom.
Gossip **abounded** in the halls and
students' bathrooms (which still
smelled **atrocious**).

NOTE: Warn students of run-on sentences. Note also that there are several ways to write this Caught'ya correctly.

47. sycophant incorrigible Paragraph – new topic Types of Sentences – simple; compound with **;** Punctuation – use of **;** in compound sen. Commas – unnecessary appositive Other Skills – discuss 3 reasons for semicolons; sing. poss.; discuss collective nouns like "everyone"(see *Grammar, Usage, and Mechanics Guide*)	**B -** orson odious and his main **sycophant** danny dapper attempted to make everyones life as miserable as possible and they were **incorrigible** and they made nasty comments to everyone **C -** Orson Odious and his main **sycophant**, Danny Dapper, attempted to make everyone's life as miserable as possible; they were **incorrigible**. They made nasty comments to everyone.

NOTE: Since this is a long Caught'ya, you might want to do part of it orally.

48. amicable melodious witty appalling Paragraph – new topic (the teachers) Types of Sentences – simple; complex (sub. clause at end) Punctuation – use of colon before a list Commas – aside; noun list; 2 adj. where 2nd is not age, size, color, or related to noun (2 places); no **,** around "also" if it doesn't mean "too"; verb list Homophones – new/knew/gnu; their/there/they're Other Skills – vocabulary; do not begin a sen. with FANBOYS; abbreviations; capitalize names of languages	**B -** and the teachers with the exception of ms **amicable** artist mr. **melodious** music, and the new amazing english teacher ms **witty** writing wizard, were there usual stern selves. they also still did their usual routine when william or sam recited one of their **appalling** limericks stick out theyre tongues smoke slightly from there ears and noses and flicker their eyes **C -** The teachers, with the exception of Ms. **Amicable** Artist, Mr. **Melodious** Music, and the new, amazing English teacher, Ms. **Witty** Writing Wizard, were their usual, stern selves. They also still did their usual routine when William or Sam recited one of their **appalling** limericks: stick out their tongues, smoke slightly from their ears and noses, and flicker their eyes.

NOTE: Since this is another long Caught'ya, you may want to do part of it orally.

49. deplorable   witty   cinquain

Paragraph – new subject

Types of Sentences – simple; simple

Punctuation – use of dash (see *Grammar, Usage, and Mechanics Guide*)

Commas – long introductory phrase; unnecessary appositive; interrupter

Homophones – were/where; knew/new/gnu; write/right/rite

Other Skills – go over collective nouns like "crew"; who vs. whom; "ie" spell rule; sing. poss.; abbreviation; capitalize languages; use of dash to show a break in thought

Literary Devices – reference to poetry

B - happily for the crew of friends whom were getting tired of William waggishs **deplorable** limericks the new english teacher ms **witty** writing wizard taught them a knew form of poetry **cinquain**. william thankfully abandoned limericks and began to rite cinquains

C -   Happily for the crew of friends who were getting tired of William Waggish's **deplorable** limericks, the new English teacher, Ms. **Witty** Writing Wizard, taught them a new form of poetry—**cinquain**. William, thankfully, abandoned limericks and began to write cinquains.

NOTE: See Chapter 3 for the definition of a cinquain and how to write one.
   After this Caught'ya, the "i" before "e" spelling rule will be indicated only by the spelling of the word in bold for the often-confused letters.

50. penned   martinet   audacity   utter

Paragraph – new topic (writing cinquain)

Types of Sentences – complex; compound/complex

Commas – interrupted sub. clause; appositive; compound part of compound/complex sen.

Homophones – new/knew/gnu

Other Skills – sing. poss.; ordinal #s (first, etc.); discuss superlatives (least, worst, etc); abbreviation

B - william waggish as soon as he was comfortable with the new poetic form **penned** several cinquains. williams first effort was about mr math **martinet** his least favorite teacher and he had the **audacity** to **utter** it as he entered class that same day

C -   William Waggish, as soon as he was comfortable with the new poetic form, **penned** several cinquains. William's first effort was about Mr. Math **Martinet**, his least favorite teacher, and he had the **audacity** to **utter** it as he entered class that same day.

NOTE: It is almost halfway through the year. You might want to review the eight parts of speech (if you have not been doing so all along) and ask students to point them out in the Caught'yas.

Many Caught'yas in this story use the basic abbreviations. The postal code abbreviations for the states, however, are not addressed. You may wish to conduct a lesson in the use of these codes (see *Grammar, Usage, and Mechanics Guide*).

51. drones

No Paragraph – still on poem

Types of Sentences – simple

Punctuation – " around short works like poems

Commas – use of commas in poem (noun list)

Homophones – its/it's

Other Skills – capitalization of first lines of poem

Literary Devices – poem in narrative

B - he entitled his poem mindless math

math class,
its deadly dull.
the old teacher **drones** on...
numbers, equations, formulas.
boring.

C - He entitled his poem "Mindless Math."

Math class,
It's deadly dull.
The old teacher **drones** on...
Numbers, equations, formulas.
Boring.

Writing Idea #10: Poetry.

Write several cinquains on nature. Use these guidelines.

→   Write five lines. Syllables in lines – 2, 4, 6, 8, 2.
→   Write about a noun or something concrete.
→   Don't try to make each line complete or express a single thought. Each line should flow into the next.
→   Cinquains work best if one avoids using many adverbs and adjectives.
→   The poem should build toward a climax with the last line as a conclusion or link to the topic.

NOTE: See Chapter 3 for more information on cinquains.

Midterm Caught'ya Test follows on next page.

Remember, you can adapt the test to fit the needs of your students and then print copies from the CD included with this book.

If you choose not to use this test, you will need to read the passage in Part 1 of the Teacher's Key to your students so that they don't lose the thread of the story.

If you give the test, read the corrected version of the test (the key) aloud several times to your students when they have the test in front of them. In this way, they can "hear" the punctuation. You might want to go over any words for which they do not know the meaning since this is a grammar test, not a vocabulary quiz.

Some teachers like to let students mark up a copy of the test and then write the corrected version on their own. Others simply let students write in the corrections on the copy and leave it at that. Personally, I prefer the first method as it makes students think and be more careful, but if time is a factor, the second option would be acceptable.

This test is a review of most of the skills your students have learned in previous Caught'yas. There are three parts of the test, but not all three must be used. If you feel, for example, that your students are not ready to handle Part 3, skip it.

I always gave a midterm around December to check that my students were learning. I also gave one or two Caught'yas as a "quickie quiz" about once every three weeks or so to make sure students paid attention when we went over the daily Caught'ya and didn't cheat when marking the number of errors missed.

Almost Midterm Caught'ya Test

Directions for Part 1:

Students, correct the following long Caught'ya. This test will show how carefully you listen when your teacher goes over Caught'yas. You will lose two points per error, so check your work. Ask your teacher for meanings of words you do not know. This is not a vocabulary test. Follow your teacher's directions, and read the test again to yourself to help with punctuation.

Hint: There are seven paragraphs. All periods are correct. Do not change any of them. Twice, the first quotation mark has been left in to help you. There are spelling errors and one missing hyphen. Some words will need to be changed.

out of the corner of his eye william spied mr math martinet that was standing at the front of the classroom. as william **uttered** the last few words of the poem mr martinets eyes fluttered less than 8 times his tongue would protrude and his ears **exuded** curls of smoke. "aha muttered william to no one in particular cinquains work as good as limericks on these **bizarre** teachers. sam sagacious pursued his new interest the girl in homeroom whose name was alessandra **amorous**. she was a former **sycophant** of orson odious. alessandra had become **disenchanted** with the **latter** when orson who secretly loved alessandra had poped her bra in the back right in front of everyone in the lunchroom. she hadnt spoken too orson since then. orson odious of course was not pleased with this turn of events and he went out of his way to embarrass alessandra every chance he got. alessandra also avoided danny dapper and petra pulchritudinous whom still hung with there leader orson. "still stuck up arent you alessandra orson asked alessandra one day in front of sam and at least 9 other students as he past by. yes are you **spurning** me too queried petra **spitefully**. petra secretly missed the company of her former freind alessandra when she **primped** in the girls bathroom among every class but she would never let orson danny or alessandra know. alessandra muttered something

uncomplimentary in spanish under her breath but no one else heard the **affront**. orson certainly wouldnt have understood it anyway.

Directions for Part 2:

First, number the fifteen sentences on your corrected copy of the test so you don't lose track of the numbers. Then, use your corrected version of the test to identify the types of sentences of each of the fifteen sentences in this exam—simple, compound, complex, or compound/complex.

Hint: Nine are simple. Two are compound. Two are complex. Two are compound/complex.

1. _____ 9. _____

2. _____ 10. _____

3. _____ 11. _____

4. _____ 12. _____

5. _____ 13. _____

6. _____ 14. _____

7. _____ 15. _____

8. _____

Directions for Part 3:

First, invent an imaginary person who is really obnoxious. Next, give that imaginary person a name. Then, think of three or four things that this person might do that would drive you crazy (as Orson drives Alessandra crazy). Finally, write down your ideas.

Now, write a persuasive essay to this person, trying to persuade him or her to quit his or her obnoxious behavior. Be sure to support your arguments with good examples.

Almost Midterm Caught'ya Test KEY

Part 1:

Out of the corner of his eye, William spied Mr. Math Martinet who was standing at the front of the classroom. As William **uttered** the last few words of the poem, Mr. Martinet's eyes fluttered fewer than eight times, his tongue protruded, and his ears **exuded** curls of smoke.

"Aha," muttered William to no one in particular, "cinquains work as well as limericks on these **bizarre** teachers."

Sam Sagacious pursued his new interest, the girl in homeroom whose name was Alessandra **Amorous**. She was a former **sycophant** of Orson Odious. Alessandra had become **disenchanted** with the **latter** when Orson (who secretly loved Alessandra) had popped her bra in the back, right in front of everyone in the lunchroom. She hadn't spoken to Orson since then.

Orson Odious, of course, was not pleased with this turn of events, and he went out of his way to embarrass Alessandra every chance he got. Alessandra also avoided Danny Dapper and Petra Pulchritudinous who still hung with their leader, Orson.

"Still stuck-up, aren't you, Alessandra?" Orson asked Alessandra one day in front of Sam and at least nine other students as he passed by.

"Yes, are you **spurning** me, too?" queried Petra **spitefully**. Petra secretly missed the company of her former friend, Alessandra, when she **primped** in the girls' bathroom between every class, but she would never let Orson, Danny, or Alessandra know.

Alessandra muttered something **uncomplimentary** in Spanish under her breath, but no one else heard the **affront**. Orson certainly wouldn't have understood it anyway.

Part 2:

1. simple
2. compound/complex
3. simple
4. simple
5. simple
6. complex
7. simple
8. compound
9. simple
10. simple
11. complex
12. simple
13. compound/complex
14. compound
15. simple

52. proboscis refrained cringed

Paragraph – new topic

Types of Sentences – compound; simple

Commas – intro adv.; 2 intro prepositional phrases; 2 adj. where 2nd is not age, color, or linked to noun; compound sen.

Homophones – their/there/they're

Other Skills – review prepositions

B - their in the middle of the lunchroom sam wanted to punch orson in his big ugly **proboscis** but he **refrained** from doing so. alessandra **cringed**

C -   There, in the middle of the lunchroom, Sam wanted to punch Orson in his big, ugly **proboscis**, but he **refrained** from doing so. Alessandra **cringed**.

NOTE: Now that the year is almost half over, and your students have memorized the coordinating and subordinating conjunctions, it is time to memorize the prepositions. They are listed in the *Grammar, Usage, and Mechanics Guide*.

Students learn them painlessly if you chant only four new ones a day (adding four each day until you cover the entire list). Middle-school students love to chant these with a different gesture (like "the Egyptian" or raising an arm, etc.) with each set of four prepositions. When all have been added to the chant, you and your class (although *you* will never remember the gestures, *they* will) can chant and move to the prepositions each time one appears in a Caught'ya (which is most of them) until your students tire of the exercise.

Once students memorize the prepositions, they can learn not to capitalize them in a title, that when you combine one with a noun, you have an adjective or adverb in a prepositional phrase, and that when you put two prepositional phrases together at the beginning of a sentence, you must have a comma after them.

53. cad   heed

Paragraph – new topic and new speaker

Types of Sentences – simple (compound verb); simple; simple (compound subject)

Punctuation – quote within a quote; " around vernacular

Commas – quote

Homophones – no/know; one/won

Other Skills – run-on sen.; "no one" is 2 wds.; need for correct subject pronoun; friends; go over compound subjects and predicates

Literary Devices – use of teenage vernacular for verisimilitude

B - sam gently put his hand on her shoulder and said he is a bogus **cad** and no one listens to him and me and my friends pay him no **heed**

C -   Sam gently put his hand on her shoulder and said, "He is a 'bogus' **cad**. No one listens to him. My friends and I pay him no **heed**."

---

54. sycophant   noisome

2 Paragraphs – 2 different subjects

Types of Sentences – compound/ complex; simple (despite length)

Punctuation – ( ) around narrator aside

Commas – compound sen.; intro adv. (optional); unnecessary appositive

Verbs – verb tense switch; use of strong verbs in 1st sen.; go over helping verbs

Other Skills – sing. poss.; who vs. whom; dangling participle (grinning)

Literary Devices – narrator aside

B - alessandra smiled at sam and grinning back sams heart sang with hope. meanwhile orson odious and his **sycophant** danny dapper who the girls thought handsome despite his mean nature have big plans for a particularly **noisome** event

C -   Alessandra smiled at Sam, and as he grinned back, Sam's heart sang with hope.
     Meanwhile, Orson Odious and his **sycophant**, Danny Dapper (whom the girls thought handsome despite his mean nature), had big plans for a particularly **noisome** event.

55. awe-inspiring   *sotto voce*

Paragraph – new topic

Types of Sentences – complex; simple

Punctuation – *italicize* Latin phrase

Commas – no **,** before A WHITE BUS word

Homophones – new/knew/gnu; to/too/two; one/won

Verbs – affect (influence) vs. effect (cause); review helping verbs

Other Skills – abbreviation; sc**ie**nce (doesn't follow rule)

B - ms stern sceince displayed a particularly **awe-inspiring** demonstration of teacher weirdness after william recited sotto voce one of his new cinquains to see how it would affect the teacher. sam concluded that cinquains had an even greater affect on the bizarre teachers than limericks

C -   Ms. Stern Science displayed a particularly **awe-inspiring** demonstration of teacher weirdness after William recited *sotto voce* one of his new cinquains to see how it would affect the teacher. Sam concluded that cinquains had an even greater effect on the bizarre teachers than limericks.

Writing Idea #11: Expository/Explanatory/Informational Essay.

Surely, you have had a "weird" teacher in your eight years (including kindergarten) in school. Perhaps this was a good weird (like a teacher who gave "really cool" assignments or did unusual things to make the class interesting), or perhaps the teacher's weirdness was annoying. Without using the teacher's name (make up a name instead), write an essay explaining exactly how this teacher was different from most of your other teachers. Be sure to give lots of specific details about the teacher's "weirdnesses."

56. protrusion   utterance

No Paragraph – same topic

Types of Sentences – compound

Commas – noun list; compound sen.; extra info

Homophones – no/know

Verbs – do not split verbs; "rise" (transitive) vs. "raise" (intransitive)

Other Skills – science; abbreviation; not...only...but; fewer (can count) vs. less; than (comparative) vs. then (adv.); write out #s to 120

B - ms stern science had not only done the usual eye fluttering smoke curling and tongue **protrusion** but she had also raised and lowered both arms no less then 5 times during the recitation of the poem once with the **utterance** of each line

C - Ms. Stern Science not only had done the usual eye fluttering, smoke curling, and tongue **protrusion**, but she also had raised and lowered both arms no fewer than five times during the recitation of the poem, once with the **utterance** of each line.

NOTE: Your students have heard the word "pronoun" many times in previous Caught'yas. This may be a good place to review the seven different kinds of pronouns. If they can learn these well (especially the subject, object, and possessive pronouns), they will have a better chance to use them and spell them ("its" in particular) correctly. See "Pronouns" in the _Grammar, Usage, and Mechanics Guide_.

57. monotonous   droned   latter laboriously   drivel

Paragraph – new topic

Types of Sentences – complex; simple

Punctuation – " around title of short works; ( ) around narrator aside

Verbs – do not use "would" to denote past tense (it is conditional); story in past tense; do not split infinitives

Other Skills – vocabulary; review demonstrative pronouns (this/that/ these/those); abbreviations; sing. poss.; plural poss.; sc**ie**nce; antecedent/pronoun agreement (each is singular); capitalize lines in poem

Literary Devices – narrator aside; metaphor in poem

B - this poem is entitled ms. **monotonous** science because ms stern science would **drone** on and on about the days science topic which sounded like all the other days topics while covering the board with her notes. she would require each student to **laboriously** copy the **latter** into their notebook

science,
dreary subject...
monotonous drivel...
every day the same thing from one
dull prof.

C -   This poem was entitled "Ms. **Monotonous** Science" because Ms. Stern Science **droned** on and on about the day's science topic (which sounded like all the other days' topics) while covering the board with her notes. She required each student to copy the **latter laboriously** into his or her notebook.

Science,
Dreary subject...
Monotonous drivel...
Every day the same thing from one
Dull prof.

NOTES: *Star Trek* was wrong. "To boldly go where..." should be "To go boldly." Infinitives should never be split.

If your students still are confusing plurals and possessives (as in putting apostrophes in plural nouns), you might want to start putting apostrophes in future Caught'yas whenever a word ends in "s." In this way, students will have to think about whether to use that apostrophe. No matter how many times you explain that no apostrophe is needed in a plural noun, students (and adults—look at signs in your town) put in unnecessary apostrophes. Putting an apostrophe with every noun ending in "s" proved to be effective in getting my seventh-graders to use apostrophes only in possessive nouns and contractions. Try it. I have put in extraneous apostrophes in the "B" sentence in the next two Caught'yas for illustration.

58. regale

Paragraph – new speaker

Types of Sentences – simple; simple; simple

Punctuation – **!** needed for emphasis; quote within a quote; **"** around vernacular

Commas – direct address

Verbs – affect vs. effect; use of pluperfect

Other Skills – fri**e**nd; sing. poss.; who vs. whom; contraction; plurals vs. possessives

Literary Devices – use of teenage vernacular; hyperbole

B - wowzer man whispered jesse to his friend sam, who also had witnessed the effect of william's poem on the teacher. this rock's. i cant wait to **regale** the rest of our freind's with this latest affect of william's poem's

C - "Wowzer, man!" whispered Jesse to his friend Sam, who also had witnessed the effect of William's poem on the teacher. "This 'rocks.' I can't wait to **regale** the rest of our friends with this latest effect of William's poems."

59. fervent

Paragraph – new speaker (narrator)

Types of Sentences – simple; intro. participial phrase

Commas – intro word

Homophones – peace/piece; wrote/rote

Other Skills – plurals vs. possessives; demonstrative pronouns (this/that/these/those); p**ie**ce; abbreviation; go over poss. pronouns

B - yes this was another piece to add to the puzzle of the bizarre teacher's. inspired by william's success' and by ms witty writing wizard's **fervent** teaching jesse rote a cinquain of his own

C - Yes, this was another piece to add to the puzzle of the bizarre teachers. Inspired by William's success and by Ms. Witty Writing Wizard's **fervent** teaching, Jesse wrote a cinquain of his own.

NOTE: The first letter of each line of the poem is capitalized.

60. amicable   hue

No Paragraph – same topic

Types of Sentences – simple; complex (sub. clause at end)

Punctuation – " around work of art

Commas – unnecessary appositive

Homophones – wear/ware

Other Skills – who vs. whom (object of preposition); review prepositions; demonstrative pronouns (this/that/these/those); do not end sentence with a preposition

B - he dedicated his to his favorite teacher ms **amicable** artist, that he had a small crush on. he entitled his composition art in pink because ms **amicable** artist loved to ware that **hue**

> frothy
> teacher in pink.
> daily we create and mold.
> she guides our hands...creative things
> spring forth.

C - He dedicated his to his favorite teacher, Ms. **Amicable** Artist, on whom he had a small crush. He entitled his composition "Art in Pink" because Ms. **Amicable** Artist loved to wear that **hue**.

> Frothy
> Teacher in pink.
> Daily we create and mold.
> She guides our hands...Creative things
> Spring forth.

Writing Idea #12: Descriptive Essay.

Get a partner. Silently stare at your partner for five minutes and take notes on his or her appearance (include other things in addition to clothing since that changes from day to day) and personality as revealed in his or her appearance. Take lots of notes.

    Now, use your notes to write an essay describing your partner.

Alternative Writing Idea #12: Descriptive Essay.

Your teacher will show you a copy of a painting. Write a critique of that painting. Be sure to include a description of the painting, your perception of the artist's purpose and audience, an analysis of the colors and subject used, and finally, why you do or do not like the painting.

NOTE: You will need a large print of a painting. You can buy poster-size reproductions at local art galleries for less than $20, but your art teacher probably has a few on hand. If there is a humanities teacher in your school, he or she may have a few as well. My students *loved* Van Gogh's art.

61. audibly Paragraph – new topic Types of Sentences – complex; simple; simple Punctuation – need **!** for emphasis Commas – sub. clause at beginning Other Skills – review prepositions	**B -** when jesse repeated his poem **audibly** in art class within hearing of his favorite teacher he watched her actions. nothing happened. he said the poem again **C -** When Jesse repeated his poem **audibly** in art class, within hearing of his favorite teacher, he watched her actions. Nothing happened! He said the poem again.
62. emitted 2 Paragraphs – 2 new speakers Types of Sentences – compound; simple Punctuation – use of semicolons in a series of indep. clauses Commas – direct address; quote; compound sen.; introductory word; quote Other Skills – contraction; abbreviation; go over 4 uses of semicolons; **wei**rd; discuss use of comparative (**wei**rder)	**B -** thats a nice cinquain jesse said ms amicable artist but her eyes never fluttered her tongue never protruded and her ears and nose never **emitted** smoke. yes this gets weirder and weirder Jesse muttered **C -** "That's a nice cinquain, Jesse," said Ms. Amicable Artist, but her eyes never fluttered; her tongue never protruded; and her ears and nose never **emitted** smoke. "Yes, this gets weirder and weirder," Jesse muttered.

63. unremittingly

Paragraph – new subject

Types of Sentences – simple; simple (compound verb)

Homophones – its/it's; new/knew/gnu

Verbs – verb tense shift

Other Skills – go over collective nouns (See *Grammar, Usage, and Mechanics Guide*); antecedent/pronoun agreement 2 times; then (adv.) vs. than (comparative)

B - the group **unremittingly** continues to test their teachers with the knew poetry form. everybody wrote their own cinquain and than they tried it out

C - The group **unremittingly** continued to test its teachers with the new poetry form. Everybody wrote his or her own cinquain and then tried it out.

NOTE: I suggest again that you continue to insist that your students write out "it is" instead of using the contraction "it's." It is the only way they will learn the difference between the possessive pronoun and the contraction.

64. majority   critique

No Paragraph – same topic

Types of Sentences – simple; simple

Punctuation – " around vernacular

Commas – noun list; interrupter

Verbs – accept vs. except

Other Skills – plural poss.; abbreviations

Literary Devices – use of student vernacular

B - it was sweet to watch the **majority** of the teachers reactions to the poems. ms amicable artist mr melodious music and ms witty writing wizard however still did not react in any way accept to **critique** the poems

C - It was "sweet" to watch the **majority** of the teachers' reactions to the poems. Ms. Amicable Artist, Mr. Melodious Music, and Ms. Witty Writing Wizard, however, still did not react in any way except to **critique** the poems.

65. perplexed   blatant   pondered

No Paragraph – same topic

Types of Sentences – simple; simple; simple

Homophones – new/knew/gnu

Verbs – subject/verb agreement; affect vs. effect

Other Skills – go over collective nouns; go over superlatives (most); abbreviations; science

Literary Devices – building suspense

B - the crew were getting even more **perplexed**. the cinquain had the most **blatant** affect on ms stern sceince and dean dread. sam **pondered** this gnu development in the mystery

C - The crew was getting even more **perplexed**. The cinquain had the most **blatant** effect on Ms. Stern Science and Dean Dread. Sam **pondered** this new development in the mystery.

Writing Idea #13: Personal or Fictional Narrative.

Think about any mystery you have ever encountered and then solved. It could be a mystery as simple as losing something that you *know* where it was the day before. Write a story telling exactly what happened in your personal mystery. Be sure to give details and write a satisfying ending. Try to build suspense if you can. You may, of course, make something up if you prefer.

NOTE: Since it has so many words ending in an "s," this is an appropriate Caught'ya to play with plurals and possessives again in order to make students think twice before using an apostrophe. I have put in extraneous apostrophes. Take them out if you think this is too much for your students.

66. odoriferous   milled

Paragraph – new time; new subject

Types of Sentences – simple; complex

Punctuation – " around sounds

Commas – intro adverb; interrupter; optional after short intro adv.; sub. clause at beginning

Homophones – week/weak; their/there/they're

Other Skills – antecedent/pronoun agreement (review collective nouns); plural poss.; hyphen in 2 wds. acting as 1

Literary Devices – onomatopoeia ("boom"); personification ("'boom' erupted")

B - a few week's later though theyre was an **odoriferous** incident that distracted the group from their experiment's with the bizarre teacher's. one day as the student's **milled** about in the hall's between classe's a loud boom erupted from the boy's bathroom in the seventh grade hallway

C -   A few weeks later, though, there was an **odoriferous** incident that distracted the group from the experiments with the bizarre teachers. One day, as the students **milled** about in the halls between classes, a loud "boom" erupted from the boys' bathroom in the seventh-grade hallway.

NOTE: At this juncture in the school year, seventh-graders "should" be ready to learn the three questions an adjective could answer and the five questions an adverb could answer, especially if their sixth-grade teacher did Caught'yas. See the *Grammar, Usage, and Mechanics Guide*. I liked to teach this and then post the questions on the wall somewhere for reference. Note that there are six adjectives and five adverbs (mostly prepositional phrases) in Caught'ya #66.

67. noxious   reeked
   a plethora of   noisome
   billowed

No Paragraph (same topic) then ¶ (new action)

Types of Sentences – simple; compound; simple

Punctuation – put " around sound

Commas – compound sen.; no , bet. 2 adj. (2nd adj. is color); participles; list of participles

Homophones – their/there/they're

Other Skills – do not split verbs; bad (adj.) vs. badly (adv.); plural poss.; write out #s to 120;

Literary Devices – action; onomatopoeia; use of "that" to avoid quote; metaphor

B - the boom was immediately followed by a bad **noxious** odor that **reeked** bad of rotten eggs. the door to the boys bathroom suddenly burst open and **a plethora of noisome** grey smoke **billowed** out. 2 boys emerged from the smoke coughing hacking giggling and holding theyre noses

C - The "boom" immediately was followed by a bad, **noxious** odor that **reeked** badly of rotten eggs.

   The door to the boys' bathroom suddenly burst open, and **a plethora of noisome** grey smoke **billowed** out. Two boys emerged from the smoke, coughing, hacking, giggling, and holding their noses.

---

68. perdition   dearth of

No Paragraph – same topic

Types of Sentences – complex; complex (both with sub. clause at end)

Commas – unnecessary "who" clause; introductory adv. (optional); no , before "as" since sub. clause is at end

Verbs – loose vs. lose

Other Skills – do not use "that" to refer to people; who vs. whom; then vs. than; review A WHITE BUS words

Literary Devices – building suspense

B - isabelle and felicia that were standing nearby thought they recognized orson and danny as they ran out of the bathroom. than all **perdition** broke lose as students scattered in all directions to flee the noxious smoke and the **dearth of** fresh air

C - Isabelle and Felicia, who were standing nearby, thought they recognized Orson and Danny as they ran out of the bathroom. Then, all **perdition** broke loose as students scattered in all directions to flee the noxious smoke and the **dearth of** fresh air.

NOTE: It is a good idea to stress the use of "a plethora of" and "a dearth of." Students like using these phrases. Besides, they can never remember if "a lot" is one word or two.

B – Sentences for the Board	C – Corrected version of the CY
69. stentorian bellowed garbed foreboding Paragraph – new topic Types of Sentences – simple; complex Punctuation – **?** needed in question Commas – 2 adj. where 2ⁿᵈ is not age, color, or linked; adj. list Verbs – sit (intransitive) vs. set (transitive) Other Skills – who vs. whom; plural poss.; hyphens needed in 2 wds. acting as 1 Literary Devices – building suspense; description within action	**B -** a booming **stentorian** voice echoed from down the hall. who set off a stink bomb in the boys bathroom **bellowed** a tall black **garbed foreboding** looking man **C -** A booming, **stentorian** voice echoed from down the hall. "Who set off a stink bomb in the boys' bathroom?" **bellowed** a tall, black-**garbed**, **foreboding**-looking man.
70. ubiquitous loomed No Paragraph – same topic Types of Sentences – simple; complex Commas – 2 adj. where 2ⁿᵈ is not age, size, or linked Verbs – story in past tense Other Skills – do not use "that" to refer to people; who vs. whom; between vs. among; hyphen needed in 2 wds. acting as 1 Literary Devices – personification (smoking bathroom); still building suspense	**B -** it is the feared seemingly **ubiquitous** dean dread that was ever present in the halls and lunchroom. he **loomed** over and rushed between the scurrying seventh graders as he proceeded towards the still smoking bathroom **C -** It was the feared, seemingly **ubiquitous** Dean Dread who was ever present in the halls and lunchroom. He **loomed** over and rushed among the scurrying seventh-graders as he proceeded towards the still-smoking bathroom.

Writing Idea #14: Summary and Prediction.

Write a summary of the story so far, and then end your summary with a detailed account of what you predict will happen next. Write at least a paragraph about your prediction and be sure to give a plethora of details about what will happen to the major characters involved in the latest incident.

---

71. putrescent   stench

Paragraph – new topic

Types of Sentences – simple; compound

Commas – narrator aside (also appositive); compound sen.

Other Skills – who vs. whom (here object of preposition); review prepositions; CVC + suffix = double second consonant

Literary Devices – action

B - felicia for who spells never worked panicked. the **putrescent stench** of the stink bomb filled her nostrils and gaged her

C -   Felicia, for whom spells never worked, panicked. The **putrescent stench** of the stink bomb filled her nostrils, and it gagged her.

---

72. incantation   dispel

No Paragraph – same topic

Types of Sentences – simple; simple

Commas – introductory participial phrase; interrupter beginning sen.

Other Skills – bad (adj.) vs. badly (adv.)

B - without thinking she muttered an **incantation** to **dispel** the smoke and odor. of course it backfired bad

C - Without thinking, she muttered an **incantation** to **dispel** the smoke and odor. Of course, it backfired badly.

---

73. mauve   reeked

No Paragraph – still same subject

Types of Sentences – simple; compound

Commas – compound sen.

Other Skills – sing. poss.; bad (adj.) vs. badly (adv.)

Literary Devices – personification (smoke changing); metaphor (rotten eggs)

B - felicias fingernails turned **mauve**. the smoke changed from grey to **mauve** but it still **reeked** badly of rotten eggs

C - Felicia's fingernails turned **mauve**. The smoke changed from grey to **mauve**, but it still **reeked** badly of rotten eggs.

74. culprits   obstreperous

No Paragraph (same topic) then ¶ (new action)

Types of Sentences – simple; simple

Punctuation – " around short works like poems

Commas – intro phrase; 3 unnecessary appositives

Homophones – their/there/they're; hair/hare; to/too/two

Other Skills – do not begin sen. with FANBOYS; capitalize 1st letter of each line in poem

Literary Devices – building suspense

B - oddly enough their were mauve streaks in the hair of the two fleeing **culprits** orson odious and danny dapper. william waggish also on the scene muttered his newest cinquain entitled orson the **obstreperous**

there is
one bad person.
a mean boy...a troublemaker...
he loves to torment the helpless.
bad kid.

C - Oddly enough, there were mauve streaks in the hair of the two fleeing **culprits**, Orson Odious and Danny Dapper.

William Waggish, also on the scene, muttered his newest cinquain entitled "Orson, the **Obstreperous**."

There is
One bad person.
A mean boy...A troublemaker...
He loves to torment the helpless.
Bad kid.

75. cadence

Paragraph – new action

Types of Sentences – complex; compound

Commas – intro adverb (optional); compound sen.

Other Skills – "ly" denotes adverb

B - immediately dean dread waved his arms up and down in **cadence** with the poem as smoke curled from his ears and nostrils. his tongue protruded from his mouth and his eyes fluttered uncontrollable

C -   Immediately, Dean Dread waved his arms up and down in **cadence** with the poem as smoke curled from his ears and nostrils. His tongue protruded from his mouth, and his eyes fluttered uncontrollably.

Writing Idea #15: Strong, Vivid-Verb Paragraph Writing.

Write a strong, vivid-verb paragraph using the topic sentence, "_____ is weird." (Please make up a name so that no one is insulted or hurt.) This paragraph must have a title, a topic sentence similar to the one given, five strong, vivid-verb sentences that explain why that person is weird, and a concluding sentence that may use a "dead" verb.

---

76. stellar

No Paragraph – continuation

Types of Sentences – compound; simple

Commas – transition; compound sen.

Verbs – never split infinitives

Other Skills – run-on sen.; review simple (and good) transitions; _____ names of long works; w**ei**rdness; make adj. a noun by adding "ness"

Literary Devices – simile; literary reference

B - in addition his legs seemed to completely buckle and he wobbled like the scarecrow from the movie the wizard of oz and it was a **stellar** performance of teacher wierdness

C - In addition, his legs seemed to buckle completely, and he wobbled like the scarecrow from the movie The Wizard of Oz. It was a **stellar** performance of teacher weirdness.

NOTE: *Star Trek* was wrong. "To boldly go where..." should be "To go boldly." Infinitives should never be split.

77. lapse No ¶ (same topic) then ¶ (new speaker) Types of Sentences – complex; simple Commas – sub. clause at beginning; unnecessary appositive; quote Verbs – use of imperative	**B -** when dean dread recovered from his momentary **lapse** he took charge of the situation. get the custodian mr fixit he bellowed to a nearby teacher **C -** When Dean Dread recovered from his momentary **lapse**, he took charge of the situation. "Get the custodian, Mr. Fixit," he bellowed to a nearby teacher.

NOTE: Warn students of the unclear meaning due to the use of too many pronouns.

78. striplings Paragraph – new speaker (narrator) Types of Sentences – complex (sub. clause at end); simple Homophones – their/there/they're Other Skills – then vs. than; dangling participle (frowning); unclear due to use of too many pronouns; sing. poss.; fewer (can count) vs. less; write out #s to 120; review prepositions; hyphen in 2 wds. acting as 1	**B -** than frowning his eyes bulged when he spied the mauve smoke that had been grey less than 4 seconds before. he also saw two **striplings** with matching mauve streaks in there hair sprint out the door of the seventh grade wing **C -** Then as he frowned, the dean's **(or Dean Dread's)** eyes bulged when he spied the mauve smoke that had been grey fewer than four seconds before. He also saw two **striplings** with matching mauve streaks in their hair sprint out the door of the seventh-grade wing.

NOTE: If your students have progressed enough to understand, now would be a good time to point out the difference between a clause (has a subject and a verb) and a phrase (a group of words, serving as one part of speech, that lack either a subject or a verb or both). A sentence, for example, is an "independent clause" since it has a subject and a verb and can stand on its own.

B – Sentences for the Board	C – Corrected version of the CY
79. receding No ¶ (same topic and speaker) then ¶ (new speaker) Types of Sentences – simple; simple Punctuation – ! after emphatic command Commas – direct address; quote Homophones – to/too/two Other Skills – between (2) vs. among (3+); write out #s to 120; fewer (can count) vs. less; then (adv.) vs. than (comparative); use of caps to denote loudness; use of imperative	**B -** he made a connection between the 2 in less then a second. you boys stop dean dread roared two the **receding** backs of orson and danny **C -** Dean Dread made a connection between the two in less than a second. "You, boys, STOP!" Dean Dread roared to the **receding** backs of Orson and Danny.
80. brisk pace exacerbated Paragraph – new action Types of Sentences – simple; simple Homophones – to/too/two; their/there/they're Other Skills – CVC + suffix = double 2nd consonant; except vs. accept; write out #s to 120; do not use "that" to refer to people; who vs. whom; hyphen in 2 wds. acting as 1 Literary Devices – building tension	**B -** all boys in the hallway stoped accept the 2 in question that were headed for the sixth grade wing at a **brisk pace**. this **exacerbated** the possibility of theyre guilt **C -** All boys in the hallway stopped except the two in question who were headed for the sixth-grade wing at a **brisk pace**. This **exacerbated** the possibility of their guilt.

81. miscreants

Paragraph – new subject

Types of Sentences – complex; compound

Commas – sub. clause at beginning; interrupter

Verbs – pluperfect tense

Other Skills –write out #s to 120; farther (can measure) vs. further; sing. poss.

B - if they had run 5 steps further the **miscreants** might have escaped dean dreads eye. dean dread however moved quickly

C -   If they had run five steps farther, the **miscreants** might have escaped Dean Dread's eye. Dean Dread, however, moved quickly.

Writing Idea #16: Imaginative Narrative.

Orson and Danny get into a lot of trouble. I'm sure you can think of some students at your school who are always in trouble. Think of the kinds of trouble some seventh-graders get into and the naughty things they do, make some notes, plan out your story, and write a story about a mis-adventure of a miscreant. Be sure to include the consequences of the miscreant's actions in your story. Try to incorporate (use) humor in your story.

---

82. malefactors   reprobates

No ¶ (same speaker) then ¶ (new speaker)

Types of Sentences – simple; simple (imperative); simple

Commas – long intro adv.; direct address; quote; 2 adj. where 2nd is not age, color, or linked to noun

Homophones – their/there/they're;

Other Skills – comparatives (quicker); use "an" before a vowel; write out #s to 120; use of imperative

Literary Devices – aphorism (quicker than the blink...); foreshadowing

B - quicker than the blink of an eye he had the **malefactors** by the back of their shirts. you two **reprobates** come with me to my office. we need to investigate this incident he said in a low menacing tone

C - Quicker than the blink of an eye, he had the **malefactors** by the back of their shirts.

　　"You two **reprobates**, come with me to my office. We need to investigate this incident," he said in a low, menacing tone.

B – Sentences for the Board	C – Corrected version of the CY
83. jubilantly jeered scalawags Paragraph – new topic Types of Sentences – simple; simple (compound verb) Punctuation – ! needed for emphasis Homophones – there/their/they're Verbs – use of strong verbs Other Skills – review collective nouns; who vs. whom; do not use "that" to refer to people; antecedent/pronoun agreement; write out #s to 120; hyphen between 2 wds. acting as 1 Literary Devices – alliteration	**B -** orson and danny cringed. the crowd of seventh graders that witnessed this clapped there hands in delight and **jubilantly jeered** at the 2 **scalawags** **C -** Orson and Danny cringed. The crowd of seventh-graders who witnessed this clapped their hands in delight and **jubilantly jeered** at the two **scalawags**!
84. apprehended castigated transgression No Paragraph – same subject Types of Sentences – simple; simple Commas – intro word (optional) Homophones – their/there/they're Verbs – use of pluperfect; do not split verbs (2 times) Other Skills – further vs. farther (can count); then (adv.) vs. than (comparative) Literary Devices – dénouement (natural conclusion)	**B -** the class tormenters had finally been **apprehended** for something. farther they might even be **castigated** and than suspended for their **transgression** **C -** The class tormenters finally had been **apprehended** for something. Further, they even might be **castigated** and then suspended for their **transgression**.

85. putrescent   congregated

No ¶ (same topic) then ¶ (new time)

Types of Sentences – simple; complex

Commas – interrupter; sub. clause at beginning

Verbs – gerund phrase; use of pluperfect

Other Skills – review collective nouns and pronoun and verb agreement; review A WHITE BUS words

B - setting off a stink bomb after all was a major offense. when the **putrescent** smoke had been cleared everyone **congregated** around felicia fey

C - Setting off a stink bomb, after all, was a major offense.

When the **putrescent** smoke had been cleared, everyone **congregated** around Felicia Fey.

NOTE: I see no reason to teach students about gerunds (verbs acting as nouns) since they will use them naturally, and there are no commas involved. Why confuse the issue? I include them just in case...The one in this Caught'ya is "Setting off...was."

Writing Idea #17: Expository Essay–Problem/Solution.
Everyone has good days and bad days. Think of your worst day. Write an essay that briefly explains why it was your worst day and then spend most of the essay (at least three paragraphs) talking about some solutions that would have made that day better. Be sure to give details.

---

86. extolled   diffidently

3 Paragraphs – 3 new speakers

Types of Sentences – simple; simple; simple

Commas – direct address (in all 3 sen.); quote (in all 3 sen.)

Other Skills – well (adv.) vs. good (adj.)

Literary Devices – repartée (quick dialogue)

B - you did good girlfriend praised isabelle ingenuous. you really nailed them felicia **extolled** sam sagacious. astounding felicia said vivian virtuous **diffidently**

C -   "You did well, girlfriend," praised Isabelle Ingenuous.

"You really nailed them, Felicia," **extolled** Sam Sagacious.

"Astounding, Felicia," said Vivian Virtuous **diffidently**.

B – Sentences for the Board	C – Corrected version of the CY
87. lauded cuffed contritely 2 Paragraphs – 2 new speakers Types of Sentences – complex (sub. clause at end); simple Commas – direct address; quote; direct address; quote Homophones – to/too/two; your/you're Other Skills – need noun for clarity Literary Devices – repartée	**B -** way too go girl **lauded** jesse jocose as he **cuffed** her gently on her back. i take back all those poems about youre magic felicia william waggish apologized **contritely** **C -** "Way to go, girl," **lauded** Jesse Jocose as he **cuffed** Felicia gently on her back. 　　"I take back all those poems about your magic, Felicia," William Waggish apologized **contritely**.
88. magnanimously loathed attire Paragraph – new speaker Types of Sentences – compound; simple question; simple Punctuation – need for **?** in question Commas – direct address; compound sen. Homophones – to/too/two Other Skills – contraction; spelling of all right (alright is wrong); review FANBOYS; review demonstrative pronouns (this, that, these, those) Literary Devices – sarcasm	**B -** thats alright william returned felicia **magnanimously** for she really **loathed** williams teasing poems. what am i going too do with these mauve nails. they clash with my black **attire** **C -** "That's all right, William," returned Felicia **magnanimously**, for she really **loathed** William's teasing poems. "What am I going to do with these mauve nails? They clash with my black **attire**."

NOTE: Since this is an especially long Caught'ya, you might want to consider doing it orally.

89. dénouement   incident
   nefarious   duo

Paragraph – new topic

Types of Sentences – simple (despite length); simple

Punctuation – accent on French word used in English; ( ) around narrator aside

Commas – put **,** around "too" if it means "also"

Homophones – to/too/two; their/there/they're

Verbs – verb must agree with sing. subject

Other Skills – hyphen in 2 wds. acting as 1; who vs. whom; write out #s to 120;

Literary Devices – narrator aside

B - the **dénouement** of the entire stink bomb **incident** was that orson and danny over who all the girls still all drooled and for whom some still did an extra copy of there homework were suspended for 10 days. the **nefarious duo** was sentenced to cafeteria clean up for a month after theyre return too

C -   The **dénouement** of the entire stink-bomb **incident** was that Orson and Danny (over whom all the girls still drooled and for whom some still did an extra copy of their homework) were suspended for ten days. The **nefarious duo** was sentenced to cafeteria clean-up for a month after their return, too.

NOTE: This is a good place to do a mini-lesson on who/whoever (subject) vs. whom/whomever (object of verb or preposition) if your students still confuse the two.

NOTE: Although this Caught'ya is only two sentences, it is long. You may want to do the second sentence orally.

90. reprehensible   preyed
posterior   intrepid

Paragraph – new time

Types of Sentences – simple; compound with 3 indep. clauses

Punctuation – use of **;** in 3 indep. clauses (review 4 uses)

Commas – introductory adv. (optional)

Homophones – pair/pare/pear; prayed/preyed

Verbs – verb tense shift

Other Skills – vocabulary; write out #s to 120; friends

Literary Devices – alliteration

B - after that incident dean dread and the rest of the teachers keep a watchful eye on the **reprehensible** pear for the remainder of the school year. orson still gave evil looks danny still **preyed** on the girls but the 2 ceased to be a major pain in the **posterior** of the **intrepid** freinds

C -   After that incident, Dean Dread and the rest of the teachers kept a watchful eye on the **reprehensible** pair for the remainder of the school year. Orson still gave evil looks; Danny still **preyed** on the girls; but the two ceased to be a major pain in the **posterior** of the **intrepid** friends.

NOTE: Since there are three independent clauses in this Caught'ya, this also might be a good point to go over again the difference between a clause (contains a subject and verb) and a phrase (lacks either a subject or a verb or both).

Writing Idea #18: Persuasive/Argumentative Essay.

Try to remember a time when you were in trouble with your parents or with a teacher (or the dean) at school. Write a letter to that person and try to convince him or her not to punish you too severely. Be sure to give convincing arguments with details. Be sure to use direct address.

You also must use the correct form for a business letter for headings, greeting, and closing.

B – Sentences for the Board	C – Corrected version of the CY
91. abruptly Paragraph – new topic Types of Sentences – simple; simple Punctuation – " around irony Commas – introductory adv. (optional); unnecessary appositive Homophones – one/won Literary Devices – irony	**B -** now felicia **abruptly** became miss popular. one of the teachers even recommended her for the special school for magically gifted kids marvelously magic magnet middle school **C -** Now, Felicia **abruptly** became "Miss Popular." One of the teachers even recommended her for the special school for magically gifted kids, Marvelously Magic Magnet Middle School.
92. awry Paragraph – new time Types of Sentences – complex ("on the day" acts as subordinating conj.); simple Commas – sub. clause at beginning; interrupter; interrupter; participle phrase Verbs – rise vs. raise; intransitive vs. transitive Other Skills – sing. poss.; fewer (can count) vs. less; than vs. then (adv.); write out #s to 120	**B -** on the day she was tested for admission to that school however felicias entry spell as usual went **awry**. instead of rising a pencil more than one foot but less then 2 feet off the desk as required felicia turned the pencil and her hair green **C -** On the day she was tested for admission to that school, however, Felicia's entry spell, as usual, went **awry**. Instead of raising a pencil more than one foot but fewer than two feet off the desk as required, Felicia turned the pencil and her hair green.

NOTE: At this point a review (or lesson) on the common irregular verbs which students often confuse might be appropriate. Be sure to include lie/lay, rise/raise, sit/set. In that list, the problem lies in which is intransitive (takes no object) and which is transitive (takes an object).

NOTE: Warn students that the last sentence needs to be reworded.

93. rationalized   putrid

Paragraph – new speaker

Types of Sentences – compound quote; simple question

Punctuation – **?** needed in question; note punctuation in interrupted quote

Commas – quote; appositive (only one best friend so unnecessary); quote and compound sent.

Verbs – correct use of "would" as conditional tense

Other Skills – contractions; fr**ie**nd; who vs. whom; do not end a sen. with a preposition

Literary Devices – alliteration; humor

B - i didnt want to go theyre anyway she **rationalized** later to isabelle her best friend and i didnt want to leave all of you stuck here without me. who would william direct his **putrid** poems at she concluded

C - "I didn't want to go there anyway," she **rationalized** later to Isabelle, her best friend, "and I didn't want to leave all of you stuck here without me. At whom would William direct his **putrid** poems?" she concluded.

---

94. relegated   cropped up
  clamorous   obstreperous

Paragraph – new topic

Types of Sentences – complex ("now that" acts as a sub. conj.); simple

Commas – sub. clause at beginning; extra info

Homophones – new/knew/gnu

Other Skills – vocabulary; do not capitalize names of subjects except languages

B - now that orson and danny were **relegated** to nasty stares only gnu problem students **cropped up**. carolyn **clamorous** became even more **obstreperous** with her persistent but pointed questions in math

C -   Now that Orson and Danny were **relegated** to nasty stares only, new problem students **cropped up**. Carolyn **Clamorous** became even more **obstreperous** with her persistent, but pointed, questions in math.

95. **jabbering** **incessant** **inane** **audible** **querulous** **quarrels**

No Paragraph – same topic

Types of Sentences – simple (compound subject); simple

Commas – 2 adjectives where 2nd is not age, size, color, or related; unnecessary who clause

Verbs – do not use "would" to denote past tense (it is conditional)

Other Skills – vocabulary; comparatives; who vs. whom

B - john **jabbering** and his **incessant inane** chatter grew to be more **audible** and more annoying. quincy **querulous** who always would argue with everyone tried to pick more **quarrels**

C - John **Jabbering** and his **incessant**, **inane** chatter grew to be more **audible** and more annoying. Quincy **Querulous**, who always argued with everyone, tried to pick more **quarrels**.

Writing Idea #19: Personal Narrative.
Everyone quarrels with someone at some time. Think of a quarrel you had with someone. Write about the subject of that quarrel. Be sure to include some details and some conversation. Be sure to include an introductory paragraph and a satisfying conclusion.

---

96. vociferously

No Paragraph – same topic (more details)

Types of Sentences – simple; simple

Other Skills – abbreviation; gerund; review prepositions; who vs. whom; review object pronouns; never use "that" to refer to people; need a noun for clarity

Literary Devices – specific details

B - he went so far as to complain **vociferously** to ms stern science about copying the notes from the board. she punished him by requiring him to make an extra copy of the notes for someone that was absent

C - Quincy went so far as to complain **vociferously** to Ms. Stern Science about copying the notes from the board. She punished him by requiring him to make an extra copy of the notes for someone who was absent.

B – Sentences for the Board	C – Corrected version of the CY
97. droll slovenly monotony No ¶ (same topic) then ¶ (new event) Types of Sentences – simple; complex (sub. clause at end) Homophones – to/too/two Verbs – verb tense shift Other Skills – sing. poss.; participle (verb as adj.); CVC + suffix = double 2nd consonant; comparatives Literary Devices – humor	**B -** even jesses usually **droll** jokes fall flatter than usual. skateboarding steven **slovenly** provided a welcome break in the **monotony** of school when he accidentally dropped his saging jeans to his ankles as he jumped too touch the top of a doorway **C -** Even Jesse's usually **droll** jokes fell flatter than usual. Skateboarding Steven **Slovenly** provided a welcome break in the **monotony** of school when he accidentally dropped his sagging jeans to his ankles as he jumped to touch the top of a doorway.
98. slovenly inadvertently No Paragraph – same topic Types of Sentences – simple; simple Punctuation – " around idiomatic expression Commas – 2 adj. where 2nd is not age, size, color, or linked; no **,** before "boxer" since they are a kind of shorts Homophones – right/rite/write Other Skills – review object pronouns Literary Devices – idiomatic expression	**B -** it seemed that dean dread was rite behind he. steven **slovenly** thus **inadvertently** mooned dean dread with his bright orange and blue striped boxer shorts **C -** It seemed that Dean Dread was right behind him. Steven **Slovenly** thus **inadvertently** "mooned" Dean Dread with his bright, orange and blue, striped boxer shorts.

99. retribution No Paragraph – same incident Types of Sentences – simple; compound Punctuation – " around idiomatic expression Commas – compound sen. Homophones – new/knew/gnu Verbs – never use "would" to denote past tense (it is conditional); verb tense shift Other Skills – need noun for clarity; write out #s to 120; review collective nouns; hyphen in 2 wds. acting as one Literary Devices – humor	**B -** he would maintain afterwards that the **retribution** of 3 days of in school detention was worth mooning the dean. everyone talks about the incident for weeks and steven became the new hero for that time **C -** Steven maintained afterwards that the **retribution** of three days of in-school detention was worth "mooning" the dean. Everyone talked about the incident for weeks, and Steven became the new hero for that time.
100. quest unravel otiose 2 Paragraphs – 2 new topics Types of Sentences – simple; simple Commas – noun series; noun series Homophones – their/there/they're Verbs – use of pluperfect Other Skills – write out ordinal #s	**B -** william jesse and sam intensified there **quest** to **unravel** the mystery of the bizarre teachers and their strange behavior. sam jesse and olivia **otiose** had taken music for the 2nd year **C -** William, Jesse, and Sam intensified their **quest** to **unravel** the mystery of the bizarre teachers and their strange behavior. Sam, Jesse, and Olivia **Otiose** had taken music for the second year.

Writing Idea #20: Dialogue.
Write a one-page conversation among William, Jesse, and Sam as they discuss Steven's "accidental mooning" of the dean and what they plan to do to unravel the mystery of the strange teachers. They also could discuss why they think that poems have such an effect on their teachers.

101. loathe   buffoon

No Paragraph – elaboration of topic sentence

Types of Sentences – simple; compound

Punctuation – " around vernacular (and pun) and what Jesse said

Commas – appositive; appositive; compound sen.; appositive

Verbs – use of pluperfect

Other Skills – use "like" only when comparing nouns; who's vs. whose; fewer/less

Literary Devices – use of vernacular; pun on word "tubular"

B - sam like he had the previous year played the oboe. olivia **loathe** to learn a new instrument stuck to her clarinet and jesse always the **buffoon** played the trombone which allowed him some tubular slides

C - Sam, as he had the previous year, played the oboe. Olivia, **loathe** to learn a new instrument, stuck to her clarinet, and Jesse, always the **buffoon**, played the trombone which allowed him some "tubular slides."

102. pique   fervent   pithy

No ¶ (same topic) then ¶ (new topic)

Types of Sentences – compound; simple

Commas – intro phrase; compound sen.; appositive

Other Skills – demonstrative pronouns (this/that/these/those)

B - for the most part the trio liked the subject and the teacher but classical music did not **pique** their interest. jesse whos attitude towards classical music was less than **fervent** directed a **pithy** cinquain at the music teacher mr melodious music

C - For the most part, the trio liked the subject and the teacher, but classical music did not **pique** their interest.

Jesse, whose attitude towards classical music was less than **fervent**, directed a **pithy** cinquain at the music teacher, Mr. Melodious Music.

B – Sentences for the Board	C – Corrected version of the CY
103. oeuvre devotee sentiment No ¶ (same topic) then ¶ (new subject) Types of Sentences – simple; simple Punctuation – " around title of short works; note normal punctuation used in poem; note first letter of each line of poem is capitalized; hyphen in 2 wds. acting as 1 Commas – extra info; noun series; appositive; long intro phrase; appositive Other Skills – need noun for clarity Literary Devices – musical references	**B** - he entitled his **oeuvre** music misery we play poorly, off-key. bach, beethoven, mozart, 3 ancient composers, long dead, haunt us. in spite of the mention of his favorite composers mr melodious music a **devotee** of classical music did not appreciate the **sentiment** **C** - Jesse entitled his **oeuvre** "Music Misery." We play Poorly, off-key. Bach, Beethoven, Mozart, Three ancient composers, long dead, Haunt us. In spite of the mention of his favorite composers, Mr. Melodious Music, a **devotee** of classical music, did not appreciate the **sentiment**.
104. engross No ¶ (same topic) then ¶ (new speaker) Types of Sentences – compound; simple Commas – compound sen.; quote Homophones – to/too/two Other Skills – need noun for clarity	**B** - he sentenced jesse too playing bach on the trombone to **engross** the crowd at lunch for a day but he did not react in any other way to the poem. strange murmured sam **C** - He sentenced Jesse to playing Bach on the trombone to **engross** the crowd at lunch for a day, but Mr. Melodious Music did not react in any other way to the poem. "Strange," murmured Sam.

105. anomalous

Paragraph – new speaker

Types of Sentences – complex (sub. clause at end)

Punctuation – quote inside quote; " around vernacular

Commas – interjection; direct address; quote

Homophones – your/you're

Verbs – correct use of "would" as conditional tense

Other Skills – friend; demonstrative pronouns who vs. whom; good vs. well

Literary Devices – use of vernacular; humor

B - bogus your toast my friend whispered olivia for whom writing a poem for the fun of it would be **anomalous** even though she was good at it

C -   "'Bogus,' you're toast, my friend," whispered Olivia for whom writing a poem for the fun of it would be **anomalous** even though she was good at it.

Writing Idea #21: Expository/Explanatory Essay.
There are all different kinds of music from classical to rock to rap to hip-hop to the latest in popular music. Write an essay to explain to your teacher which kind of music is your favorite and why it is your favorite. Be sure to come up with three reasons why you love your favorite type of music and support those reasons.

For example: I love classical music the best because it doesn't have words like the modern music. I can sit in my favorite chair and read a book while listening without having the words interfere. Not having words to my music also lets me concentrate on the music itself more, and images can swirl around in my head, not hampered by words, etc.

106. mulled over peers Paragraph – new speaker Types of Sentences – complex; simple Punctuation – " around vernacular; quote within a quote; use of ellipses to indicate incomplete thought Commas – interjection and direct address; quote Verbs – use of pluperfect Other Skills – review pronouns (7 kinds); friends	**B -** bummer dudes said jesse jocose to his freinds as he **mulled over** the misery of having to play bach on his trombone before his **peers**. if only he had let me play jazz **C -** "'Bummer, dudes,'" said Jesse Jocose to his friends as he **mulled over** the misery of having to play Bach on his trombone before his **peers**. "If only he had let me play jazz..."
107. *sotto voce* Paragraph – new subject Types of Sentences – simple; simple Punctuation – put Latin phrase in *italics* Commas – short intro adverb (optional) Verbs – accept vs. except (not a verb) Other Skills – abbreviation; superlatives (best); review object pronouns; superlatives Literary Devices – use of Latin	**B -** in english ms witty writing wizard also did not react to the poems in any way except to analyze them for form. william waggish recited *sotto voce* one of his bestest efforts **C -** In English, Ms. Witty Writing Wizard also did not react to the poems in any way except to analyze them for form. William Waggish recited *sotto voce* one of his best efforts.

B – Sentences for the Board	C – Corrected version of the CY

108. subordinating conjunctions
(A WHITE BUS words)

No Paragraph – same subject

Types of Sentences – complex (sub. clause at end); simple

Punctuation – " around short works; " around incongruous word use ("dead verb"); note punctuation in poem (semicolon use)

Commas – no **,** before A WHITE BUS word; interrupter

Other Skills – need noun for clarity; w**ei**rd; gerunds (singing and chanting); capitalize first word of each line of poem; review semicolon uses; parallel construction (to sing...to chant)

Literary Devices – personification ("dead" verbs)

B - he had entitled it writing wacko because the new english teacher was indeed a little crazy. ms writing wizard required her students to sing dead verbs and the **subordinating conjunctions** and chanting prepositions and the coordinating conjunctions

> writing
> weird stuff.
> poems, essays, stories;
> singing "dead" verbs; chanting the preps.
> strange class.

C - He had entitled it "Writing Wacko" because the new English teacher was, indeed, a little crazy. Ms. Writing Wizard required her students to sing "dead" verbs and the **subordinating conjunctions** and to chant prepositions and the coordinating conjunctions.

> Writing.
> Weird stuff.
> Poems, essays, stories.
> Singing "dead" verbs; chanting the preps.
> Strange class.

NOTE: This is a good point to review the subordinating and coordinating conjunctions, prepositions, and the helping ("dead") verbs.

109. critiqued   stringent
       customary

2 Paragraphs – new persons speaking (2nd is narrator)

Types of Sentences – simple; simple

Commas – direct address; quote; interrupter; appositive

Homophones – your/you're

Other Skills – abbreviation; do not capitalize subjects

Literary Devices – building mystery

B - william **critiqued** ms writing wizard youre last line needs work. in social studies however the new teacher ms **stringent** social studies reacted in the **customary** fashion to the poems

C -   "William," **critiqued** Ms. Writing Wizard, "your last line needs work."

        In social studies, however, the new teacher, Ms. **Stringent** Social Studies, reacted in the **customary** fashion to the poems.

110. mock   dreary   stringent unethical

No ¶ (same topic) then ¶ (time change)

Types of Sentences – simple; complex (sub. clause at end)

Punctuation – note normal punct. in poem

Commas – unnecessary who clause; 2 intro prepositional phrases (adv.)

Homophones – wrote/rote

Verbs – do not split verbs

Other Skills – vocabulary; who vs. whom; contraction; review superlatives (least); capitalize first letter of each line of poem; review poss. pronouns; abbreviation; "no one" is 2 wds.; antecedent/pronoun agreement ("no one" is sing.); superlatives

B - isabelle ingenuous who didnt usually like to **mock** anyone wrote a cinquain for her least favorite class

> history.   (Say it in two syllables.)
> we study dates, facts,
> and people who are dead...
> a good class to catch a good nap.
> **dreary**.

towards the end of the period isabelle recited her poem under her breath when ms **stringent** social studies was walking the aisle to make sure noone was being **unethical** on their test

C - Isabelle Ingenuous, who usually didn't like to **mock** anyone, wrote a cinquain for her least favorite class.

> History   (Say it in two syllables.)
> We study dates, facts,
> And people who are dead...
> A good class to catch a good nap.
> **Dreary**.

Towards the end of the period, Isabelle recited her poem under her breath when Ms. **Stringent** Social Studies was walking the aisle to make sure no one was being **unethical** on the test.

Writing Idea #22: Poetry Writing.
It's time to write some more poetry. Compose at least five cinquains using nature as a subject.

111. spontaneous lank Paragraph – change of topic Types of Sentences – simple, simple (looks compound) Commas – object list; **,** between dependent and indep. clauses Homophones – their/there/they're; hair/hare Other Skills – use "an" before a vowel; abbreviation; not only...but; fewer (can count) vs. less; comparatives; then vs. than (comparative); write out #s to 120 Literary Devices – description within action	**B -** theyre was a immediate and **spontaneous** reaction by ms stringent social studies. not only did her eyelids flutter her tongue protrude and smoke curl from her ears but her **lank** grey hair stood on end for more than 2 but less then 3 seconds **C -** There was an immediate and **spontaneous** reaction by Ms. Stringent Social Studies. Not only did her eyelids flutter, her tongue protrude, and smoke curl from her ears, but her **lank** grey hair stood on end for more than two but fewer than three seconds.

NOTE: Now would be a good time to review the differences between clauses and phrases again.

112. overtaxed 2 Paragraphs – 2 new speakers Types of Sentences – simple; simple Punctuation – quote within quote; need to put vernacular in quotes; quote with question Commas – 2 interjections; quote Other Skills – relative pronouns who vs. whom	**B -** oh wow that rocks said jesse who witnessed the event. what is all this whined pauline for who anything out of the ordinary **overtaxed** her ability to cope **C -** "Oh, wow, that 'rocks,'" said Jesse who witnessed the event. "What is all this?" whined Pauline for whom anything out of the ordinary **overtaxed** her ability to cope.

B – Sentences for the Board   C – Corrected version of the CY

NOTE: You might want to read this one out loud to your students for clarity.

113. barrage   egregious

2 Paragraphs – new speakers (2nd is narrator)

Types of Sentences – simple; simple; deliberate use of fragment; simple (compound subject)

Punctuation – 3 question marks needed

Commas – prep. phrase list; noun list

Homophones – to/too/two; hair/hare

Other Skills – contraction; then (adv.) vs. then (comparative); discuss fragments

Literary Devices – humor

B - i had gotten used to the smoke the flutter and the tongue but hare standing on end. whats next she moaned. sparks. jesse, william and sam then wrote and recited a **barrage** of **egregious** cinquains

C -   "I had gotten used to the smoke, the flutter, and the tongue, but hair standing on end? What's next?" she moaned. "Sparks?"
    Jesse, William, and Sam then wrote and recited a **barrage** of **egregious** cinquains.

---

114. articulate   epitome

No Paragraph – same topic and speaker

Types of Sentences – simple; simple

Commas – unnecessary phrase (appositive)

Verbs – verb tense shift

Other Skills – relative pronouns (which vs. that and who vs. whom)

B - alessandra also writes one that she gave to sam to **articulate**. sam for who alessandra was the **epitome** of female beauty was thrilled right down to his toes

C - Alessandra also wrote one which she gave to Sam to **articulate**. Sam, for whom Alessandra was the **epitome** of female beauty, was thrilled right down to his toes.

NOTE: Warn students that this one is particularly difficult.

115. reek

No Paragraph – same topic, same speaker

Types of Sentences – simple; compound with semicolon

Punctuation – quote within quote; note normal punct. in poem; " around short works; use of colon (never after a verb); " around euphemism; use of ; in 2 compound sen. (one in poem)

Commas – intro phrase

Homophones – course/coarse

Verbs – verb tense shift

Other Skills – who vs. whom; do not use "that" to refer to people; do not end sen. with prep.; sing. poss.; capitalize first letter of each line of poem

Literary Devices – euphemism ("bites" instead of "sucks," which is the current, popular phrase)

B - of course he tried her cinquain on every teacher that he came into contact with. alessandras cinquain is entitled horribly hard middle school bites it goes like this

> school "bites."
> teachers assign
> piles of homework and projects.
> bathrooms **reek**; lunchroom is noisy.
> why us?

C - Of course, he tried her cinquain on every teacher with whom he came into contact. Alessandra's cinquain was entitled "Horribly Hard Middle School 'Bites;'" it went like this:

> School "bites."
> Teachers assign
> Piles of homework and projects.
> Bathrooms **reek**; lunchroom is noisy.
> Why us?

NOTE: This would be an excellent time to review the three uses of the semicolon. See NOTE for Caught'yas #38 and 62.

Writing Idea #23: Expository–Problem/Solution.

All people have problems. Think of some problem that you have. Now write down at least three possible solutions to your problem. Then write an essay that explains your possible solutions and why each might work. Your problem could be anything from too much homework to a little brother or sister who gets into your things or a bully at school or something more serious.

116. upbraided   pejorative

2 Paragraphs – new subject; new speaker

Types of Sentences – simple; complex

Punctuation – quote around euphemism; quote within a quote; " around referred-to word

Commas – direct address; quote

Homophones – know/no; your/you're

Other Skills – abbreviation

Literary Devices – euphemism ("bites")

B - ms witty writing wizard **upbraided** sam for his use of the **pejorative** word bites. as you know young man your use of the verb to bite is improper she scolded

C - Ms. Witty Writing Wizard **upbraided** Sam for his use of the **pejorative** word "bites."

"As you know, young man, your use of the verb 'to bite' is improper," she scolded.

117. flourish   blathering

No ¶ (same speaker continued) then ¶ (new speaker)

Types of Sentences – compound with semicolon; simple; complex with question (2 sub. clauses at end)

Punctuation – ? needed

Commas – quote

Homophones – your/you're; to/too/ two

Verbs – lay (intransitive past) vs. laid (transitive past)

Other Skills – use "an" with vowel; unclear pronoun (who rarely listened?) so need noun

Literary Devices – humor

B - you have to bite something it is a transitive verb. your using it as a intransitive verb she finished with a **flourish** as she lay down the chalk. what is she **blathering** about whispered olivia too isabelle since she rarely listened in class when a teacher spoke

C - "You have to bite something; it is a transitive verb. You're using it as an intransitive verb," she finished with a **flourish** as she laid down the chalk.

"What is she **blathering** about?" whispered Olivia to Isabelle since Olivia rarely listened in class when a teacher spoke.

NOTE: This is a good place for a final review of transitive vs. intransitive verbs. You might want to review the most often confused ones: lie/lay, rise/ raise, sit/set, etc.

It is also a good place for a final review of "your/you're."

118. exuberantly extemporaneous aversion guise

2 Paragraphs – new topic and speaker (narrator); new speaker

Types of Sentences – compound; complex

Commas – compound sen.; 2 adj. where 2nd is not age, size, color, or linked; interjection; quote

Verbs – story in present tense

Other Skills – vocabulary; abbreviation; use "an" before vowel; sing. poss.; note lack of caps of "what" due to continued quote

Literary Devices – metaphor (teacher is a "grammar book")

B - ms witty writing wizard overheard olivias question, and she **exuberantly** launches into an extensive **extemporaneous** lesson on verbs that take a object and verbs that do not. oh brother murmured olivia as she rolled her eyes upwards in **aversion** she really is a grammar book in the **guise** of a person

C -   Ms. Witty Writing Wizard overheard Olivia's question, and she **exuberantly** launched into an extensive, **extemporaneous** lesson on verbs that take an object and verbs that do not.

"Oh, brother," murmured Olivia as she rolled her eyes upwards in **aversion**, "she really is a grammar book in the **guise** of a person."

Passage to be read out loud to students

NOTE: Take a break from the Caught'yas (it's near the end of the year anyway) and read the following to your students several times. The following, read out loud, will continue the story up to the last seven Caught'yas and the final exam which will bring the seventh-grade part of the story to a conclusion.

Before you read the passage, write the vocabulary on the board, go over, and require students to put them in their vocabulary notebooks.

As you read, you will want to point out correct grammar, mechanics, usage, spelling, etc. as a review for the year. You may wish especially to point out the correct form of the skills you know are going to appear on the final exam.

If you have more time, you can put the following passage into Caught'ya form. Remember, there are seven more Caught'yas to go before the final exam.

Isabelle and Sam just grinned; Olivia Otiose was being her usual **otiose** self. She was very intelligent, but somehow **abhorred** to do anything that might make her do homework or study.

Other teachers reacted differently to Alessandra's poem. Mr. Math Martinet, Ms. Stern Science, and Ms. **Stringent** Social Studies did the usual: fluttering eyes, smoking ears, protruding tongue. In addition, their hair either stood on end for fewer than three seconds, or they raised their arms in the air in **cadence** with each syllable of the poem. When Sam recited Alessandra's poem in the vicinity of Dean Dread in the cafeteria, he rewarded the seventh-graders with a startling show of silver sparks that **emanated** from the tips of his fingers. The show stopped as **abruptly** as it had begun.

"Wow, Pauline," said Jesse Jocose in admiration, "you called it! Sparks!"

Principal **Punctilious**, who had lunchroom duty that day and who did not show any overt reaction to the poem, promptly used his radio and called Mr. **Adept** Fixit. The **latter** arrived in fewer than five seconds and then exited with Dean Dread following behind him. Jesse Jocose recited the poem again as the two passed by his table, but while Dean Dread reacted in the usual manner, Mr. Adept Fixit did not even **grimace**.

The art and music teachers, like the new creative writing teacher, showed no **overt** reaction except utter disgust at the use of the **epithet** "bites."

One day at lunch, Sam, William, Jesse, Isabelle, Pauline, Vivian, Alessandra (who now hung around with her hero, Sam), Felicia, and Pauline analyzed the new information that they were **amassing** on their bizarre teachers.

"This is getting stranger and stranger," said Sam. "Why did our **intractable** English teacher last year react to the poems while the creative writing teacher this year does not?"

"Hey, guys, why are they all reacting more obviously this year?" asked Vivian Virtuous.

Jesse Jocose, who always looked for an excuse to be funny, suddenly stood up on the bench and recited a **spontaneous** cinquain in a **strident** voice.

> There are
> Five things I hate
> About lunch: awful food,
> Piercing noise, hard seats, no freedom,
> Stale rolls.

When he had finished his poem, Jesse sat down on the **inflexible** seat mentioned in Jesse's poem. Felicia (who secretly liked Jesse) **surreptitiously** threw a stale roll in Jesse's direction. Jesse, laughing, pitched an apple core into Felicia's lap.

William, not to be outdone and remembering that Dean Dread had left the room, flicked his tray and **launched** his uneaten, **sodden** vegetables into the air and yelled, "Food fight!"

Immediately, the air became **rife** with flying bits of food and trash. Bits of spaghetti dangled from the ceiling fans. Greasy sauce plastered everyone's hair and smeared most **visages**. Bits of "mystery meat" lay in brown blobs on the now-filthy floor. The **cacophony** of shouting and laughing student voices drowned out Mr. Punctilious Principal who stood on stage and shrieked **futilely** into his microphone.

119. visage wrath Paragraph – new time and action Types of Sentences – simple; simple Commas – intro adv. (optional); 2 adj. where 2nd is not age, size, color, or linked; extra info about subject in predicate Homophones – there/their/they're Other Skills – use of strong, vivid verbs; review use of active vs. passive voice Literary Devices – metaphor ("visage" and "picture")	**B -** all at once the doors to the cafeteria flung open. a tall menacing figure stood their his **visage** a picture of righteous **wrath** **C -** All at once, the doors to the cafeteria flung open. A tall, menacing figure stood there, his **visage** a picture of righteous **wrath**.
120. din amplification raucous Paragraph – new speaker Types of Sentences – simple imperative; simple Commas – direct address; quote; intro phrase Other Skills – review prepositions	**B -** students stop this immediately he boomed over the **din**. even without **amplification** his **raucous** voice could be heard by all **C -** "Students, stop this immediately," he boomed over the **din**. Even without **amplification**, his **raucous** voice could be heard by all.

Writing Idea #24: Descriptive Essay.

Write an essay to describe the cafeteria in your school. Be sure to include colors, furniture, wall decorations, the food, and any other distinguishing feature.

121. stentorian   fearsome

Paragraph – new speaker (narrator)

Types of Sentences – complex (sub. clause at end); simple; compound

Commas – intro adv. (optional); verb list; compound sen.

Verbs – transitive "set" vs. intransitive "sat"

Other Skills – accept vs. except; need hyphen in 2 wds. acting as 1; sing. poss.

B - amazingly the cafeteria was suddenly silent accept for the drip of the spaghetti as it fell from the fans. students froze in place. they stood leaned or set mid hurl at the sound of dean dreads **stentorian** and **fearsome** voice and they stared in his direction

C -   Amazingly, the cafeteria was suddenly silent except for the drip of the spaghetti as it fell from the fans. Students froze in place. They stood, leaned, or sat, mid-hurl, at the sound of Dean Dread's **stentorian** and **fearsome** voice, and they stared in his direction.

NOTE: This is a great place for a final review of the subordinating conjunctions. Note that this Caught'ya also includes three of the four types of sentences—a good review before the final which will require students to identify types of sentences.

122. appalling   boded   dire
intoned

Paragraph – new speaker

Types of Sentences – complex; complex; complex

Commas – quote; 2 adj. where 2nd is not age, size, color, or linked; direct address; quote

Homophones – their/there/they're

Verbs – do not split verbs; sit vs. set (intransitive vs. transitive)

Other Skills – vocabulary; use of imperative

B - i will absolutely not tolerate such **appalling** behavior dean dread continued in a deadly low tone that **boded** disaster and punishment. set down children he ordered. theyre will be **dire** consequences for this he **intoned**

C -   "I absolutely will not tolerate such **appalling** behavior," Dean Dread continued in a deadly, low tone that **boded** disaster and punishment. "Sit down, children," he ordered. "There will be **dire** consequences for this," he **intoned**.

B – Sentences for the Board	C – Corrected version of the CY

123. jabbering   mute   querulous   bristled
 	
3 Paragraphs – new speaker (narrator); new subject; new speaker
 	
Types of Sentences – simple; simple; simple (compound verb); complex
 	
Punctuation – ellipses for unfinished quote; quote within quote for what was said before
 	
Commas – participial phrase; unnecessary "who" clause; quote
 	
Verbs – sit vs. sat
 	
Other Skills – vocabulary; review collective nouns; then (adv.) vs. than (comparative)
 	
Literary Devices – simile ("like an...")
	B - everyone sat, stunned into silence. even john **jabbering** was **mute**. than quincy **querulous** who always had to argue with everybody broke the silence and said but. i said silence repeated dean dread as he **bristled** like an angry warthog
	
	C - Everyone sat, stunned into silence. Even John **Jabbering** was **mute**.
	    Then Quincy **Querulous**, who always had to argue with everyone, broke the silence and said, "But..."
	    "I said 'silence,'" repeated Dean Dread as he **bristled** like an angry warthog.

124. querulous ominously miscreants Paragraph – new speaker (narrator) Types of Sentences – compound; simple; simple (compound verb) Commas – compound sen.; interrupting adv. Other Skills – vocabulary	**B -** quincy **querulous** was **querulous** but he was not stupid. he did not attempt to speak again. dean dread stalked **ominously** to the front of the cafeteria where he stood hands on hips and glared at the **miscreants** **C -** Quincy **Querulous** was **querulous**, but he was not stupid. He did not attempt to speak again. Dean Dread stalked **ominously** to the front of the cafeteria where he stood, hands on hips, and glared at the **miscreants**.

NOTE: You might want to do this Caught'ya orally.

125. postponed   gobbet
      persisted   comport

Paragraph – new speaker

Types of Sentences – compound/complex; compound with semicolon; simple

Punctuation – continued quote (no caps); use of ; in compound sen.

Commas – transition (and quote); quote; compound sen.; noun list; transition; quote; transition; quote

Homophones – your/you're; their/there/they're; piece/peace

Verbs – do not split verb

Other Skills – transitions; hyphen in 4 wds. acting as 1 and 2 wds. acting as 1

B - first he said classes will be **postponed** and you will stay here until every strand of spaghetti every drop of milk every piece of paper and every **gobbet** of sauce is cleaned and this cafeteria shines. second he **persisted** all end of the year field trips are cancelled for all seventh grade students instead your required to write a series of essays on how to **comport** yourselves in public. third he pronounced theyre will now be assigned seats in the cafeteria for the rest of the year

C -   "First," he said, "classes will be **postponed**, and you will stay here until every strand of spaghetti, every drop of milk, every piece of paper, and every **gobbet** of sauce is cleaned, and this cafeteria shines. Second," he **persisted**, "all end-of-the-year field trips are cancelled for all seventh-grade students; instead, you're required to write a series of essays on how to **comport** yourselves in public. Third," he pronounced, "there will now be assigned seats in the cafeteria for the rest of the year."

Writing Idea #25: Persuasive/Argumentative Essay.

Write a business letter to Dean Dread (as if you were a seventh-grader at HHMS) to convince him not to give such harsh punishments. Include at least three good arguments with detailed support for each one. Include correct headings, greeting, and closing.

Caught'ya Final Exam follows on next page.

Remember, you can adapt the test to fit the needs of your students and then print copies from the CD included with this book.

Caught'ya Final Exam

Directions for Part 1:

Students, correct the following long Caught'ya. This test will show how carefully you listen when your teacher goes over Caught'yas. You will lose two points per error, so check your work. Ask your teacher for meanings of words if necessary. This is not a vocabulary test. Follow your teacher's directions, and read the test again to yourself to help with punctuation.

Hint: There are twelve paragraphs. All periods are correct except one which needs to be changed to a question mark. There are spelling errors and four missing hyphens. Some words need to be changed.

after dean dread made this pronouncement he crosses his arms in front of his enormous chest and just stared. the seventh graders cleaned the cafeteria under his watchful eye and noone opened his or her **maw**. and noone not even orson misbehaved in any way. even john **jabbering** was **mute** and beth bibliophilic didnt turn pages in her book little women by louisa may alcott until dean dread stoped talking. after they cleaned up the mess the seventh graders filed **mutely** out of the cafeteria. no one spoke until the cafeteria was no longer in sight. its not fair to cancel our field trips exclaimed william. why do we have to rite essays too complained olivia that hated to write. why is he so mean whines pauline to her freinds. hey you guys said isabelle that always calmed her friends when they were agitated we *were* guilty you know. we *did* throw food and in fact we began the food fight ourselfs because we threw the first **salvo**. i know **retorted** sam but did he have to take away all our end of year field trips. its to much he concluded. orson and his **sycophant** danny a to handsome young man chose that moment to angrily pass by. nice going losers **jeered** orson to who everyone who was not in his crowd were a loser. danny **aghast** at the thought of having to write a bunch of essays in front of the teachers which meant he actually would have to write them by himself was really **livid** at the thought. he **lashed** out. your nothing but unsightly stupid trash he hissed. your a pimple on dean dreads **posterior** too. everyone in the group of friends glared at orson with there best **withering** gaze. they still **loathed** orson and danny because the 2 were so mean. luckily the end of the school year quickly arrived. despite the lack of the much desired field trip to the amusement park and the extra essays they had to write the school year ended on a upbeat note. ms amicable artist mr melodious music and ms witty writing wizard got together and staged an afternoon in a nearby park. the HHMS jazz bands members provided music and they played good. students made impressions of leaves and flowers onto special paper. vivian recited some of her favorite poetry including i dream a world by langston hughes. all 3 subjects were covered so that it could be **dubbed** educational.

Directions for Part 2:

Use your corrected version of the test to identify the types of sentences of each of the first fifteen sentences in this exam—simple, compound, complex, or compound/complex. Number the sentences so you don't get confused. Sentence #15 ends with the comment about everyone who was not in Orson's crowd being a "loser."

Hint: Two are compound/complex. Two are compound. Four are complex. The other seven are simple sentences.

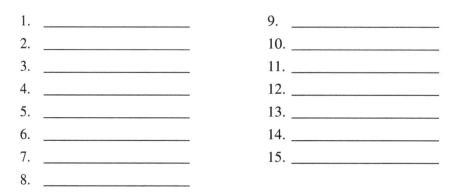

1. _____   9. _____
2. _____   10. _____
3. _____   11. _____
4. _____   12. _____
5. _____   13. _____
6. _____   14. _____
7. _____   15. _____
8. _____

Directions for Part 3:

Read the end of the Caught'ya story. Then write the end of the story for Sam, Isabelle, and friends. How will they uncover the mystery in the eighth grade? Support your answers. Write as clearly as you can, and provide lots of details. Include a topic sentence and a concluding sentence for each paragraph. Use transitions and similes. Vary sentence structure. Most importantly, put passion and flair into your answer.

Soon the last day of school arrived. Exams had ended. The friends, except Sam Sagacious, of course, promptly forgot about their strange teachers and concentrated on their summer plans.

The girls had **diverse (different)** ideas about how to spend their summer. Isabelle Ingenuous had imaginative projects to do. Olivia Otiose had to go to summer school for math because she had been lazy and had not done her homework; nor had she studied for tests. She hoped to spend time with her new friend, Alessandra, though, because she also thought that learning more Spanish might be fun. Felicia Fey planned to **hone (improve by practice)** her magical skills (but she really didn't want to leave her friends to go to the school for **mages (wizards)**). Pauline Puerile didn't know what she was going to do that summer since no one yet had suggested anything that appealed to her. Alessandra Amorous and her family planned a trip to Puerto Rico to visit relatives. Vivian Virtuous had signed up for a writing course. Beth Bibliophilic would, of course, read as much as she could, but she hoped to travel with her family as well.

The boys had plans as well. William Waggish hoped to laze around in the morning, write poetry, and play sports at the local Boys Club in the afternoons. Sam Sagacious decided to go to the library daily for research but also was on a baseball team with William and Jesse. Jesse Jocose was going to summer school by choice to learn about computers. He hoped to spend his afternoons playing basketball and baseball.

It looked as if it would be a good summer for all the friends. They didn't have to deal with Orson Odious or Danny Dapper (whose parents were going to send them to their grandmothers for two months), and homework (except for Olivia Otiose) already was a **vague (slight, unclear)** memory.

On the last day of school (after all the students had left), all was silent at Horribly Hard Middle School except for muffled sounds from the art, music, and seventh-grade language arts rooms, the "clack" of computer keys in the main office, and the muttered **epithets (swear words)** of Mr. Adept Fixit in the dean's office.

Caught'ya Final Exam KEY

Part I:

After Dean Dread made this pronouncement, he crossed his arms in front of his enormous chest and just stared. The seventh-graders cleaned the cafeteria under his watchful eye, and no one opened his or her **maw**. No one, not even Orson, misbehaved in any way. Even John **Jabbering** was **mute**, and Beth Bibliophilic didn't turn pages in her book, Little Women, by Louisa May Alcott until Dean Dread stopped talking.

After they cleaned up the mess, the seventh-graders filed **mutely** out of the cafeteria. No one spoke until the cafeteria was no longer in sight.

"It's not fair to cancel our field trip!" exclaimed William.

"Why do we have to write essays, too?" complained Olivia Otiose who hated to write.

"Why is he so mean?" whined Pauline Puerile to her friends.

"Hey, you guys," said Isabelle who always calmed her friends when they were agitated, "we *were* guilty, you know. We *did* throw food, and, in fact, we began the food fight ourselves because we threw the first **salvo**."

"I know," **retorted** Sam, "but did he have to take away all our end-of-year field trips? It's too much," he concluded.

Orson and his **sycophant** Danny, a too handsome young man, chose that moment to pass by angrily. "Nice going, losers," **jeered** Orson to whom everyone who was not in his crowd was a "loser."

Danny, **aghast** at the thought of having to write a bunch of essays in front of the teachers which meant he would actually have to write them by himself, really was **livid** at the thought. He **lashed** out.

"You're nothing but unsightly, stupid trash," he hissed. "You're a pimple on Dean Dread's **posterior**, too."

Everyone in the group of friends glared at Orson with his or her best **withering** gaze. They still **loathed** Orson and Danny because the two were so mean.

Luckily, the end of the school year quickly arrived. Despite the lack of the much-desired field trip to the amusement park and the extra essays they had to write, the school year ended on an upbeat note. Ms. Amicable Artist, Mr. Melodious Music, and Ms. Witty Writing Wizard got together and staged an afternoon in a nearby park. The HHMS Jazz Band's members provided music, and they played well. Students made impressions of leaves and flowers onto special paper. Vivian recited some of her favorite poetry, including "I Dream a World" by Langston Hughes. All three subjects were covered so that it could be **dubbed** "educational."

Part 2:

1. complex
2. compound
3. simple
4. compound/complex
5. complex
6. complex
7. simple
8. simple
9. simple
10. complex
11. compound/complex
12. compound
13. simple
14. simple
15. simple

CHAPTER 8

125 Caught'yas for Eighth Grade

Introduction to the Eighth-Grade Story
125 Caught'ya Sentences for Grade Eight

→ Almost Midterm Caught'ya Test and Key
→ Caught'ya Final Exam and Key
→ Twenty-Five Ideas for Writing Assignments

The first section is to be read aloud to your students to set the scene for the Caught'ya story that follows. You might want to read this section more than once in order to place the characters' names and the setting firmly in your students' minds. A copy of the entire uninterrupted story can be found in **Chapter 5**. You may wish to print out a copy or two of the seventh- and eighth-grade parts of the story to have in your classroom for any student who joins the class after the first week of school.

If the sixth- and seventh-grade English teachers in your school are *not* using this book, you will need to read those parts of the story to your students in order to keep them abreast of what happened to our intrepid heroes in the earlier grades.

After the introduction, you will find 125 Caught'yas. Each Caught'ya consists of two to four sentences of the story, a vocabulary word or five, and a plethora of errors. There is a suggested writing assignment every five Caught'yas or so. A midterm and a final exam have been included in the middle and at the end of the Caught'yas. Finally, there are sections where you will be instructed to read a page or two to the class so that the story can be fully developed.

Please note that words in bold type are vocabulary words that may be repeated in the subsequent Caught'yas. It is a good idea to go over their meanings and to use them in your daily parlance and in vocabulary games so that your students will retain their meanings and become comfortable with them.

A review of the vocabulary, particularly those used in the names, certainly can't hurt as many of the words are repeated in the earlier parts of the story. You will find all vocabulary words that are used in the

Caught'yas in this chapter are listed by Caught'ya number in **Chapter 4** of this book.

Introduction to the Eighth-Grade Story

As the August morning sun chased the shadows from the roofs of houses and painted the sky gold, once again there was an **eerie** silence at Horribly Hard Middle School. In the dawning light, you could not see into the classrooms because of the light-blocking curtains at every window. No early teacher rushed out of a car in the parking lot to set up a lab or to get an early start on preparation for the first day of school. Horribly Hard Middle School was like a spooky mansion: closed, dark, and abandoned.

In contrast, across town, as the sun rose a bit higher in the sky, Marvelously Magic Magnet Middle School (popularly known as MMMMS) burst with energy and noise. Coffee perked in the teachers' lounge. Cars roared into the parking lot, parked, and spilled out teachers of different sizes, shapes, and complexions. Boxes, books, bags, and piles of "stuff" filled their arms as they walked into the school early to be ready for the first day of classes for the year.

Finally, four cars drove up to the **dormant** and silent Horribly Hard Middle School: a new mauve Lexus sedan, an old blue Ford pick-up truck, a new red Chevy sedan, and an old, battered, tan Subaru station wagon that had seen better days. A middle-aged man, Mr. **Punctilious** Principal, stepped out of the Lexus. Another middle-aged man, the custodian, Mr. **Adept** Fixit, exited the blue pick-up.

The man who exited the Lexus wore a suit and tie, and carried a battered briefcase. The owner of the Ford climbed out of his pick-up, walked to the back, and lifted a tool chest from the bed of his truck. He **sported** a denim shirt and overalls, a red handkerchief in his upper pocket, a wrench that hung out of his lower pocket, a purposeful air, and a worried look on his face.

The door of the Subaru creaked open and out fell construction paper and magazines, followed by a **harried**-looking woman. She was dressed in a long, loose purple dress with a purple flower in her thick blonde hair and a **myriad** of colored pencils in her mouth. The two men nodded solemnly to each other and smiled at the woman as she gathered the stuff that had fallen from her car.

The red Chevy parked next to the Subaru. The door swung open in **tandem** with the trunk. A man, dressed in a tri-corner hat and military uniform of 300 years ago, awkwardly stepped out of the car. He nodded to the lady in the purple dress, smiled, and walked to the open trunk.

After lifting out the biggest of the boxes in the trunk and placing it on the ground, he closed the trunk, picked up the box, and headed towards the eighth-grade wing of the school.

The men **trekked** in different directions: the suited one toward the school office, the man in overalls toward the custodian's office, and the one with the box towards the farthest wing of the school. The woman gathered her materials from the pavement and **ambled** slowly to a building set slightly off from the main part of the school. No other human soul could be seen in the dim light of early morning.

Slowly, one after the other, classroom lights came on in HHMS. Soon the school was **ablaze**, and all classrooms were lit, but apart from Mr. **Adept** Fixit, who rushed from room to room to open doors and turn on lights, no sounds of people could be heard on the campus. This was the first day of school?

If you listened carefully in the main office near the door to the principal's room, you could hear the faint click of computer keys as Mr. **Punctilious** Principal, a man who was always concerned with correct procedure, checked and rechecked the procedures which would be followed that first day of school as well as the list of students who would enter the **portals** of the HHMS in less than an hour.

If you **strolled** over to the art room, you could hear faint singing of an old Beatles tune and the rustling of paper.

Five minutes later another car pulled up in front of the still silent Horribly Hard Middle School. A man in a **dapper** blue suit who was humming a Mozart sonata **ambled** toward a nearby dark classroom. He was burdened with various-sized instrument cases. He wore his favorite purple tie that was decorated with yellow musical notes. His tie was **askew**, and his glasses perched unevenly on his nose, ruining the effect of his handsome blue suit.

Before the man with the instrument cases could close the trunk of his car, a final **vehicle**, an ancient white Volvo sedan, **careened** into the lot and parked next to the **decrepit** tan Subaru. A pleasingly-plump middle-aged woman with curly grey hair jumped **animatedly** out of the Volvo, nodded **genially** to the man who hummed the Mozart sonata, and turned back to her car.

The **stout** woman then opened the hatch and removed an obviously heavy box that was **brimful** with books. She heaved the box for better **leverage** and trudged slowly with her heavy burden in the direction of the seventh-grade wing of the school.

The staff parking lot of Horribly Hard Middle School once again fell silent. Only six cars awaited their drivers.

On another side of the school, forty-five minutes later, a long, curved line of school busses arrived, one by one. Each **disgorged** a bunch of chattering students, each with his or her backpack. Other students who had walked to school **ambled** slowly onto the school grounds to join the **hordes** being let off by the busses. Horribly Hard Middle School came alive with voices, and a new school year began.

A young man, whose vast, faded, too-big trousers sat **precariously** low on his hips, rode a much-decorated skateboard on one of the sidewalks. Mysteriously, a **foreboding** figure appeared. It was the **dreaded** Dean **Dread**. As usual, he was **garbed** in black. His long, narrow face showed neither humor nor compassion.

Dean Dread raised his **menacing** voice so that the **miscreant** could hear, and he said in a deadly tone, "Steven **Slovenly**, give me that skateboard. Skateboards are **banned** on campus. Sagging pants without belts also are not allowed. Come to my office right now to get a piece of **twine** to use as a belt for those **outsized** pants you insist on wearing. Didn't you learn anything last year when your pants dropped to your ankles right in front of me?"

Steven Slovenly knew he was **culpable**. He hung his head, mumbled something about "forgetting," got off his board, put it under his right arm, gripped the waistband of his trousers, and followed Dean Dread to the **latter**'s office. Every few steps, Steven hitched up his pants with his left hand. A few students pointed at Steven and **jeered**.

Steven Slovenly kept repeating, "I forgot. I forgot," as he **trudged dejectedly** after Dean Dread.

Meanwhile on the other side of the school, seven students, who had just walked to school together, stood on a corner of the sidewalk waiting for the bus of one of their friends to arrive.

Isabelle **Ingenuous**, an **animated**, perky young lady, twirled with an excess of energy. One of Isabelle's friends, Olivia **Otiose**, slouched next to her. Another friend, Pauline **Puerile**, whined in a babyish manner about the summer being over, but she perked up when Alessandra **Amorous**, another member of the group, diverted her attention by recounting a story of her summer in Puerto Rico with her relatives. The fourth girl in the **assemblage** was dressed and **coiffed** in an odd manner. Her long hair was light sea green. Her shorts and t-shirt also were green, but their color was more like that of a lime.

NOTE: Do not use the first definition of "fey" which is "to be fated to die soon." I used "fey" to mean "enchanted one" or "enchanter," meaning that Felicia has some magic powers.)

This was Felicia **Fey**, who was known for casting spells that always went **awry** (except once in the seventh grade when one of her spells **nabbed** the **perpetrators** of a stink bomb in the boys' bathroom).

B – Sentences for the Board	C – Corrected version of the CY
1. puerile ingenuous uttering Paragraph – new topic Types of Sentences – simple; simple Commas – no commas around "Pauline Puerile" because appositive is necessary (Felicia has more than one friend) Homophones – to/two/too Other Skills – "i" before "e" spell rule; sing. possessive; possessive pronouns Literary Devices – alliteration	**B -** felicia began to mutter words of a spell too encourage her freind pauline **puerile** to cheer up. isabelle **ingenuous** put her hand over felicias mouth two stop her from **uttering** her spell **C -** Felicia began to mutter words of a spell to encourage her friend Pauline **Puerile** to cheer up. Isabelle **Ingenuous** put her hand over Felicia's mouth to stop her from **uttering** her spell.
2. obliterate Paragraph – new speaker Types of Sentences – simple; simple question Punctuation – quotes go around what is said out loud; all commas and periods always go inside quotes; **?** needed in question Commas – direct address; quote; before added rhetorical question Homophones – know/no; your/you're; new/gnu/knew Verbs – verb-tense shift (story in past tense) Other Skills – compound word (backfire); contraction Literary Devices – alliteration; rhetorical question	**B -** you know it will backfire on you felicia cautions isabelle ingenuous. you dont want to **obliterate** youre knew hairdo do you **C -** "You know it will backfire on you, Felicia," cautioned Isabelle Ingenuous. "You don't want to **obliterate** your new hairdo, do you?"

B – Sentences for the Board	C – Corrected version of the CY
3. retorted indignant Paragraph – new speaker Types of Sentences – simple (compound subject); simple; simple Punctuation – quotes around what is said out loud; . and , always go inside quotes Commas – quote Other Skills – subject vs. object pronouns; "i" before "e" spell rule; contraction; comparatives; adjective/adverb confusion (good vs. well) Literary Devices – use of strong, vivid verbs	**B -** me and my other magic friends practiced all summer **retorted** a slightly **indignant** felicia. im getting a little gooder at it. im doing good **C -** "My other magic friends and I practiced all summer," **retorted** a slightly **indignant** Felicia. "I'm getting a little better at it. I'm doing well."
4. garbed puckish waggish Paragraph – new speaker Types of Sentences – complex Punctuation – quotes around what is said out loud; all , and . go inside quotes; **?** needed in question Commas – interjection; direct address Homophones – your/you're; whose/who's Verbs – verb-tense shift (story in past tense) Other Skills – relative pronouns (whose) Literary Devices – use of strong, vivid verbs	**B -** hey felicia how come your not **garbed** in black as you were all last year asks a boy whos **puckish** expression mirrored his **waggish** personality **C -** "Hey, Felicia, how come you're not **garbed** in black as you were all last year?" asked a boy whose **puckish** expression mirrored his **waggish** personality.

NOTE: Do not use the first definition of "fey" which is "to be fated to die soon." I used "fey" to mean "enchanted one" or "enchanter," meaning that Felicia has some magic powers.

5. fey   retorted   waggish
   egregious

Paragraph – new speaker (narrator then Felicia)

Types of Sentences – compound

Punctuation – " around what is said out loud; . and , always go inside "

Commas – quote; interjection; direct address; no **,** before "and" as not a list or compound sen.; compound sen.

Homophones – role/roll; rite/write/right

Other Skills – vocab. lesson; consonant-vowel-consonant (CVC) spell rule (double final consonant when suffix added); "ie" spell rule; go over general spelling rules; parallel construction (may...may); use of superlative

Literary Devices – alliteration

B - felicia **fey** rolled her eyes and **retorted** hey william **waggish** i may dress weirdly and my spells may backfire but you right the most **egregious** poetry

C - Felicia **Fey** rolled her eyes and **retorted**, "Hey, William **Waggish**, I may dress weirdly, and my spells may backfire, but you write the most **egregious** poetry."

Writing Idea #1: Expository Essay in a Friendly Letter.
Write a letter to a friend to explain to him or her the "weird" and different traits that make up your personality. Be as specific as you can, giving examples of each personality trait. Use the correct heading, greeting, and closing for a letter.

NOTE: All the nine comma rules except those in a letter will be included in the first 20 Caught'yas. To this end, you might want to point out the correct use of commas in this friendly letter.

When you teach the headings of a letter in order for your students to be able to complete Writing Assignment #1, you might want to make certain that your students understand how to write the postal code for your state and the states where they have relatives. (Florida, for example, is FL.) You can find a list in the *Grammar, Usage, and Mechanics Guide* on the CD.

6. lame   vapid   barbs

Paragraph – new speaker (narrator)

Types of Sentences – simple; compound; simple with compound objects

Commas – infinitive phrase; compound sen.; put commas around "too" if it means "also"; noun series

Homophones – to/two/too; hear/here

Verbs – verb-tense shift

Other Skills – "no one" is 2 words; collective pronoun (everyone) needs singular possessive pronoun to follow (his or her); sing. possessive; go over possessive pronouns; "i" before "e" spell rule

Literary Devices – alliteration

B - to hide his admiration of felicia william waggish makes a tasteless but funny joke about girls. noone listened and everyone turned their head in alessandras direction to here her story. they too were used too williams **lame** poems **vapid** jokes and friendly **barbs**

C -   To hide his admiration of Felicia, William Waggish made a tasteless but funny joke about girls. No one listened, and everyone turned his or her head in Alessandra's direction to hear her story. They, too, were used to William's **lame** poems, **vapid** jokes, and friendly **barbs**.

---

7. sagacious   mutely   clamor

Paragraph – new topic

Types of Sentences – complex with subordinate clause at end (no comma); compound

Punctuation – use of parentheses around extra info

Commas – unnecessary appositive (Sam has already been identified); 2 adj. where 2nd adj. is not color, age, size, or linked to noun

Other Skills – vocab. lesson; collective noun (troop); _____ or *italicize* titles of books and long works (see **Grammar, Usage, and Mechanics Guide**); capitalization of titles; sing. possessive; who (subject) vs. whom (object); never use "that" to refer to people

B - the last member of the troop sam **sagacious** simply stood wisely and **mutely** as he waited for the **clamor** to die down. he held a huge heavy book nortons anthology of poetry in his hand and pretended to read it but he really was watching alessandra amorous who he liked

C -   The last member of the troop, Sam **Sagacious**, simply stood wisely and **mutely** as he waited for the **clamor** to die down. He held a huge, heavy book (<u>Norton's Anthology of Poetry</u>) in his hand and pretended to read it, but he really was watching Alessandra Amorous whom he liked.

B – Sentences for the Board	C – Corrected version of the CY
Literary Devices – use of literary reference; alliteration	

NOTE: Even though this is the second week of school or so, it is good to point out to students the difference between a clause (subject and verb) and a phrase (a group of words without a subject or verb or both).

NOTE: Warn students of the need to rewrite part of the sentence.

8. regaled   pupils   eloquent

Paragraph – new subject

Types of Sentences – compound/ complex (sub. clause at beginning); simple

Punctuation – use of **:** to denote shift in structure; hyphen in 2 wds. acting as 1

Commas – sub. clause at beginning of sen.; compound part of sen.; 2 intro adjectives; appositive

Homophones – new/gnu/knew

Verbs – use of pluperfect

Other Skills – "no one" is 2 wds.; "ie" spell rule; misplaced modifier (the   composition didn't have a brown face, William did...); sing. poss.; who (subject) vs. whom (object); never use "that" to refer to people

Literary Devices – literary reference; alliteration

B - since his joke had fallen flat and noone had laughed william waggish **regaled** his friends with a knew limerick about girls that wear green. brown faced with expressive dark **pupils** williams composition of mischievous poems to hide his real aspiration to be as **eloquent** a poet as his secret hero langston hughes

C -   Since his joke had fallen flat, and no one had laughed, William Waggish **regaled** his friends with a new limerick about girls who wear green. Brown-faced with expressive dark **pupils**, William composed mischievous poems to hide his real aspiration: to be as **eloquent** a poet as his secret hero, Langston Hughes.

9. emanated

No ¶ (same topic); then indented poem; then ¶ (new topic)

Types of Sentences – simple; simple

Punctuation – " around short works; punctuation same in poem as elsewhere; " around double entendre

Commas – appositive in poem

Homophones – there/their/they're; whose/who's

Other Skills – put " around short works like poems, articles, etc.; sing. poss.; contraction; who vs. whom (adj. clause); do not use "that" to refer to people; first letter of each line in poem is capitalized

Literary Devices – double entendre ("fey" as name and "enchanted one")

B - he entitled it the heroine

> their was a young lady in green
> whose spells often cause a big scene.
> shes "fey" as they come
> but smarter than some
> like orson who really is mean.

a faint wisp of smoke **emanated** from both ears of a teacher that was standing just barely within earshot

C - He entitled it "The Heroine."

> There was a young lady in green
> Whose spells often cause a big scene.
> She's "fey" as they come
> But smarter than some,
> Like Orson who really is mean.

A faint wisp of smoke **emanated** from both ears of a teacher who was standing just barely within earshot.

NOTE: My students never knew which form of "their/there/they're" I would use and got angry when I spelled it correctly. Mix them up so that your students have to think. I told students that "their" must be followed by something that is owned. You can substitute "here" for "there," and forbid the use of "they're" or, for that matter, "it's" in the classroom for the year.

10. protruded   sagacious

No ¶ (same topic) then ¶ (new topic)

Types of Sentences – compound; simple (compound verb)

Commas – transition; compound sen.; verb series

Homophones – new/knew/gnu

Other Skills – fewer (can count) vs. less (can't count); poss. pronouns; write out #s to 120; double negative

B - first her tongue **protruded** slightly and next she froze in place for less then 3 seconds. this wasnt nothing new. sam **sagacious** glanced at the teacher put his book in his backpack and laughed

C - First, her tongue **protruded** slightly, and next, she froze in place for fewer than three seconds. This was nothing new.

Sam **Sagacious** glanced at the teacher, put his book in his backpack, and laughed.

B – Sentences for the Board	C – Corrected version of the CY

(go over use of "anything" and
"nothing")

Literary Devices – alliteration

NOTES: After this point, the literary device of alliteration as used in the names of the characters will no longer be listed in the skills.

To teach the simple transitions to students, I have found it very effective to sing them to a simple tune. I like to use the song "She'll Be Coming 'Round the Mountain" and sing the following words:

> Topic sentence, first, next, then,
> Finally and a conclusion.
> Topic sentence, first, next, then, finally-y
> And end with a conclusion.

Writing Idea #2: Persuasive/Argumentative Essay.

Think of a friend who has a bad habit (like writing stupid poetry or smoking cigarettes), and write a letter to your friend to convince him or her to give up the bad habit. If you can't think of a friend with a bad habit, make one up. Be sure to give examples and details to bolster your arguments. Use the correct heading, greeting, and closing for a letter.

NOTE: Refer to the note after Writing Idea #1.

11. discombobulate

Paragraph – new speaker

Types of Sentences – simple; simple; compound; simple question

Punctuation – " around what is said out loud; . and , always go inside "; ? in question

Commas – direct address; introductory word; compound sen.; parenthetical expression

Homophones – it's/its; your/you're

Other Skills – contraction; affect vs. effect; avoid splitting verbs (still can affect); "ie" spell rule; then (adverb) vs. than (comparative); relative pronoun "which"; comparatives (greater)

B - its working. you haven't lost youre touch william. yes you can still affect and **discombobulate** some of the teachers and last year in fact you recited cinquains which had an even greater effect on the teachers than the limericks. are you going to go back to limericks this year

C - "It's working. You haven't lost your touch, William. Yes, you still can affect and **discombobulate** some of the teachers, and last year, in fact, you recited cinquains which had an even greater effect on the teachers than the limericks. Are you going to go back to limericks this year?"

NOTE: I never understood why "it's" and "its" are difficult words for students to differentiate when they write. But, the truth is that they constantly confuse them in their writing. I solved the problem by forbidding the use of "it's." Students had to write out "it is" instead, leaving "its" to its proper use as a possessive pronoun.

Another trick is to request students to try to use "his" every time they want to use "its" or "it's." Of course, "his" does not work if you wish to say "it is..."

12. exasperating

Paragraph – new speaker

Types of Sentences – simple; compound

Punctuation – " around what is said out loud; , and . always go inside "; interrupted quote

Commas – introductory word or expression; quote; no , before "William" as is necessary

B - nah says his friend william waggish i still like composing limericks just to be **exasperating** like a constant drip. i does good at annoying you all and besides its fun

C - "Nah," said his friend William Waggish, "I still like composing limericks just to be **exasperating**, like a constant drip. I do well at annoying you all, and, besides, it's fun."

appositive (he has many friends); compound sen; interrupter (besides); simile that's extra info	
Homophones – its/it's	
Verbs – verb-tense shift; subject/verb agreement	
Other Skills – "ie" spell rule; well (adv.) vs. good (adj.); interrupter	
Literary Devices – simile	
13. deter tittered	**B -** six pairs of eyeballs rolled at this comment. felicia fey threatened to zap william but that didn't **deter** him. she than furrowed her brow stuck out her tongue at him and good naturedly muttered something rude under her breath as the rest of the girls **tittered**
Paragraph – new speaker (narrator)	
Types of Sentences – simple; compound; complex (sub. clause at end)	
Commas – compound sen.; verb series	
Other Skills – hyphen in 2 wds. acting as 1; then (adv.) vs. than (comparative); oft confused words "breath" (noun) and "breathe" (verb)	**C -** Six pairs of eyeballs rolled at this comment. Felicia Fey threatened to zap William, but that didn't **deter** him. She then furrowed her brow, stuck out her tongue at him, and good-naturedly muttered something rude under her breath as the rest of the girls **tittered**.

NOTE: I know this is early in the year, but it is important that your students learn the eight parts of speech. It is a good idea to put an acronym for the eight parts of speech somewhere on a wall in your classroom. I used NIPPAVAC or PAVPANIC.

The second week of school, I challenged my students to figure out the acronym. It usually took a week or so until some bright student figured it out (or heard it from a sibling who had been in my class in a previous year).

Once the acronym is identified, you and your students can chant the parts of speech until you and they memorize them: Noun, Interjection, Preposition, Pronoun, Adverb, Verb, Adjective, Conjunction (NIPPAVAC). Once your students memorize the parts of speech, you can begin asking them to point them out in subsequent Caught'yas. I suggest that you do this, one part of speech at a time, all year long.

14. insipid

Paragraph – new speaker

Types of Sentences – simple; simple question

Punctuation – " around what is said out loud; . and , always go inside "; ? needed in question

Commas – 2 intro prepositional phrases; direct address; no , before "Jesse" as appositive is necessary; interjection

Homophones – your/you're; write/ rite/right

Other Skills – contraction; "ie" spell rule; double negative (can't... nothing); accept (verb) vs. except; review pronouns so far; demonstrative pronouns (this, those)

Literary Devices – reference to poetry

B - for the benefit of youre friends william cant you and your freind jesse write nothing except those **insipid** limericks and cinquains felicia teased. hey how about giving us a break and trying another form of poetry this year

C - "For the benefit of your friends, William, can't you and your friend Jesse write anything except those **insipid** limericks and cinquains?" Felicia teased. "Hey, how about giving us a break and trying another form of poetry this year?"

NOTE: As with "it's," I forbade my students to write the contraction "you're." I insisted that they write out "you are" instead. This helped them learn the difference between the homophones.

15. jibe   loped   malevolent odious   dapper   pulchritudinous

Paragraph – new speaker (narrator)

Types of Sentences – compound; simple

Commas – interrupter; compound sen.; 2 adj. where 2nd is not age, size, color, or linked to noun; unnecessary appositive

Homophones – it's/its

Other Skills – vocab. lesson; sing. poss.; "ie" spell rule; use of participle (followed); write out #s to 120

B - isabelle ingenuous of course smiled at williams poem and felicias freindly **jibe** but her smile immediately turned to a frown at the sight of a recognizable hulking figure that **loped** towards them with a **malevolent** grin on its face. it was orson **odious** followed by his 2 pals danny **dapper** and petra **pulchritudinous**

C - Isabelle Ingenuous, of course, smiled at William's poem and Felicia's friendly **jibe**, but her smile immediately turned to a frown at the sight of a recognizable, hulking figure

B – Sentences for the Board	**C** – Corrected version of the CY
Literary Devices – alliteration; metaphor ("hulking figure")	that **loped** towards them with a **malevolent** grin on its face. It was Orson **Odious** followed by his two pals, Danny **Dapper** and Petra **Pulchritudinous**.

Writing Idea #3: Paragraph Writing.

Write a strong, vivid-verb paragraph using the topic sentence, "_____ (put in a fictitious name) is a real pain in the neck." Then write the rest of the paragraph (seven-sentence minimum) to explain what this person does that drives you nuts. It is a good idea to think of several people who drive you nuts and combine their traits into one made-up person.

This paragraph must have a title, a topic sentence similar to the one given, five strong, vivid-verb sentences that explain why this person drives you insane, and a concluding sentence that may use a "dead" verb. Be sure to vary sentence structure and include at least one of each type of sentence.

→ Teachers, see *Blowing Away the State Writing Assessment Test* (Kiester, 2000)

**16. derided   odious   nemesis
reek   wafted**

2 Paragraphs – 2 new speakers in conversation

Types of Sentences – simple; simple (subject implied)

Punctuation – " around what is said out loud; . and , always go inside "; hyphen in 2 wds. acting as 1 adj. (ultra-strange); quote within a quote; " around made-up show

Commas – intro word; business name; quote; direct address; unnecessary appositive (the nemesis); participial phrase

Homophones – its/it's

Other Skills – vocab. lesson; contraction; collective noun (cast); antecedent/pronoun agreement; breath vs. breathe

Literary Devices – alliteration; dialogue (repartee); personification ("reek," "wafted")

B - well if it isnt the super strange cast of weirdo incorporated and their famous witch **derided** orson **odious** the **nemesis** of the group. seen dean dread today orson asked sam sagacious wrinkling his nose against the **reek** of stale cigarette smoke that **wafted** from orsons clothes and breath

C -   "Well, if it isn't the super-strange cast of 'Weirdo, Incorporated' and its famous witch," **derided** Orson **Odious**, the **nemesis** of the group.

"Seen Dean Dread today, Orson?" asked Sam Sagacious, wrinkling his nose against the **reek** of stale cigarette smoke that **wafted** from Orson's clothes and breath.

17. putrescent   misdeed   culpability

Paragraph – new speaker

Types of Sentences – complex (sub. clause at end); complex (sub. clause at end)

Punctuation – " around what is said out loud; . and , always go inside "

Commas – no , before "stink" as is linked to noun

Homophones – hair/hare

Other Skills – write out ordinal #s; sing. poss.

Literary Devices – sarcasm; summary of previous incident

B - set off any **putrescent** stink bombs lately inquired william with a trace of sarcasm in his voice as he referred to the incident in the 7th grade when orson had been caught for his **misdeed** by dean dread. his **culpability** was revealed when a misfired spell of felicias put mauve streaks in his hare that matched the smoke

C -   "Set off any **putrescent** stink bombs lately?" inquired William with a trace of sarcasm in his voice as he referred to the incident in the seventh grade when Orson had been caught for his **misdeed** by Dean Dread. His **culpability** was revealed when a misfired spell of Felicia's put mauve streaks in his hair that matched the smoke.

18. sycophants   dapper   pulchritudinous

Paragraph – new topic

Types of Sentences – complex (sub. clause at end)

Commas – intro adverb (optional); unnecessary appositive; parenthetical expression

Homophones – their/there/they're

Verbs – verb-tense shift

Other Skills – sing. poss.; "ie" spell rule

Literary Devices – building suspense

B - suddenly orson's **sycophants** danny **dapper** and petra **pulchritudinous** came up behind him ready to back up there friend just as orson spies a teacher approaching

C -   Suddenly, Orson's **sycophants**, Danny **Dapper** and Petra **Pulchritudinous**, came up behind him, ready to back up their friend, just as Orson spied a teacher approaching.

19. cohorts   epithets   ominously

2 Paragraphs – new topic; new speaker

Types of Sentences – complex; complex (both with sub. clause at beginning)

Punctuation – quote within a quote; put " around idiomatic expression; put " around what is said out loud; all , and . go inside "

Commas – sub. clause at beginning; sub. clause at beginning; adj. series; quote

Homophones – passed/past; air/heir

Other Skills – "ie" spell rule; verb "breathe" vs. noun "breath; incorrect use of object pronoun and word order

Literary Devices – idiomatic expression

B - when orson and his **cohorts** strutted by Isabelle and friends they muttered a few nasty choice **epithets** and threats under their breathe as they past by. as he raised a fisted hand in the air orson threatened **ominously** me and my freinds will make toast of you later

C -   When Orson and his **cohorts** strutted by Isabelle and friends, they muttered a few nasty, choice **epithets** and threats under their breath as they passed by.

    As he raised a fisted hand in the air, Orson threatened **ominously**, "My friends and I will make 'toast' of you later."

---

20. bravado   infuriate
    pulchritudinous   ingenuous

3 Paragraphs – different speakers

Types of Sentences – simple; complex (sub. clause at end); simple

Punctuation – " around what is said out loud; , and . always go inside "

Commas – quote; quote

Homophones – see/sea

Verbs – subject/verb agreement; avoid splitting verbs (**has** already **changed**)

Other Skills – vocab.; incorrect use of object pronoun and word order; further (can't count) vs. farther (can count); plural poss.

Literary Devices – sarcasm; repartée

B - me and my friends is trembling william said with false **bravado**. isabelle hushed him before he could **infuriate** orson any further. i see that petra **pulchritudinous** has already changed her clothes in the girls bathroom commented Isabelle **Ingenuous**

C -   "My friends and I are trembling," William said with false **bravado**.

    Isabelle hushed him before he could **infuriate** Orson any further.

    "I see that Petra **Pulchritudinous** already has changed her clothes in the girls' bathroom," commented Isabelle **Ingenuous**.

NOTES: After this point, "quotes around what is said out loud" will no longer be pointed out in the skill list. Nor will "commas and periods *always* go inside quotation marks" or "? needed in a question." I suggest that you point these punctuation skills out to your students each time they appear. In addition, there are so many examples of the "i" before "e" spelling rule, that, from now on, the word only will be listed under the "Other Skills" section with the unusual spelling in bold type.

If you have required that your students write the complete date above each Caught'ya, all the comma rules, except in the greeting and closing of a letter which you can cover in Writing Idea #1 and the comma required between a city and state, have been covered in the first 20 Caught'yas. If you wish to do a review at this point, it might be a good idea. The comma rules are listed in the *Grammar, Usage, and Mechanics Guide* that is on the CD.

Writing Idea #4: Problem/Solution Expository Essay.

Everyone has problems; every institution has problems. Think of a problem in your school (such as bullies like Orson or dress-code problems). In the first paragraph of your essay, explain the problem and briefly propose some solutions. In the body of the essay, expand on those solutions, giving examples and details of how each solution might solve the problem. Write a concluding paragraph to wrap it all up. Put some passion into your essay.

21. putrid   jocose   alacrity

No ¶ (same speaker) then ¶ (new speaker—narrator)

Types of Sentences – compound; simple; compound

Commas – compound sen.; quote

Homophones – know/no

Verbs – verb-tense shift; do not split verbs

Other Skills – use of semicolon (see note below); friends; review poss. pronouns

Literary Devices – use of strong, active verbs

B - i no her family and her mother would never let her wear a skirt that short to school she finished. another **putrid** yellow school bus pulls up to the curb. jesse **jocose** leapt off the bus with **alacrity** he walked quickly up to his freinds

C - "I know her family, and her mother never would let her wear a skirt that short to school," she finished.

    Another **putrid** yellow school bus pulled up to the curb. Jesse **Jocose** leapt off the bus with **alacrity**; he walked quickly up to his friends.

NOTES: 1) With Caught'ya #21, you might want to teach the four reasons for using semicolons: A) a series of independent clauses; B) instead of a coordinating conjunction in a compound sentence (as in this Caught'ya)*;* **C) when there are too many commas in a compound sentence; and D) in a list, to avoid confusion because there are too many commas. This may avoid future abuse of the semi-colon. (See the *Grammar, Usage, and Mechanics Guide*.)**

    2) Now that students have encountered compound sentences quite a few times, it might be a good idea to begin memorizing the FANBOYS (coordinating conjunctions—for, and, nor, but, or, yet, so). Students enjoy chanting them over and over with different body movements that I call out. For example, recite while clapping hands over the head, then in front, then between legs, then do an "Egyptian" or a "shower," etc. Students should continue to recite the FANBOYS every time one appears in a subsequent Caught'ya.

    Students love this and memorize the conjunctions quickly. Once the conjunctions are memorized, students easily can learn never to put a comma before FANBOYS unless in a list or a compound sentence. Students also can be told never to capitalize one in a title or begin a sentence with one until they get their driver's license. This will give them time to mature their writing so that every other sentence doesn't begin with "and" or "so."

    I actually have given a special "FANBOYS Driver's License" to an outstanding writer, giving that student permission to judiciously use conjunctions for effect at the beginning of a sentence.

NOTE: Since this is such a long Caught'ya (5 sentences), you may want to do part of it orally.

22. regale   sultry   simmering

Paragraph – new speaker

Types of Sentences – simple question; simple; simple; complex (sub. clause at end); simple question

Punctuation – " around vernacular (Dudes and Lades); " around slang (hack)

Commas – interjection; direct address; 2 adj. where 2nd is not age, size, color, or related to noun; interjection; direct address; interrupted quote

Homophones – new/knew/gnu

Other Skills – contractions; note no caps on "got" as is interrupted quote

Literary Devices – use of slang and teenage vernacular; alliteration

B - hey dudes and lades hows it going. i cant wait to **regale** you with all i learned at the tubular computer camp i attended this **sultry simmering** summer. now i can really hack. hey william he said as he thumped his buddy on the back got any new poems

C - "Hey, 'Dudes and Lades,' how's it going? I can't wait to **regale** you with all I learned at the 'tubular' computer camp I attended this **sultry, simmering** summer. Now I can really 'hack.' Hey, William," he said as he thumped his buddy on the back, "got any new poems?"

B – Sentences for the Board	C – Corrected version of the CY

23. ambled   ebony

Paragraph – new topic and speaker (narrator)

Types of Sentences – simple; simple (no subject); simple; simple

Punctuation – _____ or *italicize* titles of long works

Commas – always put **,** around "too" if it means "also"; interrupter

Homophones – hair/hare; one/won; to/too/two

Verbs – use of pluperfect

Other Skills – collective noun; antecedent/pronoun agreement; demonstrative pronoun

Literary Devices – literary reference

B - everyone rolled their eyes and groaned. another girl exited her bus and **ambled** over to the group to. she had intricately braided **ebony** hair and a hardback book as usual in her hand. this one was entitled pride and prejudice

C -   Everyone rolled his or her eyes and groaned. Another girl exited her bus and **ambled** over to the group, too. She had intricately braided **ebony** hair and a hardback book, as usual, in her hand. This one was entitled <u>Pride and Prejudice</u>.

NOTE: This is an appropriate point at which you may want to teach the seven types of pronouns. (See *Grammar, Usage, and Mechanics Guide*.) Then, as you encounter examples of each in subsequent Caught'yas, you can point them out to your students. You also might want to go over collective nouns (see *Grammar, Usage, and Mechanics Guide* again) and the reason why they require singular verbs and pronouns.

24. virtuous   bailiwick

No ¶ (same topic); ¶ (new speaker)

Types of Sentences – complex; simple; simple; simple; deliberate fragment

Punctuation – use of **!** in fragment denoting excitement

Commas – sub. clause at beginning; direct address (2); quote

Homophones – its/it's; new/gnu; your/you're

Other Skills – contractions

B - as she was greeted the usually shy vivian **virtuous** turned to the boys with excitement. william jesse i learned a gnu form of poetry in my summer writing course she bubbled. youll love it. its in your **bailiwick**. haiku

C - As she was greeted, the usually shy Vivian **Virtuous** turned to the boys with excitement.

    "William, Jesse, I learned a new form of poetry in my summer writing course," she bubbled. "You'll love it. It's in your **bailiwick**. Haiku!"

Literary Devices – literary reference;
hyperbole (over-praising)

NOTE: Eighth-graders are capable of comprehending the real truth behind the reason for a comma if the subordinate clause is at the beginning of the sentence. A subordinate clause always is an adverb. If the clause is at the end of the sentence, the adverb is where it belongs (after the verb). If it begins the sentence, the adverb is out of place. When children diagram sentences, the lightbulb sometimes dawns as they see the subordinate clause positioned under the verb.

Recognizing a subordinate clause will become easier once they learn A WHITE BUS words (suggestion after Caught'ya #35).

---

25. rejoined   portals   lingered

2 Paragraphs – new speaker then narrator

Types of Sentences – simple (no subject after "but"); complex with compound verbs and sub. clause at end

Commas – quote; intro phrase; verb list

Homophones – its/it's; their/there/they're

Other Skills – sing. poss.; who (subject) vs. whom (object); write out #s to 120; use of hyphen in 2 wds. acting as 1; then (adv.) vs. than (comparative); friends

Literary Devices – literary reference

B - at least its different from limericks and cinquains **rejoined** isabelle whom really liked williams poems but pretended otherwise. on that note the 9 friends gathered there stuff walked to the double **portals** where eighth grade homerooms were posted checked out the lists found their names and then **lingered** together until the warning bell rang

C - "At least it's different from limericks and cinquains," **rejoined** Isabelle who really liked William's poems but pretended otherwise.

On that note, the nine friends gathered their stuff, walked to the double **portals** where eighth-grade homerooms were posted, checked out the lists, found their names, and then **lingered** together until the warning bell rang.

Writing Idea #5: Personal/Imaginative Story.

Think about all the things that happened the first day of school this year. Write a story telling your reader about the events of that day. You may exaggerate and fictionalize if you wish. Be sure to include lots of details in the body of your story. Make sure that you end the story in a satisfactory manner. Humor is good...

---

26. insufferable   dejection

Paragraph – new speaker

Types of Sentences – complex (sub. clause at end)

Commas – interjection; intro word; direct address; quote

Homophones – no/know

Verbs – verb-tense shift

Other Skills – use "like" only to compare 2 nouns; ordinal #s

B - oh no guys it looks like some of the most **insufferable** teachers followed us to the eighth grade moans pauline puerile in **dejection** as she frowned

C -   "Oh, no, guys, it looks as if some of the most **insufferable** teachers followed us to the eighth grade," moaned Pauline Puerile in **dejection** as she frowned.

---

27. intolerable

Paragraph – new speaker

Types of Sentences – simple; compound/complex

Commas – interrupter; direct address; compound part of sen.; quote

Homophones – are/our/hour

Verbs – avoid splitting verbs (really can flip)

Other Skills – use "like" only to compare 2 nouns; then (adv.) vs. than (comparative)

B - hey vivian, tell me about haiku poetry. maybe we can really flip out the **intolerable** ones this year like we did last year and then we can discover why they react to our poems said william

C -   "Hey, Vivian, tell me about haiku poetry. Maybe we really can flip out the **intolerable** ones this year as we did last year, and then we can discover why they react to our poems," said William.

---

28. reiterated   discombobulate

Paragraph – new speaker

Types of Sentences – simple with relative pronoun clause; compound with semicolon; simple; simple

Punctuation – quote within a quote; put " around vernacular

Commas – interjection; always put **,** around "too" if means "also"

Homophones – its/it's; their/there/they're; heard/herd

Verbs – avoid splitting verbs (always was ready)

Other Skills – who (subject) vs. whom (object); fewer (can be counted) vs. less (can't be counted); write out #s to 120; contractions; then (adverb) vs. than (comparative); run-on sen.

Literary Devices – use of vernacular (sweet)

B - yeah **reiterated** jesse who was always ready to try any prank that would **discombobulate** there teachers. ive herd of haiku its sweet. its only 3 lines too. thats 2 less lines then in a cinquain

C - "Yeah," **reiterated** Jesse who always was ready to try any prank that would **discombobulate** their teachers. "I've heard of haiku; it's 'sweet.' It's only three lines, too. That's two fewer lines than in a cinquain."

NOTE: This is a good point to go over the history and composition of the poetry form of haiku. See Chapter 3 for historical information on haiku as well as some examples. Every time one appears, you might want to review the form again as in a later writing assignment, students will be required to compose some.

29. diffidently   earnestly

3 Paragraphs and poem – 3 new speakers (last one narrator)

Types of Sentences – simple; simple; simple; compound; compound in poem

Punctuation – " around short works; note normal punctuation in poem

Commas – quote; quote; compound sen.; unnecessary appositive; compound sen. in poem

Homophones – one/won; your/you're; new/gnu/knew; right/rite

Other Skills – contraction; fr**ie**nd; 1st letter of each line in poem is capitalized

Literary Devices – repartée; metaphor (casts spells upon the wind)

B - i made up one this summer said vivian virtuous **diffidently**. lets hear youre poem said isabelle **earnestly**. vivian recited her haiku. it was about her new friend felicia and it was entitled my freind

> my friend casts her spells
> upon the wind, and she hopes
> that one will go right.

C - "I made up one this summer," said Vivian Virtuous **diffidently**.
  "Let's hear your poem," said Isabelle Ingenuous **earnestly**.
  Vivian recited her haiku. It was about her new friend, Felicia, and it was entitled "My Friend."

> My friend casts her spells
> Upon the wind, and she hopes
> That one will go right.

30. noisome   alleged

2 Paragraphs – 2 new speakers

Types of Sentences – simple; simple; simple

Punctuation – need for ! to show emphasis

Commas – quote; direct address; quote

Homophones – your/you're; there/their/they're

Verbs – note use of future tense

Other Skills – "well" (adv.) vs. "good" (adj.); fewer vs. less; contraction

B - isabelle pointed out youre spell on that **noisome** stink bomb sure worked good last year felicia! maybe less of your spells will go wrong this year. their are a few ive been practicing **alleged** felicia hopefully

C - Isabelle pointed out, "Your spell on that **noisome** stink bomb sure worked well last year, Felicia! Maybe fewer of your spells will go wrong this year!"
  "There are a few I've been practicing," **alleged** Felicia hopefully.

Writing Idea #6: Expressive Essay.

Write an essay to express why it is important to practice something, like spells, a sport, an instrument, reading, etc. You can draw on your own experience for one or two of the examples in the body of your essay.

31. sniggered

Paragraph – new subject

Types of Sentences – simple (compound subject); compound (with compound subject of first clause)

Commas – noun list; adj. clause ("who" clause that is extra); compound sen.

Verbs – do not split verbs (really were impressed)

Other Skills – relative pronouns "who" (subject) and "whom" (object); never use "that" to refer to people; among (more than 2) vs. between (2 or fewer); sing. poss.

B - pauline olivia and alessandra smiled. william and jesse whom stood between the girls **sniggered** but they were really impressed with vivians poem

C -   Pauline, Olivia, and Alessandra smiled. William and Jesse, who stood among the girls, **sniggered**, but they really were impressed with Vivian's poem.

NOTE: Warn of parallel construction ("stuck" instead of "sticking").

32. emitted garbled incoherently

No Paragraph – same topic

Types of Sentences – simple
(compound verb)

Commas – adj. clause with "who";
verb list

Homophones – their/there/they're

Verbs – do not split verbs (always
was observant)

Other Skills – relative pronouns
"who" (subject) and "whom"
(object); never use "that" to refer to
people; write out #s to 120;

Literary Devices – simile; use of
strong, vivid verbs

B - sam that always was observant
noticed that 2 teachers standing in
nearby classroom doorways twitched
emitted curls of smoke from their
ears and noses **garbled** almost
incoherently some phrase over and
over sticking out there tongues with
each word like lizards

C - Sam, who always was observant,
noticed that two teachers standing in
nearby classroom doorways twitched,
emitted curls of smoke from their
ears and noses, **garbled** almost
incoherently some phrase over and
over, and stuck out their tongues with
each word like lizards.

**NOTE: Your students have heard the word "pronoun" many times in
previous Caught'yas. They may be ready to learn the seven different kinds
of pronouns. If they can learn these (especially the subject, object, and
possessive pronouns), they will have a better chance to use them and spell
them ("its" in particular) correctly. See "Pronouns" in the** *Grammar,
Usage, and Mechanics Guide***.**

33. perceive

No ¶ (same topic); ¶ (new subject)

Types of Sentences – compound;
simple

Commas – compound sen.; intro
word

Other Skills – perceive; friends;
antecedent/pronoun agreement
("group" is a collective noun and
requires a sing. poss. pronoun);
review subject and poss. pronouns

Literary Devices – foreshadowing
(Sam determined...)

B - sam couldn't **perceive** exactly
what they muttered but he was
determined to find out. indeed the
group of freinds did have some of
their same teachers from previous
years

C - Sam couldn't **perceive** exactly
what they muttered, but he was
determined to find out.

　　　　Indeed, the group of friends did
have some of the same teachers from
previous years.

**34. amicable   melodious
martinet**

No Paragraph – same topic

Types of Sentences – simple; simple
(compound subject)

Punctuation – **.** needed in
abbreviations (this will not be noted
in future CYs)

Commas – parenthetical expression
(much to...); interrupter; always put **,**
around "too" if it means "also"

Homophones – too/two/to

Verbs – use of pluperfect tense

Other Skills – abbreviations; write
out ordinal #s; sing. poss.; hyphen
between 2 wds. acting as 1

B - mr math **martinet** had followed
them to the 8th grade much to olivias
dismay. ms **amicable** artist and mr
melodious music however taught 8th
graders to

C - Mr. Math **Martinet** had followed
them to the eighth grade, much to
Olivia's dismay. Ms. **Amicable** Artist
and Mr. **Melodious** Music, however,
taught eighth-graders, too.

35. scintillating   pondered omnipresent

No ¶ (same topic); ¶ (new speaker)

Types of Sentences – simple; complex (sub. clause at end)

Commas – interjection; appositive (unnecessary); quote; 2 adj. where 2nd is not age, size, color, or linked

Homophones – their/there/they're; new/gnu/knew

Other Skills – do not capitalize subjects except languages; abbreviation; do not begin a sen. with FANBOYS unless you treat it as an interjection as in this sen.; consonant + "y" = change "y" to "i" + "es" plural rule

B - and their was a new teacher for social studies mr **scintillating** social studies. i wonder what he's like **pondered** isabelle as she played with one of the **omnipresent** plastic butterflys in her hair

C - And there was a new teacher for social studies, Mr. **Scintillating** Social Studies.

"I wonder what he's like," **pondered** Isabelle as she played with one of the **omnipresent**, plastic butterflies in her hair.

NOTE: Now that your students know the coordinating conjunctions by chanting the FANBOYS and that a subordinate clause is really a long adverb, it is time for them to begin learning A WHITE BUS words, the subordinating conjunctions. Take the mnemonic device A WHITE BUS to help students learn them.

A   after, although, as

W   when, while, where
H   how
I   if
T   than
E   even though

B   because, before
U   until, unless
S   since, so that

Students enjoy chanting and chanting these in a sing-song voice every time one appears in a Caught'ya. I added "hey" at the end as we kicked up a foot. Once they memorize the subordinating conjunctions, students can be taught that they *never, never* (well, almost never) put a comma before one and that if A WHITE BUS word is combined with a subject and a verb, it is a subordinate clause which is almost always used as an adverb. In this way, they can learn to begin a sentence with "because" and have a chance to complete the sentence.

Tread carefully, though. I have had students in tears as I made a liar out of their beloved fourth-grade teacher who had told them *never* begin a sentence with "because." I informed my kids that, now that they are in middle school, it is OK, just as they can't begin a sentence with any FANBOYS until they get a driver's license.

Writing Idea #7: Explanatory Essay.

Isabelle always has a butterfly of some sort in her hair. It is a defining characteristic of her personality. Think about yourself (or a friend). Make a list of defining characteristics that make you or your friend an individual, different from all others. Now write to explain what two or three quirks make you or your friend unique. Be sure to explain why and how each trait or quirk (like Isabelle's butterflies) defines you. (If you can't think of a trait or quirk, feel free to make one up.)

---

36. despicable   automaton   witty

2 paragraphs – 2 new speakers

Types of Sentences – simple; simple

Commas – adj. list; quote; interjection; intro word; appositive

Homophones – its/it's

Other Skills – who (subject) vs. whom (object); do not use "that" to refer to people; capitalize languages; abbreviation; write out ordinal #s

Literary Devices – metaphor ("automaton" for "teacher"); exaggeration

B - its probably just another horrible **despicable** boring **automaton** moaned pauline who always saw only the negative. oh no that nice english teacher we had last year ms **witty** writing wizard stayed in 7th grade complained olivia

C -   "It's probably just another horrible, **despicable**, boring **automaton**," moaned Pauline who always saw only the negative.

"Oh, no, that nice English teacher we had last year, Ms. **Witty** Writing Wizard, stayed in seventh grade," complained Olivia.

NOTE: I suggest that you continue to ban the use of "it's" in your classroom. You can go over the difference *ad nauseum*, but until the lightbulb dawns, students will persist in confusing these two homophones.

37. griped   arduous

No Paragraph – same speaker, same subject

Types of Sentences – compound; simple

Commas – compound sen.; always put **,** around "too" if it means "also"

Homophones – there/their/they're; to/too/two; it's/its

Verbs – never split an infinitive

Other Skills – abbreviations; contraction; put hyphen in 2 wds. acting as 1 adj.; further (cannot be measured) vs. farther (can be measured); use "an" before a vowel; sc**ien**ce

Literary Devices – foreshadowing

B - we have ms grammar grouch again and theirs ms stern science on the eighth grade list too olivia **griped** further. its going to probably be a **arduous** year

C - "We have Ms. Grammar Grouch again, and there's Ms. Stern Science on the eighth-grade list, too," Olivia **griped** further. "It's probably going to be an **arduous** year."

NOTE: *Star Trek* **was wrong. "To boldly go where..." should be "To go boldly." Infinitives should never be split.**

38. incessant   predicted   eerie

Paragraph – new speaker

Types of Sentences – simple; simple

Commas – intro word; 2 adj. where 2nd is not age, size, color, or related; quote

Homophones – their/there/they're

Other Skills – abbreviations; among (3+) vs. between (2-); "an" before a vowel

Literary Devices – foreshadowing

B - well between ms grammar grouch and mr math martinet i see lots of homework. i also see william and jesse getting into trouble with theyre **incessant** stupid poems **predicted** felicia fey in an **eerie** spooky voice

C - "Well, between Ms. Grammar Grouch and Mr. Math Martinet, I see lots of homework. I also see William and Jesse getting into trouble with their **incessant**, stupid poems," **predicted** Felicia Fey in an **eerie**, spooky voice.

**39. promptly   a plethora of
    assess   omnipresent**

Paragraph – narrator speaking again

Types of Sentences – compound/
complex; simple

Commas – compound/complex
sen.with sub. clause in 2nd half

Homophones – waist/waste; no/know

Verbs – do not use conditional tense
to denote past (would)

Other Skills – received; do not end a
sen. with a preposition (if possible);
plural poss.

Literary Devices – strong, vivid verbs

B - william and jesse wasted no time and after they recieved a few lessons from vivian virtuous they **promptly** composed **a plethora of** haiku which to **assess** their teachers reactions with. sam would keep notes on the various instructors reactions in his **omnipresent** notebook

C -   William and Jesse wasted no time, and after they received a few lessons from Vivian Virtuous, they **promptly** composed **a plethora of** haiku with which to **assess** their teachers' reactions. Sam kept notes on the various instructors' reactions in his **omnipresent** notebook.

NOTE: It is a good idea to stress the use of "a plethora of" and "a dearth of" as students like using these phrases a lot. Besides, students never can spell "a lot" correctly anyway...

40. astute   manifesting protrusion

Paragraph – new time

Types of Sentences – complex (sub. clause at beginning)

Punctuation – parentheses for narrator aside

Commas – intro adverb; noun series; sub. clause at beginning

Verbs – rise (intransitive) vs. raise (transitive)

Other Skills – sing. poss.; abbreviations; fewer (can count) vs. less; then (adv.) vs. than (comparative); write out #s to 120

Literary Devices – narrator aside; strong verbs

B - one day when one particularly **astute** poem of jesses made mr math martinet freeze in his tracks and raise his arms in the air for no less then 2 entire minutes besides **manifesting** the usual ear smoke eye flutter and tongue **protrusion** sam knew that they were on the right track

C -   One day, when one particularly **astute** poem of Jesse's made Mr. Math Martinet freeze in his tracks and raise his arms in the air for no fewer than two entire minutes (besides **manifesting** the usual ear-smoke, eye-flutter, and tongue **protrusion**), Sam knew that they were on the right track.

NOTE: At this point a lesson on the common irregular verbs which students often confuse might be appropriate. Be sure to include lie/lay, rise/raise, sit/set. In that list, the problem lies in which form of the verb is intransitive (takes no object) and which is transitive (takes an object). See *Grammar, Usage, and Mechanics Guide*.

Writing Idea #8: Dialogue.

Write a one-page conversation among William, Jesse, Sam, and the rest of the crew as they discuss the actions of each of their bizarre teachers. They also could discuss why they think they get a more pronounced reaction out of the teachers with haiku. Alternatively, they could explain to each other exactly what haiku poetry is and how to write it.

41. mirth speculated superlative devoid vision

Paragraph – new topic

Types of Sentences – simple; simple; poem is simple

Punctuation – " around short works

Verbs – incorrect form of the verb "to be"

Other Skills – vocab. lesson; affect (influence) vs. effect (cause); capitalize first letter of each line of poem

Literary Devices – personification (numbers and homework fill); double entendre (vision)

B - jesse jocose entitled the poem no **mirth**. sam sagacious **speculated** that it be the **superlative** vocabulary that produced the added affect

> numbers and homework
> fill his mind that seems **devoid**
> of **mirth** and **vision.**

C -   Jesse Jocose entitled the poem "No **Mirth**." Sam Sagacious **speculated** that it was the **superlative** vocabulary that produced the added effect.

> Numbers and homework
> Fill his mind that seems **devoid**
> Of **mirth** and **vision**.

42. exasperated mused

2 Paragraphs – narrator; new speaker

Types of Sentences – simple; poem is compound; simple

Punctuation – " around short works; use of ellipses to denote unfinished thought

Commas – 2 adj. where 2nd is not age, size, color, or linked

Homophones – their/there/they're; no/know

Other Skills – further (can't count) vs. farther (can count); abbreviations; accept (verb) vs. except (comparative); sing. poss.; capitalize 1st letter of each line of haiku; contraction

Literary Devices – personification ("Her brush strokes")

B - sam also noted further that ms amicable artist had no reaction accept a sweet **exasperated** smile for williams poem that was entitled brush magic

> her brush strokes paper
> and colorful images
> appear like magic.

mr melodious music didnt react to the haiku either except to comment on there content. i wonder **mused** sam

C -   Sam also noted further that Ms. Amicable Artist had no reaction except a sweet, **exasperated** smile for William's poem that was entitled "Brush Magic."

> Her brush strokes paper,
> And colorful images
> Appear like magic.

   "Mr. Melodious Music didn't react to the haiku either except to comment on their content. I wonder...," **mused** Sam.

B – Sentences for the Board	C – Corrected version of the CY
43. scintillating **disregarded** **uttered** Paragraph – new topic Types of Sentences – simple; complex (sub. clause at end) Commas – intro adv.; unnecessary appositive; intro adv. (optional) Homophones – new/gnu/knew; no/know Verbs – use of pluperfect; never use conditional (would) to denote past tense Other Skills – don't capitalize subjects except languages (and as a name); use contraction; "like" to compare 2 nouns and "as if" in all other situations	**B -** surprisingly the gnu history teacher mr **scintillating** social studies didnt react to the poems either. usually he would simply **disregard** them as he went on with his lesson like no poem had been **uttered** **C -** Surprisingly, the new history teacher, Mr. **Scintillating** Social Studies, didn't react to the poems either. Usually, he simply **disregarded** them as he went on with his lesson as if no poem had been **uttered**.
44. arduous 2 Paragraphs – new speaker; narrator Types of Sentences – simple; complex (sub. clause at beginning) Commas – quote; sub. clause at beginning Homophones – to/two/too Verbs – note use of "dead," passive, helping verbs (is, had) vs. active, vivid verbs (noted, proved) Other Skills – demonstrative pronouns (this...); comparatives (more); write out ordinal #s; than (comparative) vs. then (adverb) Literary Devices – building suspense	**B -** this is becoming more and more curious noted sam too william. since the students had even more homework 8th grade proved more **arduous** than 7th grade **C -** "This is becoming more and more curious," noted Sam to William. Since the students had even more homework, eighth grade proved more **arduous** than seventh grade.

NOTE: This is a good point to review the subordinating and coordinating conjunctions, the helping ("dead") verbs, and the seven different types of pronouns. (See *Grammar, Usage, and Mechanics Guide*.) Prepositions will be addressed after Caught'ya #49.

> ## Writing Idea #9: Writing Poetry.
> Review with your teacher how to write a haiku poem. Then write three of them. You may write about nature, a single incident, or a picture of an emotion.

45. malicious   bibliophilic

No Paragraph – same topic (arduousness of 8th grade)

Types of Sentences – compound with adj. clause

Punctuation – use of colon (never after verb); " around vernacular

Commas – 2 adj. where 2nd is not age, size, color, or related; compound sen.; noun list; interrupter

Other Skills – demonstrative and poss. pronouns; write out #s to 120; who (subject) vs. whom (object); do not use "that'" to refer to people

Literary Devices – vernacular

B - orson odious was again up to his usual **malicious** tricks and this year he picked mainly on three victims isabelle ingenuous shy beth **bibliophilic** and of course felicia fey who had ratted on him the previous year

C - Orson Odious was again up to his usual, **malicious** tricks, and this year he picked mainly on three victims: Isabelle Ingenuous, shy Beth **Bibliophilic**, and, of course, Felicia Fey who had "ratted" on him the previous year.

**46. dapper   comeliness
bibliophilic   derision**

Paragraph – new topic

Types of Sentences – simple (no subject after "and"); simple

Punctuation – hyphen in 2 wds. acting as 1 adj.

Commas – intro phrase

Homophones – prey/pray

Verbs – do not use conditional (would) to denote past tense

Other Skills – contraction; who vs. whom; never use "that" to refer to people; use "like" only to compare 2 nouns; wrong use of pronoun—need subject pronoun as "did" is implied; review 7 types of pronouns

B - once again otiose danny **dapper** took advantage of his **comeliness** and would pray on super shy girls like beth **bibliophilic** to do his homework for him. petra pulchritudinous would show **derision** towards any girl that didnt dress like her

C -   Once again, otiose Danny **Dapper** took advantage of his **comeliness** and preyed on super-shy girls like Beth **Bibliophilic** to do his homework for him. Petra Pulchritudinous showed **derision** towards any girl who didn't dress as she did.

NOTE: Now that your students have memorized the coordinating and subordinating conjunctions, it is time to memorize the prepositions. They are listed in the *Grammar, Usage, and Mechanics Guide*. Students learn them painlessly if you chant only four new ones a day (adding four each day until you cover the entire list). Middle-school students love to chant these with a different gesture (like "the Egyptian" or raising an arm, etc.) with each set of four prepositions. When all have been added to the chant, you and your class (although *you* will never remember the gestures, *they* will) can chant and move to the prepositions each time one appears in a Caught'ya (which is most of them) until your students tire of the exercise.

Once students memorize the prepositions, they can learn not to capitalize them in a title, that when you combine one with a noun, you have an adjective or adverb in a prepositional phrase, and that when you put two prepositional phrases together at the beginning of a sentence, you must have a comma after them.

**47. malevolent   devious
  insecure**

No Paragraph – same topic

Types of Sentences – simple

Commas – long intro phrase; unnecessary appositive; put **,** around "too" if it means "also"; extra info or explanation, comparative list

Homophones – to/too/two

Verbs – subject/verb agreement; collective noun (trio) requires sing. verb

Other Skills – do not begin sen. with FANBOYS; who vs. whom; do not use "that" to refer to people; per**cei**ved; superlatives (most) and comparatives (weaker, smaller) incorrect pronoun use ("is" is implied so subject pronoun "he" is needed); go over collective nouns

B - to make matters worse the most **malevolent** trio were joined by a new student dalbert **devious**. dalbert two liked to pick on anyone that he percieved as weaker more **insecure** or smaller than he

C - To make matters worse, the most **malevolent** trio was joined by a new student, Dalbert **Devious**. Dalbert, too, liked to pick on anyone whom he perceived as weaker, more **insecure**, or smaller than he.

Midterm Caught'ya Test follows on next page.

Remember, you can adapt the test to fit the needs of your students and then print copies from the CD included with this book.

If you choose *not* to use this test, you will need to read the passage in Part 1 of the Teacher's Key to your students so that they don't lose the thread of the story.

If you give the test, read the corrected version of the test (the key) aloud several times to your students when they have the test in front of them. In this way, they can "hear" the punctuation. You might want to go over any words for which they do not know the meaning since this is a grammar test, not a vocabulary quiz. It is a good idea to write the vocabulary words on the board during the test. I also required my students to put those words into their vocabulary notebooks.

Some teachers like to let students mark up a copy of the test and then write the corrected version on their own. Others simply let students write in the corrections on the copy and leave it at that. Personally, I prefer the first method as it makes students think and be more careful, but if time is a factor, the second option would be acceptable.

This test is a review of most of the skills your students have learned in previous Caught'yas. There are three parts of the test, but not all three must be used. If you feel, for example, that your students are not ready to handle Part 2, skip it.

I always gave a midterm around the end of November or early December to check that my students were learning. I also gave one or two Caught'yas as a "quickie quiz" about once every three weeks or so to make sure students paid attention when we went over the daily Caught'ya and didn't cheat when marking the number of errors missed.

Almost Midterm Caught'ya Test

Directions for Part 1:

Students, correct the following long Caught'ya. This test will show how carefully you listen when your teacher goes over Caught'yas. Be very careful, and check your work when you're finished. Ask your teacher for meanings of words you do not know. This is not a vocabulary test. Follow your teacher's instructions.

Hint: There are eight paragraphs, a few spelling errors, and two missing hyphens. Some words will need to be switched around.

one morning however just before school orson danny and dalbert were caught smoking behind the eighth-grade wing. this affected some **drastic** changes for the better and it got rid of a problem. it seems that just as orson was taking a last drag behind the 8th grade **edifice** dean dread came around the corner and he spied the **miscreants**. what do you think your doing he said in his deadly **monotone** voice. me and my freinds didnt do nothing coughed orson as he swallowed the cigarettes smoke. oh its nothing sir mumbled dalbert and danny in unison as danny stuck his hand with the still-lit cigarette which he held among 2 fingers into his **voluminous** trousers. ouch he yelps as the lit cigarette **scorched** his leg and he **inadvertently** revealed his guilt. dalbert **devious** living up to his sneaky personality had quickly crushed the evidence of his guilt under his shoe and dean dread saw nothing. but orson and danny on the other hand could not plead innocence. follow me you **varlets** snarled dean Dread as he marched them toward his office. your parents will be notified immediately and your suspended for no less then 10 days. we do not **tolerate** illegal use of substances of any kind on this campus and your guilty. the result of this incident was that orson who had a long list of **egregious transgressions** in his records was sent to the alternative school. danny came back after 10 days of suspension a **subdued** young man that no longer made fun of others. dalbert escaped with a few days of in school detention because their was a lack of evidence in his case but he remained as **conniving** as ever. now the group of friends only had to contend with one of there tormentors and of course the ever-**haughty** petra pulchritudinous too. william and jesse continue to recite their haiku poems in an attempt to discover the mystery of theyre teachers reactions.

Directions for Part 2:

First, number the first fifteen sentences (up to "Now the group of friends") on your corrected copy of the test so you don't lose track of the numbers. Then, use your corrected version of the test to identify the types of sentences of each of the fifteen sentences in this exam—simple, compound, complex, or compound/complex.

Hint: Five are simple. Four are compound. Three are complex. Three are compound/complex.

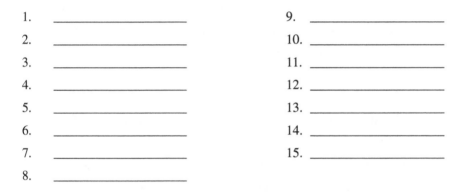

1. _____

2. _____

3. _____

4. _____

5. _____

6. _____

7. _____

8. _____

9. _____

10. _____

11. _____

12. _____

13. _____

14. _____

15. _____

Directions for Part 3:

First, invent an imaginary person who does something that you think he or she shouldn't do, like smoke, be mean, get bad grades, etc. Next, give that imaginary person a name. Then, think of three or four arguments that you could give this person to convince him or her to quit doing this thing. Finally, write down your arguments and some supporting evidence.

Now, write a persuasive essay to this person trying to persuade him or her to quit his or her obnoxious habit. Be sure to support your arguments with good examples.

Almost Midterm Caught'ya Test KEY

Part I:

One morning, however, just before school, Orson, Danny, and Dalbert were caught smoking behind the eighth-grade wing. This effected some **drastic** changes for the better, and it got rid of a problem. It seems that just as Orson was taking a last drag behind the eighth-grade **edifice**, Dean Dread came around the corner, and he spied the **miscreants**.

"What do you think you're doing?" he said in his deadly, **monotone** voice.

"My friends and I didn't do anything," coughed Orson as he swallowed the cigarette's smoke.

"Oh, it's nothing, sir," mumbled Dalbert and Danny in unison as Danny stuck his hand with the still-lit cigarette (which he held between two fingers) **[NOTE: commas are OK as well]** into his **voluminous** trousers. "Ouch!" he yelped as the lit cigarette **scorched** his leg, and he **inadvertently** revealed his guilt.

Dalbert **Devious**, living up to his sneaky personality, quickly had crushed the evidence of his guilt under his shoe, and Dean Dread saw nothing. Orson and Danny, on the other hand, could not plead innocence.

"Follow me, you **varlets**," **[commonly known Shakespearean insult meaning a knavish person, a rascal]** snarled Dean Dread as he marched toward his office. Your parents will be notified immediately, and you're suspended for no fewer than ten days. We do not **tolerate** illegal use of substances of any kind on this campus, and you're guilty."

The result of this incident was that Orson, who had a long list of **egregious transgressions** in his records, was sent to the alternative school. Danny came back after ten days of suspension a **subdued** young man who no longer made fun of others. Dalbert escaped with a few days of in-school detention because there was a lack of evidence in his case, but he remained as **conniving** as ever.

Now the group of friends only had to contend with one tormentor and, of course, the ever-**haughty** Petra Pulchritudinous, too. William and Jesse continued to recite their haiku poems in an attempt to discover the mystery of their teachers' reactions.

Part 2:

1. Simple
2. Compound
3. Compound/Complex
4. Simple
5. Complex
6. Complex
7. Compound/Complex
8. Compound
9. Simple
10. Complex
11. Compound
12. Compound
13. Simple
14. Simple
15. Compound/Complex

B – Sentences for the Board	C – Corrected version of the CY
48. stickler manifested lisped Paragraph – new time Types of Sentences – simple then quote is compound using semicolons Punctuation – use of **;** in compound sen.; use of colon Commas – intro adv. (optional); unnecessary appositive; noun list; verb list Homophones – four/for; their/there/they're Other Skills – abbreviations; write out numbers to 120; use of dash in 2 wds. acting as 1; fewer (can count) vs. less Literary Devices – narrator aside ("ever the stickler...")	**B -** one day ms grammar grouch ever the **stickler** for correct punctuation and grammar **manifested** her usual symptoms froze for 10 seconds and **lisped** over and over for more than 30 seconds but for less than 60 seconds the following phrase their are 4 uses of semicolons there are 4 uses of semicolons **C -** One day, Ms. Grammar Grouch, ever the **stickler** for correct punctuation and grammar, **manifested** her usual symptoms, froze for ten seconds, and **lisped** over and over for more than thirty seconds but for fewer than sixty seconds the following phrase: "There are four uses of semicolons; there are four uses of semicolons."

NOTE: You might want to review the four reasons for using semicolons *See the Grammar, Usage, and Mechanics Guide* **or the note after Caught'ya #21. You also might want to go over the rules of colon use—never after a verb or a preposition but use before a list; to denote a shift within a sentence; and in a letter. See the** *Grammar, Usage, and Mechanics Guide* **for more.**

NOTE: Warn students of the misplaced modifier and the need to rearrange the first sentence after the poem.

49. adroit   prose   surreptitiously   bibliophilic   dumbfounded   antics

2 Paragraphs (new topic; new topic); indented poem

Types of Sentences – simple; (Poem: simple, simple question, deliberate use of fragment); compound

Punctuation – use of " around short works; need for **?** in poem; use of ( ) for narrator aside

Commas – 2 adj. where 2nd is not age, size, or linked to noun; unnecessary "who" clause; compound sen.; extra info (participle)

Verbs – use of pluperfect

Other Skills – vocab. lesson; capitalize title and first letter of each line of poem; contraction; abbreviation; who vs. whom; never use "that" to refer to people; sing. poss.; spell rule—CVC = double 2nd consonant before suffix; misplaced modifier; antecedent/pronoun agreement ("he" is sing. and requires "his" or "the" to follow)

Literary Devices – narrator aside

B - william had recited an **adroit** clever poem he entitled no fire

> she likes correct **prose**.
> wheres her imagination
> her creative fire

dalbert devious whom sat in his usual place in the back row of ms grouchs class stoped **surreptitiously** poking beth **bibliophilic** with his feet that sat in front of him and he stared **dumbfounded** at the **antics** of their teacher

C -   William had recited an **adroit**, clever poem he entitled "No Fire."

> She likes correct **prose**.
> Where's her imagination,
> Her creative fire?

Dalbert Devious, who sat in his usual place in the back row of Ms. Grouch's class, stopped **surreptitiously** poking Beth **Bibliophilic** (who sat in front of him) with his feet, and he stared, **dumbfounded**, at the **antics** of the **(or his)** teacher.

50. pondered   discombobulated

2 Paragraphs – new speakers (2nd is narrator with indirect quote)

Types of Sentences – simple; simple; complex

Punctuation – quote within a quote; use of " around vernacular

Commas – interrupted quote; sub. clause at beginning

Homophones – their/there/they're

Verbs – use of pluperfect

Other Skills – interjection; contraction; odd spelling of "weird"

Literary Devices – teenage vernacular

B - whoa he **pondered** this is really 'bogus. maybe these 'weirdo nerds arent so wierd after all. after they left the class dalbert asked william what he had said that had **discombobulated** there instructor and made her freeze

C -   "Whoa," he **pondered**, "this is really 'bogus.' Maybe these 'weirdo nerds' aren't so weird after all."

After they left the class, Dalbert asked William what he had said that had **discombobulated** their instructor and made her freeze.

Writing Idea #10: Persuasive (Argumentative/Point-of-View) Essay.

Obviously, poetry writing has become important to William, Jesse, and their friends. Think of something that you do that is important to you. It could be writing, a sport, a hobby, anything. Think about why and how this is important to you and what arguments you could use to convince a friend to like it as well.

Now, write an essay to convince your friend (give him or her a name) to like what you enjoy doing. You must come up with two or three strong arguments to convince your friend. Be sure to include details and incidents to make your arguments more effective.

51. entreated   rejoined

2 Paragraphs – 2 different speakers

Types of Sentences – simple; simple; simple; simple

Punctuation – quote within a quote; " around vernacular

Commas – quote; intro word; quote

Homophones – its/it's; too/to/two

Other Skills – contraction

Literary Devices – teenage vernacular; play on words ("words"); satire

B - please tell me what you did to make the teachers do all that he **entreated** william. its to sweet for words. words thats all it is. its just poetry **rejoined** william waggish

C -   "Please tell me what you did to make the teachers do all that," he **entreated** William. "It's too 'sweet' for words."

   "Words, that's all it is. It's just poetry," **rejoined** William Waggish.

NOTE: If your students still are confusing plurals and possessives (as in putting apostrophes in plural nouns), you might want to start putting apostrophes in future Caught'yas whenever a word ends in "s." In this way, students will have to think about whether to use that apostrophe. No matter how many times you explain that no apostrophe is needed in a plural noun, students (and adults—look at signs in your town) put in unnecessary apostrophes. Putting an apostrophe with every noun ending in "s" proved to be effective in getting my eighth-graders to use apostrophes only in possessive nouns and contractions. Try it. I have put extraneous apostrophes in the "B" sentence in the next Caught'ya for illustration.

52. regaled   apparent   bizarre

Paragraph – new speaker (narrator)

Types of Sentences – complex

Punctuation – hyphen in 2 wds. acting as 1

Commas – phrase list; sub. clause at beginning

Verbs – do not split infinitives

Other Skills – sing. poss.; affects vs. effects; write out ordinal #s

Literary Devices – irony; strong verbs

B - when william **regaled** him about the limerick's affect's on the teacher's in the 6th grade the cinquain's effect's on the teacher's in the 7th grade and the even more **apparent** affect's of the haiku this year dalbert resolved to whole heartedly join in the effort to unravel the mystery of hhms's **bizarre** teacher's

C -   When William **regaled** him about the limerick's effects on the teachers in the sixth grade, the cinquain's effects on the teachers in the seventh grade, and the even more **apparent** effects of the haiku this year, Dalbert resolved to join whole-heartedly in the effort to unravel the mystery of HHMS's **bizarre** teachers.

NOTE: *Star Trek* still is wrong. "To boldly go where..." should be "To go boldly." Infinitives should never be split.

53. beseeched   implore   affable

No ¶ (same topic); ¶ (new speaker)

Types of Sentences – simple; complex

Commas – intro word; direct address; sub. clause at beginning; quote

Homophones – write/rite/right

Verbs – do not split verbs; never split infinitives

Other Skills – who vs. whom; infinitive phrase (to teach); breath (noun) vs. breathe (verb)

B - he even politely **beseeched** vivian virtuous to quickly teach him how to write a haiku poem. please vivian as i live and breath i **implore** you to teach me how to rite a haiku pleaded dalbert who was suddenly **affable**

C - He even politely **beseeched** Vivian Virtuous to teach him quickly how to write a haiku poem.
     "Please, Vivian, as I live and breathe, I **implore** you to teach me how to write a haiku," pleaded Dalbert who suddenly was **affable**.

54. shoddy   stern   topple

Paragraph – new speaker (narrator)

Types of Sentences – simple; simple; compound

Punctuation – hyphen in 2 wds. acting as 1

Commas – gerund list; compound sen.

Homophones – its/it's

Verbs – gerunds; subjunctive (as if she were)

Other Skills – affect vs. effect; abbreviation; odd spelling of "science"; use "like" to compare nouns only; not only...but

Literary Devices – strong verbs; irony

B - dalberts first effort was not **shoddy**. its effect on ms **stern** sceince was amazing. not only did she do the usual smoking tongue wagging and freezing but she wobbled as well like she was going to **topple** over

C -   Dalbert's first effort was not **shoddy**. Its effect on Ms. **Stern** Science was amazing. Not only did she do the usual smoking, tongue-wagging, and freezing, but she wobbled as well as if she were going to **topple** over.

NOTE: I see no reason to teach students about gerunds (verbs acting as nouns) since they will use them naturally, and there are no commas involved. Why confuse the issue? I include them just in case...There are several in this Caught'ya: smoking, tongue-wagging, freezing...

Similarly, let subjunctives fall where they may until high school unless you have a particularly advanced or sophisticated group of students.

55. wily   automaton   incessant

No Paragraph – same topic

Types of Sentences – complex (sub. clause at end); simple; (poem–simple); simple

Punctuation – " around short works; regular punctuation in poem

Commas – noun list

Other Skills – capitalize first letter of each line of poem

Literary Devices – string of nouns (used as intro to sentence); humor

B - this pleased dalbert to no end as he loved to be **wily**. dalbert entitled his poetic effort the **automaton**

> science is her life.
> facts figures **incessant** notes
> she is not human

C - This pleased Dalbert to no end as he loved to be **wily**. Dalbert entitled his poetic effort "The **Automaton**."

> Science is her life.
> Facts, figures, **incessant** notes;
> She is not human.

Writing Idea #11: Strong, Vivid-Verb Paragraph.

Dalbert loves to be wily and devious. What is your favorite thing to be??? Write a strong, vivid-verb paragraph using the topic sentence, "I love to be _____." Then write the rest of the paragraph (seven-sentence minimum) to explain why and how you love to be _____. It is a good idea to think ahead and plan your verbs.

This paragraph must have a title, a topic sentence similar to the one given, five strong, vivid-verb sentences that explain your premise, and a concluding sentence that may use a "dead" verb. Be sure to vary sentence structure and include at least one of each type of sentence.

→   Example (because this is a difficult topic): Strong verbs are in *italics*.

Dalbert loves to be wily and devious. He *sneaks* around and bothers people when they try to work. When he eats in the cafeteria, he always *spits* food in people's faces. Some mornings, he *slinks* behind the building and *smokes*, and then, while others get caught, he *gets* away with it. In addition, Dalbert *teases* and *taunts* the shy girls who would never tell on him. To top off his deviousness, he *puts* snakes in teachers' drawers and gum on their seats, but no one ever *catches* him.

---

56. deviousness   cogitating   peers

Paragraph – new topic (now effect on Dalbert)

Types of Sentences – simple; simple

Punctuation – " around slang; hyphen between 2 wds. acting as 1

Verbs – use of gerund as subject (writing haiku)

Other Skills – affect vs. effect; sing. poss.; use of reflexive pronoun (himself); use of demonstrative pronoun; between (2) vs. among (3+)

Literary Devices – use of slang

B - the affect of dalberts poem on dalbert himself was to focus his **deviousness** on composing haiku instead of **cogitating** how to torment his **peers**. writing haiku became the in thing between the 8th graders that year

C -   The effect of Dalbert's poem on Dalbert himself was to focus his **deviousness** on composing haiku instead of **cogitating** how to torment his **peers**. Writing haiku became the "in" thing among the eighth-graders that year.

NOTE: This is an appropriate point at which you may want to review again the seven types of pronouns. Then, as you encounter examples of each in subsequent Caught'yas, you can point them out to your students.
     You also may want to review the eight parts of speech.

---

57. slovenly   unanticipated

No ¶ (same topic); ¶ (new time)

Types of Sentences – simple; compound

Punctuation – " around short works; use of dash for break in thought and structure

Commas – 2 adj. where 2nd adj. is not color, age, or linked; compound sen.; noun list

Homophones – there/their/they're

Other Skills – friends; use "an" before vowels

Literary Devices – irony; humor

B - even skateboarding steven **slovenly** wrote on his skateboard in huge block letters the phrase haiku rules. the year progressed and william jesse and the other freinds were joined in there efforts at haiku writing from a **unanticipated** source danny dapper

C - Even Skateboarding Steven **Slovenly** wrote on his skateboard in huge, block letters the phrase "Haiku Rules."

　The year progressed, and William, Jesse, and the other friends were joined in their efforts at haiku writing from an **unanticipated** source—Danny Dapper.

---

58. subdued   sycophant
**　　scurrilous   superlative**

2 Paragraphs – new topic; new speaker

Types of Sentences – simple; simple; simple; complex (sub. clause at end)

Punctuation – use of ! for emphasis

Commas – appositive; quote; quote

Homophones – its/it's; there/they're/their

Other Skills – vocab. lesson; reflexive pronoun (himself)

Literary Devices – irony

B - a **subdued** danny former **sycophant** of the **scurrilous** orson odious even composed a haiku himself. its easy he marveled. there short. use **superlative** vocabulary in it so that it has an even greater effect on the teachers instructed sam sagacious

C -　A **subdued** Danny, former **sycophant** of the **scurrilous** Orson Odious, even composed a haiku himself. "It's easy," he marveled. "They're short!"

　"Use **superlative** vocabulary in it so that it has an even greater effect on the teachers," instructed Sam Sagacious.

59. fervently   heeded
    foreboding   garbed

2 Paragraphs – new speaker; narrator

Types of Sentences – simple; compound; simple

Punctuation – " around words used out of context; ( ) in narrator aside; use of colon

Commas – quote; compound sen.

Other Skills – sing. poss.

Literary Devices – strong verbs; narrator aside

B - i will said danny **fervently**. danny **heeded** sams advice and he asked beth bibliophilic in a nice tone for a change for some suggestions. he used the following words **foreboding** and **garbed**

C -   "I will," said Danny **fervently**.
    Danny **heeded** Sam's advice, and he asked Beth Bibliophilic (in a nice tone for a change) for some suggestions. He used the following words: "**foreboding**" and "**garbed**."

---

60. foreboding   garbed

No Paragraph – same topic

Types of Sentences – simple; simple; poem is simple

Punctuation – " around short works

Homophones – piece/peace

Other Skills – reflexive pronoun; write out ordinal #s; capitalize 1st letter of each line of poem; caps in titles; regular punctuation in poems

Literary Devices – personification and metaphor (garbed in a black expression); sarcasm in poem title

B - he entitled his poem my favorite dean. it was the 1st peace of work danny had completed by himself all year

> a **foreboding** man
> **garbed** in a black expression
> looms over students

C - He entitled his poem "My Favorite Dean." It was the first piece of work Danny had completed by himself all year.

> A **foreboding** man
> **Garbed** in a black expression
> Looms over students.

Writing Idea #12: Problem/Solution Expository Essay.

Think of a foreboding person who scares people. This could be a real person, a made-up one like Dean Dread, a comic-book character, or a character in a movie or TV show. Think of two or three things you could do to change this person so that he or she were not as foreboding and scary.

Now, write an essay to propose your solutions, making sure you give support that would show why your solutions would work. Be sure to explain in your first paragraph just what it is about this person that makes him or her so scary. Remember, this is an essay about solutions.

B – Sentences for the Board	C – Corrected version of the CY
61. marveled palpable metaphor Paragraph – new speaker Types of Sentences – simple; compound Punctuation – ! needed for emphasis Commas – appositive (with "whose"); compound sen. Homophones – who's/whose; your/you're Verbs – subject/verb agreement Other Skills – conjunction; friends; incorrect use of object pronoun; put others first Literary Devices – irony	**B -** thats not bad **marveled** william whos dislike of danny was **palpable**. me and my friends is impressed with your **metaphor** and youre actually a good poet he **marveled** **C -** "That's not bad!" **marveled** William, whose dislike of Danny was **palpable**. "My friends and I are impressed with your **metaphor**, and you're actually a good poet," he **marveled**.

NOTE: Warn of the need for five hyphens (one is provided).

62. mammoth wind-milled Paragraph – new topic (now about Dean Dread) Types of Sentences – compound/ complex (sub. clause at end) Punctuation – hyphen in 2 wds. acting as 1 (many examples) Commas – 2 intro prep. phrases; gerund list; compound part of sen.; 2 adj. where 2nd is not age, color, or linked Verbs – rise (intransitive) vs. raise (transitive); need for subjunctive (as if he were) Other Skills – sing. poss.; use "like" only to compare 2 nouns Literary Devices – simile	**B -** in reaction to dannys poetic effort dean dread did the usual eye fluttering ear smoking and tongue protruding but he also rised his **mammoth** trunk like arms into the air and **wind-milled** them like he was a plane revving up to take off **C -** In reaction to Danny's poetic effort, Dean Dread did the usual eye-fluttering, ear-smoking, and tongue-protruding, but he also raised his **mammoth**, trunk-like arms into the air and **wind-milled** them as if he were a plane revving up to take off.

NOTE: This is a good place for another review of the common irregular verbs which students often confuse. Be sure to include lie/lay, rise/raise, sit/set. In that list, the problem lies in which form of the verb is intransitive (takes no object) and which is transitive (takes an object).

63. lisped   authority   buckled

No Paragraph – same speaker

Types of Sentences – compound; compound (or 2 simples)

Punctuation – **;** in compound sen.

Commas – intro phrase (optional); quote; always put **,** around "too" if it means "also"

Homophones – to/too/two

Other Skills – fewer vs. less; than (comparative) vs. then (adv.); do NOT begin sentence with FANBOYS, but if you must use it, set it off by a **,** like an interjection; too many pronouns for clarity (noun needed)

B - in addition he also **lisped** the clause i am the **authority** i am the authority. he repeated this for more than 4 but less then 5 seconds. and he **buckled** at the knees to almost falling over

C - In addition, he also **lisped** the clause, "I am the **authority**; I am the authority." He repeated this for more than four but fewer than five seconds. Dean Dread **buckled** at the knees, too, almost falling over.

NOTE: This also is a good time to point out again to students the difference between a clause (subject and verb) and a phrase (a group of words without a subject or verb or both). You might want to review the FANBOYS (coordinating conjunctions) and the four uses of the semicolon as well.

64. blatant Paragraph – new speaker Types of Sentences – simple; simple; compound (with imperative) Punctuation – quote within quote for slang Commas – quote; compound sen; direct address; quote Homophones – there/their/they're; here/hear Other Skills – comparatives; w**ei**rd; contraction	**B -** theyre is something wierd going on here said sam. theyre reactions are becoming more and more **blatant**. i never thought id say this but way to go danny **C -** "There is something weird going on here," said Sam. "Their reactions are becoming more and more **blatant**. I never thought I'd say this, but 'way to go,' Danny."

**65. loped   gawked   ajar
     uncharacteristic**
 	
2 Paragraphs – new speaker; narrator again
 	
Types of Sentences – complex; simple
 	
Commas – quote; unnecessary "who" clause; extra info (her mouth)
 	
Other Skills – vocab. lesson; do not use double negative; who vs. whom; do not use "that" to refer to people; write out ordinal #s
 	
Literary Devices – strong verbs
	B - it wasnt nothing murmured danny as he blushed at the unaccustomed praise and **loped** off. alessandra amorous that had hung around with Danny in the 6th grade **gawked** at danny her mouth **ajar** in shock at his **uncharacteristic** behavior
	
	C - "It was nothing **(or "It wasn't anything")**," murmured Danny as he blushed at the unaccustomed praise and **loped** off.
	       Alessandra Amorous, who had hung around with Danny in the sixth grade, **gawked** at Danny, her mouth **ajar** in shock at his **uncharacteristic** behavior.

Writing Idea #13: Personal (or Imaginative) Narrative.

Just as Danny Dapper changed from a freeloading person who hung with the bully and used people to someone who liked the "nerds" and actually began to work, other people can change their character as well. Think of a person whom you know (or make one up) who noticeably changed his or her character. (This happens often in middle school.) Write a story about that change—how that person was before he or she changed, what brought about the change, and how the change showed in that person's actions.

B – Sentences for the Board	**C** – Corrected version of the CY
66. reiterated Paragraph – new speaker Types of Sentences – simple; simple; simple Punctuation – need **!** for emphasis Homophones – its/it's Other Skills – capitalize names of languages; then vs. than; spelling of "truly"; who vs. whom; do not use "that" to refer to people; reflexive pronoun Literary Devices – foreign language; sarcasm	**B -** es increíble. its unbelievable she said in spanish and then **reiterated** in english to anyone who listened. danny truely wrote something himself **C -** "Es increíble! It's unbelievable!" she said in Spanish and then **reiterated** in English to anyone who listened. "Danny truly wrote something himself!"
67. pulchritudinous *modus vivendi* episode Paragraph – new topic Types of Sentences – compound; simple (even though long) Commas – compound sen.; 3 prep. phrases at beginning; extra info Homophones – there/their/they're Other Skills – *italics*; *italics* for Latin phrases; write out ordinal #s; use "an" before a vowel; plural poss. Literary Devices – Latin phrase; building suspense	**B -** danny may have written something on his own but petra **pulchritudinous** hadnt changed her *modus vivendi*. that same evening at the second school dance of the year there was a **episode** with petra **pulchritudinous** that temporarily at least pushed thoughts of the bizarre teachers out of the friends minds **C -** Danny may have written something on his own, but Petra **Pulchritudinous** hadn't changed her *modus vivendi*. That same evening at the second school dance of the year, there was an **episode** with Petra **Pulchritudinous** that, temporarily at least, pushed thoughts of the bizarre teachers out of the friends' minds.

NOTE: Since it has so many words ending in an "s," this is an appropriate Caught'ya to play with plurals and possessives again in order to make students think twice before using an apostrophe. I have put in extraneous apostrophes. Take them out if you think this is too much for your students.

68. subdued   adorned

Paragraph – new topic (now descriptive)

Types of Sentences – simple; simple; compound

Commas – noun list; compound sen.

Other Skills – sing. poss.

Literary Devices – descriptive writing; personification; strong, vivid verbs

B - the cafeteria was beautiful with **subdued** light. all the table's lined the wall's with red and blue paper draped over them. mound's of artfully arranged chip's cookies' cake's veggies' and fruit **adorned** tablecloth's in the school's color's

C - The cafeteria was beautiful with **subdued** light. All the tables lined the walls with red and blue paper draped over them. Mounds of artfully arranged chips, cookies, cakes, veggies, and fruit **adorned** tablecloths in the school's colors.

69. cascaded   garlands   strident   strummers

No Paragraph – description continued

Types of Sentences – compound; simple

Commas – compound sen.; unnecessary appositive

Verbs – strong, vivid verbs

Literary Devices – descriptive writing; strong, vivid verbs; personification; alliteration

B - a fountain of pink punch **cascaded** into a huge bowl and **garlands** of paper flowers hung from the ceiling. a live band the **strident strummers** warmed up on a low platform

C - A fountain of pink punch **cascaded** into a huge bowl, and **garlands** of paper flowers hung from the ceiling. A live band, The **Strident Strummers**, warmed up on a low platform.

70. strident   reverberated

No ¶ (same description); ¶ (new speaker)

Types of Sentences – compound; complex (sub. clause at end)

Commas – compound sen.; interjection; quote, verb series

Homophones – their/there/they're; herd/heard

Literary Devices – description; strong verbs

B - theyre **strident** music boomed from large speakers and the walls **reverberated** with the bass. ah breathed petra as she entered the room glanced around and herd the music

C - Their **strident** music boomed from large speakers, and the walls **reverberated** with the bass.

"Ah," breathed Petra as she entered the room, glanced around, and heard the music.

Writing Idea #14: Descriptive Writing.

Think of a place that you like. It could be outside under a tree, at a park, at a playground, in your bedroom, in a video room, or any place you like. Go there. Listen to the sounds. Look around. Smell the smells. Absorb the atmosphere. Take notes on what you see, smell, hear, and possibly feel and taste.

Now, write three or four descriptive paragraphs to describe this place. Use personification, strong verbs, and vivid language. Try to avoid the use of "dead" verbs (helping verbs). Keep your paragraphs in the past tense.

71. azure   garments
inappropriateness

No Paragraph – continued quote

Types of Sentences – complex (sub. clause at end)

Punctuation – " around what parent said; hyphen needed in 2 wds. acting as 1

Commas – quote; repeated phrase (too short, too tight); additional info

Homophones – wear/ware; their/there/they're

Verbs – subject/verb agreement

Other Skills – vocab. lesson; correct use of subject pronoun; plural poss.

B - me and my friends is going to have a blast tonight she said as she ducked into the girls bathroom to change to her too short too tight black skirt and spaghetti string **azure** blouse **garments** that her mother would not let her ware because of there **inappropriateness** for her age.

C - "My friends and I are going to have a blast tonight," she said as she ducked into the girls' bathroom to change to her too-short, too-tight black skirt and spaghetti-string **azure** blouse, **garments** that her mother would not let her wear because of their "**inappropriateness** for her age."

72. comely   pulchritudinous

Paragraph – new slant on topic

Types of Sentences – complex; simple (no subject after "and")

Punctuation – hyphens needed in 2 or 3 wds. acting as 1

Commas – sub. clause at beginning; unnecessary "who" clause

Verbs – use of pluperfect

Other Skills – use "like" only to compare 2 nouns; who vs. whom; plural poss.

Literary Devices – description within action

B - since petra had plastered so much makeup on her now not so **comely** face she looked like she had been painted. petra whom thought she looked **pulchritudinous** exited the girls bathroom and found her freinds

C - Since Petra had plastered so much make-up on her now not-so-**comely** face, she looked as if she had been painted. Petra, who thought she looked **pulchritudinous**, exited the girls' bathroom and found her friends.

73. ebony No Paragraph – same topic (can be argued new topic–Orson and Dalbert added) Types of Sentences – compound Commas – compound sen.; participial phrase; adj. list Other Skills – no longer...but; use of participle as adj.; review preps; too many pronouns for clarity Literary Devices – description within action	**B -** orson no longer attended hhms but dalbert devious dressed in an **ebony** tank top and tight black leather pants found her without delay **C -** Orson no longer attended HHMS, but Dalbert Devious, dressed in an **ebony** tank top and tight, black, leather pants, found Petra without delay.
74. surreptitiously perilously posterior garb Paragraph – same people but different action Types of Sentences – simple; complex; simple Commas – sub. clause at beginning Homophones – there/they're/their Verbs – verb-tense shift Other Skills – farther (can count) vs. further; sing. poss.; review A WHITE BUS words (sub. conjunctions) Literary Devices – description within action	**B -** he sweeps petra up in his arms to dance. as the dance moved to a slow tune dalbert **surreptitiously** moved his hands farther down petras back until they rested **perilously** close to her **posterior**. theyre improper behavior and **garb** were spotted immediately **C -** He swept Petra up in his arms to dance. As the dance moved to a slow tune, Dalbert **surreptitiously** moved his hands further down Petra's back until they rested **perilously** close to her **posterior**. Their improper behavior and **garb** were spotted immediately.

NOTE: At this juncture in the school year, eighth-graders "should" be ready to learn the three questions an adjective could answer and the five questions an adverb could answer, especially if their sixth-grade teacher did Caught'yas. (See the *Grammar, Usage, and Mechanics Guide*.) I liked to teach these eight questions and then post them somewhere on the wall for reference. Note that there are two adjectives and five adverbs (including 2 subordinate clauses) in Caught'ya #74.

75. shrilled compounded gyrate

Paragraph – new speaker

Types of Sentences – simple

Punctuation – **!** needed for shouted quote; note placement of **!**

Homophones – their/there/they're

Verbs – use of imperative; never split infinitives

Other Skills – abbreviation; write out #s to 120; further vs. farther; parallel construction needed (ignoring her and continuing); adj. used as adv.

B - stop that at once **shrilled** ms grammar grouch to the 2 students who farther **compounded** there guilt by ignoring her and continued to **gyrate** slow to the music

C - "Stop that at once!" **shrilled** Ms. Grammar Grouch to the two students who further **compounded** their guilt by ignoring her and continuing to **gyrate** slowly to the music.

Writing Idea #15: Expository/Evaluative Essay.

Petra challenges the dress code. Think of two or three reasons why she does this. Now, write an essay to explain to adults why teens want to defy the rules of adults (like dress codes).

---

76. bailiwick

Paragraph – new speaker

Types of Sentences – simple; simple; compound

Punctuation – use of **;** to form compound sen.; review 4 uses of **;**

Commas – direct address

Homophones – their/there/they're

Verbs – use of imperative

Other Skills – demonstrative pronoun; write out #s to 120

B - dean dread you must come see this. this is your **bailiwick**. these 2 students must leave this dance at once we must call their parents

C - "Dean Dread, you must come see this! This is your **bailiwick**. These two students must leave this dance at once; we must call their parents."

77. laden

Paragraph – new speaker (narrator)

Types of Sentences – complex; simple (compound verb)

Punctuation – hyphen needed in 2 wds. acting as 1

Commas – sub. clause at beginning; unnecessary "who" clause (and extra info); 2 intro prep phrases

Other Skills – review A WHITE BUS words (see note after #35); who vs. whom; review poss. and reflexive pronouns; further vs. farther; between vs. among; spell rule—CVC = double 2nd consonant when adding suffix

B - as dean dread approached petra who already was in trouble with her mother panicked and ran. in her haste to farther the distance among herself and dean dread she triped over a tablecloth and toppled over a food **laden** table

C -   As Dean Dread approached, Petra, who already was in trouble with her mother, panicked and ran. In her haste to further the distance between herself and Dean Dread, she tripped over a tablecloth and toppled over a food-**laden** table.

78. amid   visage   wailed   wrath

No Paragraph – same topic/speaker

Types of Sentences – simple; complex

Commas – noun list; sub. clause at beginning

Homophones – there/their/they're

Verbs – irregular verbs lie/lay; transitive vs. intransitive verbs

Other Skills – vocab. lesson; between (2) vs. among (3+)

Literary Devices – description

B - she fell face down **amid** the food with her painted **visage** in a chocolate cake. as petra laid there between the cakes fruit and cookies she **wailed** her distress and **wrath**

C - She fell face down **amid** the food with her painted **visage** in a chocolate cake. As Petra lay there among the cakes, fruit, and cookies, she **wailed** her distress and **wrath**.

NOTE: You might want to re-teach the irregular verbs "lie" and "lay." "Lie" is intransitive and "lay" is transitive and takes an object. The difficulty lies (ha) in "lay" which is the present tense of the transitive verb and the past tense of the intransitive one—"I lay down a few minutes ago," but "I lay the pen down right now." Since "laid" is always transitive, I told students that "something has to get laid." When they stopped snickering, I made my point. "Some*thing*, an object, has to be placed after using the word 'laid.'" Then I gave them lots of examples.

NOTE: Warn of run-on sentences.

79. sniveled

Paragraph – new speaker

Types of Sentences – deliberate fragment; simple; simple; complex

Punctuation – run-on sentence

Commas – quote

Verbs – subject/verb agreement; improper form of verb "to be"

Other Skills – contraction; antecedent/pronoun agreement; friends; *italics* for emphasis; abbreviation; then vs. than

B - why me im so beautiful and me and my friends is so popular and things like this dont happen to *me* she **sniveled** as dean dread and ms grammar grouch plucked her off the cake and than walked her to the office to phone her parents

C - "Why me? I'm so beautiful. My friends and I are so popular. Things like this don't happen to *me*," she **sniveled** as Dean Dread and Ms. Grammar Grouch plucked her off the cake and then walked her to the office to phone her parents.

80. ominous

3 Paragraphs – new action; new speaker; new speaker

Types of Sentences – simple; simple; compound

Commas – quote; direct address; compound sen; quote

Homophones – your/you're

Other Skills – sing. poss.; do not end sen. with prep. (unless unavoidable); use "an" before a vowel

Verbs – pluperfect (had written)

Literary Devices – dialogue; foreshadowing

B - dean dread firmly gripped dalberts arm with his other hand. i wish i had written a poem to use right about now dalbert muttered. your in big trouble young man and you must not speak unless spoken to said dean dread in an **ominous** tone

C - Dean Dread firmly gripped Dalbert's arm with his other hand.

"I wish I had written a poem to use right about now," Dalbert muttered.

"You're in big trouble, young man, and you must not speak unless spoken to," said Dean Dread in an **ominous** tone.

Writing Idea #16: Dialogue.

Write a one-page conversation between yourself and the principal of your school, assuming that you got into trouble. Each person must say at least ten things. You may add some narrator explanation wherever appropriate (like at the beginning and the end).

B – Sentences for the Board	C – Corrected version of the CY
81. wily egregious 2 Paragraphs – new topic; new time Types of Sentences – simple; simple; simple Commas – narrator aside Homophones – week/weak Verbs – verb-tense shift Other Skills – contraction; building suspense	**B -** dalbert devious for once in his **wily** life couldn't think of a way to squirm out of trouble. he didnt even think he had done anything that **egregious**. the next weak all anyone could talk about was petra pulchritudinous **C -** Dalbert Devious, for once in his **wily** life, couldn't think of a way to squirm out of trouble. He didn't even think he had done anything that **egregious**. The next week all anyone could talk about was Petra Pulchritudinous.
82. décolletage comely Paragraph – new speaker Types of Sentences – simple (compound object); compound with **;** Punctuation – accent mark needed on French word; use of **;** in a compound sen. Commas – interrupted quote Homophones – it's/its Verbs – do not split verbs; incorrect use of verb form "should **have**" Other Skills – contraction; comparatives Literary Devices – use of foreign language	**B -** its amazing said vivian virtuous petra is actually wearing long pants and tops without any **décolletage**. she looks like the rest of us shes really **comely** without all that makeup. she should of done this sooner **C -** "It's amazing," said Vivian Virtuous, "Petra actually is wearing long pants and tops without any **décolletage**. She looks like the rest of us; she's really **comely** without all that makeup. She should have done this sooner."

B – Sentences for the Board	C – Corrected version of the CY

83. escorted   mortified

Paragraph – new speaker

Types of Sentences – simple; simple (compound verb); compound (with **;**)

Punctuation – use of **;** in compound sen.; quote within a quote; **"** around non-English word

Commas – interjection; quote; verb list

Homophones – week/weak

Verbs – sit (intransitive) vs. set (intransitive)

Other Skills – sing. poss.

Literary Devices – use of foreign language

B - wow i can't believe it said alessandra amorous. petras mother actually came to school every morning for a weak set in homeroom with her and **escorted** her to 1ˢᵗ period. i bet petra was **mortified** i certainly would be mucho humiliated

C -   "Wow, I can't believe it," said Alessandra Amorous. "Petra's mother actually came to school every morning for a week, sat in homeroom with her, and **escorted** her to first period. I bet Petra was **mortified**; I certainly would be 'mucho' humiliated."

NOTE: This is a good place for a review of the uses of the semicolon and the most used irregular verbs that have like forms of which one is transitive and the other intransitive like "sit/set," "lie/lay," and "rise/raise."

84. lavatory   optimistically   intolerant

2 Paragraphs – 2 new speakers

Types of Sentences – complex (sub. clause at end); simple; simple; compound

Commas – quote; quote; compound sen.

Homophones – so/sew

Verbs – do not split verbs (only is going)

Other Skills – contractions; plural poss.; CVC spell rule = double 2ⁿᵈ consonant if add suffix

B - maybe shell be nice when we bump into her in the girls **lavatory** said felicia **optimistically**. dont get your hopes up said pauline puerile. she scofed at my blouse today so i think this is only going to make her more **intolerant**

C -   "Maybe she'll be nice when we bump into her in the girls' **lavatory**," said Felicia **optimistically**.
    "Don't get your hopes up," said Pauline Puerile. "She scoffed at my blouse today, so I think this only is going to make her more **intolerant**."

85. blithe   episode

2 Paragraphs – new speaker; narrator

Types of Sentences – simple; complex

Commas – quote; intro adverb (optional); sub. clause at beginning

Homophones – week/weak; its/it's

Other Skills – contractions; who vs. whom; never use "that" with people

B - shes not a **blithe** camper this week added Isabelle whom always looked for the best in everyone. soon as it usually happens with gossip talk about the **episode** at the dance and its aftermath died down

C -   "She's not a **blithe** camper this week," added Isabelle who always looked for the best in everyone.

Soon, as it usually happens with gossip, talk about the **episode** at the dance and its aftermath died down.

Writing Idea #17: Personal Narrative.

Think about gossip at your school. Now, think about one particular incident. Write down your thoughts. Now write a story telling about that incident. Be sure to include description, dialogue, a strong beginning, and a satisfactory ending.

---

86. scintillating   predecessor   humdrum

No ¶ (same topic) then ¶ (new topic)

Types of Sentences – simple; compound

Punctuation – " around name of particular day

Commas – 2 adj. where 2ⁿᵈ is not age, color, size, or linked; compound sen.; unnecessary appositive

Homophones – new/knew/gnu

Verbs – do not split verbs (certainly was different)

Other Skills – abbreviation; review prepositions

Literary Devices – stimulating interest in reader

B - the knew topic of conversation centered around mr **scintillating** social studies and his living history day incident. mr scintillating social studies turned out to be an exciting creative teacher and he was certainly different from his **predecessor** ms **humdrum** history

C - The new topic of conversation centered around Mr. **Scintillating** Social Studies and his "Living History Day" incident.

Mr. Scintillating Social Studies turned out to be an exciting, creative teacher, and he certainly was different from his **predecessor**, Ms. **Humdrum** History.

87. bizarre   unadulterated
lackluster   vernacular

No ¶ (same topic) then ¶ (new speaker)

Types of Sentences – complex (sub. clause at end); simple

Punctuation – quote within a quote; " around vernacular

Commas – 2 adj. where 2nd is not age, color, size, or linked; quote

Homophones – one/won

Verbs – verb-tense shift

Other Skills – vocab. lesson; parallel construction (to spark...to hold); contraction; who vs. whom; no , before necessary "who" clause

Literary Devices – vernacular

B - his teaching methods were somewhat **bizarre** since he liked to spark lively discussions and hold panels instead of **unadulterated lackluster** study out of the text. hes tubular murmured jesse whom always uses **vernacular**

C - His teaching methods were somewhat **bizarre** since he liked to spark lively discussions and to hold panels instead of **unadulterated, lackluster** study out of the text.
"He's 'tubular,'" murmured Jesse who always used **vernacular**.

---

88. extensive

Paragraph – new topic and new time

Types of Sentences – complex (sub. clause at end)

Punctuation – " around made-up day

Commas – , for clarity before "even though"; repetition; intro adv. (optional)

Homophones – won/one

Other Skills – capitalize name of made-up special day; write out #s to 120; fewer (can count) vs. less; sing. poss.; review poss. pronouns

B - his living history days had become legendary even though he only held one or 2 every unit or less then 4 every 6 weeks. on living history days mr scintillating social studies dressed up in a soldiers costume from his **extensive** wardrobe

C -   His "Living History Days" had become legendary, even though he only held one or two every unit, or fewer than four every six weeks. On "Living History Days," Mr. Scintillating Social Studies dressed up in a soldier's costume from his **extensive** wardrobe.

89. garbed No Paragraph – same subject Types of Sentences – compound/ complex; simple; (note run-on) Punctuation – ( ) around narrator's comment; hyphen in 2 wds. acting as 1 Commas – sub. clause at beginning; compound part of sen.; interrupter; intro adv. (optional) Other Skills – if...then; then (adv.) vs. than (comparative); capitalize name of war; use of transitions; write out ordinal #s	**B -** if they were studying the revolutionary war then he **garbed** himself in the uniform of a foot soldier one day and than he came as a sergeant or a high ranking officer the next day. the 3rd day he arrived as a cavalry officer. he even brought the mess kit and an authentic unloaded of course rifle from the period **C -** If they were studying the Revolutionary War, then he **garbed** himself in the uniform of a foot soldier one day, and then he came as a sergeant or a high-ranking officer the next day. The third day, he arrived as a cavalry officer. He even brought the mess kit and an authentic (unloaded, of course) rifle from the period.

**90. probed   era   innovative
      clad**
 	
No ¶ (same topic) then ¶ (new time)
 	
Types of Sentences – compound;
simple
 	
Commas – intro adv. (optional);
participial phrase; comparison
 	
Other Skills – discuss collective
nouns like "class"; then vs. than;
CVC spell rule = double 2nd
consonant when add suffix; capitalize
name of car and war
 	
Literary Devices – simile
	B - the class then held lively
	discussions or students **probed** the
	history of the **era** in an **innovative**
	manner. one morning mr scintillating
	social studies steped out of his red
	chevy **clad** like a true soldier in the
	full uniform of a sergeant in the civil
	war
	
	C - The class then held lively
	discussions, or students **probed** the
	history of the **era** in an **innovative**
	manner.
	     One morning, Mr. Scintillating
	Social Studies stepped out of his red
	Chevy, **clad**, like a true soldier, in the
	full uniform of a sergeant in the Civil
	War.

Writing Idea #18: Expository Essay.

Mr. Scintillating Social Studies dresses up as various soldiers to illustrate his topic. Think of how you like to dress (for an ordinary day, for church, or for a party—pick one). Think about two to three reasons why you like to dress that way.

Now, write an essay to explain to your parents (you may do this in letter form) why you like to dress the way you do. Use details and examples to support your explanations.

---

91. dangled   a plethora of

No ¶ (same topic) then ¶ (new place)

Types of Sentences – compound; complex

Punctuation – hyphen in 2 wds. acting as 1

Commas – compound sen.; sub. clause at beginning

Other Skills – use "an" before a vowel; CVC spell rule; antecedent/ pronoun agreement (a plethora of— like a group of—is sing. and requires a sing. poss. pronoun)

Literary Devices – description within action

B - a duffel bag and mess kit hung from one shoulder and an authentic rifle **dangled** from the other. as he sauntered to the eighth grade wing of the school he passed by the bus port where **a plethora of** school buses were disgorging their students

C - A duffel bag and mess kit hung from one shoulder, and an authentic rifle **dangled** from the other.
   As he sauntered to the eighth-grade wing of the school, he passed by the bus port where **a plethora of** school busses were disgorging students.

NOTE: Again, it is a good idea to stress the use of "a plethora of" and "a dearth of" as students like using these phrases a lot. Besides, students never can spell "a lot" correctly anyway...

B – Sentences for the Board	C – Corrected version of the CY

**92. conveyance   regalia
        careened   crescent-shaped**

2 Paragraphs – new speaker; new action

Types of Sentences – complex (sub. clause at end); simple; simple

Punctuation – ! in what is said with enthusiasm; hyphen in 2 wds. acting as 1

Commas – 2 interjections; intro adv. (optional); participial phrase

Homophones – its/it's

Other Skills – capitalize made-up name

Literary Devices – description within action

B - oh boy its living history day enthused jesse as he descended from his public **conveyance** and spied his history teacher in full soldier **regalia.** hi mr s. suddenly a police car sirens blaring **careened** around the **crescent-shaped** driveway

C - "Oh, boy, it's 'Living History Day!'" enthused Jesse as he descended from his public **conveyance** and spied his history teacher in full soldier **regalia.** "Hi, Mr. S."
    Suddenly, a police car, sirens blaring, **careened** around the **crescent-shaped** driveway.

---

93. ominous

No ¶ (same topic) then ¶ (new speaker)

Types of Sentences – simple; compound; simple; simple

Commas – compound sen; participial phrase; quote

Homophones – their/there/they're; your/you're

Verbs – verb-tense shift

Other Skills – write out #s to 120; abbreviations; "an" before a vowel; CVC spell rule; compound word (firearm)

B - 2 officers got out. they quickly surrounded mr scintillating social studies and there guns were drawn. your under arrest one of them says in a **ominous** tone. fire arms are not permitted on school grounds

C - Two officers got out, and they quickly surrounded Mr. Scintillating Social Studies, guns drawn.
    "You're under arrest," one of them said in an **ominous** tone. "Firearms are not permitted on school grounds."

94. constable   replica   facsimile

2 Paragraphs – new speakers

Types of Sentences – simple; simple; compound

Commas – quote; compound sen.

Homophones – your/you're; its/it's

Verbs – incorrect form of verb "to do"

Other Skills – do not begin a sen. with FANBOYS; use "an" before a vowel;   never use a double negative

Literary Devices – dialogue

B - your violating the law said the other **constable**. but its a **replica** of a antique gun spluttered mr s its only a **facsimile** and it dont have no bullets

C -   "You're violating the law," said the other **constable**.

     "It's a **replica** of an antique gun," spluttered Mr. S. "It's only a **facsimile**, and it has no bullets." (**or "it doesn't have any bullets"**)

NOTE: This is a good place to hold a final review of the three most commonly confused homophones: their/there/they're; your/you're; and its/it's.

95. horde

2 Paragraphs – new speaker then narrator resumes

Types of Sentences – simple; complex

Commas – intro word; quote; sub. clause at beginning; extra info

Homophones – their/there/they're

Other Skills – incorrect use of subject pronoun (object pron. used with prep.); write out #s to 120; antecedent/pronoun agreement (collective noun "horde" is sing.— "them" is plural)

B - well it looks like a rifle to my partner and i said one of the officers angrily. as the 2 officers prepared to drag mr s to there car a **horde** of students jesse in front of them surrounded the trio

C -   "Well, it looks like a rifle to my partner and me," said one of the officers angrily.

     As the two officers prepared to drag Mr. S. to their car, a **horde** of students, Jesse in front, surrounded the trio.

Writing Idea #19: Persuasive/Argumentative/Point-of-View Essay.

The police officers are about to arrest one of the students' favorite teachers. Think of some arguments that the students could use to convince the police officers not to arrest Mr. S.

Now, pretend you are one of the characters in the Caught'yas (pick whichever one you like), and write an essay as if you were that person to try to convince the police officer not to arrest Mr. Scintillating Social Studies. Be sure to give two to three solid arguments and to use details and perhaps incidents to strengthen your arguments.

96. implored   unison
   incarcerate   cacophony

2 Paragraphs – dialogue

Types of Sentences – compound; compound; simple

Punctuation – use of **;** in compound sen.; quote within quote; need **!** for emphasis

Commas – direct address; compound sen.; intro word; repeated word; quote

Other Skills – vocab. lesson; contraction; abbreviations; capitalize and put in **"** made-up day; demonstrative pronouns

Literary Devices – dialogue

B - you cant arrest mr s officers its living history day **implored** a bunch of students in **unison**. those are fun days and we learn a lot. no no you cant **incarcerate** mr s shouted jesse over the **cacophony** of protesting students and police sirens

C -   "You can't arrest Mr. S, Officers; it's 'Living History Day!'" **implored** a bunch of students in **unison**. "Those are fun days, and we learn a lot!"

   "No, no, you can't **incarcerate** Mr. S.," shouted Jesse over the **cacophony** of protesting students and police sirens.

97. beseeched No Paragraph – same speaker Types of Sentences –compound; simple Commas – compound sen.; quote; quote Other Skills – contractions; who vs. whom; do not use "that" to refer to people; "a lot" is 2 wds.	**B -** hes one of the few good teachers that we have and we learn alot from him he added. please dont take our teacher he **beseeched** **C -** "He's one of the few good teachers whom we have, and we learn a lot from him," he added. "Please don't take our teacher," he **beseeched**.
98. din assessment Paragraph – narrator resumes Types of Sentences – simple; compound Commas – intro adv. (optional); appositive (a participial phrase); verb list; compound sen. Homophones – principal/principle; maid/made; one/won Verbs – verb-tense shift Other Skills – then (adv.) vs. than (comparative); oft confused words— "quiet," "quite," and "quit"	**B -** at that moment mr punctilious principal roused from his office by the **din** appears on the scene. he surveyed the situation made a quick **assessment** of the crisis made a decision and than he quietly spoke to one of the police officers **C -** At that moment, Mr. Punctilious Principal, roused from his office by the **din**, appeared on the scene. He surveyed the situation, made a quick **assessment** of the crisis, made a decision, and then he quietly spoke to one of the police officers.

NOTE: There are seven prepositions in this Caught'ya so it might be a great time to do a final review of the prepositions. You can ask students to identify them in the Caught'ya. Then you can go over them and discuss their uses and the rules regarding them.

B – Sentences for the Board	C – Corrected version of the CY
99. dénouement chortled Paragraph – new topic Types of Sentences – simple (though long) with compound verb; simple Punctuation – ( ) around narrator aside; hyphen needed in 2 wds. acting as 1 Commas – verb list; interrupter Homophones – principal/principle; their/there/they're Other Skills – abbreviation; who vs. whom Literary Devices – writing a conclusion	**B -** the **dénouement** of the incident was that the officers examined the gun replica carefully handed it to the principle saluted mr scintillating social studies whom saluted back and **chortled** in amusement while getting into their car. the students however talked about the near arrest for days **C -** The **dénouement** of the incident was that the officers examined the gun replica carefully, handed it to the principal, saluted Mr. Scintillating Social Studies (who saluted back), and **chortled** in amusement while getting into their car. The students, however, talked about the near-arrest for days.
100. sauntered impart Paragraph – new speaker Types of Sentences – compound/complex (sub. clause at end) Commas – compound part of sen.; quote; extra info (infinitive phrase) Homophones – no/know; to/two/too; write/rite Other Skills – demonstrative pronoun; reflexive pronoun	**B -** this calls for a haiku and i know just the person too help me rite one said jesse jocose to himself as he **sauntered** to his homeroom eager to **impart** the news to his friends **C -** "This calls for a haiku, and I know just the person to help me write one," said Jesse Jocose to himself as he **sauntered** to his homeroom, eager to **impart** the news to his friends.

NOTES: Since there are subject, possessive, demonstrative, reflexive pronouns in Caught'ya #100, you might want to review the seven different types of pronouns one last time. (See *Grammar, Usage, and Mechanics Guide*.)

You might also want to review the subordinating conjunctions (A WHITE BUS words), coordinating conjunctions (FANBOYS), and prepositions again.

Writing Idea #20: Poetry Writing; Descriptive Writing.

Compose at least three haiku. Each should be about one incident (as taken in a photograph), one moment in nature, and one emotion. First go over the required form for haiku poetry.

Then pick the best poem, and write a few paragraphs to explain the incident, emotion, and moment in nature in prose.

---

101. commemorate   yore

Paragraph – new topic and narrator speaking

Types of Sentences – complex (sub. clause at end); simple; compound (in poem)

Punctuation – hyphen in 2 wds. acting as 1; put " around short works; normal punctuation in poem

Commas – interrupter; no **,** before "friend" since appositive is necessary (many friends)

Homophones – wrote/rote; principal/ principle

Verbs – do not split verbs; use of pluperfect

Other Skills – who vs. whom; never use "that" to refer to people; fri**e**nd; capitalize title of poem and 1ˢᵗ letter of each line; affect (influence) vs. effect (to cause)

B - it was william waggish though that rote the haiku to **commemorate** the excitement even though he had only heard about it second hand from his freind jesse. he entitled his poem mr punctilious principle to the rescue

> a fake gun of **yore**
> affects near-arrest but lo,
> principal saves day

C -   It was William Waggish, though, who wrote the haiku to **commemorate** the excitement even though he only had heard about it second-hand from his friend Jesse. He entitled his poem "Mr. Punctilious Principal to the Rescue."

> A fake gun of **yore**
> Effects near-arrest, but lo,
> Principal saves day.

B – Sentences for the Board	C – Corrected version of the CY
102. peers unison Paragraph – new topic Types of Sentences – simple; simple Homophones – there/their/they're Verbs – verb-tense shift Other Skills – between vs. among; write out #s to 120 Literary Devices – build interest	**B -** william and jesse stood up between all there **peers** and recite the poem in **unison** at lunch at the top of there voices. there were 7 teachers in the room at the time **C -** William and Jesse stood up among all their **peers** and recited the poem in **unison** at lunch at the top of their voices. There were seven teachers in the room at the time.
103. ebony proboscises **plummeted** Paragraph – new topic Types of Sentences – simple (compound verb); compound Punctuation – hyphen in 2 wds. acting as 1 Commas – verb list; participial phrase Homophones – their/they're/there Verbs – rose (intransitive) vs. raised (transitive) Other Skills – write out #s to 120; then vs. than; less vs. fewer (can count) Literary Devices – description	**B -** 4 of them and dean dread immediately rose on their toes emitted **ebony** smoke and silver sparks from their ears and **proboscises** rose theyre arms in the air and wind milled them. then 2 teachers **plummeted** to theyre knees and they kneeled theyre for less then 30 seconds blinking theyre eyes and muttering **C -** Four of them and Dean Dread immediately rose on their toes, emitted **ebony** smoke and silver sparks from their ears and **proboscises**, raised their arms in the air, and wind-milled them. Then, two teachers **plummeted** to their knees, and they kneeled there for fewer than thirty seconds, blinking their eyes and muttering.

104. inaudible   scurried

No ¶ (same topic) then ¶ (new focus)

Types of Sentences – simple; compound/complex

Commas – compound part of sen.

Homophones – principal/principle

Other Skills – antecedent/pronoun agreement ("each one" is sing. and needs a sing. poss. pronoun); abbreviation; collective pronoun (everyone) requires sing. poss. pronoun)

B - each one muttered something **inaudible** under their breath. the students gasped in shock as mr punctilious principal **scurried** into the cafeteria, and then he sent everyone to their next class

C - Each one muttered something **inaudible** under his or her breath.

     The students gasped in shock as Mr. Punctilious Principal **scurried** into the cafeteria, and then he sent everyone to the (**or "his or her"**) next class.

105. remonstrated

2 Paragraphs – dialogue

Types of Sentences – simple; simple

Commas – quote; quote

Homophones – fair/fare; its/it's

Other Skills – contraction; do not begin sen. with FANBOYS; who vs. whom

B - but, i'm not finished with my lunch," **remonstrated** isabelle ingenuous. its not fare whined pauline puerile who had eaten only a bite of her sandwich

C -   "I'm not finished with my lunch," **remonstrated** Isabelle Ingenuous.

     "It's not fair," whined Pauline Puerile who had eaten only a bite of her sandwich.

Writing Idea #21: Evaluative Essay (Expository).

Think of what, for you, would be the best lunch possible. Now write an essay to explain two or three reasons why this is the best lunch in the world. This is a hard one. Think of your reasons first, plan, and then expand your reasons to include details. Be sure to include an introduction and a conclusion.

B – Sentences for the Board	C – Corrected version of the CY
106. reiterated conjectured 2 Paragraphs – 2 speakers Types of Sentences – simple; simple Punctuation – note placement of **?** in quote Commas – quote; quote Homophones – fair/fare; Other Skills – *italics* for emphasis; abbreviation; who vs. whom; sing. poss. Literary Devices – dialogue	**B -** *life* is not fair **reiterated** ms amicable artist whom had overheard paulines comment. what do you want to bet they call in mr adept fixit **conjectured** sam sagacious **C -** *"Life* is not fair," **reiterated** Ms. Amicable Artist who had overheard Pauline's comment. "What do you want to bet they call in Mr. Adept Fixit?" **conjectured** Sam Sagacious.
107. scurry weathered visage 2 Paragraphs – new action; new speaker Types of Sentences – complex; quote Commas – sub. clause at beginning; interrupter; unnecessary appositive (extra info); no **,** before "Jesse" (necessary appositive) Other Skills – abbreviation; comparatives Literary Devices – building suspense	**B -** as the crowd hastily exited the cafeteria they indeed saw mr adept fixit **scurry** into the cafeteria toolbox in hand and a worried look on his **weathered visage**. this is getting more and more peculiar said sam to his pals jesse and william. **C -** As the crowd hastily exited the cafeteria, they, indeed, saw Mr. Adept Fixit **scurry** into the cafeteria, toolbox in hand and a worried look on his **weathered visage**. "This is getting more and more peculiar," said Sam to his pals Jesse and William.

108. atypical

No ¶ (same speaker) then ¶ (new speaker)

Types of Sentences – simple; simple; simple

Punctuation – hyphen in 2 wds. acting as 1; note placement of **?** in quote

Commas – quote

Homophones – are/our

Other Skills – spell of "truly"; do not begin sen. with FANBOYS

Literary Devices – dialogue

B - we must get to the bottom of this mystery. some of are teachers are truely **atypical** he concluded. so what middle school teacher is a normal adult asked jesse

C - "We must get to the bottom of this mystery. Some of our teachers are truly **atypical**," he concluded.

"What middle-school teacher is a normal adult?" asked Jesse.

---

109. rampant   eccentric
persevered   endeavor

No ¶ (same speaker) then ¶ (new speaker)

Types of Sentences – simple question; complex; deliberate use of fragment

Punctuation – **?** needed in question

Commas – 2 adj. where 2nd is not age, size, color, or related; **,** for clarity before A WHITE BUS WORD (speaker aside); quote; quote

Homophones – there/they're/their

Verbs – do not split verbs

Other Skills – vocab. lesson; who vs. whom

Literary Devices – metaphor (living hormones for students)

B - who would ever want to teach a bunch of **rampant** living hormones for a career there all **eccentric** if you ask me jesse finished. some of them more than others **persevered** sam for who solving this mystery was a serious **endeavor**

C - "Who ever would want to teach a bunch of **rampant**, living hormones for a career? They're all **eccentric**, if you ask me," Jesse finished.

"Some of them more than others," **persevered** Sam for whom solving this mystery was a serious **endeavor**.

110. diversion

Paragraph – new time

Types of Sentences – complex

Punctuation – ( ) around narrator aside; hyphen needed in 4 wds. acting as 1; hyphen in 2 wds. acting as 1

Commas – noun list; sub. clause at the beginning

Verbs – verb-tense shift

Other Skills – abbreviations; write out ordinal #s

Literary Devices – narrator aside

B - as the end of the year approached, mr scintillating social studies ms amicable artist mr melodious music and mr punctilious principal of all people arrange a field trip to an amusement park as an end of the year **diversion** for the 8th graders

C -   As the end of the year approached, Mr. Scintillating Social Studies, Ms. Amicable Artist, Mr. Melodious Music, and Mr. Punctilious Principal (of all people) arranged a field trip to an amusement park as an end-of-the-year **diversion** for the eighth-graders.

Writing Idea #22: Descriptive Writing.

Have you ever been to a park or an amusement park? Think about what it was like. If you choose a local park, you might want to go there and take notes on what you see, hear, feel, and smell there.

Then, think of what focal points (ceiling/floor/walls, right to left, north/south/east/west, color/shape/use, or any other focal points you can come up with) to organize your essay so that it is not just unrelated pieces of information.

Now, write an essay to describe the park or amusement park you visited. If you have never been to a park or amusement park or can't remember one, pick any place, like a playground or your neighborhood. You will need an introduction and a conclusion. In the middle should be at least three aspects of whatever you chose to describe. Each aspect (like what you see, hear, and smell) should be fully described in a "word picture" so that whoever reads your essay can picture the place in his or her mind.

111. maliciousness superlative No Paragraph – same discussion Types of Sentences – compound/complex (sub. clause at end); can break up into shorter sen. (run-on) Commas – compound part of sen. Homophones – their/there/they're Other Skills – parallel construction (for + participle...for + participle); affect vs. effect	**B -** they proposed the treat as a reward for not having a single food fight the entire year and exhibited exemplary behavior in general after orson had left hhms and danny and dalbert had turned their **maliciousness** into trying to compose haiku with **superlative** vocabulary in order to effect theyre teachers **C -** They proposed the treat as a reward for not having a single food fight the entire year and for exhibiting exemplary behavior in general after Orson had left HHMS. Danny and Dalbert had turned their **maliciousness** into trying to compose haiku with **superlative** vocabulary in order to affect their teachers.
112. elated colossal Paragraph – new focus Types of Sentences – simple; simple Commas – intro phrase (optional) Homophones – their/there/they're Verbs – pluperfect and conditional Other Skills – antecedent/pronoun agreement; collective pronouns require sing. poss. pronouns; write out ordinal #s; who vs. whom; incorrect usage (should **have**)	**B -** everyone was **elated** about their field trip. after all all there trips had been cancelled in the 7th grade due to a **colossal** food fight started by none other than william waggish who should of known better **C -** Everyone was **elated** about the field trip. After all, all their trips had been cancelled in the seventh grade due to a **colossal** food fight started by none other than William Waggish who should have known better.

113. correlated   academic

Paragraph – new speaker

Types of Sentences – simple; simple

Commas – quote; intro word (optional)

Homophones – your/you're; its/it's; principal/principle

Other Skills – abbreviation; no caps on "principal" as not used as a title

B - youre field trip needs to be **correlated** to an **academic** subject said ms grammar grouch to the principle. otherwise its forbidden by the school board

C -   "Your field trip needs to be **correlated** to an **academic** subject," said Ms. Grammar Grouch to the principal. "Otherwise, it is forbidden by the school board."

114. a plethora of

Paragraph – new speaker

Types of Sentences – simple; simple

Punctuation – hyphen in 2 wds. acting as 1 adj.

Commas – appositive

Verbs – verb-tense shift; pluperfect and imperfect; gerund as subject (verb acting as a noun—"Going to...")

Other Skills – write out ordinal #s; who vs. whom; never use "that" to refer to people; capitalize names of countries and languages; improper usage (should **have**)

B - it is pipes up ms witty writing wizard the 7th grade english teacher that had overheard the conversation. going to an amusement park provides **a plethora of** ideas for writing. we should of taken them earlier

C -   "It is," piped up Ms. Witty Writing Wizard, the seventh-grade English teacher who had overheard the conversation. "Going to an amusement park provides **a plethora of** ideas for writing. We should have taken them earlier."

115. animatedly   clambered

Paragraph – new time

Types of Sentences – simple; simple; complex (sub. clause at end)

Punctuation – hyphen in 2 wds. acting as 1

Commas – adj. list

Other Skills – write out ordinal #s; write out cardinal #s to 120; spell rule with wds. ending in "s"; CVC spell rule = double 2nd consonant if add suffix

Literary Devices – description

B - the day of the field trip dawned brightly. 5 large shiny yellow school busses lined the side of the school. 8th graders **animatedly clambered** on them as they talked non stop about the rides they planed to take

C -   The day of the field trip dawned brightly. Five large, shiny, yellow school busses lined the side of the school. Eighth-graders **animatedly clambered** on them as they talked non-stop about the rides they planned to take.

Writing Idea #23: Summary.
Write a summary of a field trip you took. Be sure to include an introductory paragraph, a concluding paragraph, and details in between. It is a good idea to list three or four highlights of the trip and give specific details about only those instead of going on and on telling *everything* that happened. Briefly summarize the parts of the trip you didn't emphasize. Try to make the summary of your trip as interesting as possible.

---

116. intrepid   flummox

No Paragraph – same topic

Types of Sentences – simple; simple

Commas – narrator comment

Homophones – their/they're/there

Verbs – do not split verbs (**all** had signed up)

Other Skills – friends

B - the **intrepid** freinds had all signed up for the same bus. they wanted to plot and plan how to **flummox** there teachers into revealing their true nature whatever it was

C - The **intrepid** friends all had signed up for the same bus. They wanted to plot and plan how to **flummox** their teachers into revealing their true nature, whatever it was.

**117. compiling   stealth
      fabricated**

No ¶ (same subject) then ¶ (new speaker)

Types of Sentences – simple (compound participles); simple; simple question

Punctuation – **?** needed in question; quote within a quote; **"** around made-up name

Commas – around adv. for clarity; quote

Homophones – to/two/too

Other Skills – collective nouns (group); antecedent/pronoun agreement; CVC spell rule = double 2nd consonant when add suffix; contraction; who vs. whom; capitalize name; antecedent/pronoun agreement ("everyone" is sing.)

B - the group spent their entire ride writing and **compiling** haiku and planning to try to get in the same area all the teachers who the poems effected. lets call this operation **stealth** volunteered vivian. does everyone have their **fabricated** excuse ready

C - The group spent the entire ride writing and **compiling** haiku and planning to try to get, in the same area, all the teachers whom the poems affected.
　　"Let's call this 'Operation **Stealth**,'" volunteered Vivian. "Does everyone have his or her **fabricated** excuse ready?"

---

118. jabbering   loquacious

Paragraph – new speaker

Types of Sentences – simple; simple; simple

Punctuation – hyphen in 2 wds. acting as 1

Commas – quote; appositive; 2 adj. where 2nd is not age, size, color, or linked; friends

Other Skills – adj. clause (whose problem)

Literary Devices – description within action

B - please include me said a familiar voice. it was john **jabbering** a nice enough fellow whose problem was that he was too **loquacious**. his tall lanky body with straw like limp hair was a familiar sight to the friends.

C - "Please include me," said a familiar voice. It was John **Jabbering**, a nice enough fellow whose problem was that he was too **loquacious**. His tall, lanky body with straw-like, limp hair was a familiar sight to the friends.

119. forte   meticulous   glee

Paragraph – new speaker

Types of Sentences – simple; compound; simple

Punctuation – quotes within a quote; " needed around idiomatic expression (detail man); quote within a quote; accent on French word

Commas – always put **,** around "too" if means "also"; quote; compound sen.; quote; participial phrase

Homophones – too/two/to; your/ you're

Other Skills – who vs. whom; never refer to a person with "that"; go over collective nouns like "group"

Literary Devices – description within action

B - me two please spoke a boy that sat nearby. your going to need a detail man too coordinate your excuses and that's my **forte** insisted mark **meticulous** his round glasses bobbing on his round face in **glee** at being included in the group

C -   "Me, too, please," spoke a boy who sat nearby. "You're going to need a 'detail man' to coordinate your excuses, and that's my **forte**," insisted Mark **Meticulous**, his round glasses bobbing on his round face in **glee** at being included in the group.

Passage to be read out loud to students

NOTE: It is almost the end of the year, and I'm sure your school has scheduled a plethora of extra-curricular events (like dances, trips, and awards). It would be a gross understatement to say that your students' minds are not on learning English. To give them a break, take a few days to read to your students the following part of the story. In truth, I did not want to cut the story short when I wrote it, but it is too long to fit into 125 Caught'yas, two to four sentences at a time. The following, read out loud, will continue the story up to the last six Caught'yas and final exam which will bring the entire story of all three years to a conclusion.

Before you read the passage, however, you will want to write the vocabulary words on the board, go over them, and require students to put them in their vocabulary notebooks. To make it easier for you, I have given you a simple meaning beside each of the vocabulary words. I realize that you know the meanings of these words, but often finding a simple synonym proves elusive. I know you are swamped at the end of the year, have your brains taxed to the max, and don't need more piled on you.

You could, if you have the time, require your students to find the meanings in groups (to make it more fun). Then play games with the words until your students know them and can use them when they write.

As you read, you will want to point out correct grammar, mechanics, usage, spelling, etc. as a review for the year. You may wish especially to point out the correct form of the skills you know are going to appear on the final exam (which follows after Caught'ya #125).

If you have more time and wish to do more Caught'yas, you can put the following passage into Caught'ya form and use as many as you need to complete the year. Remember, there are six more Caught'yas to go before the final exam.

Please note that this passage is all about a field trip and a sneaky plan, subjects near and dear to eighth-graders. Lots of funny things happen in this section. I think your students will enjoy it. It certainly was fun to write...

The group accomplished its **objective (goal)** on the **tedious (boring)** bus ride to the amusement park. Once there, they forgot all about their **clandestine (hidden)** plans as they swooped and swirled on the rides, **devoured (ate ravenously)** mounds of junk food, gossiped, laughed, and enjoyed a day of freedom with **peers (contemporaries)**. As the allotted time at the park approached, the students, **laden (piled high)** with purchases, slowly **meandered (wandered)** towards the parking lot where the busses had parked.

There, in the spaces where five yellow school **conveyances (vehicles)** marked with their county's name were supposed to be waiting, was nothing! Mr. Punctilious Principal, who had driven separately in his van in case a student had become ill or wasn't **punctual (on time)** for the return trip, took out his cell phone and made a frantic call.

"They're where?" he shouted in a **wrathful (angry)** tone with a **soupçon (French word used in English meaning a suspicion or hint of panic)**. "Why didn't the rest remain? I see. One hour, you say? It's pushing their limits, you know. You'd better call Mr. Adept Fixit." With that **baffling (confusing)** remark, he hung up.

Sam Sagacious was intrigued by hearing the Principal's end of the conversation.

"I wonder what he meant by that," Sam said, *sotto voce* **(softly)** to his friends among whom he stood.

"Let's wait and watch the teachers," suggested Isabelle Ingenuous. "Hey, Alessandra, tell us another story about your "abuela" (grandmother) and your waggish younger "primos" (cousins) in Puerto Rico. Maybe that will take our minds off of standing here **sweltering (super hot and sweaty)** like hairy dogs in the **sultry (hot)** sun with no breeze to **mitigate (make less)** the heat."

"Yes, I just love hearing about Puerto Rico," sighed Olivia whose usual otiose, **indolent (lazy)** nature did not apply to learning Spanish.

"I might be able to help," offered Felicia Fey.

"No, Felicia," said the rest of the group with **alacrity (quickness)**.

Felicia didn't listen to her friends. She muttered something under her breath, waved her hands (despite the fact that Isabelle and Vivian tried to hold them down) and "poof." A small, cool breeze **wafted (floated lightly)** by and rustled their **tresses (hair)**. A few birds flew by upside down. A white cloud turned slightly **chartreuse (yellow-green mix)**.

"At least its effects weren't too **egregious (really bad)**," said Vivian Virtuous, her ebony curls bobbing as she **gawked (stared)** upwards. "Birds flying upside down for a few moments never hurt anything, and no one saw the cloud but us."

"Way to go, Felicia," said Mark **Meticulous (super careful)**. "The **zephyr (light breeze)** feels good."

"Don't encourage her, Mark," **asserted (said forcefully)** Pauline Puerile. "She'll get into trouble when one of her spells doesn't go so well and affects a teacher."

Slightly less than an hour later, at 6 p.m., the busses pulled into the parking lot. As the students and teachers boarded them, Sam noticed that Ms. Stern Science, Mr. Math Martinet, and Ms. Grammar Grouch were moving more and more **lethargically (without energy)**. Their faces were **inert (not moving)** as if frozen. Unfortunately, each of the teachers boarded a different bus, so Jesse and William couldn't try a haiku on them. Ms. Grammar Grouch got on the bus with the intrepid friends, told the students in a slow, **monotone (boring, no variation)** voice to sit down, perched herself **gracelessly (clumsily)** in a front seat, and motioned slowly to Mr. Scintillating Social Studies (who also was on the same bus) to take over with the students. The busses took off for Horribly Hard Middle School.

Vivian Vivacious and Beth Bibliophilic took books out of their book bags that they had **secreted (hidden)** under the seats and **commenced (began)** to read. Vivian read Their Eyes Were Watching God by the **eminent (well-known)** Florida author Zora Neale Hurston, and Beth read David Copperfield by the **illustrious (famous)** British author Charles Dickens. Most of the students dozed or quietly chatted.

"Let's do it," whispered Jesse Jocose to William and Sam.

"It's now or never," agreed William. "Wake up, girls. Put down those books. Get out the haiku we wrote and get ready to recite at my signal."

Ms. Grammar Grouch sat unsuspecting in her seat. Mr. Scintillating Social Studies continued to chat **affably (nicely)** with a nearby student, unaware that a large group of students were about to **wreak havoc (cause great devastation)**.

"Now," said William.

At his signal, a dozen students rose to their feet and shouted the following poem at the top of their voices:

> Sparks, smoke **emanate (come out)**
> From their **orifices (holes)** as
> If they are on fire.

The bus driver ignored them.

Mr. Scintillating Social Studies commented, "**Incomparable (the very best)** use of vocabulary, students," and laughed good-naturedly.

Ms. Grammar Grouch, on the other hand, reacted violently. Smoke and sparks did, as usual, **emanate (come out)** from all her **orifices (holes)**. She twitched, fluttered her eyes three times, threw her arms in the air, and then froze, **rigid (stiff)** as a marble statue, eyes open, arms raised in the air. There she sat in that position, immobile.

"She's just having one of her spells," **placated (tried to make feel better)** Mr. Scintillating Social Studies as he yanked out his cell phone and dialed frantically.

The bus pulled over next to the principal's van, and the two men carried the **inflexible (stiff)** Ms. Grammar Grouch (whose arms still stuck straight up) from the bus to the van and laid her **transversely (sideways)** across the back seat. They slammed the door shut, and Mr. Punctilious Principal **vaulted (leapt)** into the driver's seat and sped off.

"That was interesting," said Sam Sagacious.

"That's a gross **understatement (means less)**," **rejoined (said back quickly)** Isabelle Ingenuous.

"OK, guys," said Sam. "Now we go to the next step of 'Operation Stealth **(sneakiness)**.' Can everyone sneak out Thursday night? Do you have your excuses ready for maximum **credibility (believability)**? Does everyone know what **comestibles (eats)** to bring so we don't starve or get caught carrying too much food in our lunch bags?"

"I will check everyone's excuse and coordinate who is supposed to be staying overnight with whom, so there should be no **glitches (problems occurring)**," said Mark **Meticulous (super careful, thorough)** with pride.

The friends spent the remainder of the long, **tedious (boring)** ride back to school **solidifying (making sure of)** their plans. Mark and Sam took **copious (lots of)** notes.

The following Thursday afternoon when school let out, Isabelle, Felicia, Olivia, Pauline, Vivian, Alessandra, William, Jesse, Sam, Dalbert, and the newest members of the group, John **Jabbering (talking non-stop)** and Mark **Meticulous**, hid, one-by-one, in a small, stuffy, seldom-used book room in the eighth-grade wing of the school. Beth Bibliophilic, a **timorous (shy)** girl, **opted (chose)** out of the adventure. The group had decided to ask Dalbert Devious to join them because he knew how to pick locks. Dalbert was **ecstatic (delighted)** to be included. Dalbert, being devious, had no problem giving his parents a **bogus (fake) pretext (excuse)** for where he was spending the night.

Isabelle had convinced their beloved, seventh-grade English teacher, Ms. **Witty (clever)** Writing Wizard (for whom she now worked as an aide), that she needed to get into a book room but wasn't sure which one.

"She didn't know which book room either, so she gave me her master key that opens all the doors. I went to the book room, took out a book as my excuse, and left a thin book to block the door slightly **ajar (open)**," she told her **cohorts (buddies)** in stealth, "but it proved **redundant (extra)**. When I went back to her room, Ms. Witty Writing Wizard forgot about the key, so I still have it.

"I've never done anything like this before. I know it's for a good motive, but I'm nervous," she whispered to her assembled friends with **trepidation (fear)**. "It was the scariest thing I ever did," she added with a **quiver (shake)** that made the **omnipresent (always there)** plastic butterflies in her hair nod in agreement.

The group of twelve remained silent as they listened to someone open most of the classroom doors in the hallway. They **lingered (stayed) mutely (silently)** until that person's footsteps echoed down the hall, and a door closed. Soon, there were no more sounds outside the book room, and Mr. Adept Fixit had left the school.

They **warily (cautiously)** exited the book room, checking to make sure the coast was clear. One by one, they checked all the classrooms in the hallway. To their **utter incredulity (absolute amazement)**, they found, in most rooms, an **immobile (unmoving)** teacher, standing like a statue in the middle of the room. Ms. Stern Science didn't blink an eye when they touched her or said a haiku. Mr. Math Martinet remained rigid and unresponsive to every attempt to rouse him. Ms. Grammar Grouch stood like a silent **sentinel (watching soldier)** in the middle of her room, totally **oblivious (totally unaware)** to the twelve students who surrounded her, recited haiku, and waved their hands in her **static (unmoving) visage (face)**.

"This is really strange," said Sam Sagacious as he wrote in his notebook. I **surmise (guess)** that these teachers are not human. I think that they are robots."

"Let's check for the controls," said William.

"Where do we begin?" asked Isabelle. "I don't want to undress a teacher, even if she is a robot, to find out."

"We'll look for a panel on the upper chest first. Have you noticed that all the teachers on whom the poems worked are always dressed in high-necked blouses or shirts and ties?" pointed out Sam.

The boys, since the chosen victim was a male teacher, loosened the teacher's **cravat (tie)** and unbuttoned his shirt halfway. Sure enough, there was a panel.

"Wow! These teachers truly are robots," **affirmed (agreed)** Jesse and Alessandra in **unison (together)**.

"Let's open the panel and see what's inside," suggested Sam.

Dalbert took out one of his **diverse (different)**, little tools and pried open the panel on the teacher's chest. Everyone twisted his or her head to peer inside. Wires branched out from switches and vanished into the **crevices (little cracks)** of his body. Little green lights blinked slowly along the wires. There was no question. The teacher was a robot.

"'Tubular,'" said Jesse. "Our teachers are robots!"

"Not all of them, I think," argued Sam. "I think some of them are human. Neither Ms. Witty Writing Wizard, nor Mr. Scintillating Social Studies, nor Ms. Amicable Artist, nor Mr. Melodious Music ever were affected by the poems."

"Oh, my gosh," **interjected (added in)** Alessandra, "they are all the creative teachers – writing, new methods of studying history, art, music."

"You're right!" agreed William.

"They probably couldn't make robots creative and **innovative (creative, imaginative)**," added Vivian.

"Wait a minute. What about Principal Punctilious?" **queried (asked)** William. "He didn't react to the poems either."

"It's a certainty that he's human as well," agreed Sam. They would need a human in charge to make all the decisions and to **assess (check out)** any situation that arose, like our field trip. Mr. Adept Fixit has to be human as well."

"Yes, I've never seen him react to any of our poems," said Jesse.

"I **deduce (figure out)** that it's Mr. Adept Fixit who turns the robots on and off," offered Sam.

"Well, we'll find out in the morning, won't we?" said Isabelle. "Now, let's try to get a little sleep."

"I set the alarm clock to wake us up on time," said Mark Meticulous who was the detail guy.

Alessandra suggested, "Let's lie down on the carpet in the teachers' lounge with books for pillows and get some shut-eye. At least it's larger than that tiny book room, and the carpet, even though it is **sullied (dirty)**, is better than the hard, **grubby (grimy)** floor."

"Good idea, girlfriend," said Felicia Fey. "Does anyone want me to try to soften those books or clean the carpet a bit?"

"No, Felicia," eleven voices shouted together.

The group of friends lay on the carpet, heads **bolstered (propped up)** on books, and slept **fitfully (restlessly)** until 5 a.m. when Mark's alarm rang with a **cacophonous (noisy and jangling)** sound.

The twelve students leapt up, went to do their morning **ablutions (washings)** in the boys' and girls' bathrooms respectively, scattered, each

secreting (hiding) himself or herself in a different classroom, and lay in wait to see what would happen.

An hour later footsteps **resonated (echoed)** down the hall. Mr. Adept Fixit entered each classroom in turn. The students observed from their hiding spots as he opened the panel(s) on each robot teacher, flipped a switch, closed the panel, and **lingered (stayed)** fewer than ten seconds for the teacher to come to life.

As he or she awoke, each robot said graciously, "Thank you, Mr. Fixit. Good morning. Have a nice day," in a **monotone (boring, no variation)** voice and proceeded to go to the blackboard to write the day's date and lesson.

As the school became alive with a **myriad (lot of different kinds)** of students, the **intrepid (loyal)** twelve **mingled (mixed)** with the crowd and went to their homeroom as if they, too, had just arrived at school by foot, car, or bus. Like a bunch of **conspirators (people who get together to plan something secretly)** in a spy novel, they had big, **covert (secret)** plans for the upcoming eighth-grade awards ceremony.

News of the truth about the robot teachers spread like mosquitoes in **stagnant (non-moving)** water among the students. Not one eighth grader "ratted" that he or she knew the **appalling (horrible)** truth of the bizarre teachers to anyone not in his or her class. For once, everyone kept a secret.

The last few weeks of school dragged by like a slow-moving train. Everyone waited anxiously for the end-of-year awards ceremony. Every few days, someone would try out a haiku on the robot teachers. Superlative vocabulary in the poems **enhanced (intensified)** the effects on the robots. The eighth-graders' **implausible (not explainable)**, **exemplary (perfect)** behavior worried the principal. He knew they were up to something but had no clue what the kids were planning.

120. *coup de grace* **(a French phrase meaning "the final blow")**

Paragraph – new topic

Types of Sentences – simple; compound

Commas – compound sen.

Other Skills – *italicize* foreign words; write out ordinal #s; than vs. then

Literary Devices – use of foreign phrase

B - william waggish had the honor of composing the *coup de grace*. every 8th grader memorized the haiku and they were more then ready

C -   William Waggish had the honor of composing the *coup de grace*. Every eighth-grader memorized the haiku, and they were more than ready.

Writing Idea #24: Strong, Vivid-Verb Paragraph– Expository.

Write a strong, vivid-verb paragraph to explain an honor you have had. It could be as simple as a time when your parents rewarded you for doing something really well, or it could be an official honor like receiving a medal or being picked to lead.

　　This paragraph must have a title, a topic sentence, five strong, vivid-verb sentences that explain why school is a drag, and a concluding sentence that may use a "dead" verb. Be sure to vary sentence structure and include at least one of each type of sentence.

121. capacity latter Paragraph – new time Types of Sentences – simple; compound Commas – transition; compound sen. Verbs – verb-tense shift; sit (intransitive) vs. set (transitive) Other Skills – use of transition Literary Devices – strong verbs in description	**B** - finally the evening of the awards ceremony arrives. the administration and teachers set on the stage and parents and students filled the cafeteria to **capacity** with the **latter** spilling out into the hallway **C** - Finally, the evening of the awards ceremony arrived. The administration and teachers sat on the stage, and parents and students filled the cafeteria to **capacity** with the **latter** spilling out into the hallway.
122. tome rapt No Paragraph – same description, same place Types of Sentences – compound/complex (sub. clause at end) Punctuation – hyphen between 2 wds. acting as 1 Commas – compound part of sen.; appositive Verbs – lie/lay (intransitive) vs. lay/laid (transitive) Other Skills – write out ordinal #s Literary Devices – building suspense	**B** - all the 8th graders were poised for the signal and even beth bibliophilic lay down her **tome** the hunchback of notre dame as she watched william with **rapt** attention **C** - All the eighth-graders were poised for the signal, and even Beth Bibliophilic laid down her **tome**, <u>The Hunchback of Notre Dame</u>, as she watched William with **rapt** attention.

NOTE: One last time, you can go over the difficult irregular verbs that are confused. "Sit" vs. "set" occur in Caught'ya #122. "Lie/lay" and "lay/laid" (in Caught'ya #123) seem to be the most difficult for students (and adults) to grasp.

B – Sentences for the Board	C – Corrected version of the CY
123. clandestine Paragraph – new action Types of Sentences – simple; complex Commas – noun list; sub. clause at beginning Other Skills – use of transition (then); then vs. than; write out #s to 120 Literary Devices – building suspense	**B -** william gave a **clandestine** sign to isabelle felicia olivia pauline vivian alessandra jesse sam dalbert john and mark. then just as mr punctilious principal had finished his welcoming speech the 12 stood up **C -** William gave a **clandestine** sign to Isabelle, Felicia, Olivia, Pauline, Vivian, Alessandra, Jesse, Sam, Dalbert, John, and Mark. Then, just as Mr. Punctilious Principal had finished his welcoming speech, the twelve stood up.
124. *coup de grace* egregious **abound** Paragraph – new speaker (all 8th-graders) Types of Sentences – simple; simple Punctuation – " around referred-to poems and short works; " around poem said loud; normal punctuation used in poem Other Skills – write out ordinal #s; *italicize* foreign words; antecedent/pronoun agreement; superlatives; capitalize first letter of each line in poem Literary Devices – use of foreign word	**B -** this was the signal. every eighth grader in the room recited the following haiku entitled ***coup de grace*** in their loudest voice why does the school board use **egregious** robots when good teachers **abound** **C -** This was the signal. Every eighth-grader in the room recited the following haiku entitled "***Coup de Grace***" in his or her loudest voice. "Why does the school board Use **egregious** robots when Good teachers **abound**?"

125. orifice   uttering

Paragraph – new topic

Types of Sentences – simple; simple; simple (compound verb)

Commas – verb list

Homophones – threw/through; their/there/they're

Literary Devices – strong verb description

B - the robot teachers on stage spluttered. sparks and smoke billowed from every **orifice**. they through there arms into the air opened their mouths and stared out at the audience without blinking or **uttering** a sound

C -   The robot teachers on stage spluttered. Sparks and smoke billowed from every **orifice**. They threw their arms into the air, opened their mouths, and stared out at the audience without blinking or **uttering** a sound.

Writing Idea #25: Persuasive/Argumentative/Point-of-View Essay.

The students at HHMS did not like the robot teachers and wanted to get rid of them and get human teachers. Think of one thing you really don't like about your school. Write a letter to your principal to explain your point of view and to convince him or her to change that thing you despise (like a dress code or a no-chewing-gum rule). Be convincing.

Think of two or three good arguments to persuade your principal. List them and then take notes on support or illustrations (in words) you can use to make your point more convincing.

Now, write a letter to your principal to convince him or her to make that change in your school. Be persuasive. Use superlative vocabulary. Give great detail. Make your voice heard!

NOTE: Students will find out the end of the story when they take the Final Exam!

Caught'ya Final Exam follows on next page.

Remember, you can adapt the test to fit the needs of your students and then print copies from the CD included with this book.

Caught'ya Final Exam

Directions for Part 1:

Students, correct the following long Caught'ya. This test will show how carefully you listen when your teacher goes over Caught'yas. You will lose two points per error, so be very careful and check your work when finished. Ask your teacher for meanings of words if necessary, but most difficult ones have been provided. This is not a vocabulary test. Follow your teacher's directions, and read the test again to yourself to help with punctuation.

Hint: There are seventeen paragraphs, not including the poem. All periods are correct except three, two of which need to be changed to exclamation marks and the other one to a question mark. There are a few spelling errors and four missing hyphens. Some words need to be changed.

the 8th graders led by the intrepid 12 quickly followed this poem by a 2nd haiku. they entitled it we want human teachers and than they shouted it at the top of there voices in perfect unison

> we **merit (deserve)** real profs.
> creativity will die.
> without humanness.

no less than 12 of the robot teachers sparked and smoked once more emitted a huge dying sigh and fell flat on their faces. the cafeteria was totally silent for a moment and then all **perdition (heck)** broke loose. parents protested loudly and **vociferously (insistently)**. we want those abominable fake teachers replaced with real people as soon as you can do it they insisted. students smiled and gave each other high fives and said we did it. as the human teachers clapped enthusiastically to they joined in the high fives with their students and they pated each other on the back. ms amicable artist murmured to mr melodious music thank heavens i couldnt take much more of those unfeeling **automatons (robots)**. after a quick phone call during which he was heard to say the jig is up mr punctilious principle banged the podium for the

pandemonium (craziness) and **ruckus (disturbance)** to die down. finally as the **din (noise)** turned to silence and all eyes glared at the principal with dislike the truth emerged. beth even lay down her book little women and paid attention. first he said I no that this is no excuse but me and the human teachers fought the school boards decision to save money by replacing real teachers with robots. they used horribly hard middle school as an experiment. frankly I am surprised that the robots lasted this long before our clever students brains figured out the secret. i think the school boards little experiment is over. i for one am relieved and delighted. thank you students for uncovering the truth. and students keep ever **vigilant (watchful)** because you never know what money saving strategy they will try next. when mr punctilious principal finished and sat down a cheer arose from the assembled 8th graders. the long nightmare of hhms was over and the mystery of the bizarre teachers was solved. theyre was only 2 questions remaining. why did the robot teachers react to the poems and why did there reactions get even more intensified when the students incorporated great vocabulary in their poems. ive got it. sam exclaimed when they exited the cafeteria between the other students. you see the teachers who were creative and individualistic were human. they had to be. robots cannot be programmed to be individualistic or creative. they just react to the program in them. ms amicable artist whom taught art mr melodious music who taught music ms witty writing wizard that taught creative writing and mr scintillating social sudies that came up with all kinds of wierd ways to present history all taught creative subjects or taught in a creative manner. all the robot teachers taught us in a rote manner by using the book exactly as written by making us copy notes or by giving us ditto sheets. they couldnt be creative at all sam concluded. than why did the **superlative (super)** vocabulary enhance their reactions to the poems asked Isabelle. well suggested jesse i think that using super vocabulary is like being creative. it takes thought. i think your rite said sam. the robots were obviously programmed only with the basic vocabulary of middle-school students. when we added those big juicy vocabulary words to our poems they only confused the robots more since those words did not compute. i think we've solved the entire mystery concluded william waggish with an air of relief and excitement.

i wonder what next year in high school will be like...

Directions for Part 2:

Use your corrected version to the test to identify the types of sentences of each of the first fifteen sentences in this exam—simple, compound, complex, or compound/complex. *Do not include the poem.* You might want to number the sentences on your exam so you don't get confused. Sentence #15 ends with "brains figured out the secret" and is in the middle of a paragraph.

Hint: Two are compound/complex. Three are compound. Three are complex. The other seven are simple sentences.

1. _____   9. _____
2. _____   10. _____
3. _____   11. _____
4. _____   12. _____
5. _____   13. _____
6. _____   14. _____
7. _____   15. _____
8. _____

Directions for Part 3:

The story of William, Isabelle, and their friends in middle school has ended with the students triumphing over the school board by discovering their little secret. Now they, like you, are ready for high school. Will they remain friends?

What about you and your friends? Will you remain friends in high school, or will your different interests, schools, and paths in life separate you? Write a brief essay to express how you think your relationship with your friends will change in high school (or not) and explain why.

Support your answers with specific details of personalities, interests, etc.

Write as clearly as you can, and provide lots of details. Include a topic sentence and a concluding sentence for each paragraph. Use transitions and similes. Vary sentence structure. Most importantly, put passion and flair into your answer.

Caught'ya Final Exam KEY

Part I:

The eighth-graders, led by the intrepid twelve, quickly followed this poem by a second haiku. They entitled it "We Want Human Teachers," and then they shouted it at the top of their voices in perfect unison.

> "We **merit (deserve)** real profs.
> Creativity will die
> Without humanness."

No fewer than twelve robot teachers sparked and smoked once more, emitted a huge dying sigh, and fell flat on their faces. The cafeteria was totally silent for a moment, and then all **perdition (heck)** broke loose. Parents protested loudly and **vociferously (insistently)**.

"We want those abominable fake teachers replaced with real people as soon as you can do it," they insisted.

Students smiled and gave each other "high fives" and said, "We did it!" As the human teachers patted enthusiastically, too, they joined in the "high fives" with their students, and they clapped each other on the back.

Ms. Amicable Artist murmured to Mr. Melodious Music, "Thank heavens, I couldn't take much more of those unfeeling **automatons (robots)**."

After a quick phone call, during which he was heard to say, "The jig is up," Mr. Punctilious Principal banged the podium for the **pandemonium (craziness)** and **ruckus (disturbance)** to die down.

Finally, as the **din (noise)** turned to silence, and all eyes glared at the principal with dislike, the truth emerged. Beth even laid down her book, <u>Little Women</u>, and paid attention.

"First," he said, "I know that this is no excuse, but the human teachers and I fought the school board's decision to save money by replacing real teachers with robots. They used Horribly Hard Middle School as an experiment. Frankly, I am surprised that the robots lasted this long before our clever students' brains figured out the secret. I think the school board's little experiment is over. I, for one, am relieved and delighted. Thank you, students, for uncovering the truth. Students, keep ever **vigilant (watchful)** because you never know what money-saving strategy they will try next."

When Mr. Punctilious Principal finished and sat down, a cheer arose from the assembled eighth-graders. The long nightmare of HHMS was over, and the mystery of the bizarre teachers was solved.

There were only two questions remaining. Why did the robot teachers react to the poems, and why did their reactions get even more intensified when the students incorporated great vocabulary in their poems?

"I've got it!" Sam exclaimed when they exited the cafeteria among the other students. "You see, the teachers who were creative and individualistic were human. They had to be. Robots cannot be programmed to be individualistic or creative. They just react to the program in them.

"Ms. Amicable Artist, who taught art; Mr. Melodious Music, who taught music; Ms. Witty Writing Wizard, who taught creative writing; and Mr. Scintillating Social Studies, who came up with all kinds of weird ways to present history, all taught creative subjects or taught in a creative manner. All the robot teachers taught us in a rote manner by using the book exactly as written, by making us copy notes, or by giving us ditto sheets. They couldn't be creative at all," Sam concluded.

"Then why did the **superlative (super)** vocabulary enhance their reactions to the poems?" asked Isabelle.

"Well," suggested Jesse, "I think that using super vocabulary is like being creative. It takes thought."

"I think you're right," said Sam. "The robots were obviously programmed only with the basic vocabulary of middle-school students. When we added those big, juicy vocabulary words to our poems, they only confused the robots more since those words 'did not compute.'"

"I think we've solved the entire mystery," concluded William Waggish with an air of relief and excitement. "I wonder what next year in high school will be like..."

Part 2:

1. Simple
2. Compound
3. Simple
4. Compound
5. Simple
6. Complex
7. Simple
8. Compound/Complex
9. Simple
10. Complex
11. Compound/Complex
12. Simple
13. Compound
14. Simple
15. Complex

Bibliography

Carolina Biological Supply Company. *Painted Lady Butterfly Kit.* Burlington, NC: Carolina Biological Supply Company, 1998.

Earth's Birthday Project. *All about Painted Lady Butterflies* [online]. Santa Fe, NM: Earth's Birthday Project, 1998. Available from World Wide Web: (http://www.earthsbirthday.org/butterflies/activitykit/2.html)

Earth's Birthday Project. *Care Instructions for Butterflies and Moths* [online]. Santa Fe, NM: Earth's Birthday Project, 1998. Available from World Wide Web: (http://www.earthsbirthday.org/butterflies/activitykit/3.html)

Florida Department of Education, *Florida Writes!: Grade 8.* Tallahassee, FL: Florida Department of Education, 2002 & 2003.

Frazier, Walt. *Word Jam.* USA: Troll Communications, 2001.

Girl Scouts of the USA. *Making Things: How to Write a Cinquain* [online]. New York: Girl Scouts of the USA, 2004. Available from World Wide Web: (http://jfg.girlscouts.org/how/make/cinquain.htm)*

Hewitt, John. *Poetry in Forms Series: Cinquain* [online]. PoeWar.com Writer's Resource Center, 2004. Available from World Wide Web: (http://www.poewar. com/archives/2004/10/24/poetry-in-forms-series-cinquain)

Kiester, Jane. *Blowing Away the State Writing Assessment Test.* Gainesville, FL: Maupin House Publishing, 2000.

__. *Caught'ya Again! More Grammar with a Giggle.* Gainesville, FL: Maupin House Publishing, 1992.

__. *Caught'ya! Grammar with a Giggle.* Gainesville, FL: Maupin House Publishing, 1990.

__. *The Chortling Bard: Grammar with a Giggle for High School.* Gainesville, FL: Maupin House Publishing, 1998.

__. "Cinquain." (Unpublished poetry unit used in classroom).

__. *Elementary, My Dear: Caught'ya! Grammar with a Giggle for Grades 1, 2, and 3.* Gainesville, FL: Maupin House Publishing, 2000.

__. "Haiku." (Unpublished poetry unit used in classroom).

__. "Limericks." (Unpublished poetry unit used in classroom).

National Geographic Society. *National Geographic Atlas of the World, Revised Sixth Edition*: Washington, D.C.: National Geographic Society, 1992.

Random House. *The Random House Dictionary of the English Language, Unabridged Edition.* New York: Random House, 1967.

Rassias Foundation. *The Rassias Method* [online]. Rassias Foundation, 2003. Available from World Wide Web: (http://www.dartmouth.edu/~rassias/foundation/themethod.html)*

Siqueira, Rodrigo. *The Art of Haiku Poetry* [online]. Laboratory of Integrated Systems, University of São Paulo-Brazil, 2004. Available from World Wide Web: (http://www.lsi.usp.br/usp/rod/poet/haiku.html)*

University of Missouri-Kansas City. *Limericks* [online]. University of Missouri-Kansas City, 2003. Available from World Wide Web: (http://www.umkc.edu/imc/limerick.htm)*

* This link is no longer available.